WOMEN OF PRAGUE

Ethnic Diversity and Social Change
from the Eighteenth Century to the Present

WOMEN OF PRAGUE

*Ethnic Diversity and Social Change
from the Eighteenth Century to the Present*

Wilma Abeles Iggers

Berghahn Books
Providence • Oxford

First published in 1995 by
Berghahn Books
Editorial offices:
165 Taber Avenue, Providence, RI 02906, USA
Bush House, Merewood Avenue, Oxford, OX3 8EF, UK

© Wilma Abeles Iggers 1995

Library of Congress Cataloging-in-Publication Data
Iggers, Wilma.
    Women of Prague : ethnic diversity and social change from the eighteenth
century to the present / Wilma Abeles Iggers.
        p.   cm.
    Includes bibliographical references and index.
    ISBN 1-57181-008-0 (cloth). -- ISBN 1-57181-009-9 (pbk.)
    1. Women--Czech Republic--Prague--History--Sources. 2. Women--
Czech Republic--Prague--Social conditions--Sources. 3. Prague
(Czech Republic)--Social conditions--Sources. 4. Prague (Czech
Republic)--Ethnic relations--Sources. 5. Women--Czech Republic--
Prague--Biography. I. Title.
HQ1610.3.Z9P754 1995   95-1636
305.4'09437'12--dc20   CIP

British Library Cataloguing in Publication Data
A catalogue record for this book is available from
the British Library.

Cover: Pastel drawing by L. Kuba.
Reproduced with permission from the Kolin Museum.

Printed in the United States on acid-free paper.

CONTENTS

to Georg

PREFACE

&

The material on which this book is based comes in part from printed sources; the rest I found in literary estates. In the case of Magdalena Dobromila Rettigová, much of the literature by and about her is contained in the 1985 edition of her famous cookbook. Besides, I found a good deal in the National Literary Archives in Strahov. Some of the impressions I absorbed on walks in the town of Litomyšl where Rettigová seems to have been the most active also found their way into this book. This may also be true of Božena Němcová in whose life Litomyšl also played an important role. I found most of the literature connected with her in the rich collection of the library of the University of Illinois in Champaign—Urbana. The unpublished diary of Josefa Náprstková was brought to my attention by Dr. Zdenek Šolle in Prague. The Leo Baeck Institute in New York permitted me to use the memoirs of Else Bergmann, the daughter of Berta Fanta. Dr. Martin Bergmann, Else Bergmann's son sent me a copy of his grandmother's diary. My trip to Jerusalem yielded several documents from Hugo Bergmann's estate in the Hebrew University Archives. Georg and Lilli Deiglmayr, Hermine Hanel's children lent me their only copy of their mother's autobiography and supplied additional information orally and in letters.

Almost all of my material about Gisa Picková-Saudková was supplied by Dr. Zbyněk Sedláček, the director of the archives of the town of Kolín East of Prague. I am especially grateful to Mrs. Bettina Adler and Professor Jeremy Adler in London, England for giving me permission to xerox unpublished material from Grete Fischer's estate, to Grete Fischer's niece Elizabeth Wolf in Darlington in Northern England and to a number of people in London who knew Grete well for rounding out my picture of her.

While I was working on Milena Jesenská, to begin with Professor Gibian of Cornell University handed me a suitcase full of material by and about her. I was, however, especially fortunate to have access to the vast collection of "Mileniana" in the possession of Dr. Marie Jirásková in Prague, unquestionably the authority on Milena, and to be able to ask her innumerable questions since I began working on this project in 1987. As literature about Milada Horáková is almost unavailable in American libraries, it would have been practically impossible to include a chapter about her in this volume without the help of her daughter, Jana Kánská of Pittsburgh, who sent me xeroxes and answered my questions in letters and on the telephone.In addition to providing the lead to Ruth Klinger, the Brod family in Munich/Fürstenfeldbruck supplied me with Ruths self-published autobiography and with letters and clippings. Besides, Stephen Jolly of London helped to complete my picture of her. Professor Vilém Prečan of the Czechoslovak Documentation Center in Scheinfeld, Germany and now also of the Czech Academy of Sciences first spoke to me about Jiřina Šiklová and supplied me with her writings which had been smuggled out of Czechoslovakia. Since then I have been seeing Jirina on my annual visits to Prague and corresponding with her. The material with which she provided me deserves to be the core of a book-length portrait of that remarkable woman.

I would like to thank my former employer, Canisius College in Buffalo, N.Y., for providing me with a typist in the early phases of this work, and Iris Pilling of Darmstadt, Dagmar Friedrich of Göttingen and Milena Klímová of Prague for critiquing individual chapters. Several librarians helped me a great deal: Waltraut Klitzke of the *Deutsche Bücherei* in Leipzig, Sally Di Carlo of the Bowhuis Library at Canisius College and Marie Kallista of the library of the University of Illinois. For invaluable help with the typing of the countless versions of chapters, as well as for thoughtful advice and moral support, I would like to thank my friend Irene Schultens in Göttingen.

Despite very basic disagreements with me about the very essence of this book, my husband Georg Iggers could always be counted on, whether I needed a sympathetic listener, or a fair arbiter in my frustrating battles with the computer. He tries to be fair to women, especially this one, and I would therefore like to dedicate this book to him.

INTRODUCTION

Wenceslas Square, 1830

*I*f you wander through the streets of Prague today, or look at a map or an aerial photograph of it, the city seems to have grown as an organic whole with its roots in the Middle Ages. However, if you begin to study the history of its inhabitants more closely, you will soon realize that at least three ethnic groups—Czechs, Germans, and Jews—coexisted there with each group concentrated in quite different areas of the city, some relatively permanent, some in a state of slow flux. Their boundaries were flexible and at times a group was gradually transformed into another. After the Thirty Years' War (1618-1648) when the Germanizing efforts of the Habsburgs proved successful, the Jews divided into two strands, one German and one Czech, and the Czechs did not reemerge until the nineteenth century. During the Second World War, most of the Jews who had not emigrated were exterminated, and a few years later almost all of the German gentiles were expelled. Thus the city was left with essentially only one ethnic group, the Czechs.

Although many people, often strangers to the city, have written about Prague—its architecture, its role in history, its atmosphere—and its multi-ethnic character, especially in conjunction with Kafka, none of this literature deals with what it was like to simultaneously brush shoulders with one's own kind and with the two and eventually three other groups which one noticed in a different way, and usually to a lesser extent and with negative feelings.

Women tend in their autobiographical writings, in contrast to men, to deal with their own social and familial milieu and to examine their own motivations and feelings. They include that sort of material which helps us to reconstruct a social and cultural climate rather than to concentrate on political and economic developments which, especially when a "lesser" people is involved, interests only some specialists.

With this reader, which includes excerpts from the writings, often autobiographical, of women who have lived in or were associated with Prague in the last two hundred years, I am trying to accomplish something much more modest than a history of multi-ethnic Prague. I hope, as much as is possible between the covers of one book, to bring a number of women from the different ethnic groups to life, to show their everyday thoughts and concerns and how they experienced the changes that took place around them. For that reason I decided to give the word to the protagonists themselves as much as possible, and to persons who knew them well.

My first criterion of selection for these women was the availability of the necessary kind of written materials—letters, diaries, an autobiography or memoirs—by a woman conscious of the unique Prague environment. Since such records were very rare before the turn of the eighteenth to the nineteenth century, that is the point in time at which I begin. I also wanted to find as great a variety of women as possible; if they mostly turned out to be famous or at least well known, it is because such records rarely exist about ordinary people. However, my search to find women representing the various groups was unevenly successful. Surprisingly, there is no dearth of women representing the Czech gentiles during the first part of our period, the early nineteenth century when attention was increasingly turned to expressions of individual attitudes and feelings. This ethnic group was then struggling to establish their identity, and to move beyond their working-class, or small tradesman status. If, especially with regard to the nineteenth century, I am presenting a much more detailed picture of the history of Czech women than of others, it is because, although they generally came from lower classes, they were much more active, and much more was written by them and about them than by and about women in the other ethnic groups. Of course it is impossible to give a comprehensive picture of these women, or to cover the same aspects of their lives in similar ways. Our sources are such that sometimes the emphasis is on their childhood and youth, sometimes on their mature years, sometimes on their reflections, sometimes on their relationships with others.

My project acquired broader and more concrete contours as I thought about my own social and cultural background (Czech, German and Jewish), and about the rural and urban influences on me through my contact with different layers of society, separate, often in conflict, yet mutually influencing me.

I decided to begin with Magdalena Dobromila Rettigová (1785-1845) because from her lifetime on, we have records of women chronologically fairly close together or whose lives overlap. Thus we can see change and continuity within each ethnic strand and growing diversity among them in a world which was allegedly becoming increasingly one.

As far as I know only two of the women to whom chapters are devoted in this book actually knew each other personally; yet the same places, and in some cases even the same people, have played a role in the lives of several of them. Ossip Schubin was born near St. Anne's Square, where Grete Fischer had her interview with a famous critic half a century later. Some of Berta Fanta's ancestors lived in Kamyk, Schubin's childhood paradise. Two of our protagonists, Milena Jesenská and Milada Horáková, born only four years apart,

Area around Prague at the time of Rettigová, now part of the city

probably did not know each other, but Záviš Kalandra, Milena's friend, was linked with Milada in the same show trials and executed with her, although they had never known each other.

We have to sketch the historical developments during the period which concerns us at least briefly, and to clear up at least one problem: it is important to realize that even vocabulary contributes to making the nationality situation of Bohemia unclear. Patriotism in the region had meant love of Bohemia for a long time, to both Czechs and Germans. The very Czech word "český" and the German word "böhmisch" (in English "Bohemian") are ambiguous, since both, until the twentieth century, referred to the language as well as to the country. More recently, however, German usage has changed, and English along with it, so that the adjective referring to the language has come to be in German "tschechisch" instead of "böhmisch" and in English "Czech" instead of "Bohemian". Thus, the movement which was referred to in German as Jung-Böhmen was comparable to contemporary movements in many other European countries from Young Ireland to Young Turkey, and was neither self-consciously Czech nor German.

The Protestant Czechs had been defeated in the Battle of the White Mountain in 1620; many of those who did not want to become Catholic—30,000 noble or bourgeois families—went into exile, and their lands were confiscated. During the war, half the population was decimated by famine, epidemics and exile. From then on, Czech was only taught in the low grades, German became the official language and the nobility and the bourgeoisie became completely Germanized. Czech became the language of peasants, small tradesmen and servants.

While the devastation of the Thirty Years' War would have constituted a tremendous setback for Bohemia by itself, the ruthless recatholization—involving a change of ownership of vast properties into the hands of foreign Catholic noble families—had a comparable impact, both psychologically and materially, on the population. The new German nobility, including high clergy, engaged in a flurry of building palaces, churches and other ornamental buildings perhaps unmatched elsewhere. A cult of ancient Czech Catholic martyrs was created to overshadow the memories of Hussitism, the indigenous Czech Protestantism. The bourgeoisie, decimated and impoverished, was Germanized, overawed and overshadowed by the splendor of the nobles. However, a contrast perhaps comparable to this between the bourgeoisie and the nobles was that between the bourgeoisie and the poor, who were ill fed and ill dressed and often had only caves dug in

The Old Town Square

the hillsides to live in. In Prague, the German element, which before had constituted a third of the population, increased, especially on the Lesser Side and below Hradčany castle.

It was not until the time of Empress Maria Theresa (1740–80) that the bourgeoisie developed a new self confidence which was reflected in the architecture and furnishings of their houses as well as in theater and music. At that time theater in Prague was almost entirely German. However, historical writing, although in German or Latin, turned increasingly to the history of Bohemia. German intellectuals thought of themselves increasingly as Bohemian (or Austrian) Germans, sometimes even of "Slavic descent" although their names were German. There was a revived interest in old Bohemian folk customs, similar to the regional folklore studies that had emerged in other European countries.

However, while the sentimental mood of the time sympathized with these tendencies, the spirit of the Enlightenment advocated working toward making the whole Empire uniformly German. Thus, elementary schools which had been Czech up until this time became German.

Probably as a reaction to the increased Germanizing efforts of Marie Theresa's son, Emperor Joseph II (1780–90), a small Czech elite developed which aimed to resuscitate the Czech language and culture. (Ironically, they had to communicate with each other in German.) Among them was Josef Dobrovský, the first serious scholar of Slavic philology, who wrote his works on the Czech language in German

Czech costumes in the nineteenth century from around Domažlice

and Latin. He, however, was convinced that Czech would never again become a living language. Still, patriotic plays—generally of little artistic value—were produced in Czech. Of more lasting importance was the Bohemian Society of Sciences, founded in 1785. Ironically, it was confirmed by Joseph II, the great Germanizer, who did not suspect that the society was to become an important nucleus of Czechization. In 1793 a chair for the study of the Czech language was established at the Prague university, and very gradually the national awakening began to manifest itself in the publication of Czech grammars, dictionaries and literary works.

Women, lacking any education, did not begin to participate in the movement until the early nineteenth century. However, by the 1820s, every town in Bohemia and Moravia had a group of men and women who organized gatherings at which there were recitations and singing with patriotic themes. In the 1820s, the first opera was written in Czech, and in 1831, the first modern Czech publishing house was founded. The Czech national awakening, in some ways more remarkable than the revival of Hebrew as a living language in modern Palestine, began to truly gather momentum in the 1830s.

As Czech social life came into its own between 1830 and 1840, political and social groups were formed which organized excursions to historic places, sang Czech songs and cultivated Czech literature. This was also the time when the first woman to whom I am devoting a chapter, Magdalena Dobromila Rettigová, became known. Her name is still a household word in Bohemia because in addition to traditional moral stories, plays, and books of advice for women, she wrote cook books, one of which is still a sort of bible of Czech cuisine.

While amateur theaters had already existed in the eighteenth century, now a permanent one was established in a wooden structure in Prague. A ball organized by Josef Kajetán Tyl, the writer of the opera *Fidlovačka* [a shoemakers' festivity], from which the song that later became the Czech national anthem, "Kde domov můj?" [Where is my home?], is taken, became a cultural landmark. It took place in February of 1840, and created a sensation by having the tickets, menus, etc. printed in Czech for the first time, rather than in German. At this and later balls small books were distributed containing poems written by Czech women. Various other social and educational activities and particularly large scale nationalistic manifestations, attended by thousands of people, made for more cohesiveness among Czechs.

At this time the foremost Czech nationalist leader was the internationally known historian František Palacký, around whom the new Czech political and cultural elite began to congregate. He was the first, in 1846, to publish a scholarly history of Bohemia—of course in German.

From the 1840s on, the Czechs demanded more autonomy in the Austrian Empire and parity with the German language. However, even those moderate hopes were crushed by the failure of the revolution of 1848. In fact, under the foreign minister Alexander Bach (1852-1859) an even more severe absolutism was imposed which lasted ten years. During that time A. Päumann, the Prague police chief, allegedly announced that in ten years there would be no more Czech nation. When all political manifestations were forbidden, Czech patriots concentrated on the advancement of the Industrial Union which promoted Czech industry. The humiliation of the Czechs, whose capital had housed the first university in Central Europe and been the seat of the Emperor, reached its peak in 1867, when Emperor Francis Joseph—in what came to be known as "The Compromise"—had himself crowned king of Hungary, but never of Bohemia.

Until 1945, most Germans belonged to the middle and upper bourgeoisie and to the nobility, which had partly come to Bohemia after the Thirty Years' War and partly been originally Czech, but Germanized; there were practically no lower-class Germans.

Let us briefly look at the numbers of population involved. In 1846, Prague proper had 66,046 inhabitants who considered themselves German, and 36,687 who considered themselves Czech. In addition, there were about 6,000 Jews, mostly living in the ghetto. Relative numbers changed considerably in the course of the century. If by about 1870, the Czechs represented a majority, this was in part due to the strong increase in industrialization, which attracted a large number of Czechs from the countryside, particularly to the lower class suburbs. In 1880 thirteen percent of the population was German and in 1900 Germans made up only six per cent of a population of 514,345. From 1892 on, all Prague street signs were in both languages rather than in German only. Successes such as this resulted in an intensified Czech struggle for dominance which in turn brought about multiple defensive measures on the part of the Prague Germans. Almost invariably, new Czech commercial and social organizations gave rise to German ones.

The split into two societies in Prague became increasingly pronounced. There were even two "corsos" where the solid middle class took their strolls; the Germans walked on Ferdinandgasse, today's Národní, the Czechs on Příkopy—Graben in German. An important caesura was the establishment of a Czech university in 1882.

Czech women felt that they had a vital role to play in this society, one that was different and in part separate from that of the men: to cultivate, in that highly Germanized environment, the Czech language, especially to teach it to their children, and to devote themselves to Czech cultural affairs. With many creative writers of this time and later, national themes predominated—in fact, several of the most prominent Czech women writers concentrated their efforts to a large extent on cultivating Czech folklore, and reproducing its themes in works of their own. Karolina Světlá (1830-1899) spent much of her time in the country dressed like a peasant, and another writer, Eliška Krásnohorská (1847-1926) wrote libretti for Smetana's operas from peasant life. These tendencies are epitomized most clearly by Božena Němcová (1817?-1862) whose *Babička* [The Grandmother], first published in 1855, is still the most revered book in the Czech language. While many Czech women in the nineteenth century expressed their patriotism in their belletristic writings, the study and writing of history still remained almost entirely the domain of men.

The history of the emancipation of Czech women is closely linked with the history of their national awakening and of their philanthropic activity. It is perhaps because Czech women were fighting on two fronts—the feminist and the patriotic, that their feminism was less militant than that of women in Germany or England. The two thrusts were linked in Eliška Krásnohorská's article "The Voice of a Pedagogue on the Women's Question"[1] in which she claimed that the whole nation can only progress when women are not left behind. She therefore chided Czech women for being ashamed to speak Czech in public and for accepting the values of those who set themselves up as their superiors: the Germans and men. Women publicly active in areas other than writing also were perceived as patriots—whether they were feeding the poor or holding educational gatherings of women. Toward the end of the nineteenth century, the unity of purpose among them became much more diffuse, but by then the tradition of a feminine presence had been well established.

Božena Němcová, who began writing in the 1840s, was the first Czech woman to produce literature of high quality. However, parallel with the development of the Czech national revival, the number of women who made a mark in Czech public life kept increasing throughout the nineteenth, century and so did the relevant written records among which we can choose.

The main and most obvious factor which characterized most Czech women in the early nineteenth century was their place on the lower rungs of the socio-economic ladder, with very few exceptions, they also had only the most rudimentary formal education. The few in the "better" classes learned handicrafts, some piano and some French— what was thought necessary to be the right wife for a good bourgeois, although there were not even enough men for all women to marry.

In addition to being less well educated than men, women had to work longer hours and at a greater variety of jobs than men, had less access to outside stimulation, could make few independent decisions and survived—if they were lucky—many unwanted pregnancies, for they were generally unprepared for the sexual side of marriage. The first woman to seriously write about female education in Prague was Honoráta Zapová. In her *Nezabudky* (1855) [Not To Be Forgotten] she deals with all the topics she thinks a woman's education should include, such as hygiene, friendship and marriage.

What seems remarkable from our late twentieth-century perspective is that educational workers, organizers, teachers, principals were all people with little or no specialized, professional training. None of the women who in many cases took up leadership positions in a variety of different areas had gone to school much beyond their mid-teens. If we bear in mind that Eliška Krásnohorská, the founder of the first women's gymnasium, had never gone to a similar school herself and yet that the level of the school was such that many of its graduates went on to university and became very successful in various professions, one may look skeptically at the institutionalization of "professional" education.

As elsewhere, the question of the right to work never concerned the laboring woman—she not only could, she always had to work—

nor the upper class woman, who rarely thought of working. But it was all the more a problem for the women of the classes between those two: as the nineteenth century progressed, women could make ever fewer objects for daily use at home, and had to buy increasingly more of them with generally no more money available in the household. It was obviously even more necessary for the woman who could not or chose not to marry to earn a living. Training of various kinds was urgently needed for those women, since the only alternative to marriage, other than entering a convent, was to be a spinster dependent on the charity of relatives.

The first Prague literary salon met in the house of Honoráta Zapová whom I mentioned as an educator and who originally came from Poland. She was used to women participating in discussions on cultural topics. Other salons were founded by wives of well-known patriots. While men continued to meet in innumerable coffee houses and taverns with different interest groups or with celebrities they admired, it goes without saying that "nice" women still could not attend.

Although the majority of Czech men were no more sympathetic to the aspirations of women than men elsewhere, impulses for women's advancement sometimes came from men. So was Karel Slavoj Amerling (1807-1884), a Saint-Simonian[2] who was considered an unrealistic fool by some, together with his wife Svatava who as early as 1844 founded Budeč,[3] the first school for girls with egalitarian tendencies.

Egg Market, 1888

Believing "women should first of all be human beings and then women ... wives, mothers", he was far ahead of his peers. Bohuslava Rajská (1817-1852), considered the first Czech feminist, was hired as the first teacher, but soon left because she considered it an even more important patriotic duty to marry F.L. Čelakovský, the most celebrated Czech poet of his time, and to take care of his four children.

After Budeč had to close its doors because of its founder's excessive ambitions, the emphasis was for a long time on women's practical training, later exemplified by the Czech Women's Production Club which was organized by Karolina Světlá, the versatile writer and most visible role model and worker for nationalist causes, in 1860. It received a small amount of support from the government, which supported forty industrial schools for Germans, some with very few pupils, but none for Czechs.

What made the situation of women in Prague unusual was that they had to be conscious of living among different ethnic groups. Czech awareness of the German presence was always there; when they struggled for a new school, they wanted to make sure that it was Czech. When they looked for foreign models in social work, they emphatically studied French or English institutions rather than German ones. In mid-nineteenth century, philanthropy also was often linked not only to feminism, but also to the Czech-German polarity.

This was the case in actions launched by Karolina Světlá, Eliška Krásnohorská and even of Vojta Náprstek, the greatest feminist, who was the husband of one of our protagonists, Josefa Náprstková (1838-1907). It was not so with Marie Riegrová (1833-1892), who was above all devoted to alleviating the suffering of the poor, especially women, but, in harmony with her husband František Ladislav Rieger (1818-1903), the most prominent Czech politician in the nineteenth century, she was not interested in also turning them into militant feminists.

It is remarkable that most of the activist women of the Czech revival were at least in part of German descent. In fact, almost as a rule, they only learned Czech as a second language, sometimes against parental opposition. Nevertheless, they took it for granted that it was their task as women and mothers to participate in the reawakening of the dormant Czech language and culture, and once that was accomplished, in the education of Czech youth. They, their attitudes, sacrifices and even martyrdom are so much a part of Czech consciousness that these facts generally are taken for granted with no attempt to explain them. This simpleminded patriotism, of course, subsided when the national reawakening was completed. The founding of Minerva in 1890, the women's gymnasium in Prague and the first in Central Europe, can be considered the last major act of patriotism of this kind.

The most outstanding examples of Czech patriotic women who only gradually learned Czech—more or less well[4]—were Terezie Palacká, the wife of the historian František Palacký, Johana Fričová the wife of J.V. Frič, the revolutionary of 1848, and Augusta Braunerová, the wife of a member of the House of Deputies in Vienna. She was raised in upper-class German speaking circles but married a prominent patriot and presided over the foremost patriotic salon of her time, although she never spoke Czech well. Karolina Světlá and her sister Žofie Podlipská (1833-1897), a popular writer, were educated in German and French and learned Czech behind their parents' backs. Several of the women with whom we shall concern ourselves belong in this category. They devoted themselves to activities related to the Czech national cause—whether it be education, politics, charity work or literature. Some Slavicized their names, e.g. Antonia Reiss to Bohuslava Rajská. However, Jindřich Fügner (1822-1864), one of the two founders of Sokol[5]—which could be called "the most Czech" organization—and his wife Kateřina seem to have been exceptions. He felt more at home with German than with Czech and when asked about his identity, he is reported to have said that he was a German speaking Praguer.

The relative numbers of middle and upper class Czechs and Germans in Prague are hard to establish, at any rate until late in the nineteenth century. Who was Czech, who was German? Names certainly would be no criterion.

The women who identified with Czech nationalism tended to reject everything German. The following narrative[6] is only one episode, told by one person. However, both the narrator, Eliška Krásnohorská and the people with whom she deals were very central to Prague Czech female society, and the episode throws so important a light on attitudes of the time that I decided have to reproduce it almost unabbreviated:

> It was perhaps in 1864 that Světlá sometimes gathered together a small circle of girls to whom she devoted long afternoons with motherly, sincerely patriotic intentions. She wanted to awaken us, to encourage us to educate ourselves, so that we would understand the significance of the times and our obligations which extended beyond the family. She did not preach to us, but proceeded quite modestly. Perhaps to make us feel even more at home, she sometimes—believe it or not—knitted a stocking while we had our coffee.
>
> One day, when we chosen ones were distinguished by such an invitation to Mrs. Světlá's, we were surprised by an event we never would have expected: a German woman was brought among us. Světlá told us that the lady wants to

know Czech society, and that it was up to us to inculcate in her respect for Czech female intelligence.

Berta Mühlsteinová [a minor poet] said to me with a self-confidence I did not have: "I am not afraid of her, I know German well."

She came. She was a young lady with a pretty, expressive face of a certain Jewish type which betrayed her origin from a patrician family which had already been Christian for a long time. Her large family which I shall call X had an excellent reputation for being honest and unusually well educated among Prague merchants. In Miss X's parental home which was not known for luxury, but for hospitality and humanitarianism, art and reading were cultivated to a much higher degree than is usually the case. They were educated and truly refined people, how would Miss X otherwise have interested Světlá?

In that house all met who stood out in spirit and education in German circles: scholars, writers, artists and the social tone which prevailed there was elegant but relaxed.

If I remember correctly, Miss X singled out an opportunity to render Světlá a small service and to speak to her.

When that young lady entered the little salon, we had no idea what mission she came to fulfill, what intentions she harbored behind cheerful conversation full of wit with which she entertained us. She, who was there for the first time, was immediately at home, while we, accustomed to being there, were timid, and somehow felt strange. It wasn't even the German language which bothered us, we knew enough to talk, but something unclear oppressed us. We felt an antagonism against Miss X as against an intruder, and despite all her communicativeness, self-assurance, free behavior and intelligent eloquence we did not like Miss X at all.

She also became a participant in subsequent gatherings. I felt clearly that she deeply admired Světlá's intelligence and knowledge, but that she viewed the rest of us very critically, without respect.

With the same tolerant scorn she judged the modest furnishings of the salon, the simple refreshments and Berta's and my poems, which to our surprise she knew well. She was not even impressed with two young women with whom—evidently as an examiner—she spoke French and English. She overwhelmed us with Spanish, Greek and Sanskrit quotations, and told us that she was still studying Sanskrit, but would soon begin studying Russian. She spoke of all her accomplishments so casually, as if they were matters of course for an educated lady.

With ironic praise she reproached me for a poem which was not designed to endear me to the Germans. She showed us subtly, what little geese she considered us.

After several such gatherings, Světlá was invited very cordially by Miss X's father to a family supper. Světlá was unable to think of an excuse and went.

In her naiveté, she put on very casual clothes, and instead of coming into a family circle, she came into a luxurious social gathering, where there were gentlemen with white ties and tuxedos, and ladies in silk dresses with low necklines. Yes, even Světlá's great heroic heart was able to grieve because of the style of her blouse.

But she could not understand why she was the center of the whole group and the object of so much interest. There were writers, artists, journalists and professors present. They spoke about scholarly, literary and philosophic topics, but put every question to Světlá. "Believe me," she told me, "it felt like an examination. I thought: I'll prove to you, you annoying Germans, that I am not an ignoramus, as you impudently assume of every Czech."

I am sure Světlá dazzled them.

A short time later she was again invited most urgently "for supper". She tried to avoid this invitation in every way she could, not understanding why she should socialize with Germans. I don't know for what reasons she decided to go after all. One was her clothing: "I don't want them to think that a Czech lady doesn't even know how to dress for company, and she went in a beautiful blue silk dress, to make up for the way she was dressed on the previous occasion. Even in this detail Czech pride demanded satisfaction.

It was the same splendid company as the first time. Suddenly Světlá heard why she was introduced into that German circle by a trick. She was told directly and emphatically: "You are wasting yourself in the narrow Czech circles. You should write in German." And the two editors present, supported by the whole gathering, began urgently to convince Světlá to write her precious books from the life of the Czech people in a world language—of course in German.

"I cannot even repeat," Světlá said incensed, "what flatteries they swept into my face together with perfidious, veiled remarks about the inferiority of the Czech world. As long as I live I shall blush that I had to suffer through all that."

Arguments were expressed such as: your society is such that you have to despair; your circles can neither appreciate nor reward you; in German society you would live like a great writer of a great nation. We do not ask you to be a renegade; precisely your love for the Czech nation makes you a new individuality. Write about your Czech people as enthusiastically as before—it is only a question of the language. I wish I could remember the fiery words with which Světlá answered her German admirers, as soon as the first shock passed, with which their proposal paralyzed her.

"Only the language?" she called; "It is precisely the life and death of a nation, and for the Czech language I want to live and die. We don't value Europe's recognition, as long as our right to a national life is not recognized and as long as the famous nations can ask enslavement and servility of the small ones. Does my Czech society seem unworthy to you? Do you think it is to the credit of the Germans, if they are ahead of us in any way? No, your culture was never wiped out with fire and sword down to its foundations, you never began after such a tragic decline! You see only shortcomings and inadequacies in our education, I see in it miracles of the greatest efforts which there ever were under the sun! I see only its development, brought about with great spiritual and moral strength such as your nation in its well-being never had any incentive to have. How could you value my insignificant writings better than Czech circles? You are not able to understand the source from which I draw them. Don't judge what you don't understand. Everything that unites us Czechs is strange to you, and serves to defend us against you."

Pointing out the greatness of our foremost national workers, she confessed that honors and personal advantages are like weeds to her.

When they objected that enmity among nationalities must finally cease and that they were honestly extending their hands to her in friendship, our honest Světlá replied: "Between us and you flow rivers of blood! On your shore stands Germany, our arch enemy, and your hands, ladies and gentlemen, will not be able to hold him back. You suggest building bridges for him across those currents? May both of my hands fall off the moment I lift a finger for that purpose!"

It was not long before Prussian cannon moved from the Czech border to Hradec Králové and streams of blood once more were spilled. [She is referring to the battle of Königgrätz in 1866].

So Světlá did not become a world famous writer with the help of the German language.

However, while Czechs and Germans avoided each other's cultural functions, almost absolutely after the Schiller-Centennary celebrations of 1859, it is not true that, as has been claimed, Prague society was totally polarized. On the German side there was, at least until late in the nineteenth century, more condescension than hostility. The portions of Ossip Schubin's (1854-1935) memoirs in this book contain several instances of mutual awareness and life together. She and Sidonie Nádherný von Borutín (1885-1950), who might have been another of our German protagonists, were partly of Czech decent and proud of their Czech connections.

It seems that while there were some social and some charitable occasions at which women of Czech and of German orientation met in Prague, there were few meetings of the minds of leading women from both camps. One interest some few women shared was the philosophy of Bernard Bolzano (1781-1848), a priest and professor of theology in Prague, a philosopher and a mathematician. He stressed striving for happiness for oneself and others, personal morality, a concern with the well-being of one's fellow man, and rejected the biblical idea, according to which there would always be free people and slaves, rich and poor. He combined his moral teachings with lessons in logic, metaphysics, psychology, and pedagogy.

Philanthropy played a very important role in the lives of Prague women in the second half of the nineteenth century. It was one of the few opportunities they had to be active outside of their household. Žofie Podlipská, even recommended it as a remedy for a disastrous personal life. As Terezie Palacká came to realize that professional skills were necessary for a social worker, she went to Paris to learn them. Having renounced what pleasure she had formerly found in the arts, she established Czech nursery schools from 1882 on, first in Prague and then in the countryside. While at first the attention of middle-class women was concentrated on the poor, especially on women and children, gradually they began focusing on the preparation for life of women of their own class.

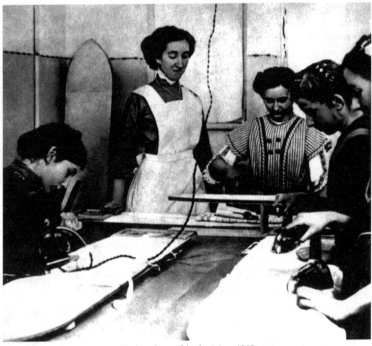

Teaching the use of the electric iron, 1910

This was also a time of important economic changes: as crafts guilds were dissolved and free enterprise was encouraged, many new Czech enterprises were established. Although they had a hard struggle competing with those supported by German and Jewish capital, this meant progress in the long run. As for emancipation, the concept was considered so radical, that in the 1860s, Bohemian women had barely heard of it. When Světlá was asked what the word "emancipistky" meant, she had great difficulty finding an editor who printed her very moderate reply. In fact, as one might expect, the impact of influential men on the history of women was mixed. On the negative side, there was the politician František Ladislav Rieger, who enjoyed immense political power and authority, who hindered the activities of Světlá and Krásnohorská. He wrote to the latter that an institution run by two female writers can neither be led correctly nor act for the general good. He merely tolerated his wife's (Marie Riegrová) untiring philanthropic work.

However, other men played a perhaps unusually positive role in this regard. We have already mentioned three: Tyl, Amerling and Bolzano. The fourth, who had the greatest and most lasting impact on the largest number of women, was Vojtěch Náprstek (1826-1894), the husband of Josefa (Pepička) Náprstková at whom we shall have a closer look in chapter 3. I know of no man who had a comparable importance to women in any society, and therefore shall devote space to him which might be considered disproportionate.

But first we have to consider his mother, Anna Fingerhutová (1788-1873).[7] Born as the last of a miller's twelve children in 1877, she lost her father early and worked as a servant from her tenth year on, and at fourteen was placed in charge of her uncle's business. After she had been married to a tavern keeper for eleven years and had three children with him, her husband died. She carried on the business herself and later married Antonín Fingerhut. With him she had two sons, Ferdinand and Vojtěch (called Vojta). Soon the Fingerhuts were able to buy the house "u Halánků" on Bethlehem Square which came to occupy a uniquely prominent place in the consciousness of Czechs. Having known poverty, Mrs.Fingerhutová (Panímaminka, literally Mrs. Mother, as she was called affectionately), regularly distributed soup to students and other poor people, as well as clothing and money. She continued her charitable activities when her husband died after nine years of marriage.

It soon became obvious that Vojta was going to be her successor. He went to study law in Vienna, and there became involved in revolutionary activities in 1848. When the revolution failed, he was forced to flee to America, and spent ten years in Milwaukee, running a lending library and a shop as well as publishing and writing for a liberal German journal. Tinka Krákorová, a pretty Czech actress he had met in Vienna, was his companion.

In 1858, Vojta returned to Prague without Tinka, of whom his mother did not approve. There he met his mother's chief helper, Josefa (Pepička) Křížková. She was an efficient, hard-working, decent woman and Vojta wanted to marry her, but on his mother's insistence had to wait for twelve years, until after his mother's death.

To Vojta, his mother was the model woman. It may seem surprising that he somehow equated her, a hard-working, independent woman, with American women and with the woman of the future. The character and appearance of his Tinka was evidently diametrically opposed to those of his mother and his wife, but our knowledge of her will forever be very limited because Pepička destroyed all written material referring to her.

Vojta developed a strong interest in ethnography and in technological progress which, to him, was closely linked to women's emancipation. Convinced of the importance of women, especially mothers, for society, he lectured about the necessity to liberate women from drudgery, in part with the help of household machines, and of elevating them intellectually and morally. In a lecture in 1865, he startled his audience by declaring: "Women are certainly as gifted as men. Why should they not participate in all higher tasks of life, if human ingenuity frees them from all kinds of lowly tasks?"[8] On other occasions he advocated women's suffrage. In 1865 he began to invite the ladies of Prague—predominantly, but not exclusively Czech—to lectures which he organized for them in the reading room of his house, and gave them access to his extensive and growing library.

One very important aspect of Náprstek's educational activity was that he and his guest speakers expressed themselves in totally unpretentious, intelligible language. Somehow it was possible for professors with international reputations in the sciences and in philosophy like Jan Evangelista Purkyně (1787-1869) and Thomas Masaryk (1850-1937) to lecture at the same time to the intellectual élite and to people who had been forced to leave school before the age of ten. Náprstek also organized excursions to museums, humanitarian institutions, factories and to the surrounding countryside for women, and they were invited to meet interesting visitors from abroad. This circle soon came to be known as the American Ladies Club, because during his ten years in America, Náprstek had become convinced that American women were much freer than Czech women to pursue their own interests, that they were more respected and that in America there was more educational equality between the sexes. He also felt that this greater freedom was expressed in the very clothing women wore, i.e. that American women, not having to be preoccupied with attracting men by their appearance, could dress simply and comfortably, as did his mother and his wife Pepička.[9]

In addition, the club was concerned with informing women about technical progress which would make their work easier. Besides the lectures, the club also organized expositions of objects useful to women. Educational materials were collected, excursions for pupils were organized, and monuments were erected in memory of famous women, first of all for Božena Němcová. Another area of the club's concern was humanitarian. With Náprstek's help, the women went on excursions with deaf mutes, and read to blind people. Their largest single accomplishment was the collection of 30,000 guilders—on the twentieth anniversary of the founding of the club in 1885—for establishing an orphanage.

After the club was launched, decisions were entirely up to the members, not to Náprstek. Five years after it was founded, the club

American Ladies Club, 1870

was notified by the police that their activities were not authorized, and were henceforth forbidden. From then on it continued its activities as the "Former American Ladies Club".

Náprstek paid from his own pocket for lectures by famous scholars, painters, writers, doctors. It goes without saying that some of the lectures were presented by women. When Náprstek decided in 1885 no longer to contribute to the cost of the lectures, they were presented by the members themselves for a few years and then ceased entirely.

The club was the first women's organization with great prestige, also among men. And its members went forth to found other important associations, such as the Physical Training Association for Women and Girls, the Women's Production Association, a cooking school, and most important, the gymnasium Minerva. A school of nursing, founded in 1875, the only one in the Austrian Empire, trained women successfully for five years, but had to be closed as a result of intrigues by German members of the Prague City Council.

In 1865 there were 4,351 volumes in Náprstek's library, twenty years later 37,037. Of these, 6,459 were in Czech and in 1894 the library had grown to 47,596 volumes. He bought books on the women's question in all European languages. Already during his stay in America he had begun to make scrapbooks on everything that had been published on the subject of women; he had nineteen scrapbooks in all.

Vojta's impact on the Czech women of Prague is best expressed in a proclamation written by Světlá (1863), addressed to him and signed by three hundred women. It says in part: "It is you, Sir, who has the honor of having been the first in our nation to have had compassion with our misery. For it is misery if a dressmaker dies of hunger despite all her efforts … it is misery if one raises a young woman only for a man, and if she enters into marriage only to be able to survive".[10]

Vojta Náprstek was undoubtedly the hero of the patriotic ladies of Prague. However, he himself was an internationalist who, to be sure, idealized America. His somewhat amateurish but important museum where he collected ethnological materials from the whole world as well as industrial machinery glorifying progress, the chief goal of which was the emancipation of women, mark him as a man of the nineteenth century in a positive sense.

It was also he, as a member of the Prague city council, who pointed out in 1878 the discrepancy between the amount allocated for boys' trade schools and that allocated for girls' schools for the following fiscal year—12,000 guilders as opposed to 1600. He stressed that this injustice can only be explained by the assumption of many men that it is the job of a woman to marry and to have children. "There are many men who … don't even think of marriage. We can neither force them nor punish them as in Sparta they punished old bachelors."[11]

The house "u Halánků" remained, until Pepička's death, the cultural center of Prague Society and a place where Czechs from abroad, especially America, could feel at home.

The 1860s, the time following Bach's absolutism, were marked by a surge of Czech patriotism. It manifested itself in a great deal of sociability and in the founding of hundreds of organizations. The most important of the latter was Sokol, already mentioned, which ultimately included large contingents of Czechs all over the world.

About that time, as in other cities with a growing bourgeoisie and an even more rapidly growing population of working class poor, charity bazaars became popular. Sellers and buyers were bourgeoises and aristocrats; the poor, the beneficiaries did not attend the functions. Although the dominance of the German language there should have been expected, it was criticized severely, as was the use of German in public generally.

About the time when the American Ladies' Club was losing momentum, a more exclusive, much smaller group of people, many of them writers or critics and more men than women, began to congregate regularly in the home of Anna Lauermannová née Mikschová. The meetings of this most famous literary salon continued from 1880 on for nearly fifty years, with its hostess the confidante of three generations of literati.

Theater had been a popular type of entertainment for a long time. As early as 1850 the drive to collect money all over the country for the construction of a national theater was launched, and the corner stone was laid in 1868. When the National Theater burned to the ground after only a few performances in 1881, money was again raised, this time more quickly and with the help of virtually the entire Czech population, so that it could be reopened in 1883. Much of the money was collected by women's organizations.

In order to convey to the reader somewhat of an idea of how limited the financial possibilities of women must have been, I present a statistical table[12] showing the relative employment of men and women which unfortunately says nothing about women in the lower strata or those employed in households:

In 1881, men and women were employed in Prague as follows:

	Men	Women
Officials:	2,636	24
Teachers	1,253	931
Lawyers and notaries	192	2
Physicians	294	2
Lower officials	667	2
Writers, artists, musicians	114	8
Actors	507	97
Painters, sculptors	205	10
Engineers, architects	261	–

National Theater

In the last two decades of the nineteenth century, when the national revival was accomplished, women remained highly motivated and active as writers and in various other areas of cultural life, in the women's movement, in politics, and later, in the twentieth century, in the anti-Nazi resistance and finally, as dissidents against the communist regime.

As early as the 1890s, the graduates of Minerva had much more diverse interests than its founders and became scientists, doctors, lawyers, artists, etc. As Prague continued to grow and to become more Czech, the number of Czech women of whom there is general awareness continued to grow, also because increasing numbers of Czechs rose into the middle class.

As we move into the twentieth century, nationalism as a common theme disappears. As a protagonist of the modern age, Milena Jesenská (1894-1944) comes to mind first. What makes her an unusually good subject for inclusion in this study are not only her personal qualities, but also the varied records about her, which enable us to view her from many different perspectives. She, one of the three twentieth-century Czech women I chose because of their different personalities, interests and careers, died in a Nazi concentration camp. The second, Milada Horáková (1901-1950) survived imprisonment by the Nazis and was executed by the Communists. Jiřina Šiklová (1935–), our youngest protagonist and at least a cousin in spirit of Milena Jesenská, was jailed by the Communists for organizing the illegal transmission of literature. For years she cleaned institutional offices and corridors, but is now back at the university, teaching and coordinating a program of gender studies.

What about Czech Jewish women? Although there had probably been Czech speaking Jewish women in the Czech villages for centuries, there seem to have been few primarily Czech speaking ones in Prague, and in the period which concerns us, almost none about whom there is any adequate written material.

Czech-Jewish society was only emerging in the late nineteenth century, although Jewish literature had first been written in Czech in the 1840s, when Siegfried Kapper had been rejected by Karel Havlíček who can almost be considered an official spokesman of the Czechs. The Jewish women portrayed in the literature written by members of the Czech-Jewish movement were probably idealized, but we can assume that the traditional roles in which they were portrayed probably correspond to reality.

When that movement began in the 1880s, it was by far the strongest in smaller towns among the less affluent, and dominated by men. It was at least a generation later that Czech-Jewish women became active, by then not as propagandists for the movement which, in fact, had come to a standstill, but as professionals of various kinds. They seemed to be engaged in practical tasks and so confident about their world—this was the time of the First Republic—that they found no time for reflective writings. The situation of the Czech-Zionist women must have been similar, but in addition, they rejected the diaspora and therefore were programmatically opposed to preserving their past.

If I am including one Czech-Jewish woman, Gisa Picková-Saudková (1883-1944), although she spent little of her life in Prague, it is because her diary covers what I believe to be the main problems in the life of a Jewish woman in her time and place who desperately wants to be accepted as a Czech in a particularly thoughtful and intelligent way.

German-gentile society, being middle and upper class in contrast to the other ethnic groups which were upwardly mobile, tried to preserve—more anxiously as time went on—its status. It maintained a mutually beneficial cultural and political symbiosis with its Jewish counterpart until the 1880s.

The German-gentile women were part of a very different society than the Czechs. For the most part proud of their status and very much aware of the contrast between themselves and the Czechs, they were remarkably inactive individually, although some took part in organizations. They became publicly active much later than the Czechs, and very much later than women in France, Germany, and England.

The educated German women knew French and English, and in general "kitchen Czech". The well-to-do traveled abroad and read the standard works of the German classics or saw them on stage. There were some writers among them who are listed in the appropriate lexica, and there was, from some time before the end of the 19th century on, at least a women artists' club, but it seems to have left little of a mark outside of its own limited circle.

Wilhelmine Wiechowsky (born 1834) stood out among her contemporaries as a woman of strong social and especially feminist concerns, but her most influential co-workers for women's education were men. Seemingly a very outer directed person, she left no personal account of her own life, but wrote a biography of her husband and devoted the money she inherited to his career. She was impressed by the dynamism of Czech women engaged in a wide variety of activities ranging from providing vocational education for women to writing outstanding novels, and felt that German society limped behind them.

Generalizing about the few German-gentile women I am able to present is problematic because of their small numbers; their very scarcity is a function of one of their main characteristics: they were modest about themselves and in their memoirs dealt largely with famous men, as if they were the main raison d'être for their writings.

The German women's educational, emancipatory organizations which continued into the twentieth century had Jewish members and benefited from the support and the prestige of male Jewish sympathizers. However, while some men actively supported women's organizations, there were no men who came forth militantly for or against women's emancipation. For example, in his speech "Bahn frei! Ein Wort für unsere Frauen" [Clear the road for our women] (Prague, 1895), evidently addressed to German-speaking women generally, Moritz Popper favors the study of medicine for women, yet strictly opposes women competing freely with men—"because they could never win"—and because it would not be good for them.

Autobiographical writings or other materials from which we can piece together even sketchy portraits of Prague German-gentile women are very scarce. Hedda Sauer, the wife of professor August Sauer, and a poet and writer herself, left memoirs which are not suitable for our purposes because they report almost exclusively about the famous men she knew, especially Rilke. Pauline Countess Nostitz, originally from Germany, published two volumes in which she concentrated on her two husbands and said almost nothing about herself. Ossip Schubin who spent much of her life in castles on country estates near Prague and traveling only left memoirs about her childhood and youth and leaves the reader with the feeling that she did not quite live in reality. She was never married and long stretches of her life seemed like a pattern without action or dynamism.

If one had polled the population of Prague about mid-century, it might have placed the Jews as the most despised ethnic group at the bottom of the social ladder. But there was among them an upwardly mobile minority whose activities and education fitted them for a higher station in life. As the century moved into its second half, Prague Jewish women, who were educated in German and read the German classics, became ladies of leisure in increasing numbers. Toward the end of the century some of them became active in German women's artistic and educational organizations. For most of them, a good marriage was the only way to gain economic security and therefore it seems plausible that most of the few who left any kind of a mark, i.e. those with imagination, luck, and intelligence, from the 1870s until the 1920s, moved abroad at an early age, mostly to Berlin "in order to make something of themselves."

Old Post Office in the Old Jewish Quarter

It seems that the question why, in the prosperous part of Prague German-Jewish society especially from the three-quarter mark of the nineteenth century on, there is no female equivalent of the well-known male intelligentsia, has never been addressed. In the writings of each of the women who moved to other cities we can find remarks about the stifling atmosphere of the Prague Jewish society which they had left behind. From their memoirs and autobiographical fiction, we learn that unlike their male relatives, their contacts had been limited to the Jewish society from which they came. Since only a few of them gradually succeeded in going on to university or in pursuing an artistic career, and even taking a job was a threat to the prestige of a good middle class family, the majority seem to have lived in a sort of holding pattern, a purposeless limbo, waiting to be matched with the socially and economically right husband. Since the eligible men also had access to gentile women for sex or marriage, the young Jewish women were caught between the Scylla of anxiety about finding someone to marry and the Charybdis of playing "hard to get".

I am devoting chapters to two women who moved to Berlin, both of whom had very colorful careers, but very different from each other: Grete Fischer (1893-1977) and Ruth Klinger (1906-1989). I also shall be dealing with one of the exceptions, Berta Fanta (1866-1918), who stayed in Prague where she played an important role in its cultural life.

Various sources agree about the situation of German-Jewish women in Prague. In P. St. Jungk's *Franz Werfel: Eine Lebensgeschichte* [A Biography], Anuschka Deutsch is quoted by the author as saying "... before the First World War ... to have a date in a coffee house ... was as impossible as if you would crawl up the wall. In our circles, meetings took place in the [families'] apartment, at parties."

Max Brod's novel *Jüdinnen* (Jewish Women) (1922) provides the best mosaic of the situation of, and attitude toward, Jewish women in Prague before the First World War.

Here a few quotations will have to suffice:

"... girls, weren't they those white and stupid creatures, to whom one brings flowers in the dance halls?"[13]

Even supposedly positive remarks about women are condescending: "I like to associate with women ... and I always notice admirable traits in them. Once their light airy dresses, another time a charming remark, quiet goodness;"[14] and "One actually never converses with girls, ... one entertains them."[15]

Older women seem worse, if anything. Thus, "Frau Weil talks a blue streak about a thousand outdated things, stream of consciousness style"[16] "... Frau Popper and Frau Rosenthal made petty, cruel remarks."[17] On another occasion "The women screeched."etc. [18]

Or "It is hard to understand these Jewesses. They are despicable, calculating, strange and tough, cunning to the bone ..."[19]

This is how the women in the families of the lively, intellectual Prague Jews of the turn of the century were perceived.

One woman will be introduced who is between ethnic categories: Hermine Hanel (1874-1944), the daughter of a Jewish mother and a gentile father, who was raised by her German-speaking Jewish grandparents. Like most of the other German women, she concentrates in her memoirs on the famous men she has known, and like most of the Jewish women, she left Prague at an early age to lead a freer life. It seems that her artistic interests and perhaps closeness to Catholicism made her decide on Munich as her final home.

Women, Jewish and gentile, had been playing a role in the cultural life of Germany, France, and England for generations. However, in Prague, and of course in the rest of Bohemia in the first half of the nineteenth century, Czech women were becoming increasingly active, but there were no German or German-Jewish women yet who are remembered for their cultural contribution. In the Czech-Jewish category, the one woman to whom I feel that I can devote a chapter, Gisa Picková-Saudková probably did not live up to the potential of her turn of the century manuscript because of the problems she had with her identity.

We can only speculate what would have become of our various protagonists if they had not been held back by, or been preoccupied with, the particular prejudices of their time or class, by family members who had power over them or by economic problems. Or did precisely those problems have an effect similar to that of the pebble in the oyster?

A Little Lesson in Nomenclature

I am sure that readers will notice that I am often referring to the protagonists by their first names. This is, of course, not a sign of condescension, but of familiarity or affection. Some explanations of Czech women's names are in order. During the time of the Czech national awakening, some Czechs gave themselves Slavic first or middle names. So Magdalena Rettigová inserted the name Dobromila (meaning the good and dear one) between her first and last names. Her husband, a lawyer, gave himself the name Sudiprav, meaning judge right. Božena Němcová, born Barbara (or Barbora) Panklová, was called by the diminutive Barunka and later Betty as a child. Božena, the name she chose for herself, was the name of an early Czech princess, meaning something like "of God", and became popular because of Němcová's fame. The name of her youngest son was Jaroslav, but in her letters she usually refers to him as Jarouš or Jaroušek. Her daughter's name, Theodora, was usually shortened to Dora, but occasionally the endearing form Dorinka was used. She also used Bohdana, the Czech translation of Dora, but it does not appear in the texts used in this chapter.

The names in the Náprstek family could almost be the subject of a separate paper. We have already discussed the Czech-German switches of this family name in the introduction. However, there is more. Members of the family were sometimes referred to by the name of an earlier owner of their house, Halánek, and therefore their house and business establishment were often referred to as "u Halánků", i.e. at the Haláneks'. Vojta is the abbreviation of Vojtěch, which is Adalbert in German; that form was used too, although rarely. Vojta's wife Josefa was sometimes called Pepa or Pepča for short, or Pepička, which are all forms of endearment. Paní Pepička [Mrs.Pepička] is a form more familiar than Mrs. plus last name. To complicate matters: the "a" at the end of women's first names becomes an "o" in the vocative, i.e. the case used when addressing someone. The form "panímaminka" [Mrs. Mother] implies affection as well as respect. Here we only have to be concerned with one masculine vocative: Zdeněk becomes Zdeňku.

Increasingly in the nineteenth century Czech children were given Czech sounding names at birth. This practice continued until recent decades.

The names of our German protagonists require little explanation. Schubin, whose actual name was Aloisia Kirschner, and to whom reference works sometimes refer as Lola, or Lula, was mentioned as Ossip (part of her pseudonym) by her cousin Hedda Sauer, and so I decided to do likewise. Similarly I often refer to Hermine Hanel as Mizzi, which is what her family called her.

Most Czech last names add -ová when used for women, omitting the "e" before the last consonant; thus Němec becomes Němcová, and Náprstek Náprstková. With hyphenated last names, the reverse of the American usage is customary on the European continent: the married name comes first, then the maiden name. Thus Picková-Saudková's maiden name was Saudková.

I used the Czech names of towns for those which were predominantly Czech at the time with which I was dealing, or which played a role in the lives of Czech protagonists and German ones for German settings. I referred to Terezín rather than Theresienstadt because it became internationally notorious when Germans no longer lived there. Mariánské Lázne or Marienbad, Karlovy Vary or Karlsbad, Teplice or Teplitz? I find either designation problematic: on the one hand, they still are to some extent known by their German names, on the other the Czech names on modern maps correspond to post World War ll reality.

NOTES

1. *Ženské listy*, [Women's Pages], 1 October 1874.
2. Member of socialist movement which believed in equality for women.
3. A name with connotations from very early Czech history.
4. As cited by Helena Volet-Jeanneret, *La Femme tchèque au dix-neuvième siècle* (Lausanne, 1988).
5. Sokol was a Czech nationalistic association patterned on the German *Turner* movement. Its main emphasis was on sports and physical training and it was ultimately extended to Slavs everywhere.
6. Eliška Krásnohorská: *Co přinesla léta* vol.2, pt. 2 (Prague 1928), p. 174–183. [What the Years Brought].
7. The family's name had been Náprstek, which means thimble in English, until sometime in the eighteenth century when a priest Germanized an ancestor's name on a birth certificate. Thus it was Fingerhut until Vojtěch returned from the USA and changed it back to Náprstek.
8. *Ženské listy* [Women's Pages], no. 3, 1876, p. 39.
9. To an extent, I believe, his perception was correct. In America, women were able to go to some colleges at the time when the club was founded and appliances such as sewing and washing machines were introduced in America earlier than in Europe.
10. *Národní listy*, [National Pages], 5.10.1881.
11. From Vlasta Kucerová, "K historii ženského hnutí: Amerlingova éra" [The History of the Women's Movement: Amerling's era], in *Ženská revue* [Women's Review] 1914, p. 1.
12. From Jeanneret, op.cit., p. 273.
13. Max Brod, *Jüdinnen*, (Leipzig 1922) p.14.
14. ibid., p. 248.
15. ibid., p. 70.
16. ibid., p. 119.
17. ibid., p. 120.
18. ibid., p. 256.
19. ibid., p. 325.

Chapter 1

MAGDALENA DOBROMILA RETTIGOVÁ

(1785–1845)

Rettigova from the 1985 edition of her 1826 cookbook.

*M*agdalena Dobromila Rettigová *is known to Czechs to this day as the author of the cook book* Domácí kuchařka *[The Home Cook], first published in 1826 and still in use. She, however, thought of herself more as a worker for the Czech national awakening, and wrote her cook book because "more people run after a good dinner than after the most beautiful poem."[1] By choosing and polishing her language carefully, Rettigová was able to teach good Czech to many housewives who may otherwise not have learned to read Czech at all.*

Rettigová has elicited vastly different, even emotional responses from critics down to our own day. In order to convey a sense of her continuing relevance, I am quoting excerpts from some of them in this chapter, following her condensed autobiography. Our picture of Rettigová will be completed by the description of a social occasion in which she was involved as imagined by a novelist and by sampling of the very varied views of her by critics in the twentieth century.[2]

In addition to cookbooks, Rettigová also wrote books of advice for the kitchen and the household, as well as children's tales and romantic stories and plays. She had been introduced to Czech literature by her husband, but her first writings, stories and a play with the characteristic name Unschuld und Edelmut *[Innocence and Nobility of Soul], were in German. Rettigová was the only Czech writer of her time who wrote in German as well as in Czech, and her famous cook book also first appeared in German. After becoming acquainted with Czech writers and a publisher, she joined a circle of Czech literati, and soon began writing only in Czech and supporting the Czech national revival. She did not write great literature; rather her fiction was written in the sentimental fashion of her time. Her letters, which were clearly not intended to be read only by their recipients, became an important link between patriots in Bohemia and Moravia and helped bring together groups for discussion—one might call them simple cultural salons. In her lifetime she became recognized as the best naive Czech poet—in fact, one of her poems acquired the status of folk songs.*

However, Rettigová's writing was always less important to her than patriotic encouragement, especially of women. She felt there could be no progress if women who raised children lived in darkness and ignorance. In 1820 she published a proclamation, urging women to become literate and to acquire an education. Through her efforts a foundation was created which awarded outstanding graduates of the girls' schools substantial amounts of money upon reaching adulthood. As one of the group of patriots who approached the Emperor on behalf of the Czech national movement, she set an example for women to take on their share of public responsibility. Of course she did not ask for emancipation.

While she dedicated most of her books to noblewomen, Rettigová was more than critical of the nobility whom she perceived as parasites. She extolled the bourgeois values of industry, thrift, veracity, self-control and the desire to acquire property while accepting its possible loss philosophically. Productive activity was most important to her. However, in her religious writings she reveals another side of her character with passages reflecting Baroque attitudes: "You food for worms, you handful of ashes! Why are you so agitated about transitory matters?"[3] Elsewhere she uses the motif of blood and the martyrdom of Christ, the skull, the cemetery, etc.

The Rettigs moved all over Bohemia, from Tábor to Přelouč, to Ústí nad Orlicí and Rychnov nad Kněžnou. Rettigová, or Dobromila as she now called herself, was a well known poet by 1834 when the family moved to Litomyšl, an important cultural center in Eastern Bohemia and famous for its schools and activities. There the soil proved especially fertile for Rettigová's endeavors, and she was most productive. Both she and her husband worked diligently to purify the Czech language of Germanisms. She invited women from all walks of life to her home, gave them advice, and lent them Czech books, which at that time were rare and censored.

Two of the Rettigs' children—out of a total of eleven—survived to adulthood. Their daughter Jindřiška, born 1813, became an actress and a well-known opera singer. Her son Josef, born 1821, was influenced by his mother's fascination with minerals, and became a mineralogist and a member of a religious order.

Rettigová continued to develop new interests throughout her life and in her sixtieth year is reported saying, "who stops, recedes". The death of her husband in 1844 had a very destructive effect on her. She began losing strength, wrote farewell letters to her friends and died in 1845, at the age of sixty. Her autobiography, very much abbreviated, only deals with the early part of her life.

I was born 31 January 1785.[4] At that time my father, František Artmann, was burgrave of Všeradice which then belonged to Count Kounic ... . When I was five, my father went as steward to Statenice, which at that time belonged to Count Špork. There my memory begins.

All my siblings died a short time after birth, and I was the only child to live, but thanks to my parents I was not spoiled. My father was preoccupied with his duties and paid little attention to my upbringing. He loved me without showing me his love, because he could not stand a lively girl around him who might disturb him in his work. I only recognized his love when he rocked me on his knees in his free moments and talked to me about what I would have to learn when I grew older. He let me know that he wasn't leaving me any riches, but rather that I would have to learn all a girl can learn. I treasured those words in my heart and fulfilled the wishes of my good father as much as I could.

The second proof of his love was: when my mother, upset by my faults, punished me too severely and treated me badly, he often criticized her with sharp words: "You have only one child, and you are going to deprive yourself of it by your unreasonable and bad behavior!" This certainly was proof of his love, though it still wasn't right for him to say it in my presence. It would not have been good for me if my mother had only punished me when my father didn't see it; I thank [her for this] still today.

Without siblings and without playmates—for I was not allowed to associate with the children from the village—I soon learned to occupy myself and to limit myself to associating with my mother. Already in my fifth year I knew more than many spoiled children in their tenth. From my fifth year on she no longer knitted for me; for my fifth birthday she gave me six pairs of new stockings, a large ball of wool and needles with the words: "From now on you will only have what you knit for yourself; you are big enough! …" For this, too, I still thank her today, for thereby I learned to be patient and industrious, which I am to this day. I already knitted … and sewed small things, but I did not learn to sew for dolls, because that kind of entertainment was alien to me and I didn't have a single doll.

When I was six, my grandfather sent me a beautiful large doll for St. Nicolas, and I began to occupy myself with it. Then my mother said: "Aren't you ashamed of yourself, such a big girl still playing with dolls!" I was ashamed, went to my room, took out the doll and cut up her silk dress. Then I carried her to the stove and threw her in the fire. When she burned, the maid screamed and cried for her, but I said it was a disgrace to play with a doll and went to my room to make padding out of the cut-up dress. When my mother found out she scolded me, but praised me for giving up playing so easily. It was my first and last doll.

I became so accustomed to working, that I even sat at home and knitted on the last days of Carnival. When a neighbor came … and told me that the ants eat work made on those days, I replied: "I'll test if it's true. If it isn't, I'll gain two days of work annually and at most I'll lose half a stocking!" And I continued knitting. Because I already knew how to do many things and because I took no pleasure from anything except my own occupations, it was my greatest pleasure to pass my skills on to others. I used to visit the daughter of a head forester who was two years older than I and I taught her various things.

At that time one wing of the castle was occupied by the widowed Baroness Sternthal. Because her small estate, Kamyk, about an hour from Statenice, only had an apartment for a steward, she asked my father to let her have some rooms which he did with pleasure. This was the happiest time of my childhood, for the baroness brought new life into our household. She had two daughters: Therese, who was already grown, and Antonia, a few years older than myself. They were fond of me and had no ugly pride as nobility. I spent most of my time with them, going for walks, and for the first time I had that happy feeling of friendship which lasts in my soul to this day. I have not seen them since … .

In 1792 my father died and I began to suffer, for only then did I come to know people. I received lessons when I was seven for which many people pay dearly for years later.

I saw … that mosquitoes dance only in sunrays; my father had hardly died, when the same people who had bowed deeply before my mother suddenly saw it was no longer necessary. I had no idea that my father was really dead, and went ten times daily to the chapel … where he lay; I pulled him by his legs, because I thought he had to get up … .

On the way to the funeral … I tried to comfort my mother, who was crying, with words from the Bible, which I had often heard and read. In my sixth year I already knew how to read and write perfectly, I copied many sentences and impressed them on my memory. After mass we accompanied the coffin to the grave, and an oppressive feeling came over me—perhaps a premonition of suffering—and I decided to throw myself on my father's coffin. When an official pulled me back I asked: "What am I going to have here without a father?" They carried me from the church unconscious, and I remained sick for several days. That was the first time a feeling of unconsolable sadness overcame me which even now often arouses the attention of my best friends.

My mother went to Prague to ask … for a pension, and took me along. The carriage stopped at the house of the official … where we usually went. But what a difference! In earlier times the windows opened before we got out, and the master and the lady were there as well as a servant, to help us upstairs and to assure us that they were our best friends. On that day also we could see a head in the window, but nobody came to meet us, and the servant told us to wait … .Finally, after five minutes, we were admitted. They expressed their condolences, but they were so cold, that even I … felt it. And this is how we fared in many places … . In those few hours I accumulated more wisdon than many people … accumulate in a long life.

Instead of a pension, Count Clary gave my mother the alternative of either choosing some secretary for a husband within six weeks, or marrying an official he would send her from his estate. Then he would give her new husband my father's position … .

My mother was twenty-six years old at the time and pretty enough for a second marriage. But as a widow who had buried her husband hardly three days before, she had to reject that kind of an offer. She replied that [the man] would choose her because of the position and not because of herself. Six weeks passed and my mother went to recommend a certain Mixta to his Excellence. "Aha," said the count, smiling ironically, "so one was found after all. And when will the wedding be?" "Your Excellency," my mother said, "he has been married for some time." He shrugged his shoulders: "You are a little fool and you will soon be sorry." He was right.

If my mother wasn't sorry … that she did not accept the count's suggestion, she had to be sorry that she asked that Mixta. As soon as he came with his family, he showed his ungratefulness to such an extent that she moved away, although she could have stayed there as long as he wanted. In Prague [in my father's inheritance] there was money for me and for my twenty weeks old brother.

The humane Baroness von Sternthal offered my grief stricken mother a rent-free apartment where we moved in the middle of winter. But we could not heat the high, elegant rooms where we stayed. The small iron stove used to be red-hot, but nevertheless it was very cold near the window. My mother suffered from worries and various troubles in connection with my father's inheritance … They managed [it] in such a way that after three years, when the estate was settled, at most four hundred guilders remained for my mother and me. My little brother had died in the meantime. After that winter my mother became sick with rheumatism, and since the doctors blamed the cold apartment, she had to rent a small, warm place. Her sickness lasted a number of years … until finally a young doctor … cured her … in a short time. Because of my brother's constant illness, her share of the inheritance was almost gone … .

I was always healthy and active. I felt very badly, having heard my mother say at my brother's bedside: "If God really wants to take one of my children, let it be the girl, not the boy." Now I see that those words were not meant badly, for one is always fondest of the sick child. But at the time those words wounded me deeply. I hid somewhere, cried bitterly, and wished to join my father in his grave.

I have dwelled on my early years so long, in order to show that in my childhood [there were] already more thorns than roses. I now want to pass over many painful memories more briefly.

When I was ten, my mother moved to Pilsen. There I went to the city school … . The hours spent there were my happiest, all the more because in those days a very different spirit prevailed than does now. I … had fifteen-to-eighteen year old classmates who knew much less than I, especially in handicrafts. The better among them approached me to learn from me; others were jealous and hated me, especially because in their cosy bee hive I was a strange bee … .

This again caused me many difficult hours, but also much pure pleasure, for about ten good, industrious girls were entirely mine. On free days I was in charge of them during private lessons; they … had to do small assignments, calculations … for me, and each had to knit an inch more than the teacher had assigned … . So it happened that the teacher marked them as industrious. On free days we recited our school lessons and knitted at the same time … . The hard workers received small gifts from me, either a painted picture, or one pricked in paper or embroidered in cross stitch. Those things were rare then, I had some from my mother, some from "mamsel" [mademoiselle], a governess with the von Sternthals. Knitting gloves was another activity [which was not even known to the teacher of handicrafts].

After one and a half years in Pilsen we returned to Prague, where my whole youth was devoted to learning and teaching … . I was glad to share [my knowledge] with others. My reward was often ungratefulness born of envy, and therefore it happened, that even as a thirteen-year old girl I withdrew more and more … and looked for a good book or for conversation with a serious matron from whom I could learn something for the household. This pleased me more than a circle of vain and superficial girls, who ridiculed me as "the nun" or "the old, wise one".

Sometimes I stayed at my mother's, sometimes at her sister's, at whose house I experienced great, unbearable sufferings. And yet I am very grateful for it, for I gained a great deal of strength for life; there I learned patience which was highly necessary in my later life.

Out of respect and love I am not betraying the name of this aunt and her daughter who particularly tortured me … . I always loved this aunt and her daughter as I do my mother … . Only later did I understand how they taught me through their behavior to patiently bear great sufferings. They also proved to me that once I love somebody, nothing can destroy that love.

In my thirteenth year I became ill with a persistent cough. I spent my time working and reading and, since pain kept me from sleeping, I read the Bible and the Life of Christ all nights through, but only at night because I was forbidden to read books. In the daytime—when nobody was watching—I read while knitting ... . I was fortunate to learn to read novels, but I picked only the noble pages from them ... .

The cough did not improve. I suffered much from my cousin, but ... I did not complain ... and also patiently bore my aunt's lack of appreciation. I swallowed everything, ... and there was a lot. I fell seriously sick with jaundice, hoped to die and longed to be taken to St. Elizabeth's hospital. My wish was granted, and I was close to death ... so that they already rang the death knoll and prayed the Hail Mary at my beside. I lay ... unconscious for many hours, but I was still able to hear, and I remember clearly the feeling which went through me when I heard them say that I was already almost dead. I had a holy inner longing for that unknown world and only reluctantly felt my life's strength return.

My youth prevailed, my health improved ... and I asked the sisters for work, which they were glad to give me. I mended napkins and marked one nun's underwear, for which they sometimes gave me a better morsel. I liked life there and I decided that the convent is a refuge from all sufferings, where one can work, read, pray and at the same time seem holy to everybody. This thought preoccupied my mind which was inclined toward melancholy, and I wanted to become a nun. But I had to go home, where they laughed about my nuns and holy thoughts. This bothered me and made me even more reserved. [My aunt and cousin] wrote my mother, complained about me ... but I looked forward to her arrival.

[I expected that they would again treat me badly and that—weakened by my illness—I again would become sick and die.] My mother arrived one beautiful, cheerful winter afternoon in 1798. ... I felt both fright and joy, while my cousin hurried to meet her. My mother entered and immediately asked excitedly where one could buy tickets to ... the nearest ball, paying no attention to me. When I kissed her hand, she did not react ... and hurried to my aunt's room. Speechless and deathly pale I staggered to a chair and moistened my work with tears, for my fervent feeling longed for her to pay attention to me before asking for tickets for the ball. I did not follow her ... and worked until they had thoroughly badmouthed me. I shall never forget the moment they called me. They reproached me for things of which I had no idea. My mother could hardly control herself with excitement and looked for a wooden spoon to punish me. But the cook who knew everything told her ... I was innocen. She then threw away the wooden spoon, came to me and for the first time I had a good cry … . The tickets to the ball were bought, and I was told I could also go along. It was the first ball I was allowed to attend, and I cried bitterly … because I considered it a sin against my desire to enter the convent. But my mother forced me … and I obeyed like a puppet … .

For a thirteen year old girl [it] could be a fairy-tale castle, but for me it was suffering; … I declined to dance. My forehead was gloomy, but my slender figure attracted many dancers … .

After several days I left the capital with my mother and accompanied her to Kamenné, to be with Countess Bredovská. I liked life in the country, and the new occupation without suffering gave me back my health and my good cheer. When the snow melted and I saw nature reawakened in all its beauty, I felt well, and when I went for a walk past the little chapel or past the statues of saints, I did not forget to present them with a little wreath of field flowers and to pray. So gradually my monastic ideals faded, and I decided that it isn't necessary to be behind convent walls to live a religious life pleasing to God. Running through fields, woods, hills and valleys, I found hundreds of new works of the Creator which … I would have to do without in the convent.

There I also learned much about the art of cooking, for the cook— an older man for whom cleanliness was the main virtue—liked me to ask him various questions and at the same time to help … . So I learned to make butter dough. Because … I tried to do everything accurately, the old man used to sit comfortably in his high chair and let me work … . The countess had nothing against it and often praised my decorative table settings, in which I displayed more taste than the old cook … . I retained a liking for that, remembered many things or noted them down … .

After that summer we returned to Prague, where I stayed with my mother and learned to tat lace at Mrs. Kasárková's. There I also learned great patience, having to constantly hold the cushion on my lap and tat from eight in the morning until twilight. She was a good lady but a strange one, but what attracted me was her four-year old daughter Josephine. The child loved me unspeakably; almost all day she sat on the little stool at my feet wanting me to talk to her. Although I strained my eyes all day, I used to read until midnight, just so that I could again tell dear Josephine something new the next day. But this pleasure did not last long. The child became sick with pneumonia … and died … . She always wanted me, day and night … and in my arms she took leave of life. I did not want to leave the little corpse … and put my ear on her mouth and heart, but little Josephine remained dead.

The day after her funeral my shoulder felt lame, like after a stroke, but it became sensitive again after I rubbed it with onion and vinegar. I was exhausted ... and came down with a throat infection ... . My time of learning ended ... . I lived with my mother and my occupation was constant work. My entertainment in free moments were books. I had no friendships with girls my age, because they thought differently. I limited myself only to contact with my mother who was my confidante and friend and whom I loved unspeakably.

I avoided young people, especially students, because of tales I frequently used to hear about the consequences of such relationships. I was more inclined toward serious men, because of what I might learn from them I lived with my mother on the third floor of a house in the rear of which some students lived. One considered it worth his effort to strike up an acquaintance with me, a fifteen-year old girl, but his plan failed because of my lack of interest. These gentlemen were second-year law students, and my later husband seemed the most serious of them. Although I did not speak to any of them, I liked best to respond to his greeting. I didn't know his name, but while hidden I often listened with pleasure to songs he sang at the open window in the evening by the light of the moon ... .

We left that apartment without my making his acquaintance. I moved to my aunt's house for the second time ... and saw many things which did not inspire great confidence in the male sex in me ... .

Later I had to watch over [the vineyard my uncle left, together with my cousin Nanette], for she was afraid to live there alone ... The overseer was a cunning rogue who soon noticed that Nanette ... was afraid of ghosts,[and wanted to make sure that he would continue to be in charge, without our interference.] The very first day he told us a number of stories about the ghost that allegedly appeared there after my uncle's death ... .

Magdalena solved the mystery of the ghost, Nanette moved back into town and Magdalena remained in charge by herself. During that time she learned much about farming...

Although I was indifferent toward the stronger sex, I was on my guard. It took great courage when here and there a little butterfly longed to come close to the isolated little flower. So it happened that a darkeyed, by the way very handsome man did not mind a two-hour walk to see me. But I considered it most unsuitable ... to receive the visits of young men in my isolation and tried hard to make the visits difficult for him. He deprived me of many hours which I could have spent reading a good book. So I decided on a trick: I said that my aunt was coming ... and dressed up a dummy aunt. I put two pillows from the sofa on the chair near the window, attached them to a pole and hung Nanette's light whig on it ... . I put a scarf over the "aunt's" shoulders, as if she were sitting with her back to the window, and waited for my knight. He sneaked past, glanced at the aunt ... and sadly returned into town. His hat had hardly disappeared ... when I took down my wooden aunt and danced [with her] ... . Once a week I left my dummy in the corner and allowed him to accompany me to the fields. People laughed about this comedy ... [but the overseer who had not forgotten the ghost episode told the visitor the truth which ended his efforts to see me ...] To this day I enjoy thinking about [it]; later I used it in prose and in drama.

With the first snow flakes I returned to Prague ... . That winter I stayed at my aunt's and learned various kinds of work which served me well in later life. Nanette was a very pretty girl, played the piano, sang and danced well, dressed fashionably ... and her parents were very hospitable. [Guests] were well received and Nanette [had] many admirers. As a poor relative ... left with my work and ignored, I had the best opportunities to observe the butterflies and grasshoppers.[5] ...

In spring I moved back to my mother's and learned various handicrafts such as embroidering veils, lacemaking, embroidery with beads, with high scales, working with feathers, making artificial flowers, hats etc. So two or three uneventful years passed ... . In 1803 I was invited by a relative of my father's to visit his family in Písek ... . In the family there were two daughters, Viktoria and Lída ... and because of poorly chosen reading material and too early love affairs ... Lída was unfortunately, as many other girls, unable to talk about anything except clothes, accessories and love. I tried to teach her in various ways, but with regard to her love affairs she—to her detriment—did not listen ... .

Such are girls. They judge superficially and often discard a genuine but inconspicuous diamond hidden in ore while adorning themselves with a sparklng little stone ...

Magdalena then tells of a sensitive and very talented man who had professional problems because of his unattractive appearance. She did her best to help him find a position which would provide a livelihood also for her if they were to marry, but he unexpectedly stopped writing her. Then she tells of two suitors who would not have been right for her.

The man who later became my husband also lived in our building then ... . I knew him as "the little student." [After a friend brought Rettig along once, he] came more frequently, sent me drawings to embroider and other things … I became his sincere friend. Because we agreed in our opinions, he became my confidant and my heart became an open letter to him, in which he could read all my joys and sufferings. …

> *Magdalena was forced by her mother to become engaged to G., a man of sixty. When she cried and prayed in church because she dreaded marrying that man, she met a young man who told her what an evil person G. was. At that point her mother relented and no longer insisted that she marry G. The young man who saved her from that marriage was very much in love with her, but she rejected him, evidently in good part because he limped.*

… I decided more and more in favor of Rettig … . I had known him for ten years … . but neither I nor anybody else thought of love or of marriage between us … He did not mention love with a single word, and so my appreciation continued to increase … .

One beautiful fall day we took a walk to Bubeneč near Prague. It was near the silver foam of St. Mary's well that we both realized our mutual feelings were sincere love … .

I suspected I would have a tough fight with my mother and my uncle ahead of me, because then my husband was only a minor official … . But love, real faithful love, based on the friendship of several years and mutual respect, did not worry about difficulties …

[That day they went dancing to a village fair, and she was bathed in perspiration on the way back.] It was a nice September evening; we walked through the beautiful meadows along the Moldau. The moon shone and a pleasant wind blew through my curls. I carried my hat in my hand, to cool off and in order that Rettig could look me in the eyes. I did not feel cold. [But she became very ill with a sore throat, spat out blood, vomited all she ate. The first and second doctor called agreed that she would be dead in three months.]

Rettigova's husband, AJS Rettig (from her cookbook).

I had to stay in my room and Rettig visited me frequently. Those were pleasant hours, but I was pained by my mother's increasing hatred [toward him]. My condition worsened day by day, and finally the observant doctor pointed out to my mother that I would die if my mental condition did not improve. Rather than let me die, my mother agreed to my marriage. I had been reconciled to [death], feeling I would gain more in the other world than would lose in this one. [Only then Magdalena's mother very reluctantly consented to the marriage with Rettig.]

The first year of married life was a year of pains, for worries, sickness and various other sufferings came right from the start. My mother was moody and my husband suffered with me... .

[When Rettig had an inflamation in his eye, Magdalena energetically interfered with the specialist who wanted to remove the lense from the diseased eye.] ... Several times I had cramps and was seriously

Tabor – city gate

ill. This was aggravated by the sufferings which my mother caused me, so that we finally had to move away from her.

We stayed in Prague a year and a half; then my husband was appointed secretary in Tábor. [There] we were for two years, and only then I came to know people. That is not possible in the capital, because in the constant rush there ... people don't observe each other.

In small towns, the advantage of which is often pleasant boredom, all people, and particularly women, know each other. Each newcomer is an important object of conversation for them. Not a thread on them remains unnoticed, and in addition characteristics and faults of the object of their observation are invented, just so they have more to talk about. I was also fortunate, being able to give them a chance to sweeten their boredom with foolishness.

In me they found much to criticize and to envy, which moved me ever farther from their hearts. Among the things they didn't like was my love of literature, because they could not understand it. It annoyed them that I used many hours more purposefully than they did ... and wrote many poems. And ... I worked more than they. May God forgive them for how I ... suffered! I have forgiven them long ago. I also spent ... cheerful hours [there], thanks to my friendship with ... Filip and Taiber ... . Although these friendships were also the objects of gossip, we didn't care, and when my husband and my friend Filip sat together, we let everyone think whatever he wanted.

My health was weakened considerably by two childbirths ... . Our little girl Jindřiška[6] died after 33 hours, and two years later, after my return from Karlovy Vary in 1811, my six months old boy died. These were the most painful experiences of those four years in Tábor. Those various small town pettinesses I overlooked easily ... .

Some excerpts from Rettigová's letters to the patriot František Dominik Kynský follow:

[undated] ... Thanks to Father Sychr, who sent me Lessing's fairy tales, I now know where you are, and I am dedicating the first hour I can steal from my household and my children to you ... I am sure you know Dr. Koráb; due to his efforts the Czechs are waking up from their deep sleep here in Ústí ... in his absence I try to take his place, for which many people make faces at me. I, however, don't let myself be intimidated, knowing that little that is worthwhile can be accomplished without difficulties. Thanks to his efforts, fines have been introduced here: a gros[7] is paid for every corrupted Czech word. With those fines we have begun to buy Czech books, and Dr. Koráb donated 30 volumes and 30 guilders in cash. Many others are con-

tributing, and I am sacrificing my sizeable German library for those who don't know Czech yet. I worked out the enclosed Czech proclamation ... I love Father Sychr, although I have never laid eyes on him, only because he is a real Czech. We would not have thought fifteen years ago, when I sat on the big green chair at the Piarists' and drank a glass of Malaga from the secret hiding place under the bed, that we would ever meet again as Czechs, for I admit that at that time I hardly knew how to read Czech, and even less how to write it. I blush when I remember that I too was once a sleeping Czech; but now I am awake and no longer asleep, no matter how many rotten Czechs I have to put up with, who ridicule and reject our language! ...

Ústí, 3. December, 1823 ... I went for a ride, not for my enjoyment, but in order to console and give good advice to a mother upset about the sickness of her child. I sat down in a so-called (cursed) Damenwurst, my Pepínek [Joseph] with the nurse came with me. The lively white horse gallopped and aimed toward the middle of the square instead of up the hill to the Church of the Virgin Mary. The coachman, who was born stupid, quickly turned the speeding horse around, and a moment later Mařenka [Rettigová herself] lay on the pavement, and Pepínek and the nurse unharmed on top of her. Mařenka had her leg under the coach, and some iron dug deeply into her leg. I couldn't get up. They carried me away, and the next day I knew that severe consequences were expected. I was in the third month ... So that unfortunate fall saved you from having to write a new lullaby. You almost might have had to think about a dirge, as I was really close to death. I am well again—the old proverb "The frost does not burn nettles" proved to be true. The main thing is that my heart is healthy and sincere, although my leg is not yet healed ... .

(4. September, 1824) ... On the 8. of March of this year my husband sat down on the judge's chair of the town of Rychnov, to judge the living—the dead have no courts.

(In Rychnov nad Kněžnou, 24. September, 1824) ... How am I? Fine, for I carry my most valuable possession, inner contentment, with me everywhere. People loved us in Ústí, here also. It is great bliss, when a superior has the confidence of his subordinates.

Alois Jirásek, one of the most influential Czech writers of a few generations ago, also lived in Litomyšl where he collected remembrances and other material about Rettigová. He wrote in A Literary Excursion Eighty Years Ago[8]: A Sentimental Idyll, an Excursion of Course to an Old Castle, of Czech Literati Together with Their Publisher [Pospíšil] and the Personel of His Print Shop.

Pospíšil went on that excursion with the Rettigs to Kunětická Mountain, and we have a detailed description of it by Rettigová. She wrote it down in a notebook covered with marbled paper. Three vehicles full of people drove down the long town square, just then quiet, out of the fortifications through the Prague gate, along the beautiful road lined with linden trees. We rode for three hours in clouds of dust. At seven-thirty we arrived without any disasters in Kunětice, i.e. at the fortress. Immediately there were lots of busy hands, a fire was built, cream and coffee and pretzels were taken to the watchman's room. The pretzels were Mrs. Rettigová's work. In the quiet ruins of the once famous castle there was suddenly activity and noise. All in all there were about twenty people, including many children. At first all ran to see the view. Rettigová was enthusiastic! Then they looked at the old walls, at the signatures scribbled or engraved on them. Then they were called to breakfast. Mrs. Pospíšilová poured and we all soaked our pretzels in the coffee. They were called Kunětické, and shall be called that forever in memory of that famous day. (See cookbook.) It was the day of John the Baptist, and so after breakfast all the Jans[9] were congratulated ... Tears were flowing, and then the seven Pospíšil children, like organ pipes, expressed their wishes to their father, one after the other.

Then all went down to the little valley, to the little church in the middle of the quiet village, where they all gave thanks to the Lord, who granted them that beautiful day. After mass they went back up to the castle. Examining the ruins, Rettigová investigated in which place "old Kuňák might have built his first court in the year of our Lord 839." Then she went further into the past of Kunětická Mountain... . In her romantic-sentimental reminiscing Rettigová arrived at the last of the Pernštejn family, Lady Febronia, and finally said: "Famous, solid ruin, who built you, who destroyed you, who was happy and mourned inside you, who despaired within you in the terrible famine, who looked out in the distance from your high window, where are they? Where is their glory? Where is their beauty? Where is their dust?"

But to what distant past did my mind fly? Back to the table! Then all ate and drank what the good mother, the good housekeeper Kateřina (Pospíšilová) cooked and baked... . There was wine and the company drank to each other's health and to the health of friends and dear patriots in Bohemia and Moravia. "Long may they live!" resounded from the old, crumbling walls.

Alois Jirásek, who also wrote a play around Rettigová's life, was not the only creative writer intrigued by her personality. As recently as 1987 Rettigová has appeared in a prize-winning German novel, Die Fassade, *by the contemporary Czech author,* Libuše Moníková.

Literary critics have differed greatly in their evaluation of Rettigová's character and talent. Arne Novák, *the most outstanding Czech literary critic of his time wrote in 1905:*

... [Ludwig] Feuerbach's statement of that time: "Eating and drinking are in themselves religious acts" is here fully realized... . The whole universe swims in a fog of kitchen steam, the menu becomes the scale of values, a table of gargantuan proportions is shown as the noble goal of women's strivings ... the fleshy matron rocks through the world without anxiety or problems; one day she gives instructions in a prayer book about how to live in peace with God, the next day she instructs the young housewife about what to do to have a satisfied husband ... a female philistine who found the world as comfortable and philistine as she imagined it in her petty soul.[10]

On the other hand, Novák's mother, Tereza Nováková, *an important writer and organizer of the women's movement, viewed Rettigová within the context of her time and acknowledged her contribution to Czech culture. Writing in 1909, she respected and praised her:*

... in her activity as a poet and novelist, as a writer of practical books, as an organizer of patriotic activities, as a teacher of young people, as a loving wife, a good mother and housekeeper—she fulfilled a number of tasks, each of which could demand her full energy ... She did not follow a well worn-path, but one which was strenuous ... and unusual.

At the turn of the nineteenth century, Czech national consciousness was minimal. It was considered disgraceful to speak Czech, it was only spoken in cottages, by peasants and by the poor. Interest in the language was limited to the minds of a few enthusiasts ... There were almost no schools for girls... . In the early nineteenth century, even learning handicrafts was considered a great luxury ... domestic skills were the main thing. Therefore every woman who rose above that level, and in addition was able to express her thoughts and feelings in Czech, was truly exceptional.[11]

This recognition was continued by Zdeněk Nejedlý, *a communist critic in 1934:*

Rettigová was the first to be concerned about women... . She realized what women can do for the revival ... She worked in small towns, skilfully and successfully... . Her cook book is not ordinary, her language is a well chosen and pure Czech. In front is her portrait: not that of a cook dressed for the kitchen, but dressed in good taste, like a lady, showing that cooking does not have to be humdrum... .

Rettigová also gathered students around her, went to their parties, on excursions and balls, and encouraged them to write poetry.... . She was concerned about their material welfare. She arranged private lessons and free lunches for them, and rewarded them with books for doing well on examinations. She attended all public performances, appeared in plays and polished the [Czech] language wherever she found mistakes. Her influence extended beyond women to students, for whom she arranged tutoring, excursions, and meals, and organized groups interested in theater.... . Her fearless march across many obstacles makes the life of this woman worthy of respect even today.[12]

Julius Fučík, a critic and communist victim of the Nazis wrote perhaps the most scathing commentary in 1940:

... reactionary, limited, conservative and philistine ... a fat matron, rocking through the world without anxiety, without problems ... or uncertainty, creating a banal, petty world full of stupid class conceit.

... Madame de Staël is writing her *Corinne,* and the great and revolutionary George Sand appears on the scene, when Mrs. Rettigová in Bohemia calls the chapters of her greatest work "Brain Dumplings", "Liver Rolls", "May Herb Soup".... . Rettigová is a rare, pure type in the Czech literature of the first half of the nineteenth century, when the need to catch up with the interrupted development ... succeeded in pressing into almost every personality Storm and Stress as well as Biedermeier, romanticism and classicism, Macpherson and Heine. You will [however] find ... nothing like that in Magdalena Dobromila Rettigová. This stately bourgeoise is only Biedermeier.

From her cookbook

... .The Czech petit bourgeoisie gratefully accepted Biedermeier as the codification of its taste, as the sum total of the rules by which it lived ... It does not like great passions ... and even less great thoughts; it trusts the average, the solid person, it wants no surprises... .

With Magdalena Dobromila Rettigová, a woman is not a real being with human proportions, only a complement of the male person, without rights or a life of her own. "A young housewife has to especially see to it", Rettigová advises … "that she removes everything her husband hates, and that she takes pleasure only in what pleases him… . Avoid unpleasantness … even if you are really right, give him a good word … . May heaven preserve you from the thought of standing up to your husband."

… She also says what to do when the "noble man" is seduced by the example of others, by self love, … perhaps by the seduction of ignoble prostitutes. Then the gentle, calm patience of "wifie" can preserve at least peace if not the lost paradise of first bliss, if not love, then at least the husband's respect. The mute face called woman must not show what she knows about her master, but should try to prove to him that he can find at home what he looks for elsewhere. And if she does not succeed, she should be quiet and diligently care for his physical well-being… .

So this is the idyll, seen "in the decent homes for which this book is written", as Rettigová herself says; an idyll seen without idealization, without moralizing, on the contrary, with an effort to preserve it. "Young Bohemia", at that time fighting for women's emancipation, did not reveal more of the abysmal misery of women's subjugation in its militant novels and tracts than this kindhearted matron with her practical advice.

"Whisper all you want", says wise Rettigová, "but obey".

As regards the idyll of Rettigová's own marriage, we have the following testimony in a letter to V. Váša from July 23, 1836:

If I were a twenty-year old girl again with my present experience, I would rather throw myself into the deepest abyss than to a husband. There I would find immediate death, while in marriage one dies gradually, as if daily stabbed and tortured to death by one pin.

NOTES

1. Rettigová in a letter to V. Váša, 23 July 1836. This letter, together with her autobiography and other materials, can be found in the edition of her cook book edited by Felicitas Wünschová, *Domácí kuchařka*, Prague, 1985.
2. All of these texts have been collected in the edition of *Domácí kuchařka* cited earlier.
3. In her prayer book Křestǎnka vzývajici Boha *The Christian Woman Appealing to God* (1827) in the poem "Piseň o nestálosti světa" Song about the Impermanence of the World.

4. ibid., p. 345 ff.
5. i.e. young men. Watching two young men pretend love for Nanette and one of them finally confess he really loved *her*, Magdalena, made her more distrustful toward men then ever.
6. Later she had another girl and also named her Jindřiška.
7. A small coin.
8. *Domácí kuchařka* Praha 1985, pp?
9. Jan is John in English.
10. Arne Novák, *Literatura česká 19. stoleti* [Czech literature of the 19th Century], vol. 3, Prague 1905, p. 205.
11. In her preface to Rettigová's *Domácí kuchařka*, Prague 1909.
12. Z. Nejedlý, *O literatuře* [About literature], (Prague, 1952) p. 224–229.

Chapter 2

BOŽENA NĚMCOVÁ

(1817?–1862)

*Božena Němcová was an unconventional and courageous
woman and an important figure in both Czech literature
and the history of the Czech national revival,[1] but her
character is difficult to capture for newcomers to the Czech
world.*

*To most Czechs for several generations Božena Němcová
has been primarily the author of a perfect work,* Babička *[The
Grandmother], with a perfect heroine in an imperfect world, but
a world still whole and acceptable if, like Němcová's grandmother, one never
questions God's creation. Němcová has often reminded men of the traditional idea
of the Virgin Mary, while women have focused on the unhappily married, misunderstood wife, the woman deserted by her lovers, the mother who—like the
Virgin Mary—lost her beloved son. The communists of course stressed her alleged
early socialism. Many readers could identify with Němcová's fate, perhaps finding it only more tragic than their own, a fate well documented in her letters.*

*Until recently, Němcová was presumed to be the daughter of a fifteen-year-old Viennese servant girl and an Austrian coachman. When she was still an
infant, her family moved to North-Eastern Bohemia to live in the servants'
quarters of Princess Sagan's castle. There eleven more children were born. These
origins are now being questioned, for there are significant indications that
Němcová was the daughter of a countess, born in 1817 rather than 1820 as her
birth certificate states.[2] If Němcová was indeed of noble birth, it would explain
not only her appearance, which was quite different from that of the rest of her
family, but also the close contact she had with her parents' employer, the mistress of the castle, and the fact that she was sent away to be educated. Barunka
Panklová (Němcová's name as a child) was badly treated by the woman until
now presumed to be her mother. Was this because she resented the illegitimate
birth of her daughter, or because she was raising a child not her own? And if
Němcová was not the Pankls' daughter, did she know it?*

Němcová, who changed her first name, Barbora, to the more Czech sounding Božena when she began writing for publication in the early eighteen forties,

*was a startling beauty, with raven hair, green eyes, a peaches and cream com-
plexion and an ideal figure. At the age of seventeen she was forced into a love-
less marriage to Josef Němec, a man fifteen years her senior.*

*During the first few years of her marriage she bore four children and moved
from town to town with her husband who was politically persecuted by the government as a Czech nationalist. When she came to live in Prague, in 1841,
she quickly became the idol of the young, patriotic, Romantic poets, for advancing the Czech cause in literature, folklore and education, and inspiring others
by her own personal heroism when an occasion called for it.*

*If Němcová did not produce as much literature as her friends and supporters
would have wished, she had a number of reasons: there was her own and her
children's poor health—her eldest and most beloved son Hynek died at the age
of sixteen; constant, sometimes violent fights with her husband; and above all
constant economic misery which ultimately included starvation as well as
slummy, damp housing and the necessity to beg for the essentials of life from
well wishers.*

*Knowing her ability to write beautiful prose of her own, many of her con-
temporaries criticized her for spending so much of her time merely collecting fairy
tales and other folkloristic materials instead of creating her own work. Much of
her work consists of tales she collected in Bohemia and Slovakia, and then
edited.[3] What Němcová preferred above all, however, was to write letters, to her
family, friends, other patriots; their literary quality only came to be appreciated
relatively late.*

Němcová is still famous throughout the Czech nation for her novel The
Grandmother. *It is many things: a Biedermeier idyll, an impeccable work of
poetic realism, a projection of her own miserable life into an ideal past which
never existed, and a portrait of a very traditional, exemplary woman, very
unlike Němcová herself. In the increasingly urban atmosphere of Bohemia
today, where memories of life long ago are generally forgotten, references to
Němcová and her grandmother are often countered with remarks about the
changing world which requires a different literature.*

When The Grandmother *appeared in 1855, the decline in Němcová's life
had already set in: her search for an ideal love—one might say mundanely her
succession of lovers—was almost over.[4] She had been abandoned by many of her
friends, her son Hynek was dead, her son Karel had not written from Germany
for almost a year, her youngest son, Jarouš, had given up his art studies in
Munich for financial reasons, and her only daughter, Dora, was constantly sick.
Her husband's career had gone from bad to worse, and he was continually being
banished to work in distant, isolated places—in Austria, in Hungary.
Němcová's portraits dramatically change from those of a young beauty to a pre-
maturely old and bitter woman.*

*Božena Němcová's life is thus full of contrasts: beauty and ugliness, a lov-
ing father and grandmother and a rejecting mother, a coarse husband and intelligent, charming lovers, friends and enemies. The writer Žofie Podlipská spoke
of her in superlative terms while Žofie's sister, Karolina Světlá, the most prominent Czech novelist of the nineteenth century, broke with Němcová because of
her lifestyle. The greatest contrast, however, is between Němcová's death in her*

early forties when she was abandoned and impoverished, and her rich and opulent funeral that turned into an orgy of national mourning.

Němcová, her life and her work, continues to fascinate Bohemists. Václav Černý, perhaps the most interesting Czech post World War II literary historian, explored the background and history of Němcová's real grandmother. Others have concerned themselves with her last publisher, Augusta, considering the possibility that his reputation of having let her starve to death is undeserved.

Němcová also has inspired prose fiction, as well as drama and poetry.

J.V. Frič, a patriot of 1848 and one of Němcová's friends

She comes to life however, above all in her letters. We are bringing a selection of them to the reader, and interspersing them with some reminiscences of people who knew her closely.

One of the earliest glimpses of Němcová is provided by the patriot Josef Václav Frič, writing about his meeting with her in 1844:

We went to Skalice, where we paid a visit to Mrs. Němcová ... We were surprised to find Professor Smetana ... paying the ... famous and truly remarkable young woman ... his respects. After an excellent meal, during which we discussed ... patriotic affairs ... our majestic [sic] hostess accompanied us through the pretty valley to the road to Náchod, always running ahead, jumping over brooks, picking flowers, gathering them into a bouquet to put on her straw hat. All this without any coquetry—she felt at home, and laughed out loud when we stood embarrassed in front of a wooden beam placed across the brook. She crossed as gracefully as a gazelle while we crossed over step by step ... she asked ... about the Latin name of an herb she had found ... It was getting dark ... She decided to return alone, after shaking hands with each of us.

... Of course, we could speak about nothing else than that natural, highly intelligent woman, who then had no idea what trials fate held in store for her.[5]

Vlasta Pittnerová, the daughter of a minor patriot, recalling this period, recorded:

... In ... Polná in the Žďár Mountains ... the Patriotic Society used to meet every Sunday in [my father's] wine restaurant. ... They read Czech newspapers, lent each other Czech books and talked about ...

a more promising future for the Czech nation. It was the time of [Josef Kajetán] Tyl's[6] naive patriotism, when reciting Czech poems, hanging up a picture from Czech history and buying Czech books were considered patriotic deeds …

On the walls of my father's restaurant there were pictures of Czech kings … Hus and Žižka, and those of Czech awakeners … The deacon used to come and get together with the two chaplains, some officials and older citizens. In 1839 this daily company was joined by Josef Bořivoj Němec … Beautiful young Němcová … having received … Tyl's work *Poslední Čech* [The Last Czech], told my father about the deep impression this novel made on her soul. My father offered [her] his library, and she quickly read through it and looked for Czech books wherever she could find them … She also encouraged … the wives of citizens to read Czech books.

… My mother used to tell us that when she went walking in the fields she often met Němcová … with field flowers in her hands, in her waist and in her hair … she used to say that she never met a more beautiful woman. However, Němcová was glad to move to Prague in 1842.

When the name of Božena Němcová appeared in Czech literature … many [Polná] families named their girls Božena. In the quiet town … the name of the famous writer always lived in honor and love …[7]

When the Němec' lived in Domažlice in Western Bohemia, an area whose rich local color and folklore Němcová first made known, she spoke of her own life in a letter to Bohuslava Čelakovská, one of the foremost educators of Czech girls:

Domžalice from the East

14 February 1846 … My dear Dora has been in bed since we came here [in August 1845]. As soon as her wounds heal, they again burst open. As a pilgrim gone astray in the Sahara desert longingly searches for a green lawn, so I yearn for the snow to melt and the flowers to awaken that I can send my poor child into God's sunlight; that is the only medicine. On top of it all we have a damp apartment. This is why all our children became sick; the dampness has also had a bad effect on me and I have become worse. After Easter I shall go to Prague to speak with [Dr.] Čejka. It is hard not to be able to spend a day without pain or not to expect any help. I keep from being depressed, otherwise I would already be under the green grass, which I would not mind a bit if it were not for my sacred maternal duties. Well, thank God, our linden tree [Czech life and literature] is turning green, is in full bloom, and will not notice if one little leaf falls off.

… The people here are frighteningly backward. They speak Czech because they do not know German, but they know beans about higher education and national feeling. And the country folk! In one village a stone mason teaches school, elsewhere it is a cabinet maker who doesn't know how to read properly, and if he wants the children to write, he has to first have someone write it out for him. One could cry bloody tears … How many talents, how many a clever head will perish before achieving the right consciousness! Very few know anything about history, or have ever read a book; they come to me from the villages where I am known to lend books and they read at night in spinning circles. Those rural people are my joy. I always perk up when a peasant woman extends her cal-

Domžalice

loused hand and asks warmly: "Why haven't you come to see us for so long?" The real catastrophe in some of these villages is that damned-to-hell Jesuitism! The Jesuits made fools of these people and impoverished them, so that they walk around like stray sheep.[8]

In a letter to her publisher, Němcová asks for a supply of books to distribute to the Czech population.

Všeruby, 17 April 1848 ... I am very concerned to have the country people educate themselves, and for the time being that can only be achieved through reading. Here people know absolutely nothing about the world ... In one village they subscribe to a Prague newspaper ... I [have asked] my acquaintances to subscribe; three communists will do so immediately ...[9]

In Všeruby, Němcová overheard a conversation between a peasant and a "gentleman", i.e. not a local person. The peasant was asked if there were any Jews living in the area, and how he felt about them. Němcová evidently sympathized with the answers:

There are many, and we like them. They live among us and make their living from us, but nobody does anything to hurt them, and nobody ever will. It is said that they cheat, but that is ridiculous; if one would kill all who cheat, there would be more Christians killed than Jews ... Why have they let that minister [Metternich] go free, who deceived all of us and did us so much harm that all the Jews together could not do it? But it is always that way, sir, when a subject, a small person, does anything ... there is a lot of noise, and he is either jailed or beaten. When a gentleman or a rich man does any wrong, people only whisper and it is hushed up ... The farmers and their wives do not need to dress up so much just for show, they should wear their old [peasant] costumes ... Then the Jew would not be constantly bringing goods to their houses ... People don't have to drink brandy either, then the Jew would stop selling it, and by the way, if no brandy distilleries were built, the Jews wouldn't rent them. In our area there are many Jews who are farmers just as we; some have rented fields, some have their own, and so they make their living here. Those who do business have to run around for their living like greyhounds, and to live very economically if they want to save anything ...[10]

The common folk told stories of Němcová which were reminiscent in tone of those handed down about Joseph II. In her old age Mrs. Podestátová, a peasant woman from around Domažlice, recalled:

I was then a young girl, but I remember her well. She liked to go to the villages, talked to the people and listened to them. Once she came to our farm for milk, but nobody knew her. She wore a little hat with ribbons and flowers. Her hair was parted in the middle. With her was a lady from town. When they wanted to go home, it began to rain. They were afraid that their hats would get wet and asked to leave them with us … We put them on the shelf, so that nothing would happen to them … My parents had a crazy hired man [Krištof] … who put the hats in the attic … One day those ladies came again and asked for their hats. I looked with my mother, but we could not find them … We asked Krištof … In each hand he held a hat and … out of one the blind heads of kittens were looking … We all laughed, and that Mrs. Němcová as well. We took the kittens out and the ladies went home … We only found out later that it was Němcová, the writer of those beautiful sayings …

… I heard that Mrs. Němcová suffered … They say she died of starvation … It's a shame about her … May God give her eternal glory![11]

Kateřina Emlerová-Dlabačová told what the local gossips had to say about Nemcová:

The ladies of Nymburk did not like Božena Němcová, she insulted them terribly when she said they know how to scold [servants], but not how to give orders … They also held against her that she wrote so many letters, that she spent a guilder a month for postage! They gossiped about her a lot.

Němcová made an excursion to see her parents [in Germany] … When she returned … Josef Němec called his wife to the back room and one could hear loud scolding, because Němcová had extended her visit … by a day.[12]

Václav Pok Poděbradský saw her from a different perspective:

Chleby is a little village scarcely a mile North East of Nymburk … Numerous guests from intelligent and authoritative circles were invited to meet there … ladies shone too, and the loveliest flower in that wreath was our gentle [national] awakener and exceedingly fertile writer, the patriotic Božena Němcová … then at the peak of her literary activity. Her *Grandmother* was going … from hand to hand and was read with real enthusiasm … She said that with her whole soul she agrees with the aims of the nationalists to liberate themselves from the … fetters which have been repressing the life of our nation for ages. She sincerely pressed the hand of each of us students … She was really ideally beautiful and each of her movements testified to the lofty spirit which resided in that harmonious body …[13]

By 1850, the Němec' were living in Prague. There Němcová met and became friends with the two Rott sisters, Karolina Světlá and Žofie Podlipská, who both became famous writers. Žofie remembers:

It was a September afternoon ... I still see her entering our living room ... she was like a radiant light falling into my soul.

Then thirty years years old, she looked like nineteen—so marvelous was her complexion, so radiant her eyes, so slender, nimble was her figure. She wore a white hat, a sand colored dress, tight fitting, with a fringed skirt, and over it a black velvet jacket down to her hips. All in extremely good taste and elegant. Her wonderful black hair was combed smoothly along her temples and twisted behind in a simple Grecian knot. Thus lives her likeness in my memory ...

... As outgoing and lively as Němcová used to be in the company of friends, she was sad when I sometimes found her at home alone. Then her heart overflowed with her sorrows. Němcová did not like secretiveness or pretense; there was not a drop of bitterness in her heart, she did not blame anybody.

She found the purest consolation in plastic art, in the statues of the old masters. Literature and music touched her heart deeply; she used to cry in the theater .... She regretted that Prague has so little ancient art ... Our northern winters were hard on her, but in spring nature always awakened her to new vigor.

She had a gentle, soft, Slavic nature. There was nothing violent, nothing excentric or affected about her. It was impossible for her to push someone aside who approached her in a friendly way, even when she noticed he was hiding bad intentions. She tolerated people around her who did not deserve it ... Everybody was an object of study for her. She easily became acquainted with people ... They confided in her ... she talked as easily to an old grandfather as to a ten year old boy ...

If there was a sick person in the house, she nursed him successfully with her household remedies ... stayed up nights and was a cheerful and entertaining companion when they became well. She read to them and never ran out of things to talk about. She was as happy at weddings and about new babies as if they were her own and sang and played with the young as if she had never experienced troubles.[14]

Theodora Němcová, Němcová's daughter, recalled:

... Wherever it was at all possible, mother kept poultry and other domestic animals. On Poříc [in Prague] she trained a little pig to walk from the courtyard up the steps to the porch and to the kitchen where we fed it. When it got a little bigger, it was sacrificed for a festive supper ... after which mother sat down at the piano ...

... Mother was an exellent cook. I still have some recipes from her written in German which she had from the chef in Ratibořice castle where she was sent to learn how to cook ...

... In Domažlice, the play *The Smugglers* was performed; all the children went to the theater to see mother ... and the neighbors commented on how nice she looked and how well she acted ...

... In Všeruby we were among Germans who were not very sociable, but [she] also tried to make closer contacts with them, to know their way of life. The area was beautiful and healthy ... Early in the morning she used to go walking ... in the dew; [my parents] frequently went swimming, and in the evening they drank Bavarian beer ... In summer they went on excursions ...

During the revolution of 1848 ... mother wore a peasant costume to be able to go to Prague [without being recognized]. Because one could not enter the city through the gates, she went on a boat and pretended to be the wife of a soldier.

... The maids were devoted to the family and stayed with us despite all the hardship and poverty ... [because of] mother's cordiality. ... [15]

Karolina Světlá hints at problems which surfaced later:

Němcová charmed me and my sister with her musical beauty, her charming directness and her marvelous mind. She immediately insisted that we be on first name terms, and when she ... moved to Prague, we saw each other almost daily.[16]

In addition to her other mental qualities, Němcová had a very wonderful moral side which was disastrous for her under the given circumstances—with her absolute generosity she was as trusting as a child. ... She gave without hesitation ... never asking if [the recipients] were worthy of her gift ...

For weeks she housed unknown girls from the country, who pretended

Karolina Světlá

an irresistible longing for education but had totally different interests ... Young men also were not ashamed to ask Němcová for money for trips to the country. Božena sometimes gave all she had in her purse. These leeches even brought her their poor underwear to be mended by her maid. [When] the maid rebelled ... Němcová ... did the work herself ... She always did this with the blissful feeling that those gentlemen would repay their nation with amazing publications ...

But my friendship for Němcová was too sincere for me not to point out to her that by such generosity she does not help her friends, and that she should control the minds of those who could be her sons instead of letting them tell her what road to take.

But I was not successful with such remarks. Němcová usually passed me off with a joke, that I should have become head courtier … She wanted to live only by the pen and perhaps even paid for it with her life.

Němcová was absolutely not the victim of hunger and poverty some people make her out to be, but consciously sacrificed herself to her most intimate, sacred conviction. … [Josef] Wenzig, the principal of Czech secondary schools, used all his eloquence to convince her to become head of a higher girls' school, but Němcová … refused, feeling that by accepting that task she would forever clip the wings of her creativity. [17]

> *Světlá felt that Němcová was not very hard working. She believed that in her childhood, Němcová had read extensively in Princess Sagan's library which was rich in the German Romantics but hardly contained any ethical or religious works. Finally, she strongly hinted that Němcová's literary friends, anxious that there also be a Czech Georges Sand, actually wrote parts of her works— "she had after all only been educated in a village school".*
>
> *Speaking to her friend Veronika Vrbíková, Němcová mentions some of the things that disturbed her, and then reminisced about her personal history:*

22 January 1851 … What kind of suffocating atmosphere is this here in Prague? … What seemed beautiful, ideal a few years ago, I now see as artificial empty form, so that I wonder how I could ever have considered it anything else. I won't repeat to you how men judge my personality, they normally lie to us and sometimes make us into angels and sometimes into devils. Reliable people say that I have a good face and very sincere, friendly eyes … people's exterior is not unimportant …

Many people complain about our wrong, unnatural education; we could turn into something different if we had better … schools. But what has happened in this respect so far? They put bandaids here and there, healing one wound and leaving ten open, but nobody looks for the root of the illness. I also was raised mostly in German, and only my grandmother, a sincere, old time Czech such as we can still find in Bohemia today, except that no one pays attention to them, admonished me to love our fatherland and told me events from Czech history. She liked most to tell me about Libuše and Přemysl [the legendary prehistoric Czech ruler and her husband] and always tried to turn me against the German language. I obeyed her as long as I was little. When I was growing up I developed a great liking for German books, and considered Czech literature and the Czech language unrefined.

I had been married for a few years when I first saw Tyl's works; they moved my heart and vividly brought to my mind my good grandmother. She stood before me splendid and beautiful, a picture of sincere, patriotic love. The memories of my childhood years were revived in my soul.[18]

> *In Prague Němcová met the (national) awakener and priest, František Matouš Klácel, who had published a proposal in 1848 to form a brotherhood of mankind, beginning with a brotherhood of Czechs. At first Němcová and her husband were the only people to join. In his letters Klácel instructed her in philosophy, communism and socialism, and made plans for communal living. He showed Němcová's letters to Ignác Jan Hanuš, a professor at the university in Prague, and he and his colleague Ivan Helcelet joined the brotherhood. Klácel wrote to Vojtěch Náprstek in 1851:[19]*

Dear Vojtěch! … I consider the greatest treasure in my miserable life the favor of this Božena. We have been corresponding for a long time [and] our letters have been becoming ever more fervent, the kind of letters which will one day become common among mankind. We have brought back the poetry which had escaped from the world … Božena …has become my sister and her husband my brother. That brotherhood did not spread beyond that …[20]

> *Němcová evidently was glad to leave Prague and go to Ďarmoty in Upper Hungary, an area later to become Slovakia, to join her husband who, because he was considered politically unreliable, had been assigned a position in this remote region as customs official. To Ignác Hanuš she wrote:*

22 June 1851 … I had hoped that I would recover a little in the Hungarian air, but I haven't had a contented moment. Not only do I constantly have stomach cramps and pains in my left hip, but another misfortune has happened. Němec was suspended for his political inclinations, and an investigation is being launched against him. My husband doesn't go anywhere or associate with anybody, except on official business. According to a denunciation he is supposed to have made statements amounting to high treason; he is supposedly a solid Czech of republican persuasion, and has great influence on the Czechs through his wife who is against the government and popular with the Czechs. [But] he has never made speeches. He is an honest official … concerned about the good of the state. As to his republicanism, that claim is particularly ridiculous, especially the thought that he would want to realize that idea in Bohemia. I myself never wrote against the government and only described peasant life … As to attitudes, I don't think they can be censored.

The informer … must be a major villain, since a denunciation by a petty one would not be taken so seriously. It is sad for us, since we have no capital … and we have to live on half of what we used to

have; we have to pay 30 guilders a month for the children in Prague
… Most likely the reward for 29 years of service will be a little job
with 400–500 guilders in a loyal province, which my husband will not
be allowed to leave … [I try] to comfort [him; he] is very depressed,
and mental suffering results in constant sickness.[21]

*Ignác Hanuš who, like many others, loved Němcová and then abandoned her,
told a friend:*

… You have never seen such an objective [sic] female, when you see
her you'll go totally crazy over her. She has experienced some tough
times in her life and enough troubles, coarseness too in part, but she
has still preserved her refined body and soul … Too bad she does not
have a different husband, or rather, it would be better if she did not
have one at all …

She is still sick in bed, and there is no hope that she will be well soon
… Němec found her an indequate apartment, especially for winter.
Perhaps due to lack of money, one room cannot be heated, and so at
night the whole family is in one room. Three boys, quite wild, make a
lot of noise … and when Božena wants peace, she has to drive them all
to the kitchen … She bears all with stoical patience, although she does
not always want to hide her dissatisfaction with her surroundings …[22]

*Hanuš and Helcelet, and even Klácel (the priest!) succumbed to Němcová's
charms, physical and personal. The following letters to Helcelet reflect her romantic mood into which she seems to have escaped, guided by the German Romantic literature she read in her youth:*

29 July 1851 … Keep well, my Ivan! I could easily slip into romantic
thoughts. The moon shines with a full face into my windows, the fragrance [of flowers] blows pleasantly into my room, all around is
silence, there is nothing lacking but the sound of a stage coach stop-
ping under the windows. Kisses from your B.[23]

17 December 1851 … you are always on my mind. The days run
like waves, as many drops of water as there are in a wave, so many
thousand thoughts run to you, dear Ivan! … But don't worry! I have
made up my mind to write quite soberly … I am not as afraid of death
as of a lingering illness. If death has to come, let it strike me like light-
ning—but not yet. There was a time when I was indifferent to dying,
but now I wish to see the children somewhat independent. I would
like to work [for] the dawn of a better future! … When I look at the
heavy gray fog, at those hollow trees, from which the yellowed leaves
fall one by one—when I observe that vague emptiness, that sadness
everywhere, I feel sad and chilly and I wish I had wings so that I could
fly like a little bird to warmer, freer, more beautiful landscapes where

a warmer, freer air blows. But when anger and sorrow force me to shed a real tear, I cry out to those demons rushing toward me and wanting to dig into my heart with their claws, to muddy my blood with their poisonous breath—and I reach for the cup my good fairies hand me for refreshment.—They drive away the gloom, turn the gray sky blue and line it with gold; they dress the earth in a green garment and breathe fresh life into the wilted blooms—and into that beautiful nature they magically place the picture of the most beautiful, free human being. You see, this is how I intoxicate myself for moments and forget the misery of reality.[24]

In a letter to an unknown addressee, without a date, Němcová escapes from her cold, damp apartment to "the land where oranges bloom":

Now to cheer up my heart I'll eat one of those oranges you gave me, and at the same time I'll fantasize about Natalie [a character in Goethe's *Wilhelm Meister's Years of Apprenticeship*] and hum Goethe's song about the land where oranges bloom. It wouldn't be bad if fate carried us there to travel in a light gondola on the sea! The beautiful landscape around Naples, the starry sky ... warmed up by wine I would sing ... But I am no longer young and was chosen not to love but to suffer ...[25]

During the time Němcová was writing her romantic thoughts to Ivan Helcelet, she visited Klácel's home town of Česká Třebová and wrote to Karolina and Žofie, describing her little holiday in such rosy colors that she did not even recognize the work four children playing in mud must have made for the maid:

10 September 1851 ... Dear Sisters, I would already have written you if I were not too busy enjoying the delights of the idyllic life here. Truly here one revives; mountains, woods, charming views, water like crystal (to work miracles!), isolation, honest to goodness cream, good bread with tasty creamed cottage cheese, a roast every day and wine—after dinner a walk in the woods to read an excellent book, for in addition to an entertaining friend [Klácel] who neither bores me with love-struck chatter nor with dry learning, an unusual library is provided. The children have a good time; they walk in the woods all day, catch trout, Karel catches butterflies, salamanders and lizards, Jarouš keeps the innkeeper's goats and Dora watches it all and also bowls with them. But every day they are so muddy; Marie [the maid] has nothing to do and laughs all day. On these two holidays there were two hundred pilgrims from the whole region at that little chapel in the woods, Germans and Czechs, all singing together in their own language ... In the evening there was dancing at the inn ... You will be amazed how well we look! I'll probably return Sunday or Monday and then I'll quickly hurry to see you.[26]

Němcová did not return to Prague as she anticipated when writing the two sisters, for Ivan Helcelet announced his visit. From fairly delicate remarks in various letters it is clear that she and Helcelet spent a memorable night together, and that the next morning Father Klácel's eyes were red from crying. Unfortunately several letters, including Nemcová's immediately following that visit, are missing.[27] Several months after this time, her communication with Klácel ceased and the other member of the brotherhood, Ignác Hanuš, ceased to love her, his love turning into passionate hatred. It seems clear that it was jealousy which disturbed the original harmony within the brotherhood and ended it.

Němcová returned to Prague with her children. By that time money had become very scarce and she never again managed without borrowing, indeed often begging, from friends and admirers, such as the famous biologist, Purkyně:

9 May 1853 … I would like to say good-bye to you, but I am embarrassed; many times I have stood at your door, but shame and fear held me back. Believe me that debt burdens me very much; I cannot get out of those depressing circumstances. Whenever I think that I'll be able to do my work, there is disease or another worry. So far my husband has not received any compensation; he even has to sue the shameful bureaucracy for the money he was awarded.[28]

In 1853 she was again on her way to join her husband in Slovakia, referred to as Hungary, with her two youngest children and the maid. The next two letters written to Žofie reflect her worsening mood:

17 May 1853 … The children (I count Marie [the maid] among them) were cheerful [during the trip]—Jaroušek was constantly teaching them, and when [they] fell asleep, he took the little dog and explained to him what various rivers are called, and preached to him how to behave on the trip. He woke up with the first daylight, and when that shining belt, the Danube, became visible, he quickly awakened Marie and Dora and they had to look.

… whoever has never seen Hungarian mud, has no idea of mud—that is antediluvian mud. We could not even always stay on the wagon because the three horses could not pull us; if it had not been for the children, I would have preferred to walk, for it is now a joy to be in the fields. Despite the cold, the grain grows much more beautifully than in Bohemia, and the trees are sprinkled with blossoms.

Němec was annoyed that I did not let him know when I was coming … He had no housing for me, just a kitchen to use with other people—it is a very inconvenient situation. Besides, the landlady with whom I have to be in constant contact is as repulsive to me as chills with a fever.

[continued] 25 May 1853 … I felt very sick and tried to ignore it, but when even my husband noticed that I don't look well, I finally had to ... lie down. I had a bad headache and a stabbing pain in my left hip, so that I could not walk or breathe freely. No sleep and no appetite, and diarrhea besides ... I am worse and worse, which frightens me ... Since I said farewell to him [probably Dr. Lambl] of whom I think constantly, I feel as if an icy hand were lying on my heart, I suppress my sorrow and every tear. But it is as if those drops were being transformed into ice and were falling on my heart. It seems to me that I am becoming cold and insensitive toward everything. It is good not to be saddened by anything, but it is sad if nothing pleases one ... you will not condemn me, will you? ...

What are you reading, how do you amuse yourself?—I have often dreamed about all of you ... Your letter was as dear to me as a bouquet in a desert landscape to a pilgrim.[29]

When Němcová wrote Světlá later, she felt desperate, both about the circumstances of her life and about her reputation:

30 August 1853 ... I don't feel free anywhere this year, clouds everywhere, everywhere I see the sword of Damocles above me. As if there were not enough unhappiness, the doctor tells me he [her son Hynek who had stayed in Prague], won't recover. I also hear such unpleasant reports ruining my reputation that I don't even know how I'll show my face in Prague. I would like best not to return until all have forgotten that I was ever in the world ... If only that child would get better! ... If I had money and if Hynek were well, I would emigrate with the children far away, perhaps to America, and believe me that I would not miss Austria, [Bohemia then was part of Austria] or perhaps to Russia ... Love me and be convinced that Božena ... is not as bad as that gang makes her out to be ... And you ... loved me even with my faults ... I myself sometimes consider myself the worst in this world.[30]

The following letter to Lotinka Staňková, is one of many, usually written to fellow patriots, begging for food or a few coins:

4 October 1857 Please Lotinko, don't be angry that I am bothering you, but we don't know where to turn. Lend me only about 40 kreuzers, I'll return them tomorrow ... For several days already I haven't been able to cook anything except potatoes, yesterday we had 3 kreuzers worth of bread for supper; my husband is strange, it is hard on him, the children are sad and only God knows how I feel. Jarouš is complaining about a pain ... If it rains, I won't be able to come. [Probably because she did not have adequate shoes] Lotinko, forgive me ... respectfully, yours B.[31]

Němcová corresponded with a friend, Josef Hostivít Hušek, a farm manager in Jindice. Here she asked him "for a few potatoes."

5 November 1853 … We suffered two heavy blows this last half-year, one so heavy it won't ever heal. First my husband was suspended from his office and pay, and then 19 October our oldest son Hynek died of tuberculosis, an excellent student of the first higher secondary school, a good boy, an honest character … I did not go with my husband to Hungary [again] because of the children's education. The youngest boy Jaroslav has had typhoid fever twice in two years and now turns out to have tuberculosis of the lungs. This year at Christmas he was so hoarse, produced so much phlegm and became so very thin the doctor thought there was no help. But then nature helped. The doctor suggested that he should spend at least a year in the country. And Dorinka was still sick with her scrofulosis. I decided to go to Hungary with the younger ones and let the older boys stay with Šumavský for room and board …

[The censorship had detained the letter telling her of Hynek's serious illness for six weeks] … I returned [to Prague] with the children, arrived on 17 October … and could just take leave of that dear child. Friends, teachers … and fellow students arranged for a beautiful funeral, and even that was considered a demonstration … One suffers from the sin of being a Czech, standing by one's nationality and loving one's brothers in language more than distant neighbors. Why this distrust of Slavs who have sufficiently proven their honesty and loyal sentiments, and why flatter the Hungarian nation which rose up so cruelly against the government?

… even if one suffers blows with the consciousness of suffering for a sacred cause, one often still lacks strength.

… I am wondering, if you ever send anything to Prague, if it would be possible for you to send us a few potatoes … don't be angry, but I have nothing for the winter … I had to borrow the money for the trip. I don't know what to do for a living. Even if in all this sorrow I could pull myself together and write, there would be no buyers.[32]

> When Němcová's unhappy life became unbearable, she escaped into memories of her childhood which she highly idealized. To these reminiscences we owe her most famous work, The Grandmother. At the end of 1854, she said in a letter to an unknown addressee:

My soul is often as a lake, where a slight wind stirs up waves that cannot be calmed. One thought chases the other as little clouds in a thunder storm, each more somber than the next, until the whole sky is covered with heavy clouds …

… when I go through the years of my life … I think … this can't be me!—If you had known me when I was twelve, thirteen years old—I like to think about that time the most. My body was already developed, but I was half maiden, half child. I was not embarrassed to climb on a tree in front of boys, or … to raise my skirts above my knees and to wade through the water, and to sit astride on a horse riding in the meadow—I was happy about new shoes, clothes and ribbons … Back then, when men used to stop and say, "That's a pretty girl!" the words did not stay in my head. To laugh, to dance, whether on the barn floor, in the servants' quarters, in the meadow—it didn't

matter as long as I could dance! I was cheerful, frisky … But I was stubborn. My mother was strict and spoke little to us children— she … ordered me to do things and immediately punished me for everything. I was always supposed to ask her forgiveness and thank her for the punishment, [but] … I would not have done it even if she had killed me … Father could get me to do anything; he knew me and always spoke to us kindly, and I would have jumped in the fire for him, when he looked at me with his

Němcová's room when she was a child

beautiful blue eyes. Even punishments from him did not hurt so much. In those days I still used to pray fervently! I liked most to read the history of Genoveva [a German legend about a woman who raised her son in the woods] and still dreamed of bewitched princesses, about improbable deeds and my favorite fantasy was to enter a convent—just because I had heard that nuns learn so much. …

When I was not quite thirteen years old, I was sent to Chvalkovice, about an hour from home, to room and board with the farm manager and learn sewing, piano and German. There I moved in a different circle and my first naive love stories began … when I married, I wept for my lost freedom and the beautiful dreams and ideals of my life that were destroyed forever. I searched for my ideal, thinking that in the love for a man I should find … the completion of myself … Many lights flashed on my road through life … but they were only will o' the wisps leading to mud … I was on the edge of despair—but I never lost my faith and love for people! Sometimes of course … I would not mind leaving the world …

You wrote that I can be proud the nation honors me and that the people respect me—you surely didn't mean it—I can only smile at it …

The castle in Chvalkovich

My honest heart, my sincere effort to perfect myself, to help the nation prosper with all my strength is the only thing that places me above ordinary women who live for nothing.[33]

Anna Cardová-Lamblová, the sister of one of Němcová's lovers, met her about this time. In the following memoir she expressed her very mixed feelings about Němcová many years after her death:

... In this apartment we lived with my parents, and here Božena Němcová used to come and visit us daily ... In 1854 ... my brother Dr. Vilém Dušan Lambl introduced me to [her] ... I like to reminisce about those Sundays and holidays spent in nature with that dear, cheerful lady. Nobody knew how to talk with ordinary people as well as she; so we used to send her to negotiate for us for what we needed ... How lively she was, how temperamental! ... She would read to us from her work while waiting for my brother ... When he came after eight o'clock in the evening, tired, and saw that Němcová was waiting for him [to correct her manuscripts], he frowned ... He had supper, while Němcová finished reading her last work aloud ... "I am finished ... I am too tired to correct and finish it", Božena would say and toss her head.

My brother took the pages ... and wrote the ending to her story. I often witnessed similar "corrections" ... That fiery, desirable, perhaps even destructive woman ... everything about her was charming ... She had many admirers and ... many women envied her and condemned her free behavior and the way she was celebrated among literati ... Mrs. Němcová was very fearless. She went ... where nobody else dared to go. Living freely, without responsibility, she bore criticism with a smile ...

... In her household there were often dry days ... one day she complained to my mother that she only had four kreuzers left, and that she did not know what to buy with them ... an ounce of coffee to drive away the sleep, a candle to be able to work through the night, or ink, because she was almost out of it. My mother often gave her something to cook ...

Of course, Němcová did not have to live in such difficulties, she was supported generously, but her character, her almost childlike inability to know the value of money, was often responsible for her dire need. I remember that once her admirers decided to collect a fairly large amount of money to help her ... Božena accepted the gift with her usual smile, but immediately offered almost all the money to a certain writer so that he could pay his debts, and that in the presence of Mrs. Světlá [who had brought the money] .... With the rest she had a splendid dinner prepared and invited her dear friends.

Her apartment was paid for, she received coupons for her dinners, she was given nice clothes by Countess Eleonora Kounic, her friends took care of her needs in all kinds of ways. If she had known how to manage her finances only a little, she could have worked in peace. Her husband, an honorable man, also had a secure income ... Božena's life could have been quite different, but this was not possible in view of her trusting, unrealistic, poetic nature.

Worries, poverty, difficulties killed her, aggravated her sickness which cut her life short ... How much love and gentleness there was in her, how much beauty, what fascinating ideas ... no, it is impossible to forget her ...[34]

In a letter to Helcelet, Němcová again returns to her childhood:

4 June 1855 ... After Hynek's death I found the slip of paper where I had written the plan for *The Grandmother* three years ago. I read it with increasing pleasure, and as a mirage the charming picture of the little valley arose before me, and in it the quiet household where the grandmother was the main person. How that memory consoled me, carrying me from the grief of life to the pleasant days of youth. I eagerly began working. My fondness for my grandmother is the reason I paid less attention to the other characters and did not describe them as I should have ...[35]

In Prague, in addition to their dire poverty, the Němec' were ostracized, in part because of Božena's unconventional life style. She seems to have been neither willing nor able to be prudent. The Czech patriot, Karel Havlíček, whom everyone was avoiding, appreciated her courage:

Only Mrs. Němcová, when she saw me on Příkopy, ran up to me ... I said to her ... don't get into trouble because of me, whereupon that Czech woman replied, "Eh, I don't pay any attention to the government!"[36]

The "cautious" attitude of Karel Jaromír Erben, a famous Czech poet with folkloristic interests very similar to Němcová's, was shared by many:

... I cannot visit her ... She is under strict police surveillance, and everybody who goes there is watched. She knows it too, and yet she is so careless that she often receives visitors; and I especially hold it against her that she gathers around herself writers of the younger generation, the head of whom is the notorious Frič, perhaps because they flatter her. Now her husband has also been here for several weeks—another reason why a person with an office has to stay away from her place …

… Once after a year I met Němcová … I found her not looking well at all, almost neglected—no wonder, now that, with all the wor-

The Old Bleach where Němcová grew up

ries about herself and her family she also has her husband on her neck. She also told me about her plan to collect fairy-tales and legends and that she needed money to do it—I shrugged my shoulders, and said that is difficult and that I don't know who would want to sacrifice money for such a project …[37]

Jan Neruda, one of the most influential nineteenth century Czech writers in several genres, wrote the following after he visited Němcová with the poet Vitězslav Hálek in her Prague apartment:

… our glances wandered over the poor worn furniture, and kept returning to the faded, bluish table cloth; to this day I see those holes in it, mended with large white stitches. We had perhaps experienced even greater poverty, but that we should have seen it with a celebrated person as the result of a life full of work …

Němcová came in a cotton skirt, with a silken but very old black collar. She sat down on the worn and bumpy sofa … she was so thin, and her deep eyes burned in a fever! … We went silently down the stairs … We too were determined to "devote ourselves to literature". We felt a chill.[38]

Marie Langhammerová, Němcová's former maid, wrote the following:

Mrs. Němcová was a precious lady … an angel! She would have gotten up at midnight to do things for anybody. But she had no thanks for it … Day after day she wrote long into the night, although she was not well. She shared her last bite with me and with the children, the poor things who also rarely ate their fill … Often we ate … prunes and … bread for two kreuzers a day … Mr. Němec was basically not a bad man, but he was not right for Mrs. Němcová. She was so gentle, calm, kind and sweet as a dove … and he, Mr. Commissar, was rash, stubborn, somber, materialistic … they married without love.[39]

The following letter to Helcelet is interesting because of Němcová's self criticism, but even more because of her very frank statements concerning her intimate life with her husband.

18–19 June 1856 ... I am often unnecessarily wordy. Neither my subject matter nor my form is anything special ... I trust your judgment; you know that somebody who supports herself by literature is a terribly poor thing ... I won't be offended if you don't take anything for *Koledy* [Carols, a magazine]. But if you keep the story, I beg you to send me [soon] at least part of the honorarium if possible ... I have found a sympathizer in Countess Kounic, who perhaps will concern herself with my material well being. She has seen to it that next month I'll go to Poříčí on the Sázava river where I can live for 3–4 months with my two boys. When I return they want to arrange for me to live in the house of a countess as her companion and have heat and board. They also want to help me get better honoraria ... She [the countess] knows how to give without humiliating ... Well, I do not know if these beautiful plans ... will materialize ... [They didn't]

I have Karel in Sagan in Germany, where my mother and sisters and brothers are—he is a helper in the prince's park. Here he has recently been a little reckless, but I have good reports ... He is sixteen and I am putting my hopes in his healthy and unspoiled heart. Dory also isn't quite well yet. Jarouš is in third grade and I would like him to go to secondary school. [Her husband objected to providing more education for their children.]

... For two months [my husband] has been earning almost nothing. It is a strange life between us, Ivan—sometimes I feel sorry for him, and I reproach myself for being so hard on him—yet when I think of his weakness, inactivity, his unconscionable recklessness, I feel a revulsion. I see to it that he has what he needs and if I had more I would give him more. We live peacefully but without joy, and when he is in a bad mood, I am quiet and I think him right to be unhappy with me, now that he would need that delight to cheer him up. That marital duty is the foundation of everything for him and he cannot get it either by threats or by begging. For a person like him it is of course terrible, and I am surprised that he likes me ... and so God knows how things would be between us if there were no separations. Perhaps when he is again employed he will go back to his old routine, and no longer having me before his eyes, he will do what he did earlier, [go to prostitutes?] and time will perhaps wipe out my insurmountable revulsion which keeps me from obeying what the priests command. And yet I would sometimes like to sacrifice in that temple of Venus. Oh, I sometimes long for it very much, and I have to muster my whole strength to overcome myself, but you know that to have human feelings is considered a sin. Hynek [Hanuš][40] of course does not believe it, to him it seems incomprehensible that I, having enough opportunities, should not enjoy what the body desires and is part of a complete life, either with my husband or with anybody else. And yet it has been so—for more than a year ... I only loosened my reins last year, without it all having a deeper substance, and experienced enough from poisonous mouths.—At any rate, I don't know a single man to whom I would dare say: "Grant me delicious moments in your arms!" Each would say to me: "Go, sinful Magdalene." I think you would also hold it against me, as against any woman ... And finally, what does it all mean where there isn't some kind of harmony or interest in common? ... It's a good thing that I have so much to do that such thoughts cannot persecute me for long.

I am fairly well, but weak and don't have healthy coloring ... Aren't you going to visit Prague? If you did, I would also come ... I want to go to Prussia to visit my mother, and I am looking forward to Dresden, the picture gallery. I would like to go somewhere with you, Ivan,[41] and I think that we would get along well together. You complain that you are getting older, but it's not only happening to you. If you could see me now ... When you first saw me, I was very wild and had no common sense ... It's a good thing that we saw little of each other, at least nothing came between us that would spoil our memories, and I cannot tell you how dear your memory is to me. Those several meetings with you are sweet melodies ... engraved into my mind with all their loveliness so they will accompany me all my life ... I foolishly refused many a proud heart, and now I am sorry.... Without a noble heart neither intelligence nor learning nor beauty will save you ... Only when someone's heart captivated me as well as intelligence, learning, and beauty, did a permanent memory remain, and that is how it was with you, Ivan!—

How did you like *The Village in the Mountains*? [one of Němcová's narrative works] ... Now I am slowly putting together *Pictures from Travels in Hungary* and in between I must work on some smaller things and on fairy tales. The countess would like to publish them in a luxury edition, and in Leipzig they would like to translate them into German. [They appeared in *Westslavischer Märchenschatz (Western Slavic Treasury of Fairy Tales*.] I am not eager for the glory of having my name in German literature. As a woman I should be a little vain, but I don't have any vanity at all. I am always embarrassed when men, for instance Palacký [the most famous Czech historian] praise me, because I do know how inadequate my knowledge is, which is fatal to my plans for larger works.

Write, Ivan, please and send everything c/o Hanuš, you know why. Stay well and think kindly of your B.[42]

Němcová wrote to her son Karel about her relatives in Germany being neither Czechs nor Germans, and explains how her nationalism fits in with the idea of human brotherhood:

24 July 1856 … Of course, a human being is a human being everywhere, and I honor a brother in every human being of any nationality, but my own nation has to be the dearest to me, and because it is not possible for one person to work for the whole world, he always has to start with the closest, the family, the community, the whole country, and only then the world. Your relatives consider it foolishness to suffer for such things.[43]

On 2 September 1856, Karel Havlíček, who was considered a national martyr, died. Němcová wrote about it to her friend and doctor, Vilém Dušan Lambl:

Dear friend, so yesterday at six o'clock in the evening we buried our Havlíček … From Vienna the directive came that no flyers were to be printed about Havlíček's death, but Ferdinand Náprstek [the brother of Vojta, see chapter 3] made sure that over a thousand were printed. People beg for them like for relics. A tailor went to America yesterday and begged for one, saying that it and Havlíček's picture were the dearest souvenirs he was taking with him. One saw how he was loved by the people. They are not ungrateful when they see real love. Halánek [Ferdinand Náprstek] took care of things for the most part. I got two guilders from him and had a beautiful crown of thorns made for the lid of the coffin, and half a wreath of laurel leaves for his forehead, and then I ordered a passion flower, and went down and put it in his hands. Halánek put the wreath on his forehead. He got away with it, I would not have. But I ordered soup and did various other errands. Citizens offered to carry the coffin … Many people came together from many towns, walking in a procession to where he lay in the coffin; this was not empty curiosity, people looking to see what the coffin and the clothing were like. Old, young, men, women, priests, soldiers, simple tradesmen and day laborers, all came quietly, with unusual reverence, and the tears which flowed at the coffin were not false. A simple mother showed him to her child "as a martyr who suffered for the nation!" One peasant, his head as white as a blooming apple tree, kneeled long next to him and cried—then getting up he took him by his hand, saying loudly: "God repay you for what you did and suffered for us!" I could write to you about many such proofs of the gratitude of the people. They also did not want the coffin to be closed.

On Friday he already looked very bluish, especially around the forehead, his ears were as blue as a corn flower; from his mouth blood was seeping, and he smelled very strongly … Four singers beautifully sang "Salve" by Palestrina, and instead of the one priest who had been ordered, two came. [A number of prominent writers and patriots carried him]. Then citizens carried him to the city gate. There was an immense crowd, one could hardly walk, it was over 5000 and all classes and estates were represented, even some whose sincerity was open to doubt. There were probably quite a few policemen out of uniform. If they heard what I heard, they had enough to talk about: "Such a person has not been born since Hus who would dare to tell them the truth like that! Well, that's the only reward we can give him, to accompany him, and to remember him" … "Only he opened our eyes—before him we didn't even know who or what we are." "That is also why they poisoned him!" "He is our holy martyr, it is right that he has the martyr's crown." "It also means that he was a writer, a poet." "A woman gave that to him."

It was the common people who talked like that, the patriots were as quiet as mice in order not to disturb that sad procession. The bastions were dark with spectators … When the coffin was to be placed in the wagon, there was loud shouting: "We'll carry him to the cemtery." It was people from Podskal. [a low class neighborhood] Palacký gently told them they should only accompany him and they obeyed.[44]

A few days later, Němcová told her son Karel of the consequences that came from her and her husband's part in the funeral:

28 August 1856 … After the funeral, when father went to ask for the travel document, they did not want to give it to him. The third day after that he was called in for questioning. It was because as a state official he went to Havlíček's funeral, and handed somebody an obituary notice. Actually they wanted to know who was in charge of that impressive funeral. They sentenced father to eight days in jail. In such a case this is an honor. Everyone wrings their hands over such arbitrary actions and lawlessness. Poor Havlíček, it isn't enough that they tortured him to death; they take revenge for him on others! Miserable scum! Father feels terrible, and I would be glad to go to jail in his stead; he is only afraid that having a police record, he will also lose his pension. I try to talk him out of it, but am afraid myself … It is clear that I cannot leave Prague now, but I have to see that the children do, they need it … They … would really like to twist the neck of every Czech.

… It is a terrible thing to live in such cruel slavery and persecution, but perhaps it won't last forever. We are also badly off financially; they have not yet sent me any honorarium from Brno and I spent the last money I had on rent. Since you left I have not bought a thread for myself to wear, for Dora only a white mantilla and shoes, poor Jarouš doesn't have any pants for Sunday, only those black ones, and I don't have decent shoes.

… I have to keep this from father, so that he doesn't suffer too much … He may be strange, but he is your father and an upright man and the only one who won't leave us even if everybody else does. Everyone has faults, I do too, and father has to have patience with me. He also wishes that I were different, and if he … had a rich wife, his situation would be better. Somebody has to give in … and I cannot ask it of him, because it is not in his nature. He also suffers [because of my activities]. I don't look well at all, and I don't even want to say how I feel. I hate to go among people.[45]

When Němcová wrote this letter to Alois Vojtěch Šembera (a linguist), the circumstances of her life had reached rock bottom:

26 August 1856 … What should I write you? One blow follows the other, my body sinks, I don't know how long I'll be able to stand it. Since my good Hynek's death I have been sick constantly, a worm against which there is no medicine eats away at my organism. Besides there is my terrible worry about my family's material wellbeing. Lately, they have even stopped all my husband's salary. He had gone on an unauthorized excursion with a friend and the gendarmes … accused them of being Russian emissaries. Well, they found nothing but proof [in my letters] that we are Slavs; I often cursed everything, and wrote against those cheating us. I cannot make a living with literature. But things are even worse with women's work. Many are out of work—so what am I to do? I was supposed to go as a companion to a lady in the madhouse. It would have been a hard piece of bread, all day and night with her among the insane—but I was attracted by the good pay—3 guilders daily. She suddenly began to rage so much, that only strong maids could be with her … If you know of anything in Vienna [a job] … I have debts … I have sold everything of any value … we are often hungry … I have buried many of my hopes and beautiful ideals.[46]

In this letter to Adéla, who seems to have been her favorite sibling, she advises her about marriage, deals with her own, and again returns in her thoughts to her childhood which she remembers as "paradise lost".

21 November 1856 … Look, Adéla, marriage can be heaven where there is love and mutual respect, but it becomes hell when it descends to meanness … I married partly due to my lack of common sense, partly due to mother's well intentioned arguments and those of [Němec].

... In the first eight days of my marriage I cried my first bitter tears! How beautiful I had imagined life at the side of a man I loved ... I saw very early ... that our natures were not suited for each other ... In the beginning I was not sensible enough to find the right tone ... Only one passion remained for me—the love for my children, and for that I suffered all the ridicule, all the vulgarity, for that I sacrificed myself to a slavery often worse than slavery in America. But everything reaches a certain degree and then a crisis comes. When I felt the most unhappy, the beautiful star of love arose for me—as if for a pilgrim groping his way in the dark! ... As if by a miracle, poetry awakened me to life in my unhappiness! It sweetens my life, and I have consecrated myself to it for eternity! It taught me to love people, it prevented me from drowning in vulgarity, it ennobled me. It also provided peace in my marriage. Through the work of my mind I can be independent of my husband, I gained the respect of all striving people; by being tolerant of the faults of others, and in return for some self-sacrificing services of love, I won over many kindred spirits. My husband now respects me, he even loves me with his whole heart—and if it were possible to revive the respect and love in my heart, things could turn out well—but sadly—one cannot command one's heart—only reason speaks for him and friendship flowing from long habit ... how much I fought and suffered before reaching the point where I am now! It takes a great deal of spiritual strength and love of mankind not to succumb in that struggle. And do you know which vision it was that spun a web around me, like sweet magic, which I always longed for, as for paradise lost ...? It was my beautiful youth, the sweet isolation in which I lived, the simple upbringing, in short my ideal life as a girl, this pure, beautiful poetry—it was that!

The first home of Němcová after her marriage (upstairs)

You see only the prose of reality in it, for me it remains paradise. I still see every rock, every flower as they were when I was a girl full of imagination, (of which mother had no idea)—and you were a child. Do you remember how I carried you on my back?

... your heart is deep ... Therefore I am afraid that you will also suffer one day. Be careful before you tie yourself down forever! ...

I wish you were here! How beautifully we would live together! I often long for a deeply feeling soul! ... But what would mother do without you? But do come to visit—and then I shall accompany you home!

Don't marry at all rather than an uneducated man! ... May God grant that you find a husband who has a heart like our father had ... Marriage is like an inflated pillow. Once there is even the smallest tear in it, all the air escapes. The lazy, heavy body remains ...

... I think I shall have to see you all again ... before I become too estranged from you.[47]

In her book, The Village in the Mountains, *Němcová expressed her view of the role of women:*

A woman must be raised to the ruler's seat next to man, not to judge, not to punish, but as an angel of peace between him and the world.[48]

Němcová spoke on the same subject with Vitězslava Paulová, whom she trusted, but who was actually a police confidant:

We spoke about women who distinguished themselves in revolutions, mostly about ... the French Revolution. She thought that women can do the most politically, and in all social classes, from the proletariat to the most educated. For who feels all the misery, physical and spiritual, around her more than a woman? She has the children, she looks into the future. A man has no time to pay attention to that, to think about it, he has to work in his profession. Therefore she has a great influence on the man ... Finally the woman has a freer relationship to life, to society, to the state. And who will dare to investigate a woman? [49]

Němcová's letter to Adéla, written in German, shows that despite her many disappointments in love and the misery of her existence, she still believed in pure love which lasts until death:

3 June 1857 ... [the heart] bears all its sorrow rather than the proud, cold calm of reason.—Oh, who could plumb the depths of this unfathomable ocean with its cliffs and pits, its rich treasures, terrible monsters, this ocean called the human heart ...! ... But once the feeling of true love has fallen into one's heart, one keeps it until death; like a bright drop of amber which can neither dry up nor sink into the ground. Such love shines in one's breast!

... If you have any clothes, let us have them. If you would see my wardrobe ... you would cry. The black top from Marie is still my Sunday best ... I take good care of my clothes, otherwise I would go barefoot and in rags.

... I am constantly getting carbuncles, I have lots of scars which hurt a lot. Everyone is shocked at how bad I look ...

... I suppose you'll get this letter, although I don't have the money for postage. I kiss you and the children many times. Keep well and remember your B.[50]

The following letter written six months earlier by Němec to his wife shows him to be much more sensitive than he is usually thought to have been:

14 December 1856 ... I am surprised we are still in this world, that we have neither died of suffering nor ended it all ourselves. It is terrible how fate plays with us, and just now when one is at the end of one's life, so to speak. We are both unhappy creatures and I would be unhappier if I didn't have you; believe me, you are the only soul that gives me strength in this misery. Who knows where I would be without you ... without you the world is empty, [and would be even] if I could lead a quite comfortable life ... I don't wish for anything more than to ... contribute to a more contented life for you ...[51]

At the same time, Němcová was writing to Václav Bendl, a student and poet much younger than herself, about one of her love affairs with which she hoped to console herself:

14 December 1856 ... don't ever close your heart to me ... I am alone, mistress of my time ... My husband likes it quite well in Villach [in Austria] ... if Vienna keeps its word, then perhaps it will be the end of our misery for some time. I have to be very economical, but ... nobody is making life hard for me. My health is also good ... my body falls and rises with my mental state. I need no other medication than contentment ... You often used to tell me that I was not as I used to be, that I was cold, indifferent, but inside I did not feel that way! I have strayed a lot, Vašku, [an endearing form of Václav], I admit it to you now, because I won somewhat of a victory over myself! I cannot say what restlessness there was in me since Jura [i.e. Dr. Hanuš Jurenka] was to come ... His picture used to accompany me everywhere ... I used to kneel before it as before a god—and now I have to run away from all those dreams ... as if I were mourning a dead person! ... the melancholy weather right now reminds me especially of the time when we met. What ... inscrutable charm ... rests in a certain person, so that a single glance of his ... can deprive us of all strength and the tremor of his voice toss us like mercury? Why does our heart beat calmly, when one friend presses our hand, and why does the hand of another pour fire into our veins? I came to know the power of that charm and submitted to it with my defenses down and with the whole fervor of my soul! Would you throw a stone at me because of that? You wouldn't,

and I also am not sorry. I would only be if I had to believe that he considered our relationship vulgar. What happened later was of course deception, but I have forgiven him! I placed him above all of you! I would have made a wreath of the most brilliant stars for his forehead, I would have carried him to heaven so that he would shine above all! I did not question his worth because I loved him ... [I wanted] to see him in the ranks of our Knights of the Spirit—as a brave fighter! I hoped that his love for me would ... drive him on ... [a prevalent romantic notion that love would inspire men to great deeds]

... I could have easily gotten over losing his body, for sexual feeling alone was never my motive for loving, but his lack of trust always insulted me most painfully. For his sake, I wish his wife remains as faithful to him as I was.

... If he wants to speak to me, talk him out of it ... But if we should see each other, I am afraid he would either repell me or I would have to love him again, and I don't want either. ... If I could at least have fulfilled the longing of your heart, I would have undertaken anything, but those were vain hopes.

... this is my first and last such letter, in the future I shall only write to you about sensible things ... I would be glad to leave this world ... Often I wish you next to me, so that I could read and discuss various things with you ...

Recently I was invited to the Palacký's for tea. One must love the old fellow. There I hear the views of various strata of society....[52]

To her husband she wrote about the domestic worries which plagued her almost constantly:

16 February 1857 ... [She is sending him a book] A week ago yesterday we had almost nothing to eat, on Monday we were at Palacký's, on Tuesday we again had nothing and I didn't know what to do ... In the morning [the writer Václav] Staněk sent me the message that he would borrow [some money for] me, so we waited—noon—two o'clock—nothing—we were cold—we had nothing to burn [for heat] ... I bought nothing on credit from those mean shopkeepers ... Jarouš went to the Vrbas' crying. He wanted to ask them to give him some lunch [for] me, but then he was afraid that I would be annoyed.... With the last 3 kreuzers Dora bought bread and she and Manka [the maid] ate it. At four o'clock Staněk sent us one guilder, [like] a bone to a hungry dog. At five o'clock Mrs. Krejčová came and brought me 20 guilders of my honorarium. ... Earlier my bitterness kept me from shedding even a tear, but then I began to cry. ... Perhaps you will also be able to contribute.

I am glad that Jarouš gets those meals; on Friday he always brings me some coffee cake from the Vrbas.... [Responding to her husband's suggestion that they move to the small town of Bydžov]: I think it would be hard to live among the petit bourgeois there. I could not go there.[53]

In a letter to Bendl a few days later Němcová reveals a dream:

21 February 1857 ... Sometimes when I go to bed in the evening I only wish I would fall asleep and sleep a long, long time ... Life is very bitter to me. Pride, shame, disgust keep me from revealing my poverty to everyone, the vulgarity of people pains and insults me ... In a dream the other night, I sat on a chair and Hanuš [Jurenka] had his head resting on my lap, I played with his hair and looked silently at the starry sky, he was silent, you smoked and told jokes! I suggested you make an impromptu poem on our situation. You ... began a very humorous improvization in a pathetic tone about us as a three-leaf clover. Jura laughed terribly and embraced you saying: "If I were the emperor, I would make you my court poet, you are a capital fellow!" You went down on your knees before me. "If I had laurels, I would make you a wreath," I said ... When I tried to go to the kitchen, there lay a large snake on the doorstep, with his mouth open. I screamed and woke up. It was bright daylight.

Continuing in the same letter a short time later, Němcová touches on literary subjects as well as her loves and everyday concerns:

4 March 1857 ... Do you know that a Czech *Plutarch* is to be published? ... It will be biographies of historic personages. Recently there was a literary soirée at the Riegers where the project was discussed. ... I was the only woman there. ... They assigned me Marie Antonie [an insignificant author], the old bag, a nun. Well, if I could say that she was in love with all the young writers, that she wrote very loving letters to Father Kamaryt, that although these letters were supposedly written in the spirit of sisterhood and brotherhood in Christ it is clear she would rather have embraced him than her heavenly bridegroom ... there would at least be some interest in it; or I could ... make an Abélard and Héloise story out of it, but that would not be permitted. ... I'd rather take Rettigová. [See Chapter 1].

In my eyes Jura has changed, and I in his. That idealism, that imagination which attracted me to him so irresistibly is no more—my yearning, the jealousy, all gone! Only that sincere sympathy which one can feel for a great number of people remains ...

... During carneval Jarouš wanted to take a little pot along and ask [the people where he gets his board] for some dinner for me. The good hearts of the children and the sincerity of some friends are all I have. Dora is now a real housekeeper ... Some friends want to take up a collection so that I would have an assured livelihood and be able to work freely ...[54]

A few days later, Němcová wrote her husband a very frank letter revealing much about herself, and to what situations her poverty led. She has been telling him about some literary, probably editorial and secretarial, jobs she has been doing for Ferdinand Náprstek, Vojta's brother, in exchange for food and drink:

13 June 1857 ... Recently he brought a pigeon [a Czech delicacy] in his pocket, and when in return I had written sixteen addresses to Slovakia, he had a stein of beer brought, and we ate the pigeon. During the meal he said: "You know, I would give you anything, and you don't want to love me even a little bit." [Němcová]: "I thought you brought me the pigeon for those addresses." "Well, you know, if you want to love me, I would dare to give you more .... "Thank you, I don't need more for myself than I have; what anyone gives me I accept in the name of my family ... Fondness cannot be bought, you should know that if you have not only kept company with vulgar females." "You are cruel" he said, "I consider you a sensible lady with whom one can speak the truth without being slapped. You know how one sometimes feels. I am a healthy fellow and discreet, and you also would not betray me. You know, I am very fond of you, more than of any woman other than my mother. Now tell me, will you be a little fonder of me?" and at the same time he wiped his mouth, because he was constantly chewing, took my hand and kissed it. As an honorable, virtuous lady I should have thrown him out the door, but as a sensible woman I started to laugh. That declaration of love with his full mouth while he was stuffing himself was a very comical study for me. "What were you thinking of to insult me like that?" "I insult you? It is a natural thing, and you are a lady who is experienced in how things go in the world, and knows that everyone looks for it where he likes it best. Or do you consider it a sin?" She: "Yes, a sin when it happens without mutual fondness, and it would disgust me ... Fondness is not a bag of hops one can buy, or a glass of beer which one drinks when one is thirsty—I like you as a good friend and as a person, but not as a man. Now you know what I think, and let us not talk about it any more." ...

I wanted you to know what all I have to listen to ... God created the horse as well as the ox ... If I were as emancipated as many think, I would have fewer worries ...

Don't think that I would not like to see you, I realize how you feel there, but if you came here it would be the same old story ... I am often very lonely and long for you … I think if you were here we would not understand each other, and so I console myself that at least I am my own boss. But I would be glad to share the burden with somebody. Sometimes the longing to lie down on your chest and cry comes to me. I know my only refuge is there … You used to say I don't value you, and that quite different ideals are in my soul—but you are not quite right. I don't deny that I once had an ideal of how marriage and a husband should be—Well, I was young, inexperienced, raised only in nature … Nobody showed me the world from the proper standpoint; you were also only attracted by my appearance and perhaps by my unspoiled feeling. If you had had the sense which you have now, you would have made me into a different woman. I was fond of you … But things happened differently, and we both suffered. My soul burned with desire for education, for something higher, and-with disgust for vulgarity. This was my fortune, but also the cause of our rift, my unhappiness …

Few women respect marital honor as much as I did and do, but I soon lost my faith in it. Where was I to see it? —All lies, deceit, privileged slavery, forced duty. My heart longed very much to be loved—but in vain. I wanted a husband… who would stand high above me, and saw only coarse despots in men. … You [plural] had my body; my desire, my longing moved beyond. Then I thought the love of another man would bring fulfillment—now I know that is not true; the children were my only delight, but their love didn't satisfy me … I sought the truth and the world taught me to lie … I seized the national idea with my whole heart, I thought that it would satisfy my yearnings. It didn't. In time, of course, that idea became a firm conviction. I came to know the world and to realize that there is no perfection. Often I took what was mud for gold … I had more than one admirer—one had a mind, the other a body, that one a heart, another intelligence, but in the end I never found what I longed for: a man to whom I would gladly subject myself.—All had their weaknesses, … I would choose none of them for a husband. The longing remains in my soul as a drop which neither dries up nor flows away, but eternally sparkles like a diamond; it is the longing for infinite beauty and goodness.

… That longing is connected with love for all of mankind, the desire to constantly improve and to approach truth. But the world finds fault with what is the most beautiful, and calls what is natural sin.

If I didn't have that love, that poetry … how would we have lived together? … for I had lost all confidence in your heart and all respect for you. If I had not come to a better understanding, things would have stayed so … When you are far away, I long for you more often, and perhaps it is the same with you.

When two people are constantly together, they do everything in front of each other … become ordinary to each other. Only habit draws them to each other. I would come to dislike any man who was around me … I envy the aristocrats and the rich who can always remain rare to each other … I wish there could be joy in everything we do and not cold duty. … [Regarding sex] men should forget that they are masters and act as lovers toward the women they value …[55]

This letter of Němec' to his wife, unlike later ones, expresses genuine respect for her:

6 July 1857 … So you smiled bitterly at my saying that I am proud that you are my wife. You think, perhaps, that I am proud of your fame, but that never occurred to me. I am proud that you are as you are, apart from your glory, because there are very few women such as you in the world, at least I don't know of a similar one.[56]

In Němcová's letter to her husband, however, written after 31 July 1857, there was room for nothing but worries:

… Worries depress me so I can hardly bear them, and I am becoming weaker every day. Things are the same with poor Jaroslav. I have written to many places, and can't get the money [for his trip to the country] … Adolf [a relative] was here recently. I was not at home, and when the children told him how badly off we are, he did not come back … Dorinka also doesn't look well.

… I can't even think of going to the country, being all ragged. The black dress is worn and the silk one would go badly with the torn shoes. My shirts are also tearing. Dorinka needs about two shirts, a skirt and shoes … God knows how things will be with my health. I am afraid; I don't sleep, all night the most terrible thoughts persecute me, it's a wonder that I am not going crazy. I have a fever every day, my body hurts terribly and I still keep getting those boils.

… If I weren't writing those fairy tales, I don't know how we would have lived these two months.

Sometime after 25 August (Hynek's name day) 1857, in the same letter to her husband, Němcová continues in the same vein:

… On Hynek's name's day I bought 5 grošes worth of flowers … Jarouš said at the grave: "He is well off there; if he would see how we are, he would be very upset." … My only joy is that those children are so sensitive … Dora embroidered three collars … she always has given me the money she received for [such jobs].[57]

In her letter to her son Karel, Němcová advises him:

18 April 1858 … My sorrow with you children is that none of you are healthy. Please don't smoke, buy yourself a glass of good beer instead, and only eat meat products. Flour and milk are not good for you during this illness [scrofulosis]. … [with regard to his infatuation with her sister Adéla, which she discourages, she writes]: Love is something else. Thinking and feeling and education have to be equal and mutual,

unlimited confidence and freedom … Listen to me, nobody loves you as I do … Father … still does not have a job and is in a very bad mood. … Leave the army alone, be glad if you don't have to go.[58]

In a letter to Karel written about two years later. Němcová writes frankly about her bad marriage:

5 February 1860 … What all have I been through! And how Dad has always behaved towards me these last 23 years we've been together! You have enough judgment to know whether I deserved it. … I would not have

Němcová in the 1850's – her last photograph

stayed with him for even a year if it had not been for you, but my conscience could not accept that you would fall into strange hands, and one day complain about me. So I suffered for you what few women have suffered, for considering my nature it is a terrible fate to be tied to a coarse man. In order not to be dependent on Dad for everything, I became a writer, for in this way I could earn more than by such work as sewing …[59]

Some of Němcová's last letters were to Vojta Náprstek—the great benefactor of Czech women already mentioned. She had gone to Litomyšl at the invitation of Antonín Augusta, her publisher, to work on the galleys of her collected works.

11 November 1861 Mr. Vojtěch! … When I left Prague, I was determined not to return to my husband … In the morning he began screaming and calling me names … and didn't care if a maid was there … When I tried to protect Dora from his beating, he hit me—and at that time I was already sick. Every day he would chase us out … and said he would not feed us … Dora and I wore one pair of shoes all

winter ... When somebody ... asked why I was not writing anything, he said: "She will never write anything again, she is dumb. She belongs in the mad house" ... When he ... saw me writing, he extinguished my lamp, and said that it was not my petroleum.

... One afternoon he came home, and I was just organizing the fairy tales into a volume. He grabbed [it], threw it on the floor and began tearing it up. At that point I became angry and tore it out of his hand, and when he did not want to let me go, I bit his hand until he began to bleed. He wanted to hit me, but Jarouš said ... "don't hit mother, she is right." ... He cursed ... proclaimed in the taverns that I slept with Lambl, that I am a bad housekeeper, that I disgrace him ... when he came home, he continued: "You good for nothing. You will croak somewhere behind a fence, nobody will even spit at you, you should be selling matches!"—and so it went on every day ... Daněk [should] not send us the rent, because he [just] puts the money in his suitcase. He gets 100 guilders a month and can pay the rent.[60]

While in Litomyšl, her condition deteriorated—she had cancer. We have the record of a note Augusta sent her saying that if her manuscript was not going to be ready by five o'clock that day, she would receive nothing to eat. In another letter to Náprstek she continued the tale of her marriage:

21 November 1861 ... You probably wonder why this Božena is not publishing *The Grandmother* [a new edition of her book first published in 1855] ... On the way [to Litomyšl] I already felt I was hemorrhaging. ... When I was alone in my room, I took out my own sheet and waxed cloth, spread them on the sofa and prepared a clean bandage. In the morning I bandaged myself so as not to dirty the floor, went to the next room and asked the old nursemaid if she knew of anyone who could launder my blood stained underwear while I waited ... She brought me a glass of milk and two crescent rolls.

Since my husband had contributed nothing toward financing Jarouš's trip to Munich [to study art], I told him that he didn't have to know [how she managed it]. For that ... he beat me so hard that he smashed the comb on my head, and if Dora had not come, he might have killed me in his anger. The next day ... I went to the police commissioner and showed him the blue marks on my head, and told him that I ... would rent an apartment for myself. He told me that nobody could prevent me from doing that. Besides I told him that ... he [her husband] used to give me 15 guilders for our expenses for five persons, then 10 and then 5, and I had to pay for everything else, including the rent ... He drove us out of the house every day and held every bite of food against us ... I was not allowed to heat the second room, so that my feet and my hands froze ... I also told the commissioner that when [my husband] became an administrator, he had two suits made for himself, and when Dora begged him for money for shoes he told her she should earn some. He gossiped about me in the taverns and called me dirty names. … Everybody … advised me to go to the country, [because] I did not look well at all. My husband came home just as I was preparing to leave [with money some people had given me] and an argument ensued about money, which ended in him locking me in the apartment, while cursing and spitting all the time.[61]

We do not have the exact wording of the whole letter which Němec wrote to Němcová on November 21, 1861, only Josef Lelek's summary.[62] Evidently he warned her against believing Augusta who was allegedly facing bankruptcy, reproached her for entering Augusta's service as a "corrector" in the print shop without his knowledge, and for recklessly leaving her family. He continued:

You are not legally divorced and therefore cannot live away from your husband without his permission. You did not even ask me and rushed into something, as usual. If I insist, you have to leave Litomyšl immediately … I shall act as an honest [man] who cares about the honor of his wife and children, without the phantasies and fixed ideas which predominate with you. If you intend to be divorced from me legally, do it in the proper place. … you spoke empty words, as usual … The children have known their loving mother for a long time. I can imagine that you won't like the way I am speaking to you … I always speak and act openly. Your still legal husband, Němec.[63]

Writing about this period, Antonín Konstantin Viták said:

In those days the famous author of *The Grandmother* also lived in Litomyšl. She was to correct the page proofs of her collected works, [for] the printer Antonín Augusta … He put us both up in the Blue Star Hotel. But Augusta sinned very cruelly against … Božena Němcová. To be sure, he rented decent housing for her in a first class hotel, but gave her only 20 hellers a day for board, which was hardly enough to satisfy one's hunger with dry bread. That excellent … woman used to cry and complain to me bitterly …[64]

Božena Němcová was brought back to Prague toward the end of 1861 by her husband and died there in poverty on February 21, 1862. Her funeral was reported in Moravské noviny *[Moravian News]:*

Božena Němcová's funeral was grandiose and entirely worthy of the writer. Both of the large courtyards "At the three lindens" and all of Příkopy were crowded with people … the procession was lead by canon Štulc [who had slandered her earlier], with numerous assistants. The hearse was decorated with laurel wreaths and an artistically embroidered Slav tree. There were colored flags donated by the "Czechoslav daughters" to the writer of *The Grandmother*, from Princess Thurn-Taxis, Countess Kounic, the Academic Club and others. On both sides Czech girls in mourning marched with lit candles, then younger writers, etc. Behind the coffin were members of the family, behind them Czech ladies, especially Mrs. Riegrová, Karolina Světlá ... Prince Thurn-Taxis, representatives of the provincial and imperial deputies, the mayor, the vice-mayor, writers, doctors, professors, students, etc. and an endless multitude.

... eternal glory to her memory![65]

Vítězslav Hálek wrote the obituary in Národní listy *on February 24, 1862:*

Němcová fell into real poverty ... But certainly material need was not as hard on her as the philanthropy of our patriots ... Some contributions were collected to relieve her worst worries ... She was expected to account for how she spent contributions which were so modest that they are not worth mentioning. A beggar can do as he pleases with a donated penny, but Němcová became a minor to her benefactors!

... Thousands work for bread, a creative spirit works for hundreds of thousands [of people]. And these gentlemen "patriots" ... did not have enough shame to keep from asking the left what the right was doing ... It is [terrible] when the spiritual mob wants gratitude from such a spirit. Němcová, who had enough friends earlier, remained isolated in her sickness ... Her home which used to be a gathering place was later avoided. Fie to these "patriots"!

It would be proper to say something about our publishers ... who condemn manufacturers who prosper from the callouses of their workers. ... our publishers become rich from the blood of our fore-

The hotel where Němcová lived shortly before she died.

most spirits ... who write their testament early, to be buried on Vyšehrad [where famous Czechs are buried].

[Němcová's] tombstone will be taken care of by the newspapers and by the "grateful nation" ...[66]

In his obituary, the poet Jan Neruda commented:

... here almost only Božena Němcová ... was comparable to those outstanding foreign women writers ... Němcová, to be sure, did not have the electrifying spark of genius of a [Georges] Sand, she did not exuberate with the aphoristic spirit of [Anna Louise Germaine] de Staël ... but what raises her [above others] is her pure genuine poetry which germinated in Czech poetic soil, a wholly Slavic poetry. Social questions did not attract her very much, and it was not her great forte to depict social conditions, but she knew national life and all its poetic aspects; she loved and depicted them as nobody else has ...[67]

This sober but too brief evaluation by Neruda provides a striking contrast to the telegram Karolina Světlá sent in 1888, on the occasion of the unveiling of a statue of Božena Němcová near her childhood home. (But a perhaps more striking contrast to this telegram were the comments Světlá herself made about Němcová when she was still living!)

Fervent thanks to you, honored gentlemen, for your efforts which made it possible to mark this memorable place forever, where the precious spirit of a Czech woman first spread its wings to begin its blessed flight, where our honoree learned so amazingly her artistic control of our mother tongue, both oral and written, where the root of her astonishing moral strength was planted in her soul, where fate placed a crown of thorns on her forehead; giving her a soul which changed every drop of blood flowing from it into roses, the lovely fragrance of which did awaken the elevated spirit that lived in her heart, a fragrance which will do the same in other hearts as long as Slav sounds are heard in our lands, the silencing of which, God forbid, will never take place thanks to the barrier of eternally blossoming works which were created by her blessed hand for the pleasure and honor of all, past and present. In Prague, August 1888.[68]

NOTES

1. Andreas Guski, ed. *Zur Poetik und Rezeption von Božena Němcovás Babička* [The Poetics and Reception of Němcová's *Grandmother*], (Berlin, 1991): in it, Susanna Roth: "Božena Němcová und *Babička* im Urteil tschechischer

Gegenwartsautoren: Ergebnisse einer Umfrage" [Božena Němcová and *The Grandmother* in the View of Present Day Czech Authors: Results of an Inquiry], p. 260 ff.

2. Helena Sobková: "Nové úvahy o narození a původu Boženy Němcové" [New Deliberations about the Birth and Origin of Božena Němcová], in *Marginálie* [Marginal comments] (Prague, 1988), an anthology published on the 80th anniversary of the Association of Czech Book Lovers.

3. It seems to be a particular irony of history that Slovaks now, at the close of the twentieth century, are so critical of the love and enthusiasm with which Czechs like Němcová "discovered" Slovak folk art.

4. Němcová is said to have had amorous relationships with Václav Bolemír Nebeský, Josef Čejka, Vilém Dušan Lambl, Ignác Hanuš, Jan (Ivan) Helcelet, Hanuš Jurenka, František Matouš Klácel and perhaps others.

5. Josef Václav Frič, *Paměti I* [Memoirs], (Prague, no date) p. 257–8.

6. Josef Kajétan Tyl was a patriotic writer of the early 19th century.

7. Zdeněk Záhoř: *Božena Němcová. Hlasy o osobnosti a o díle* [Božena Němcová. Opinions of her Personality and Work] (Prague 1927), p. 49 ff.

8. Božena Němcová, *Knihovna klasiků*, [Library of Classics] (hereafter refered to as *K.K.*), *Listy I*, [Letters], (Prague, 1951) p. 37 ff.

9. Záhoř, op. cit., p. 103.

10. in *Sebrané spisy Boženy Němcové*, vol.9 [Collected Writings of Božena Němcová] (Prague, 1910), p. 183 f.

11. Záhoř, op. cit., p. 58.

12. ibid., p. 60.

13. ibid., p. 61.

14. ibid., pp. 80ff.

15. ibid., p. 114.

16. Karolina Světlá, *Z literárního soukromí* [From a Private Literary Life] (Prague, 1880), p. 65.

17. ibid., pp. 60f.

18. Němcová, *K. K.*, *Listy I*, op. cit., p. 159 ff.

19. See my introduction for an understanding of Náprstek's importance.

20. Záhoř, op. cit. p. 63.

21. Němcová, *Korespondence*, (Prague, 1930), p. 225 ff.

22. Záhoř, op. cit. p. 64.

23. Němcová, *K.K.*, *Listy I* op. cit., p. 174 ff.

24. ibid., p. 160 ff.

25. Němcová, *Sebrané spisy Boženy Němcové, Korespondence II*, (Prague, 1914), p. 402f.

26. Němcová, *K.K, Listy II*, op. cit., p. 132 ff.

27. However, the insipid and verbose letter Helcelet wrote to Němcová terminating their affair does still exist, and I am including parts of it to illustrate the sort of lovers Němcová encountered. It is from *Sebrané Spisy Boženy Němcové*, Sv. XIII, cor.vol. 11, (Prague, 1914) p.33 f.

It must have seemed strange to you, dear friend, that I didn't write for several months, and you will be anxious to read the content of this letter which will give you the reason ... for my sudden silence. If you already have an opinion about it, it will probably be wrong; and I ask you not to be more shocked about it than about the whim of a friend. I announce to you that I have decided to stop our correspondence, although I would regret if our initial favorable mutual attitude would suffer. How to go about it was the problem which made me hesitate so long about taking care of this letter. But why all that? Don't look for any intrigues from third persons; it is solely due to unfavorable coincidences, outward circumstances and to my strange character which could not resist them. It is perhaps one of my good qualities that I am somewhat sensitive to everything beautiful; but what is even greater is my sensitivity to everything that disturbs, insults beauty, and therefore sins against it. Don't think that I want to atone … for a delightful sin. In my belief a beautiful sin has its moral dignity and merit, and contains its own (ab)solution; what is not beautiful about it contains its own punishment. That of course is unfortunate, and difficult to repair. It is not your relationship with your husband that bothers me, although I suspect that that would happen in time; what are unbearable to me are the dissonances which come from my close connection with Hynek [Prof. Ignác Hanuš], from your and my relationship with Matouš, [Klácel] and from my inability to swim without harm in this whirlpool of lies and pretenses. Shrug your shoulders about my brains, make faces about my clumsiness, but leave alone the bitterness for which you would have cause. Extend your hand to me for the renewal of our former friendly relationship, and let us not correspond except when there is a real, factual reason. If you want to, tell Matouš about this intention of mine … send me a message by him, that you are accepting my suggestion without bitterness.

But even if you should feel more bitter about the matter than I want you to be, I want you to know that nothing will keep me from always remaining an unprejudiced admirer of your good qualities and your sincere friend.

28. Němcová, *K.K.*, *Listy II*, op. cit., p. 16 f.
29. ibid., p. l9 ff.
30. ibid., op, cit., p. 37 ff.
31. Němcová, *K.K.*, *Listy III*, (Prague, 1960), p. 137.
32. Němcová, *K.K.*, *Listy II*, op. cit., p. 45 ff.
33. ibid., p. 82 ff.
34. Záhoř, op.cit., p. 67.
35. Němcová, *Korespondence* (Prague, 1952), p. 95 ff.
36. ibid., p. 317.
37. Rudolf Havel, ed. *Božena Němcová ve vzpomínkách* [Božena Němcová is Remembered], (Prague, 1961), p. 35.
38. Jan Neruda, *Národní listy*, January, l887, feuilleton reprinted in Záhoř, op.cit. p. 87 ff.
39. Záhoř, ibid., p. 85.
40. Ignatius (Ignaz in Czech).
41. The Russian form of Jan.
42. Němcová, *K.K.*, *Listy 11*, p. 199 ff.
43. ibid., p. 212 ff.
44. ibid., p. 219 ff.
45. bid., p. 225 ff.
46. Němcová, *Korespondence*, (Prague, 1952), p. 268 ff.
47. Němcová, *K.K.*, *Listy II*, p. 255 ff.
48. Reprinted without a date in Mojmír Otruba, *Božena Němcová*, (Prague, 1964), p. 216.
49. M.D. Rettigová, *Domácí kuchařka*, [The Home Cook], (Prague, l985), p. 18.

50. Němcová, *K.K.*, *Listy III*, op. cit., p. 71 ff.
51. Němcová, *Korespondence*, (Prague, 1952), p. 320 ff.
52. Němcová, *K.K.*, *Listy II*, op. cit., p. 268 ff.
53. Němcová, *K.K.*, *Listy III*, op.cit., p. 25 ff.
54. ibid., p. 33 ff.
55. ibid., p. 77 ff. This is a summary from sixteen printed pages.
56. Záhoř, op. cit. p. 345.
57. Němcová, *K.K.*, *Listy III*, op. cit., p. 113 ff.
58. ibid., p. 242 ff.
59. Němcová, *K.K.*, *Listy IV*, (Prague, 1961) p. 74 ff.
60. Záhoř, op.cit. p. 47.
61. ibid., p. 49 f.
62. Josef Lelek, *Božena Němcová* (Prague, 1920), p. 230ff.
63. ibid., p. 227.
64. Záhoř, op.cit., p. 90.
65. *Moravské noviny*, [Moravian News] 28. February, 1862.
66. Vitezslav Hálek, *Národní listy*, [National Pages] 24 January, 1862.
67. Záhoř, op.cit., p. 336 ff.
68. ibid., p. 79.

Chapter 3

JOSEFA NÁPRSTKOVÁ

(1838–1907)

Josefa Náprstková, known by her affectionate nickname Pepička,[1] was unquestionably an interesting woman. She was guided by tradition, by common sense,
and by her husband Vojtěch, but never seems to have been aware of any conflicts
among these forces. She was the least educated, the plainest looking, the hardest working and the most unselfish, charitable, down-to-earth of all the women
in this book and a true representative of the nineteenth century work ethic.

A girl from a poor family, she felt extremely lucky to have been chosen by
Vojtěch Náprstek to be his wife, the man who probably did more for the
advancement of Czech women and much more for Czech education in general
than anyone else. There are some veiled remarks in Pepička's diary, indicating
her life was not always happy, but we do not know to what they refer; she may
have had in mind the poverty of her youth, deaths in her family or difficulties
with employees in the Náprstek family establishment.

Although Pepička seems not to have written for an audience, she considered
it possible that her diary would be read. She began writing late in life, at the age
of fifty, and wrote down what was uppermost in her mind, whether it was her
feelings, memories from her youth, recent events or expectations for the future.

She believed in living simply and economically, not in order to accumulate
money, but to have money for charity and for additions to the collections in
Vojtěch's museum.

She enjoyed traveling abroad, but most of the time worked long days running the complex Náprstek operations. We can assume that some of her basic
convictions acquired more definite contours during marriage, particularly her
Czech patriotism and her emphatic but not always convincing atheism.
Although from a working class background, she came to identify with the prop-
ertied class against the socialist workers, but only with owners who worked as
hard as the workers. If one were to ask her what gave her stability, she would
have said "work, and more hard work."

The following text is from a collection of memories and was written by
Julius Zeyer, a friend of the Náprsteks and a famous Czech poet and writer.[2]
It is followed by excerpts from Pepička's Diary.

... She came from a poor family, her father ... worked in a brewery, her mother was a servant. They were ... hard-working people. In order to bring a little money into the household, mother Křížková used to go with a bucket to breweries to ask for yeast which she then sold in homes. Often teenage Pepa had to take the bucket on her back ... she once ... declared, that she would rather drown herself [than continue to work so hard.] Her mother ... took her by the hand: "So come right now!" and took her to the mills [by the river.]

At the age of seventeen, Pepička came as a helper to Mrs. Fingerhutová's[3] who soon came to find her work indispensible. However, it was a different story when Vojtěch wanted to marry her. So she became Mrs. Náprstek only after the death of her employer.

Trained in the tradition of "panímaminka,"[4] she saw to it that everything was done as it had been during her rule. Perhaps in this anxious observance she went too far ...

The couple had a good relationship; their cordial notes testify to that, not only from the time after the wedding, but also from later

Josefa and Vojta Náprstek

years, when they left each other "telegrams", regular messages, with a pleasant greeting. Náprstek, who always viewed women from a respectful distance, behaved the same toward his wife. His ... signs of attention toward her were touching; on the counter in their storeroom ... there were always flowers which he brought her from town. Sometimes it was a little gift ... Until her death she had in her room ... a large gingerbread heart ... with the inscription "Pepička". ... Hers was ... also the first sewing machine to appear in Prague.

Mrs. Pepička totally adjusted to her husband ... She even began to learn English. Her written pages with sentences, which she translated from Czech, are preserved with Vojtěch's corrections. Just as Náprstek [almost] always wore his jacket with tails, so Mrs. Náprstková created clothes always of the same style for herself ... She dressed even more simply at home. Over her simple grey dress with a big apron she wore a brown jacket when it was cold, on which as a rule she had pinned several ... notes about what to do or to tell Vojtěch. At home she wore a white lace kerchief on her head over smoothly combed hair, parted in the middle. When she went anywhere, for a lecture, a meeting ... or very rarely ... visiting, her dress was of better material, and she wore a velvet cloak over it. On her head she wore a small, narrow, black velvet hat, rather a hood, without striking decorations... .

Her behavior toward people was friendly and simple. When anybody addressed her "milostpaní" (a respectful form of address like "gnädige Frau" in German), she interrupted "Náprstková, please. Only Náprstková!" What title could she have acquired more honorable than to be the wife of Vojtěch Náprstek?

She defended her opinions firmly even toward "prominent" people ... She also was not impressed with titles ... The Náprsteks met the governor, his Excellency Franz Count Thun and his wife and were invited to their residence ... Náprstek did not feel like going. "Pepičko, go alone. If I went, people would say of me that in my old age I run after counts!" So Pepička went by herself and had a nice chat with the countess. The hostess ... complained about Franz ... "Never mind", Mrs. Náprstková consoled her, "a wife has an apron to hide her husband's faults under."

Her husband ... sometimes took extensive trips with her. In the summer of 1876 [they] stayed ... in the Austrian Alps, in ... 1877 they went ... via Germany to Holland, where they stayed for almost three weeks. She received the tickets ... with a note: "Handed to my beloved wife Pepička for that long desired trip to [see] my competitors [i.e. the Dutch liqueur manufacturers Bols] by Vojta, orderly and clean." The excursion ended in Hamburg. Mrs. Náprstková brought back souvenirs from everywhere ... which then filled the glass case in her room.

She had her "own" little room with a little vestibule. Between her room and Náprstek's was the large reading room and ... the parlor. On the walls there were lots of photographs of people she respected ... Of course there also was a shelf of books by writers she liked, some of them given to her with dedications by the authors.

Her interests were parallel to Vojtěch's, except that she was also active in women's circles. Again and again she thought of more enterprises in which Czech women ... should participate ... Often an outstanding countryman or a foreigner was honored with a gift of Czech handicrafts, but it also could be an organization or an institution. For these gifts—sometimes quite expensive ones ... Mrs. Náprstková often made up the difference when funds were insufficient.

She never recovered after Vojtěch's death ... it seems that her motivation to live was broken. Life ... "u Halánků"[5] died as it were and only continued mechanically ... Even when there was a happy occasion, Mrs. Náprstková refused to participate, as if it were an offense against Vojtěch's memory. I remember when E. St. Vráz went on his expedition via Siberia and Japan to New Guinea and spent all of his money on ... the most beautiful artifacts with the instructions that they be exhibited. These true treasures of taste, beauty and ... skill were of course destined for the house "u Halánků". How often did we beg [her] to look at that splendor! "Since Vojtěch didn't see it, I don't want to see it either!"

The flood of 1890

She died after a long illness—tuberculosis—quietly 13 September 1907, not quite completing her sixty-nineth year—at the same age as her dear Vojtěch.

Pepička began writing her diary[6] on 3 June 1890:

I wanted to begin writing on May first, but I always have more good intentions than time. That day caused a lot of people worries and trouble, and many people will have reminders of it for life, for many laborers were fired from work because of their behavior. So they will suffer;

nowadays working people do not save as they should; they treat themselves and their children to all enjoyments, and many families spend more than they take in. It would be nice if the first of May were a holiday of labor, but where the working people on that day want to have meetings against their employers, the owners ... cannot participate, because who has his capital invested in a business has more worries and obligations than a worker, who lives from day to day and only has his own work to worry about; if the workers lived as my father did, there would not be all the complaints about bad conditons; my father had six guilders a week, and altogether about 10 guilders. He had us five children and in addition, my mother's father, and his own father in the country to support. We children did not know what beer or meat tasted like ...

Since 1885 my head has not had any rest; that year Šimáček[7] died. His words were: "Pepičko, I recommend my boys to you; help them with your advice". A week later he, a strong man full of life, was dead. It was terrible, and I still cry. Why did he have to go and why could I not have gone instead?—Then building the museum, the arrival of the American Czechs, my husband's sickness in his legs which lasted until May 1894, in September the flood; getting everything in order by September 28th, St. Wenceslas' day; then in 1891 my father's illness which also lasted 4 months; transporting the collections into the new building, mainly the work of our mothers, all that always only on Sundays and holidays. The Kottners help us vigorously with everything, otherwise I don't know how we would have managed all the work; so a good genius sends us good people; may this friendly relationship last among us for the rest of our lives! As for myself, I want to do all I can not to cause any unpleasantness.—All the work and cleaning up there was after that flood, what money and problems, all that is behind us. Now we are looking forward to the exhibition—may all turn out well! Whenever we pass by the exhibition grounds, I always say to myself: I don't care what happens to me, as long as things go well with the exhibition. When I see the damage the flood caused even in that area, I see that our house was paradise by comparison: what human efforts came to nought, what took months to create was destroyed in a day and had to be begun over again.

The exhibition was a marvelous success; we shall never forget that pearl of human skill. For the rest of my life I shall gratefully remember that I had the good fortune to live through those blissful moments ... Why did poor Mrs. Riegrová[8] not live to see that! When I heard about her death I asked myself: Why did that lady have to go, why was she taken away from her husband now that he would need her the most? At the funeral when Father Neklas [Niklas] prayed at the tomb, he also prayed: "Lord, what moved you to wrest this good, noble woman from the arms of her loved ones, and to take this thoughtful benefactress from the poor?"

At the last meeting in the City School for Continuing Education, before her departure for Italy she said to me: "How are you doing in that cooking school of yours, you are doing little good for the poor there." "It is true", I said. For one thing, the ladies there did not penetrate very deeply into the conditions of the poor, and secondly, according to their experiences, it is not always right to support the poor; from the standpoint of various observers, it is best to provide work for people. Even Tolstoy recognizes that it is only possible to free oneself from human misery through work. Therefore, it is necessary mainly to teach people the love of work, for the rich and the poor only live from work.

I remember how once Skrejšovský rode in his carriage along the Moldau like a prince; Vojtěch and I stopped and watched him; he looked around triumphantly, seeing my husband walking on foot. Think of the poor people whose savings enabled him to live like that! When they moved to Prague, Mrs. Skrejšovská had … everything so simple in her household; they said she only had colored canvas comforter covers. Later she had to have fillings for pillows which cost 10 guilders each. Where did that woman learn all that? They say that if a man allows himself larger expenditures, the wife should be ten times thriftier to make up for them; the man belongs to the public and the woman to the household; she should always guard the hearth so that it does not crack or the fire go out … The larger the household, the greater the responsibility for the wife, and therefore she has to be all the more circumspect; I know from experience, how often I am, to say it straight out, desperate when I see the responsibilities we took on, and how hard it is to do everything; panímaminka did not have the responsibilities I had, with gratitude I can say that they were in part carried out as if by miracle. It was hard, but still it was done.

Nothing went smoothly for me in life, I had to do everything several times before I succeeded; I always told myself: "Just be patient, patience brings roses." For our panímaminka, as she often used to tell us, everything went as if by magic; when she had supplies, goods rose in price; when she bought, it was cheap; with Vojtěch and me, things were the opposite: speculations did not turn out, and we had work and more work … Therefore I always liked to work; the more work we have in the business [a brewery], the happier I am, and I see to it that everybody is satisfied with the service. I like to be in the business, although I would be happier if it were different. I have to listen to many bitter words about such businesses; I am consoled by the thought that our drinks contribute to the health and advantage of people and are not intended to do harm, but may even be considered medicines.

It was my father's last visit at the exposition; he lay down on 15 November, and on the 21 he died. ... When I wanted to feel sorry for myself, I always told myself that it would be ungrateful of me, for our dear father lived to be eighty-one years old. He retired completely when he was sixty. (My husband is sixty-seven, and his work and obligations are still growing) ... When I saw how my father always had to work, I wished that he still would have some years of rest, and this wish was generously fulfilled. I wish for it also for dear Vojtěch, but it would take a miracle for my husband to live only for himself ... We have so much to straighten out, and ... the plant leaves us very little time. ...

The mother of Professor Čeněk Šercl came to see me 30 June with a letter in which Prof. Šercl informed us that according to Dr. Dejl he must stay in a dark room for fourteen days; when he was in Prague at the Jubilee Exhibition, Prof. Schoebl assured him that his eyes were entirely healthy, although he already had an inflammation. Having been reassured, he did not spare his eyes, and they became worse during the winter. Now it is feared that he may turn blind. His poor mother had a tough life ... with the man who was never a faithful husband for forty-eight years. She told me: "I still visit his grave, and I always whisper `although you destroyed my whole life, may the Lord forgive you.'" These words moved me very much. When she said to me: "I don't know why I lived", I answered: "So that you could give the Czech nation a son who made the learning of the Czech nation known in England and in Russia." This consoled her. She said: "Of course to me the love of my son has to make up for everything; if I could only take that eye ailment from him onto myself". I consoled that rare mother ... she has experienced worse things than I ...

My head spins when I think of how they will treat the things and the books after we are gone. May a good spirit protect ... what has been collected with so much love. There will be enough people who will criticize; some people only know the value of money and nothing else. Even our panímaminka clasped her hands when she saw those books and sighed: "Such a lot of money!" Certainly, when she was living, times were different and she meant no harm with those words. Proof of that is that she did not try to stop Vojtěch from founding the Czech Industrial Museum. She only was always afraid that he might be sacrificing everything for that institution and then be dependent.

Therefore she handed down the house at the Black Eagle on Poříč to the Industrial Museum, to be set up by Vojta Náprstek, on condition that as long as her sons live, they share the clear profit, so that for the rest of their lives they would have something to live on. What we could, we always deposited in the bank ... Now it would be hard to save as we did earlier; taxes are much higher, and the laws about the sale of alcoholic beverages are such that everybody is afraid to sell; we did what we could. I enjoy work as long as I am healthy, and would like to continue running the business for a long time, if only there were people who also enjoy the work.

I thank my guardian angel who suggested to me to take a liking to the ethnic embroideries. I am not a bigot; I don't like people who, with bowed head, fold their hands toward heaven and spend much time sitting in church; my religion is love thy neighbor as thyself; I don't believe in life after death, but if there is, I'll be pleasantly surprised. I have had many good ideas, and profited from many undertakings; I also was responsible for the idea of the lotteries for the

Czech costumes from the nineteenth century

National Theater,[9] although I had not intended it, for when it was a question of building a national theater, I thought that our small theater was good enough ... and that an orphanage should be built instead, we need that more urgently ... The very next day people began sending gifts for the lottery; and, because of my letter about the orphanage, the lottery for the National Theater quickly materialized. Now we have the theater *and* an orphanage, but so far the orphanage does not have an adequate building... .

The gift of honor to the French Sokol[10] gymnasts in 1889 was also my idea and it turned out beautifully; so the gifts for the cities of Nancy and Lvov materialized in 1892. The trips to those two cities were undertaken by Podlipný and his wife. The picture "The Judgment of Libuše"[11] by Pavlík was bought for the City Girls' School; I succeeded in that, too. All of you who helped make my ideas a reality please accept my warm, sincere thanks; I would never have been able to do it alone, but with unity and good will all turned out well. I also thank all those who helped me collect folkloristic embroideries, for if they had not sent me those specimens I never could have assembled the collection. My obligations did not permit me to travel in the countryside. As a stranger I could not have entered many cottages where the items had to be sought ... I have known many good people in my life, and remember them all with gratitude. My thanks for every instructive word. I don't hold a grudge against those who harmed me, although it pained me very much, but everyone has his friends and enemies.

In 1876 my husband and I went to the exhibition in Munich. There we met with Dr. Šebek of the Prague Chamber of Commerce. He asked my husband why the Czech Industrial Museum does not have German inscriptions. My husband replied that it is a Czech institute; Dr. Šebek argued with him, but my husband did not change his mind. Then he suggested that the Chamber of Commerce should establish a crafts museum. In those days they were inclined toward the German side in the Chamber of Commerce. They accepted the proposal, and so one could say a competing museum was established. Mr. Bondy, the President of the Chamber of Commerce came to see my husband to tell him; he pointed out that my husband should stick more to industrial objects and procedures which was done. ...

When we began to collect national embroideries in 1877, and embroideries generally, the experts of course recognized that it was nice, and that similar embroidery could be introduced in the schools and in Czech households. There were plenty of them in the Industrial Museum. Some teachers wanted those precious old things to be loaned to schools, so that the pupils could work according to them. They were told that no museum loans such items, but that one goes to the museum and copies what is necessary. For some people this was not sufficient, and they formed an association for the popularization of ethnic embroidery. The association applied to the city for support, to buy old embroideries which would be loaned to schools. The association for the propagation of national embroideries at that time bought old embroideries and placed them in boxes in the higher city school, where always on Thursdays and on Saturdays the teachers were allowed to select and to copy the samples. It was a good idea to arrange an exhibition of old embroideries and of new ones made according to the old.

What pleased me the most was that just this exhibition, the first in the museum about women's crafts and skills, opened on panímaminka's birthday, namely 24 April 1887 … the exhibition lasted a week, and 220 guilders were taken in, a nice amount to buy new exhibits.

It always hurts me the most that, in return for our willingness to help, we are treated with lack of consideration; whenever people can, they humiliate us.

I hope that we can still build that section which panímaminka originally set up for collections and where things were ruined because there was half a meter of water there in 1890. That room cannot be used for anything … she meant well and wanted to satisfy Vojtěch … it's a good thing that she never knew [about the water damage]. If I could at least have the knowledge that the exhibits are in an adequate building with me … If we can still carry this out, I shall go calmly, and with eternal thanks to the good spirit, to what we call eternity. What is awaiting me? More bad than good or the opposite? May only my Vojtěch stay healthy for me, so that we still live together a few years; the time we have known each other went like a beautiful dream. In 1860 I found out that he was fond of me and in 1875 we were married; now we have lived together for seventeen years; I don't know if happily; at least people say that we are as if we had just been married; I do all I can so that he is … happy. The matter of whether I'll be rewarded I have to leave up to fate. I would not like to survive him, and yet I would be glad if he always had everything according to his wishes and for his comfort.

I used to have to be in panímaminka's room at six in the morning to take everything out of the pantry according to her instructions. We all worked enthusiastically. Now, work is too much trouble for everybody. They consider work their enemy, and yet we all live from work, the rich and the poor. A woman has a hard life in an enterprise where order and precision are needed. My life is not enviable, having to work with people all day and putting up with annoyances; how lucky is a woman who only has her household to worry about!

In February of 1875 we were married, and in September of that same year I took four children—orphan girls—into the house. The oldest was sixteen ... When they all left us after ten years ... I said ... I would never take anybody into the house again. I won't describe here all I had to listen to and suffer; I was accused of being unfair when I wanted to have order and raise the girls properly; so my contentment in marriage lasted from 25 February until 15 September 1875; that day four children came into the house and troubles began and are continuing, for now instead of the children there are people for whom nothing is enough, and who complain about too much work, especially now that socialism drills everywhere. A woman who has to work with them has bitter experiences; they never dare to behave toward a man as they do toward a woman. People from earlier times would not even believe what demands working people make nowadays; now we have to expect new whims which we cannot afford ourselves.

May my Vojtěch meet with no misfortune so that he can carry everything out. When my husband has a major obligation, I feel everything with him, and I am afraid for him. I must try not to remember that he is already sixty-seven because that pains me. The thought that he might leave forever shakes me up, and I feel then that I would not be able to live.

Recently we were at Choděra's for supper. I always give my husband some from my plate. ... There was a man sitting across from us; he got up and told us how pleased he was to see husband and wife behaving toward each other in that way, and that he hopes that one day when he gets married, things will be like that also. My husband strives for a good atmosphere and contentment in our household, so much so that sometimes I am sorry that he treats people in such a way that in their ignorance they think they are something special, and then it is difficult to work with them. He has never associated with that kind of people, and does not know how they embitter one's life. If everyone would live up to his obligations, I think that there would be paradise on earth.

Now every girl wants to be a school teacher; they don't like housework. When I think of all I had to do when I came to the house when I was almost seventeen, to work in the store room with the beer every day until one o'clock in the morning, and to be at the store again at seven in the morning: On Sunday we did the laundry, which was entertaining, and all that we were glad to do ... but now the more they are paid, the less they work. I had twenty-one guilders for a quarter of a year of service; now the kitchen maid has the same pay. And yet, when I first got the twenty-one guilders, I thought all of Prague belonged to me. I did not drink beer and therefore received no money for it, but it did not occur to me that I was shortchanged. … Now I am the lady of the house and as they say "Mrs. Náprstková", but where is my cheerful mind and my contentment? They will never come back, for now I have great obligations and responsibilities for everything that happens in the house. When I was single I was responsible only for myself; I did my job and that was it. Fate gave me a position which I never dreamed of. I am always grateful for everything, and only wish that I can carry out as much as possible for the good of others …

Prof. Kroupa came again from Edinburgh on 1 August. After dinner, he began telling me about his troubles. He said he would give up his position in Scotland and deposit the money in an English bank, which will give him an annual income until his death, and that after his death the money would go to the bank. When I asked why he does not set up an endowment, he said: "Nobody gave anything to me, why should I give anything?" After I tried for a long time to convince him, he said: "In Hamburg there are six thousand marks deposited, half of that is for you for the Czech Industrial Museum; do anything you want with the other half; any endowment you wish."

"The more the state looks after people, the less they look after themselves; people only have their self-interest in mind."

I often think of the journeyman mason who was coming from work in Munich. He saw a little girl in the street in front of a house crying, and women all around. When he asked the women why the child was crying, they answered that her mother had died, and they did not know what to do with her. The fellow took the little girl by her hand and asked her: "Do you want to go with me?" The child smiled and nodded; so he took her on his shoulders and carried her home. He figured that he would try to save what the child would need. Then he saw that he could support another child, and soon there was an opportunity to find another orphan. He told his friends and they all contributed something. He then saw that more children could be taken care of. When there were six of them, he took them to the nuns in the convent. He was always looking for children, and deposited the money which was coming in, and after several years he was able to build an orphanage. All that was done by a poor journeyman mason. This is further proof that the less a person has, the more appreciative he is, and the more he has, the more selfish he will be. Of course there are exceptions, but they are so rare that all of mankind should be ashamed, because the number of good people is so tiny.

I shall now describe how Vojtěch and I became husband and wife. In the year 1856 I came to the house on 19 January. In October 1855 I was sixteen, in other words I was not quite seventeen. Old Mrs. Náprstková[12] said to father who was a distiller in the brewery house: " Adolf, I would like to try out your daughter, have your wife bring her." When he told my mother at home, she started crying: "What am I going to do at home without Pepa? She is my right hand." I said: "Mother, don't cry, I am not suitable for "u Halánků", panímaminka will send me right back, I don't know how to sell." My mother said: "Dear girl, she won't send you back; I know you, you adjust to everything." And my good, wonderful parent was right. When I came home a week later, my mother asked me how I liked it. I began to sob that I don't know if I can get used to that noise and activity, that my head is spinning, and so on. Mother listened quietly and said: "Listen Pepo … you will go and ask panímaminka how satisfied she is with you, and if she is not, or if she sends you home, you will not even stay home overnight, but I'll send you to serve as a nursemaid. That would be too bad, such a house, such a job, such food; at home nothing but

The Náprstek house from the rear

potatoes, and you dare say that you don't know if you can get used to it. I thought that you would jump with joy, and you whine; when I was a servant, I starved. In the evening I baked myself potatoes to fill up. I had to do laundry all night. And all that for twenty guilders a year. You have twenty in silver for a quarter of a year." When I heard my mother talking in this way, I realized in my soul that she was right. I did not make a sound, kissed her hand and cheek and went back. A few years later, I found out that after I left, my mother told my brothers and my sister all about what I had to go through while they sat at home as if behind glass. A few days later when I came home again, my mother asked again how I was doing. I began to praise "u Halánků", how pleasant it was there. After my mother had talked to me, I recognized that she was right. I did not have to pretend that I was satisfied. In a house with so many people, I was not on a bed of roses. Anyone who has experienced anything similar will understand. I tried to get along with everybody. I enjoyed my work … I was so happy … I danced along the pavlač[13] and skipped on one foot like a little girl. Everything pleased me. I had only one dress for every day and one for Sunday, and when I received my pay for the first time after a quarter year, I felt as if all of Prague were mine. The first thing I did was to give my mother two guilders.

In those days the German language was still considered better than Czech; also few people spoke Czech, and people who spoke German expected more respect. Also many Germans came into our business. Panímaminka did not know German well, and wanted me as the youngest to learn it, and to read German books as much as possible. In the house there still was a bookkeeper, the former teacher of the sons, Ferdinand and Vojtěch. He was a native German and spoke Czech only when he had to; his friends were all Germans. Apart from that he was an excellent man. Whenever we wanted advice about anything, we went to ask what Mr. Kraemer thought of it.

On 25 February 1858, Mr. Vojtěch, as everybody called him, came to Prague after a ten—year stay in America. It was a Thursday, and everything was readied for supper. It was decided that only Mr. Ferdinand would go to the station. We in the house watched for the carriage to arrive and wanted to run out to meet him. But as soon as the carriage … stopped, a figure jumped out and with one jump he was upstairs in panímaminka's room. None of us house people saw Mr. Vojtěch; his mother was the first to see the face of her son. From surrounding streets people came to ask if it was true that he came from America and what he looked like; if he was still white or whether, there in America, he had turned black. They had all kinds of other questions … we did not dare ask, and the chamber maids did not tell us anything. They came for beer and did not talk; we all thought that this was a matter for the family and not for the public. We looked at our masters with respect. The next morning I was in the back store-room, when around 10 o'clock panímaminka brought Mr. Vojtěch, and showed him how everything was arranged. From then on, instead of panímaminka, Mr. Vojtěch started coming to the storeroom and wrote the bills which formerly Mr. Kraemer used to write. He started to pay attention to the business and to the facilities.

… Karolinka[14] gave notice and went home. Panímaminka called me and told me that now I was going to be the senior woman employee. Of course, at first I was afraid of the responsibility, but then I adjusted to everything, so that panímaminka often said to me: "Pepo, if only I could make two halves of you, one to leave below and one to take with me upstairs or outdoors", or "where Pepa is, I don't have to be." This praise pleased me so much, that I tried all the more to please everybody.

In 1860 the Prague typographers had their first ball. My brother Emil was a typesetter in the Haase printshop. He purchased a ticket and persuaded me to go with him. Panímaminka did not like it, but still she gave me permission. That evening I was afraid that I would cry at that ball. My mother and father, my sister Uška, later Šimáčková, my brother Čeda, the doctor, my brother Emil … and I prepared for the ball and went. When we went into the hall—it was in the Konvikt building—the music brought tears to my eyes, I don't know why. When Emil saw it he took me to dance. We danced a second and a third dance. Then the organizers of the ball came and told me that Mr. Náprstek was there also. I replied "So?" … I looked at the gallery and saw Mr. Vojtěch Náprstek, who looked at me with a smile; I am writing this after thirty-three years, and my heart begins to pound. I think of that moment reverently and with gratitude. Before you could count to five, Mr. Vojtěch stood next to me and said to my brother Emil: "May I?" My brother stepped back and Mr. Vojtěch said to me "Pepičko, are you here alone?" I said I was with my mother and father and Uška and two brothers. Then Mr. Vojtěch said: "I don't mean it that way. I mean does anybody have a claim to you?" I blushed and said "nobody." From that moment on I danced only with Mr. Vojtěch, and not at all with my brother. I was so blissful and happy that to this day I feel what I felt in my soul.

You can imagine what stir this caused. It was the ball of a large family, and everyone knew everyone else, and now the young master "u Halánků" who was so distinguished chose a very ordinary common girl. There were more attractive girls present, but only I was treated with such distinction. It seems to me that it was all a dream. We all went home together at six in the morning, I to "u Halánků" with Mr. Vojtěch and my parents with my sister and my brothers. When I first came home after that ball, my dear mother took me aside and said: "My girl, yesterday all envied us the honor Mr. Vojtěch paid us when he danced with you the whole time. You looked nice together. But what's the use? Don't think of a gentleman's love. As they say, it jumps after rabbits. Therefore, dear child, think of your honor and of what you owe yourself and your family. I am not afraid because I know you, but it is my duty as your mother to tell you." She kissed me and never mentioned it again, only sometimes she referred to how well we ate at the ball, and that Mr. Vojtěch paid for everything.

I never found out if panímaminka knew about it. I only know that one day in 1867 on a Sunday evening at the time when Mr. Vojtěch used to always read to her and I used to come and ask if panímaminka had any wish I could fulfill, Mr. Vojtěch jumped up toward me, took me by my hand, put his arm under mine and walked up to paní-maminka, who was sitting on the sofa, and said: "Panímaminko, how would Pepička and I look together?" Panímaminka said "nice", and Mr. Vojtěch said "So, you wouldn't have anything against my marrying Pepička?" Panímaminka replied: "I have nothing against it, but as long as I live, I want to be the only lady of the house." Then Vojtěch: "Is this your last word?" and she replied: "You know me." I pulled myself from under his arm. I don't know what else mother and son discussed. Neither panímaminka nor Mr. Vojtěch said anything to me, and I didn't ask. We continued to live as before, and I did my work as before, only I was convinced that Mr. Vojtěch and I were fond of each other.

So the years passed for us, sometimes in contentment and some-times not, as is common in human life. I can only say that I did not have a happy youth. It could have been better, but it also could have been worse.

When my dear mother fell ill with pneumonia ... I said: "My dear mother, I shall do everything you wish." She said: "You see, Pepšo, I feel that I am nearing the end." When I objected, she said: "Let me finish, I have something on my mind, and I'll feel better if you let me speak. If I died, what would father do? Therefore promise me that, if it should happen, you will come home and not stay "u Halánků". I said: "I promise, but I know that you will be well." She shook her head sadly, and I quickly changed the subject. Then on 26 August my dear mother died; before that she said calmly: "I am dying peacefully because I have your promise." After a while she said: "Pepšo, I'll tell you something." I bent over my good mother and she said: "You and I." She sighed, and then did not move any more.

Those were her last words ... What meaning am I to make of these words: "You and I?" I often think about what could be added to them, but in vain ... A dream which I had in those days came back to me later: I dreamed that I was at a celebration with my mother. There were many people present and I lost her; I looked and cried and could not find her. Suddenly Vojtěch appeared and said to me: "Don't cry, I am she." At that moment I woke up, and really, he always lived up to those words, although I didn't tell Vojtěch about that dream until after we were married.

After the funeral I asked my father to tell paнímaminka that he was taking me home. My father was afraid to tell paнímaminka, for he saw himself that she would be upset, and he asked Mr. Vojtěch to prepare paнímaminka. Vojtěch replied that this was not possible, and that my father could more easily take care of his household than I, Pepička, could leave the business. Whatever damage he would have, he would make up for, but Pepička had to stay in the house ... I was dissatisfied with that reply, because my promise was sacred to me; therefore I tried to convince my father to ask paнímaminka himself. He said: "I know paнímaminka, she will not say anything; she will let you go, and after a while she will let me go, and then we are both going to be at home, and then the question will be what we are going to live on ... I am old and won't find a job so easily." What was I to do? I went to the cemetery to my mother's grave and asked her to forgive me for not living up to my promise to take care of my father's household, so that all would be done as my mother used to do. It is too bad that my dear mother did not live to enjoy the pleasures she longed for, such as reading and theater, but she left us when she was forty-seven years, never to return, in August 1860.

My youngest sister married Šimáček—in those days we all knew him by the name of Vojtěch Bělák. The wedding took place in 1863 ... It was simple, at six o'clock in the morning at St. Jiljí's. From church the Šimáčeks went home, changed and came to my father's house at Betlemská no. 262 for breakfast. I had bought a coffee cake and made coffee, and that was the whole wedding.

My sister Uška went to the shop. She had a business with American sewing machines in the house "u Lemanů" in Perlová Street, Šimáček went to his editorial office; my father to work "u Halánků", and I also went to the store. When I saw paнímaminka that day, she asked me if I was sorry that I was not married, and that my younger sister had gotten ahead of me [literally: pulled out the stool from under me] ... She said: "You will get what is destined for you," and that turned out to be true.

When, a week before panímaminka died, I helped her undress, she said, "Pepo, you take care of me as if you were my own daughter. God will reward you." And I said, "Why, panímaminka also takes care of us like a mother." On Sunday she was well, and a week later she was dead from a cold she contracted on an outing. Nothing could be done.

Our wedding on 25 February 1875 was simple. The ceremony took place at the Old Town Hall at ten o'clock in the morning. When we returned home, we immediately went to the store. The employees had what they call a double dinner, and we had dinner as usual. Our people each received gifts of money and books. Inspired by that, they collected money among themselves and handed it to my husband as a contribution to the Industrial Museum instead of a bouquet, because they knew my husband's and my view that one should save whenever possible for the museum collections.

I could say all kinds of things about how I did not have a bed of roses, but I don't want anybody who reads this to feel sorry for me, I want people to be inspired to work by what I say, for only through work do we get what we need. If everyone worked and did not rely on the help of others, the Czech nation would prosper. Work makes everybody happy. The fact that work pleases everyone can best be seen in children ... they are happy when they can help adults. If children were raised to help adults from childhood on, they would not have such a revulsion to work as adults. A good proverb tells us: "A bad example spoils good habits."—In our family there wasn't anybody who did not love work, and in the country where my father came from we have many friends who also work and therefore live in contentment. The welfare of the family depends mostly on the mother. If

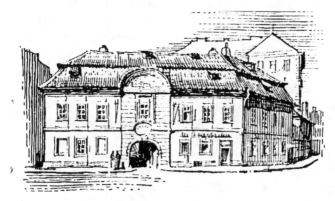

The Náprstek museum

our mothers would raise their children so that they would do their duties with love, not only the family but the whole nation would be happy. There should be this rule in every family: "You can lose everything, only from what you have learned can you yourself and others profit." These rules are valid for the poor and even more for the rich. Now an event comes to my mind which I want to mention.

Today, 4 July, marks the celebration of American Independence; in 1879, the day my sister Šimáčková died; and this year, the day of the jury's decision about the statue of Hus. Yesterday three artists came from Paris with the painter Brožík to deliberate with the gentlemen of our jury. When, at the general meeting, the architect Mr. Jan Zeyer proposed that the Frenchmen be asked to judge the models of the statue, none thought that they would determine honoraria for themselves. They decided on quite splendid ones, namely 1600 franks each. They were expected to come for one or two days, and the hotel bill and the return trip were to be paid for them. This is how it was done with the English engineer Hawksley, who was asked by the city council to evaluate the drinking water in Lahovičky. However, the Frenchmen are not such gentlemen. Three Frenchmen and Brožík, at 1600 franks, makes 6400 franks or 3200 guilders!! It will be a long time before the Czech nation saves up that amount again... since... Czech money is being sent abroad again. And on top of it, they are taking them to the theater today—that will be two boxes, and tomorrow they have a banquet on Sophie's Island at 4 guilders a person, and the Frenchmen will have everything paid for. Only the Czech nation can act like that, for as everybody knows, the Czechs have the character of doves ...

On 28 November 1893 my brother Dr. Čeněk suddenly died. He got up at six in the morning, sat down at his desk, after a while he sank to the floor and did not even sigh any more. May I also leave the world with a similar death ... lie down at night, not get up in the morning. I alone know what I felt. I had three brothers and then I had none. Two died in their youth, Emil, a typesetter, aged twenty-three, Jindřich, a technician, at twenty-one, and the last, whom I loved so much and who considered me an ideal woman, he changed entirely when he got married ... Perhaps his worries as a doctor had such an effect on him. As a doctor he was very concerned, sometimes even too much so. It is a mystery what changes a person ... one would wish that it were always for the better.

Today, 4 December I wrote to Dresden to ask about the conditions under which they cremate corpses; I would like us to have everything prepared in case of death ... so that others don't have to take care of those things.

People think good and bad characteristics are hereditary. One can also say that of our family. My mother's mother was a strange woman. As the daughter of a rich miller on the Lesser Side she inherited everything from her parents. She was their only daughter. Her brother studied for the priesthood and became a priest in Picín near Příbram; we all called him uncle Samek. Grandmother was not economical, and the whole inheritance was soon spent. Grandfather was born in Graz ... he spoke Czech very badly. He worked as a coachman for Count Buquoy, later he became a coachman for the miller Novotný, who owned Sophie's Island. Grandfather was very goodnatured. He handed over his tips and wages to grandmother, who always needed money. They had three children: Kateřina, Anton and Marie. Anton studied for the priesthood, Kateřina and Marie actually weren't led to anything; they wasted time at home, entirely carefree. When Anton saw this, he asked the lady at whose house he tutored if she would take Kateřina as a servant. The lady agreed, and Kačenka[15] went to work, but Marie did not want to work. Kačenka then got so far as to become a cook at the home of Mr. Erben, who was a Bohemian government official. In this service she met my father, and in 1837 they were married. Uncle Anton, who had become a priest, performed the ceremony. My parents lived in a happy marriage. There were six of us children. The last, Pepíček, died six months old. From that time on my mother was always sick.

My brother Čeda was supposed to become a priest; this is what our parents wanted, but when my mother wrote this to her brother ... he wrote [in German] "Kati, your son can become anything, but he should not be a priest." [Actually the German derogatory expression "Pfaffe" was used.] A priest himself, he wrote like that.

Grandmother was very mean and did not get along with anybody. When people found out that my father was about to marry her daughter, they warned him, but my father replied that he was not marrying the mother but the daughter. He was right, my mother was a model woman, hard working, ready to help everyone. In the daytime she served others and only at night she finished her housework. She was the caretaker in number 264 of Betlemská Street where there were twenty-six tenants. All adored my mother. She had advice and consolation for everybody, and was always full of good cheer and told lots of jokes. As long as she was well, she organized a ball in the house every year. The landlord built carriages, which were stored in a room on the ground floor. In winter of course there was no supply of them, and the room was empty. My mother hired a woman to whitewash the walls, she helped with that, and with the help of the neighbours she decorated the room with paper chains and green brushwood. She hired an organ grinder, baked doughnuts and made coffee and invited all citizens from Betlemská and Konviktská Streets. The dancing began at 5 o'clock for all the children. At 8 o'clock each child was given a doughnut and a mug of coffee and went home. After 8 the single and married adults all danced as one family; at 10 o'clock there were frankfurters and beer, and at 3 o'clock coffee and filled doughnuts. At 5 o'clock everyone went home to look after their chores. At 10 o'clock the room was again as it had been before. Everybody was glad to give a small amount for the music. Doughnuts, coffee, frankfurters and beer were paid for in a neighborly way. Mother was pleased when people spoke about how she could arrange things. My father only wondered that she wanted to do all this voluntarily besides all the work and worry she had. My mother paid no attention, and the next year she again planned everything with the neighbors.

In 1856 the military rented that whole building for the police, and all tenants had to move out. People cried and complained a lot. My parents rented an apartment in the same street, number 262/I. It seems that my mother was not so pleased by the peace and quiet she now had; she began to fail and in August of 1860 she died. I already had been "u Halánků" since 1856; I thought that I would not be able to live without my good, precious mother; but time and work helped to ease my pain. I always remember with gratitude the energy of that

The Náprstek library and reading room, 1875

model lady who always derived pleasure from doing things to please others. Although she was very strict, there was order everywhere, and she worked and led all of us to work. Her motto was: "We live from work, the rich and the poor." When my brothers came from school, they had to take brooms and sweep the courtyard ...

Today it is exactly eighteen years since I came to "u Halánků." Mrs. Barbara Serafinová (panímaminka's sister) had different views than her sister. She did not approve of panímaminka giving away so much. She would say: "You are turning people into lazybones, and that is not good. They come and start whining, and those who are truly poor suffer." This pleased me, as I felt the same. Our panímaminka was very strict, even with her own children, but on the other hand she was too kind to people who know how to complain and pretend. But still she had rare qualities and was a second mother to me. I can see her smiling face as she takes both of us by our hands and whispers: "May God give you strength." How often, when she saw those books in the library, she clasped her hands and said: "My God, all that money!" Of course, in those days the value of books was not appreciated, and a book was a luxury. But although panímaminka came from those times, still she remarked: "May it be for a good purpose." When my husband was in London in 1863, she had the stove fixed ... for the library, so that it would be warm there for dear Vojtěch. She was mainly afraid that Vojtěch would spend the entire inheritance ... for books, etc. ... otherwise money was not important to her. She did not spend unnecessarily, and she did not save unnecessarily ... We had no idea what, in view of the modest beginnings, could be accomplished. In 1873, when Vojtěch had paid for everything according to her last will, there were 9000 guilders left in the bank ... the amount by which this increased had to be saved. How I economized, knowing Vojtěch's task! ... In 1885 we could start building. Whenever I go among the collections I say to myself: It was all collected by miracle; a good genius gave us strength and helped us, as he also sent us good people who worked with love, for work out of love prospers more than work that stems from obligation.

May the Good Spirit who helped us realize all that watch over the collections ... [and] in the future and preserve them from disaster ... May it be preserved for the good of the Czech nation, so that Czech youth may benefit from it ... and for the glory of our country. Every piece is dear to my heart, for I know the patience with which it all was put together. ...

Today, 14 March 1894, in the morning at six o'clock, Prof. Kořenský returned from his trip around the world. May my husband be allowed to live a few more years, so that he can enjoy listening to Prof. Kořenský's experiences. According to him, Japan is full of the wonders of the world. Industry, art, the economy, gardening and fruit-growing are all on a high level. Only the Japanese nation has such skill in drawing and in everything, and I am grateful that Prof. Kořenský left us almost everything he brought from Japan. If we had known how he would buy, we could well have sacrificed 500 guilders for that purpose. Well, we are going to order as much as possible. He told me that he thought of us everywhere, and that we should have seen the beautiful things one can buy in Japan for next to nothing.

If I had seen everything and could not bring it to Prague, I would waste away with sorrow. When I was in Nurenberg and saw what rich collections they have, I began to turn gray with regret. In other countries, the government makes sure there are museums, but in Bohemia we have to get everything ourselves. Besides, we send millions to Vienna in taxes, and in return the governor declares a state of emergency when we ask for our rights. Now things are confused, and it is hard for the Young Czechs to work, when not only the Germans, but also Czech newspapers attack them. The Old Czechs, who should be glad about the radical actions of the Young Czechs, are angry instead.

I think many thousands of guilders are given away in Prague at Christmas, and there are more and more poor. Our parents would have been ashamed if some organization would have clothed us, as is done now. My mother worked and my father also, and they led us to work and not to begging.

Today, 17 April 1894, my husband celebrated his sixty-ninth birthday; I hope that we are going to enjoy good health together for a long time. I realize the time is approaching when we will have to part. I can't believe it and yet it is so. We did all we could; of course much more remained a mere wish. So today when we went to the cemetery past the Pštros- and Canarian-Gardens, I said: "Too bad that that piece of land is not ours; without hesitation we would give it to the Prague community with the provision that it must be maintained as a city garden. Future generations should not find it all built up."

Today, 14 April. Prof. J. Durdík, Prof. Prokop Vavřínek, Dr. Kovář and Miss Machová met at our house. They were talking about Prof. Kurz's proposal that instead of Greek and Latin, modern languages should be taught in the schools. Prof. Durdík was against it, because if those two languages were dropped, more attention would be paid to German. None of us agreed. ...

There was a meeting at our house. Miss Machová began to talk about the women's question; I don't agree with her. In my opinion if a woman is the least bit sharp, she can do more than a man in every profession. Of course, she mustn't think that because she is a woman everything should be made easy for her. In my opinion, the man should always be first in the family and in national life. A man rules with his head, and a woman rules with her heart. The woman's emotion, when it is used for the good ... is beneficial in the family and in public life. If I could choose, I would always prefer a strict husband.

Therefore I will advocate that women should carry out the same functions as men. Of course, there should be women doctors, because many diseases and operations could be avoided if we had women doctors, as they have in Switzerland and in Russia, for a woman always trusts only a woman. With her, she does not have to be embarrassed and can say everything openly. I wrote Prof. Albert about this. I begged him fervently to take care of this for the good of mankind and especially of women. The letter was written early in 1893, and today, 24 April 1894, I still have no reply. He probably told himself: "These women want a lot!" Besides I also wrote Dr. Eiselt, as long as he was still a deputy, that it would be good if, in addition to health science in girls' schools in the last year, they would also teach human anatomy, because girls don't learn what they should really know for life. She gets married, has children and doesn't know from what small cause a disease can come for her husband or her children. Or she becomes a governess, and children are entrusted to her. I know from experience how a hernia comes about. The doctor may say that it is fat, just to satisfy them ... and after a while an ailment may develop from it which causes problems all one's life, while it could have been cured if it had been detected early. I also asked about lectures on anatomy, but so far in vain. When will they become a reality?

NOTES

1. See "A Little Lesson on Nomenclature", pp. 27.
2. Quoted in Stanislav Kodym *Dům u Halánků* [The Halánek House], Prague, 1953.
3. See the general Introduction for comments on these names.
4. Panímaminka, literally "Mrs. Mother", contained the idea of mother and "patronna".
5. "U Halánků" is the name of the Náprstek's house, brewery, etc. which still stands today and houses the museum the Náprsteks established. It was named "at the Haláneks'" after earlier owners.
6. The manuscript is in the Náprstek Museum on Betlemské Náměstí in Prague.

7. Her brother-in-law.
8. An active philanthropist, the wife of the important Czech political leader, František Rieger, and the daughter of the historian František Palacký.
9. See the introduction.
10. The Czech nationalistic physical training association.
11. The mythical ruler of Bohemia.
12. Actually Mrs. Fingerhutová; see general Introduction.
13. The porch extending along the backs of houses.
14. Karolinka seems to have been employed in a supervisory capacity.
15. Diminutive of Kateřina.

Chapter 4

OSSIP SCHUBIN

(1854–1930)

O*ssip Schubin, actually Aloisia Kirschner, is one of the very few Prague German women whom we know well enough to include in this book. Not surprisingly, her ancestors also include Czechs, Italians and probably Jews. What we
know about her self-awareness, the circumstances of her childhood and youth
and her later lifestyle seems more like what we know in German than in Jewish settings. Seeing her in a larger framework, her preoccupation with death and
decay is reminiscent of the characteristics in Austrian literature which have been
pointed out by Claudio Magris.*[1]

*The texts of this chapter mostly inform us about Aloisia's childhood and
youth. We know that she wanted to become a singer, and that allegedly due to
a mistake made in the training of her voice it was irreparably ruined, so that she
had to give up her hopes of a singing career. Her earliest stories, thought to have
been written by a man because of her pseudonym, were highly praised. However,
her reputation soon stabilized as the writer of sentimental love stories, often about
nobles from different countries and only occasionally about Czech peasants.*

*Ossip Schubin—she took the name from a novel by Turgenev—regretted
the gradual disappearance of the glittering world of nobility, and although she
had to make her own living, she was on the whole opposed to higher education
for women.*

*What she had to say on that subject is worth quoting. After mentioning the
study of French, English and piano, she states:*

For a talented child that is quite enough. In my opinion there is nothing unhealthier for the female brain than excessive cramming. I'll
accept female doctors, they are nurses with a scientific foundation, but
oh, these poor female doctors of philosophy! I have never met one
who did not make the impression on me as if all the springs of her
brain were paralyzed. Wit, spirit, quickness, everything that makes a
conversation with a woman stimulating and attractive—I have never
found it in one. Almost all of them pass their examinations excellently
and ... are useless for the rest of life.[2]

The birthplace of Schubin.

She published profusely—forty-three novels—many of them in several volumes. Together with her sister Marie, a painter, Schubin often lived abroad—in Paris, Brussels etc.—but sometimes they also leased castles in Bohemia. Schubin is known to have engaged in some literary feuds, one involving her and Marie Ebner von Eschenbach's relative merits, about whose much greater fame she was particularly sensitive.

In her last years she lived in Prague. Although in her novels Czechs were generally members of the servant class, she greatly esteemed President Masaryk and Karel Čapek. Perhaps in the story of her childhood she gave so much space to her family's poor treatment of Bedřich Smetana because she wanted to atone for this neglect.

Here follows Schubin's story of her childhood almost in its entirety:

I was born on 17 June, in the year of our Lord 1854. My mother used to claim that my entrance into the world caused her no trouble at all, that I jumped into life exuberantly, from one moment to the other, with her hardly noticing it. It was at noon, in the bright sunshine of a beautiful summer day, but between two thunderstorms, as often happens in June. Perhaps both affected me, the sunshine and the charged atmosphere.

Since I was the second daughter, my appearance was not welcomed with enthusiasm. A pair of unusually beautiful blue eyes with black lashes, and the (unfulfilled) promise of physical grace reconciled my family to my existence during the first years of my childhood. I spent those years in the house of my grandfather on my mother's side. The house was extremely ugly, a large box painted blue and pink, with the usual gingerbread around the windows, but at any rate there was something unusual about it. It was the last of a long row of houses and actually had five corners and a four-sided facade.

The one facade looked out over an unevenly paved square lined with houses of uneven size and at a dark building with a small statue in the old fashioned curved gable; it was a former convent which had later become the editorial offices of a newspaper. Turning to the left, the second facade faced the old Post Street. There on the upper floors, the petite bourgeoisie hid their near-poverty in shame behind starched cotton curtains and … green potted geraniums, while the common people exposed their misery on the ground floor with an almost cynical lack of concern. To the right of Anne's Square, also parallel to Post Street, one looked from my grandfather's house over the narrow Coloredo Street straight into the windows of a very old, distinguished palace of nobility. Then, around a sharp corner, came the main facade. It looked far out over Francis' Quay, over the wide, solemnly rustling Moldau decorated with islands extending almost to the hill where the old royal castle, the Hradschin, is enthroned between a retinue of churches and palaces; it looked into the historical past of Prague and into the wide world.

Perhaps no other house in my old city enjoys a more beautiful view, certainly none on the right side of the Moldau … .

Since none of my grandfather's heirs were fond of the house, it was

The castle steps

sold after his death. I think I was influenced by the house of my birth. All my life I have seen the world from four different sides.

My mother?

All who met her in her later years ... claimed that she was not only one of the most intelligent, but also one of the most attractive old ladies. But she needed many years to reach that stage of perfection.

In her youth she is supposed to have been delightful, in her middle years she was very excitable and violent, unjust and extreme in her goodness as well as in her anger, and unfortunately just as unreasonable as she was intelligent. And yet we only owe our truly interesting existence to her glorious unreasonableness which simply did not accept the impossibility of our being able to raise ourselves from that most miserable, mundane daily life into which fate had pressed us.

My first memory of her is of a pale young woman with romantic, long, parted wavy hair and wonderfully shining dark eyes, such as I have only seen on Theodor Mommsen. I remember her rocking my little brother on her knees and humming softly "Malbrouck s'en va-t-en guerre; qui sait, quand reviendra ..."

With this song, as she told us, she accompanied the three of us as we entered life, and the sad refrain of the little French folk song accompanied me into old age as a kind of leitmotif.

We are more or less all Malbroucks who go to war, the great war of our lives in which we have to fight as best we can.

My father ?

The sharpest contrast imaginable to my terribly clever (I use that word intentionally), feverishly energetic mother. ...

His father was a bailiff, born in Karlsbad, his mother's maiden name was Mikšovská, a real Slav. My father took after her and despite his strict loyalty [to the Habsburgs], took the side of the Slavs (as did my mother), although he was German and studied in Vienna.

In contrast to my grandfather Kirschner, who was good and sensible but very slow, the embodiment of an inflexible, stubborn, narrow and upright Bohemian German, my father was characterized by an exaggerated Slavic softness: capable of exertion, but inclined to indifference, very attractive, of medium height, with plain black hair and blue eyes in an oblong face with regular features and a slightly upturned nose.

Despite his handsome appearance, he made an inferior impression next to my very impressive mother. Only much later did I tell myself that I had viewed him unfairly. His yielding, dependent nature simply could not prevail next to my mother's stormy superiority.

Originally an excellent official, namely an "assessor" in a ... pre-

1848 institution, the common law, which at that time was the epitome of … legal prestige, his eagerness subsided when the common law was abolished and replaced by less exclusive institutions. This meant that Bohemian land owners had to become reconciled to no longer being represented in their "rights" by a special authority.

After lengthy hesitation, my father decided to turn to agriculture. We left our nice apartment with a romantic view of the Hradschin and moved to Smíchov, at that time a practically non-existent suburb … of Prague, since the largest part of the area now covered with mammoth, ugly building complexes consisted then of fields belonging to my great-grandfather's estate. My father rented the estate, and after brief training began to experiment on it.

We moved into the so-called manor. Today it would hardly be good enough for a manager, but in those days one was modest.

I don't remember much about the move, as I was very little; only that big stacks of pewter and all kinds of other dishes stood around everywhere in the new apartment, that my little soul felt oppressed by the low ceilings and especially the doors, and that the horribly painted walls—brown curlicues on a green background in the children's room—seemed like grimaces to me and tortured and frightened me in my dreams. Furthermore I remember that my mother worked terribly hard, perhaps unreasonably so, and that my father stood around helplessly, playing the … role she had assigned him. With his idle hands in his pockets, his eyes full of tears of enthusiasm, he repeated again and again "Anna, Anna, you should be canonized!" …

That evening I cried myself to sleep—I don't know if it was because there were no regular meals that day … I was an extremely sensitive child and suffered much because of it.

However, the next morning I had a delightful impression. While half asleep, I heard a strange, soothing, humming, singing sound, today I would say it was as if swarms of bees were whirring around trees in spring …

Awakening slowly to my … limited consciousness, I asked our old nanny … what the sounds meant that had awakened me. She answered that it was the voice of the dear Lord speaking to people because it was Sunday.

I don't know why she used these sentimental expressions to explain the sound of the bells, perhaps it was simply that she was a Slav who had such legends in her blood, as do members of all peoples which have not yet become sober from "too much science". For a long time afterwards … I thought that I heard the voice of God talking to people in church bells …

Over the orchard with all its blossoms, behind the farm yard was the ancient Vyšehrad with its towering churches and lovely gardens. Today they all are covered with buildings—but to this day I remember the gold-woven, gold-shimmering soft harmonies of color which then lay over the hill surrounded by romantic, heroic legends—which returned to my mind later when I saw a Fra Angelico or a Puvys de Chavannes ...

Even today, as an old woman with a soul beaten brown and blue by the prose of life, I cannot escape the feeling that Sunday is an exceptional day and we have the right to expect something special from it ... .

At any rate on that day I became reconciled to our new home, and drew the lesson that the most modest existence is bearable if there is a window through which one can look out at something beautiful. Adjoining our old garden where I spent most of my time as a preschool child, there was another garden which was separated from ours by a wall. Although it cannot have been very high, it was higher than I, and that bothered me very much. My imagination was always occupied with the mysterious things that went on behind walls over which one could not see.

A playmate of my sister's, a monster full of good-for-nothing ideas—a much younger stepbrother of my mother's—applied his whole ingenuity to arousing my curiosity. His name was Ferdinand, probably in honor of our retired emperor.

This mean, nine-year-old Ferdinand and my eight-year-old sister had concluded an alliance of superiority against poor little me, and he told me that the strangest things were going on in the neighbor's yard. They claimed that the princess from a fairy tale of which I was particularly fond held Mr. Mordi captured there because he wasn't handsome enough for her after all, but that according to some people it was allegedly Mr. Mordi who held the princess captive because, despite of all his efforts, she refused to love him, and that the happy end of the fairy tale was an invention. But regardless who lived there, the garden was supposed to be of a fantastic beauty, full of flat marble basins with gold fish ... full of rock grottoes and quiet paths lined with cypresses. As I found out later, mean Ferdinand had taken all these descriptions from the *Tales from 1001 Nights* of which I had been given an illustrated selection for Christmas. I asked if the garden was even more beautiful than the Lobkowitz Gardens on the Lesser Side, since these really wonderful gardens, to which we had access thanks to my grandfather's connection to the princely family, were to me the epitome of horticultural splendor.

"Oh, much, much more beautiful," the monster insisted and added: "The servants are particularly beautiful. No stupid lackeys with leggings and shiny buttons, no, all slaves have knickerbockers made of gold brocade and turbans and strings of pearls. And they are all pitch black like the Moor in the circus, and when their masters come near the princess or Mordi, they put both hands up to the turban and bow to the ground ..." Ferdinand told me [of a child who] "could not control his curiosity, and two days after his espionage died of a sun stroke... ."

My wish to look over the wall became more and more urgent. Dying didn't frighten me. After death, one would go to paradise which our nanny had described to me almost as vividly as the monster had described the fairy tale garden. Actually, I was looking forward to walking in paradise, holding the hand of the Mother of God who would introduce me to many nice little angels; so I was very determined to take the chance of looking over the wall.

The decision was easier than the deed, because ... the wall was at least twice as tall as I. Besides, Nanny almost never let me out of her eyesight. Finally, she once had to go into the house for a moment; she ordered me not to move and believed me safe, because the only exit ... from the garden was through the farm yard ... .

I had noticed an old pear tree with branches reaching over our wall into the other garden. Quick as a cat, I climbed up, but before I had reached the desired lookout ... the branch broke, and I would have broken my neck or at least some limb if I had not fallen on a pile of rubbish.

When I got over the first shock, I looked around. I saw an orchard—just like ours, but infinitely more ... neglected. No people were to be seen, only an ugly black dog on a very long chain. He had yellow paws and eye brows, and it was obviously his task to watch a few cherry trees. When I fell into the yard, he began to bark wildly, running back and forth as if he were particularly anxious to catch me by a corner of my clothes. But I sat motionless beyond his reach. Suddenly, I began to sob, not because I had scraped my knees or because I was afraid of the ... dog, no, I sobbed because instead of the expected fairy tale, I had found the ugliest, most ordinary scene.

Of course I did not die of my disobedience. Instead of the Mother of God, a woman in rags came to see why the dog was excited. Just when she was asking me a few questions about how I had gotten over the wall, we heard the great lament of ... Nanny, who was looking for me in vain. The woman picked me up by my shoulders and lifted me over the wall. I received a big scolding.

I think most children in the early stages of their development ... are afraid of life, and surely my fears were unusually strong. From my third to my sixth year, I constantly had the feeling of being surrounded by all kinds of terrible secrets.

Our surroundings were the kind that would stimulate the mind of a child inclined to be frightened. Unfortunately, one could not only see the Vyšehrad from our nursery. If one turned one's head a little to the left, one saw above a gray wall between our house and the barn ... a high, dark building. It was clay-yellow and the mortar on its walls was largely broken, so that it looked as if covered with wounds. The small windows, set deep in the walls, were partly patched with paper, and an unnaturally high shingle roof rested upon it, like a dark burden of obtrusive sadness.

As I found out later, it was ... in the midst of a yard surrounded by many dwellings of paupers and depressing taverns. The whole complex was called Jáma in Czech, which means mass grave. [She is wrong about the meaning of this Czech word which actually means pit.]

Facing the street there was ... a house painted pink, with green window frames and red curtains. In the evening there glowed an evil red light through these strictly closed curtains; at the same time one could hear the dark sounds of ... provocative, miserable music, such as is usual in that kind of a tavern, in order to stimulate the animal instincts of people, the harmonica and the barrel organ played at the same time as the falsetto of a trumpet ... These two houses ... were among the most painful of the many painful impressions of my childhood.

At that time I was already plagued by frequent sleeplessness. I trembled at night in my little bed when I thought of the two houses where, as I was told in answer to my many questions, "the common people" live ... . Gradually my imagination arrived at the idea that "the common people" was a terrible kind of a monster which waited for me in our immediate vicinity—no, not one monster, a great number of them.

One night I was suddenly awakened ... and noticed how Nanny, the cook and the chamber maid were helping my mother to hurriedly pack objects which they had taken out of open wardrobes into blankets. At the same time, I heard people screaming, cows mooing, poultry cackling ... and in between a ... sound which was new to me, but which I later understood to have been fire engines.

"There is a fire in the Jáma, and our stables have caught on fire." ...

It was possible to extinguish the fires, and we children ... were put back to bed again where we, exhausted from the ... excitement, slept long into the next day.

Then came one of the experiences of my childhood which not only made a deep impression on me then, but on my whole life. The fire had torn down the wall between our farm yard and the Jáma; one could look into it unhindered. The Jáma was surrounded by barracks of different sizes ... with two and three floors, and in the middle of the yard there were the remnants of the brown house which had burned down together with some sheds leaning against our wall. It was summer. Innumerable children crawled around, bowlegged and with a rash on their faces, half naked, dirty and entirely without shame. A man with a fiery red face walked up and down on one side of the yard, swinging his arms and mumbling to himself viciously. His very big feet stuck in big, high stove pipe boots and I had the clear feeling that if he stepped on me, he could grind me to a pulp.

A woman with red, long unkempt hair hanging around her grey cheeks kept making the same downward gesture with a bottle, to show that it was empty. She grinned idiotically and showed her upper jaw which had no teeth except for two very long incisors. A few women stood in the doorways. In front of every doorway was a pile of garbage and a puddle, stench everywhere and cynically exhibited rubbish.

So that is the common people, I said to myself and began to howl. Nobody understood why. The view of the great misery made a deeper impression on me than the loss of my illusions about the neighboring garden ... I could not shake off the terrible impression. I felt pity and disgust, but my feeling of horror was even stronger ... [it] seemed to constrict my throat and my arteries—a horror also of a world order that allowed such conditions to exist ... and of the fact that two decent and kind and so well educated people as my parents lived next to this stinking, unhealthy, moral and physical misery without thinking about it.

I was especially surprised about my mother. With her excellent knowledge of history and with her strong inclination toward romanticism, she had, as a young girl, already been enthusiastic about the Declaration of Human Rights of 1789, and when the revolution broke out in Prague in 1848 she had, for the sake of historical local color, cut off her wonderful long hair ... . Indeed, while all around "the people" were shooting in the windows, she stood by her window and sang the Marseillaise. The fact that she ... took poverty for granted, despite her enthusiasm for the revolution, proves how much of a mere facade the revolutionary aims were at that time. Actually, they only wanted to satisfy some sensibilities of the middle class. Nobody was concerned with improving the conditions of life of the masses, my mother did not either. For them ... the common people were a class, almost a species by itself, which one had to avoid as much as possible, of course in a friendly way, because through closer contact one could get disease, vermin or vice.

Years later, when I asked my dear mother, how such blindness and indifference were possible, she answered, not without a certain embarrassment: "That is the way it was then, and it will always be that way!"

Thank God she was wrong and things have changed, at least in part. Our old house still stands today as it did sixty years ago, now behind the very neglected little front yard. It is the last remnant of a time which has passed and has partly been overcome. All around there are new, not particularly beautiful buildings, but which are much more hygienic than the Jáma that still sometimes emerges in my soul in a bad dream.

Originally, death did not frighten me. It was simply an occasion for funerals, and in my childlike view, funerals were something beautiful. They were among our main entertainments.

We had an old aunt who lived in Aujezd, a dark street on the Lesser Side, on the second floor of a house which was called "The Swan", and which was passed every day by a few funeral processions. Afternoon coffee, pastries, and of course a torte were served to us by our friendly aunt ... as early as possible, so that we could go to the window and not miss any of the splendor ... .

We were always looking forward to the pompous hearses with the silver angels supporting the black canopy and the innumerable wreaths loaded on another coach, to the grave diggers on horseback and on foot with their pitch torches flickering red in the daylight, and to the priest in his robes with his retinue of junior priests and altar boys. It was even more beautiful when there was music, and most beautiful when a general was buried, and his own horse walked in deep mourning behind the hearse (if I am not mistaken, in front of all the relatives); in measured intervals three ... funeral marches were played, always the same: by Beethoven, by Mendelssohn, by Chopin. Being extremely musical, I reveled in the tragic sounds of trumpets, in the roll of drums, and in the melancholy melodies of French horns, which floated up to me with the fragrance of incense, burning wax candles, laurel and wilting wreaths ... One more or less had the feeling that ... the dead person was being escorted ... straight into paradise.

But after the ... charms of the neighboring garden had proven to be a mere deception, I no longer believed in the ... beauties of paradise. And when my revered grandfather Polak suddenly died and my mother put on black clothes for days, looked terribly sad, and again and again burst into tears, it became rather clear to me that death meant something else than to be transported in a gala coach from the worries of earthly existence into paradise –that is to say into Cocaigne[3] where milk and honey flows, and where delightful angels play around the Mother of God.

I was afraid to turn to the higher authorities with my questions. I was not a popular child, first of all because of my frequent depressions, and secondly because of my uncomfortable curiosity with which I often embarrassed those authorities. I did not believe that Nanny was very knowledgeable, and so there was nothing left for me to do but to turn once more to the monster, Ferdinand, with my concern. For although my faith in his veracity was shaken, my faith in his … wisdom remained. "What is … death?" I asked him.

The monster raised his eyebrows … "How should I explain it to you?—At death all states of man cease … to die means … to cease being. All human beings must sooner or later cease being."

… I remember exactly how I spitefully stamped my foot and declared: "Then I don't want to die at all. I want to go on living forever, pick flowers and go for walks." … A few days later … he showed off with his … gun which he had gotten for his birthday … In all land-owning families, boys from age ten on were taken hunting; actually only very rarely did accidents result … [He] began … by shooting green apples from the trees, but since this did not satisfy his disruptive impulses, he tried hitting birds … .

Eventually, when I was once listening with great enjoyment to the twittering voice of a small feathered creature, which fluttered its wings up from the bushes to the blue sky, I … heard a bang. Almost at the same time the bird fell down before my feet. I saw him tremble, then he lay still with spread-out wings and contracted claws. The monster however ran triumphantly toward him to ascertain his death. …

Now I finally understood what it meant to be dead. I got into such a state of sympathetic despair … that … even Ferdinand tried to help Nanny calm me down … .

A few days later, I found the bird on the lawn where the gardener had simply thrown him instead of burying him. A repulsive smell came from the small corpse, and worms crawled around the coagulated blood of the wound. It took me a long time to get over my horror of death. Not fear of destruction tormented me, but the terrible accompanying sights and sounds … I still ask myself if nature could not have spared us this, if, instead of slowly experiencing repulsive decay, we could not turn to ashes without the elaborate fuss of an elegant, but still awkward crematorium.

Since I did devote this chapter to the great horror, I shall … describe how I was often haunted by it and what finally freed me of it.

I had the most violent attack in my seventeenth year. At that time, fear of destruction came to the foreground. I held on to my belief in immortality, but instead of simply accepting it with thoughtless piety like other Catholic children, I passionately looked for scientific proof. Since that kind of thing is to be found at most in spiritistic books of consolation—then unknown and inspiring no confidence in me to this day—I began to be tortured by ever more severe doubts. Besides, I developed an ever intensifying disgust of meat. The idea that a poor animal enjoying life had to die to satisfy me, was unbearable. I began to cry when I saw a bowl with roast chicken. From morning to night I felt eternity burdening the short span of time I would at best be permitted to live. No occupation pleased me. I always told myself: It makes no sense, why try? It leads to nothing.

I began to look so miserable that my mother noticed it and finally asked about the reason for my constantly growing melancholia. When I explained my condition to her, she did her best to strengthen my shaky faith. She quoted the loftiest statements of philosophers, poets and theologians. Suddenly, realizing how questionable her consolations were, she hesitated and looked at me sympathetically: "Oh, don't brood so much" she called ... "What will be, will be. See to it that one day you won't find your short life too long!"

I never forgot the sad glance in her large dark eyes. What she said revealed her mood at that time ... She did help me very cleverly to overcome my disconsolate, unhealthy state through all kinds of occupations and ... diversions that preoccupied me ... and took my thoughts away from eternity.After a few weeks my depression subsided—not for good, but for long stretches of time. But again and again, although in weaker form, the old horror reemerged, until I was healed from it once and for all by a very simple experience.

It was in Paris, at the Père la Chaise Cemetery, where we had dutifully noted the various monuments marked in our travel guide. ... the whole world dissolved in a blue fragrance, from which individual high buildings protruded like cliffs in a wild ... ocean. I was in a good mood—death had never seemed farther from me than at that time, on the peak of this overpopulated city of the dead.

"Père la Chaise seems to me like a place of refuge, to which one flees from the exaggerated activity of Paris," I said, and then: "Mother, you still owe us one of the important sights ... I would like to see the morgue ..." "But you have always been so afraid of death. You have never seen a dead body," my mother said. "Today I am not afraid, and I would finally like to see one!" I replied.

My mother reflected for a moment, and then decided to do as I wished. She asked the carriage waiting for us below the cemetery to go to Notre Dame ... and then went with us to the world famous house of the dead ...

My mother said: "I still need to convince myself that you are not foolhardily taking a chance with your nerves. I would not like to expose you to too repulsive an impression ... " Now my heart did begin to beat very excitedly. But I was ashamed to admit my cowardice.

A few seconds later my glances attached themselves for the first time to a corpse. Above the metal apron with which the dead ... are covered from the neck to the knee, there rested ... the head of an old man, framed with long, gray hair and a beard.

I shall never forget his countenance. It was a countenance, not an ordinary face, full of a lofty nobility separating him from us by an infinite distance and with the expression of such deep, contented peace, that it penetrated into my soul like the gentle coolness of a summer evening after a hot July day. And besides peace there was something in the expression like deep gratitude, gratitude for being freed from a great burden.

So this is how a dead body looked ...

I left the morgue in deep thought and took with me a feeling of great liberation. Since then, I never again had an attack of fear of inevitable destruction. Now I know that that state of heightened clarity, which so unsparingly makes clear to us the tragically ridiculous insignificance of our existence—taking its course for a short time between two abysses— is totally pathological. Providence, which has by all kinds of tricks subsequently patched so many gaping tears in creation, has given us a delusion to safeguard our lust for life, and it is closely linked to our health. Whenever too strong and painful an impression tears holes in this delusion—through which we then see otherwise hidden or half hidden things too clearly—we become nervous for a little while, and if the delusion tears totally, we become insane or we kill ourselves.

Now, as a totally healthy and very sensible old woman, I can admit to myself that in my youth I must sometimes have been dangerously close to insanity. But if fate often tore holes into my delusions, they always closed up again—and the delusion was never torn totally.

My mother's fear that I might find this short life too long did not materialize. Today, at the age of seventy, despite bitter and humiliating disappointments which my days have brought me, despite the pressure which the war has exerted on me, despite the painful ... deprivations which have sometimes sorely tried my patience, I enjoy life gratefully, including trifles, look forward to tomorrow when I lie down in the evening—to the moment when my chambermaid opens my blinds and windows, to the wonderful fragrance of the meadow before my window, to the forest beyond them—and when toward evening I begin to be tired, I look forward to a long, undisturbed rest.

I hope, when one day my hour strikes, that the same pleasant drowsiness overtakes me, that I ... welcome death cheerfully saying ... it's you? I thank you!...

Kamaik, the estate in the Elbe Valley, my mother's home, was originally only a rented farm which my great-grandfather had given his

Area around Kamaik

eldest daughter on her wedding, so that she could spend her honeymoon pleasantly. Always having been the most popular summer refuge of the whole family, the farm later had become the property of my widowed step-grandmother. There must have been a magic about the place. In Kamaik my oppressive feeling of misery ... dissolved. There I became a normal child and was happy.

Poor dear, long vanished Kamaik! What was so special about you that one had to love you? To be honest, I don't know. I have seen much more beautiful country homes. I have lived for many years in charming castles and felt so much at home there that I was very indignant when our aristocratic landlord suddenly remembered after a dozen years that the castle did not belong to us ... and gave us notice. I always had a hard time parting with these Bohemian castles we furnished so charmingly. I loved Bonrepos, I loved Krusko, but this love was insignificant compared with the feeling which Kamaik aroused in my anxious heart.

There were places in the Middle Ages, where an outlaw could hide, where he was safe from his would-be-capturers. Kamaik must have had something of the loving, calming, protective atmosphere of these hallowed places.

Whoever stepped over the threshold of this extremely primitive manor house left his worries, his ambitions and, I believe, also his regrets behind. It was as if our savior himself stood in the doorway in order to take everyone who arrived in his arms and to say to him: "Leave all burdens behind you. Here you shall be healed."

There was no official head of the household since the death of my grandfather, only a housewife, grandfather's young widow, to whom he had left the estate. But she made no claims to any special rights … All those present worked on the menu every evening, and the servants, the old furniture and utensils, much more familiar to the older members of the family than to the beautiful young lady of the house, mother, stepmother and step-grandmother, they were there for everybody.

… My great-grandfather had practically been given Kamaik by Prince Schwarzenberg who was one of his clients and had a high opinion of old Hirsch … .

Kamaik was for those seeking to escape from people … A great part of its character rested on the fact that not a single actually usable road connected it with the "world" … One really had to love Kamaik … to expose oneself to the dangers … on the road between Theresienstadt and our little village … . When I think of it, I don't understand how a wheel could have stayed on its axle … .

When we approached our goal, Kamaik … I saw … Ferdinand. In order to look out for us, he had climbed on the crumbling baroque pedestal of an old statue of St. John, which stood somewhat outside the village among old linden trees. He laughed all over his face, waved his straw hat like crazy, and before the carriage had time to stop, jumped down and onto the running board. There, holding on to the edge of the coachman's seat with one hand, he began … telling us the strangest stories.

In the village a calf was born with two heads, and Aunt Batsche, my step-grandmother's sister, had married a musician, a nut who always went for walks with a pleated circular cloak which was, to be sure, beautifully lined in red, but had a terribly worn velvet collar, and the new Uncle (it was too funny, Ferdinand said, to call the crazy fellow uncle), always forgot to take off the coat, so that he perspired terribly. He was always preoccupied with his opera, and actually imagined that he could write one. The monster grinned sarcastically.

Then the carriage rattled through the high gate in front of which two wonderful old nut trees stood guard, into the large farm yard. In front of the house, among the cheerful, fresh, good-looking people who welcomed us, there stood by contrast a pale short man with round glasses, and with long, straight, black hair which hung down to the collar of the carbonari coat which had been described so dramatically by Ferdinand. He had a black pointed full beard and large, soft, white hands. The man was Bedřich Smetana, and the opera which he "actually thought he could compose" was *The Bartered Bride*.

To this day, it is terribly embarrassing to me to think of the humiliating role he played among us. I turn red with shame, when I think of it. I am convinced that if one had taken the trouble to know him, one would have found things in his deep and rich soul going far beyond the very humdrum level of Kamaik conversation. But no one suspected that, and even if they had, they would have considered it disturbing. He was too serious and too great for the milieu he had come into through his marriage.How proud I would be today to be able to count him among my friends! Unfortunately, he died long ago. Having turned stone deaf, he became insane out of despair over not being able to hear his marvelously beautiful music, and died in an insane asylum. When already deaf, a short time before the outbreak of his insanity, he is reported to have said he would gladly die, if only he could regain his hearing for a few hours to hear his last opera *Hubička* [The Kiss]. He was not granted that mercy.

He was the only person who did not feel comfortable in Kamaik. I remember exactly how he stayed away from the merry company which let him know so inconsiderately that he did not fit in. Most of the time he walked up and down a distant garden path lined by high raspberry bushes, humming to himself softly, and sometimes he sat there crouched on a bench and scribbled something in a huge notebook.

In the dining room there was a piano with yellow polish, with square legs and twelve pedals of which I do not remember what they were for, and in front of which my late grandfather is said to have kissed his first wife for the first time.

It was a terrible piano with a thin, tubercular tone reminding one of … harps accompanying ballads about murderers, but it was a piano, a means of musical expression, and when I came to sit next to the genius Smetana during a meal, I noticed how he sometimes glanced at it furtively. He probably longed to tell us something by means of the keys which spoke his own language, but nobody felt like listening to him.

The monster Ferdinand told us that Uncle Smetana once fantasized on the piano, and that it was unbearable.

In order to silence the terrible conductor from Goetheborg, they used the piano as a buffet, i.e. stacks of plates, pitchers and cups were left on … the grand piano, so that he could not open it.

This is how things remained. Until one day the master in his red-lined carbonari with the worn velvet collar climbed into the carriage which was to take him down the life-threatening road to the train — and never came back.

Then the plates and cups also disappeared from the piano. It was opened, and we were allowed to strum on the yellowed keys to our hearts' content. La donna e mobile, etc … . I participated in this musical nonsense particularly enthusiastically, for I loved music tenderly, or what I thought to be music, and played all kinds of song hits by ear, or sometimes for a change Chopin's funeral march.

Kamaik was a paradise, and therefore such a sad person and genius as Bedřich Smetana did not belong there. He did not have the ability to transform himself into a child … .

The blissful feeling of arrival … when after the ride on the hot and dusty road, turning along abysses, after riding up and down sharp-cornered rocks, one entered the dear, cool house! First a few steps lead to the ground floor, then very steep turning stairs to the upper story with the guest rooms.

After a brief, refreshing washing—even the water there felt different than in Smíchov—we went to the dining room. There the table was already set, with (I am almost ashamed to confess to such luxury) genuine Old Vienna china, white, decorated with delicate garlands of vine leaves … a stiff Biedermeier bouquet of white and fire lilies, mixed with … sage and lavender in the middle.

Oh, the fragrance which greeted us from the bouquet … And along with it the fragrance of the old woodwork and chalk-white walls, of clean scrubbed floors and pine boards, and the fragrance from the garden …

A long, enthusiastic, detailed description of the garden, its flowers and fruit, follows.

To the left of the house the garden ended in a low hill; there, among mighty old pear trees, Ferdinand's tutor lived now, in the log house which originally had been built for "the Englishman."

He spent all summers in Kamaik and in return for food, lodging and friendship taught the young Polaks English and to eat with knife and fork … .

My mother lived with us three children in one room, where enough space also had to be found for my father, who came every Saturday from cholera-infested Smíchov. The English nanny who replaced our old one slept next door as did a fifteen-year-old boy, a cousin of mine. They each had their private little room separated by … chintz curtains.

Conditions were "paradisiac" in other respects as well … naively cheerful decency was a matter of course …

While Ferdinand remained … the inseparable playmate of my … sister, his sister—who was only a year older than I—and I were inseparable. Her name was Hedwig.[4] She was called Wigsa and controlled me completely, as did most people who had anything to do with me over a longer period of time, for I am weak and good natured … and up to a certain point pliable. Beyond that point nobody got anywhere with me … This is the part where my subtle ethics, sensitive feeling of decency and my stubborn sense of justice take over …

Wigsa liked playing at "being something" best. She decided to represent the Empress of Russia, I was only allowed to rise to Queen of Spain. She determined that she had eight children, I was only allowed to have six … Our husbands played a very shadowy role. I don't even know if we had any. During the endless discourses about our imaginary children … we mostly sat in a small octagon gazebo which was partly papered with amusing cutouts … partly with portraits of famous French generals. Among the cutouts, I was always particularly struck by the picture of the memorable baron von Münchhausen, portrayed in the moment when he holds on to the soul of his butler who just died, in order to undertake an excursion to heaven. I was particularly interested in the representation of the soul. It looked like an enormous ink spot of elongated triangular shape. "It looks more like the soul of a dead piano than of a person," claimed the monster Ferdinand.

… In the evening after supper, we sat on the small wooden staircase, which lead from the dining room to the garden … . It was the real salon of Kamaik. Adults and children sat there together. … Ferdinand took over his old job of frightening us by telling the most sensational ghost stories.

We had no neighbors except for a sister of my father, who was married to the director of an estate of Count Nostitz … I see Aunt Mathilde clearly before me. She had a very nice face, was heavy and somewhat clumsy and had a golden heart with very much common sense. She represented our poorer bourgeoisie with all its unpretentious, simply reliable qualities. …

Afternoon coffee was an important factor in our life. In good weather, we had it in the woods, where … the "house slaves" brought … china, silver and refreshments in large baskets on their backs. …

There is, in my memory, a dark, dull spot, like a scar … the farewell from Kamaik, I don't remember anything about it except that it hurt.

In Fall 1861, my parents bought an estate. It was one hour by coach from Prague, the landscape was not beautiful and the soil not especially good, but it was part of that land which gave the voice of its owners as much weight as the Princes Schwarzenberg in matters concerning landed property.

It was, despite the light soil, not unprofitable, and besides, my father had leased the extremely fertile adjoining property for a low rent. God gave His blessing and it all prospered beautifully. We were not rich, but well-to-do, lived well and entertained a great deal without having to restrict ourselves.

In 1863, we took a trip to the spa Teplitz for the sake of my mother's health. I remember very clearly that we went first class, with a chambermaid and the English nanny, and that the carriage we sent ahead waited for us in Teplitz.

We had a charming apartment in Schönau, with a balcony above the gardens; we went walking every day in the so-called castle garden, and on outings every afternoon. Teplitz was very fashionable and very elegant.

My little brother, who had just turned six, wore a very attractive, green Scottish outfit ... and when he went to the castle garden, the ... band played "O'er the hills to Charley." We children noticed ... how the people stared at him and whispered. They thought that we must be descendants of the Stuarts who ... still lived on the Hradschin, in national costume.

I also remember that a Lady Clarendon and her delightful daughter ... always smiled at us kindly when they met us ... Nobody associated the pale, elegant woman with the elegantly dressed children chattering in English with the plain "Mrs. Kirschner with family and servants" registered in the guest list.

So gradually ... legends developed around my little brother's Scottish outfit, which then ... inevitably were destroyed in the most prosaic way. The English nanny of a very rich baroness K. once came up to our nanny with the polite, almost humble request, if her little charge could play with us. ... our bourgeois origin became known, and we no longer aroused any interest in ... the other guests.

The following year my permanently sick mother was sent to Venice ... Meanwhile through an unfortunate speculation in grain, we suffered some financial setbacks. Of course, there was no longer a chambermaid or a nanny accompanying us. We only took along a clumsy Bohemian cook for housekeeping. Since mother was too tired to go out with us ... our main diversion consisted in looking out the window of which we soon tired ... My mother felt sorry for us, and one day, when she did go walking with us ... a gondola landed, and Lady Clarendon and her daughter climbed out. They ... passed us with glances of indifferent recognition. Although I was only nine years old, it became clear to me in that moment, how unimportant one is to people in general if one is not surrounded by the aura of some kind of prestige, whether it be inherited or personally acquired. And ... I made the firm decision ... to acquire such prestige. ...

At the end of October, my father came to Venice, to take us home. From then on, my mother's health, strangely enough, improved steadily, but our financial worries intensified. ... We went home second class ...

We did still spend the winter in Smíchov, as always, and continued to go to Prague for our lessons, but we felt ... that through some invisible cracks worries had come into our existence and that the foundation of affluence, which until then we had enjoyed as a matter of course, wobbled under our feet ...

My father was a gambler and wanted to become rich quickly. All that was needed, he told himself, was to be a little enterprising ...

Poor father! Actually he simply became the victim of an epidemic; the sixties and seventies were a time of ruined landowners. Among the various young officials and officers from our circle who married rich girls and became landowners, none lasted in that position; and even as many of those born in that class, of high and low, old and new nobility, tumbled. And that although grain prices ... were very high, and the wages of laborers pitifully low.

The cause of these many financial catastrophes was the sudden greed, which at that time had also overcome my father. Not satisfied with the profits from agriculture, they all ... tried to get ahead through the addition of industry.

Without expertise, they sprinkled these enterprises thoughtlessly over their lands, sugar factories, distilleries, breweries which, like children of love, are hardly brought into existence before they are left to their fate. An architect and a few "knowledgeable business people" were asked about the productiveness of the enterprise, and naturally they said that there was no doubt it "would pay."

And it paid for the architect. My father built a brewery. Since Lochkov suffered from a water shortage in dry weather and the ... new brewery was dependent on a single well ... a sensible businessman would naturally have considered bringing water in through pipes. My father ... had a different idea: if there was a shortage, the water simply had to be brought in barrels from the Beraun, the nearest river, of course with four horses, for Lochkov was situated on a mountain plateau, and the Beraun flowed in a deep valley, a good half hour away and was linked with Lochkov only by a miserable path through the fields. ...

All the big land owners in Bohemia were like that in those days, and my father simply followed famous models.

He also followed their example in other ways. Elected delegate to the Bohemian Parliament, he joined the federalistic party of ... the Old Czechs, who for purely practical reasons demanded autonomy for Bohemians. Of course, this autonomy, because of the lowering of taxes and the concentration of its great riches on his own land, would have been of immense importance. Although inclined to be lazy and perhaps placing too much emphasis on externals, my father had an excellent head for law and politics and predicted many events which fate still kept hidden. He maintained that sooner or later the hour of independence would come for the Bohemians ... .

[Now] I would like to tell simply how the great misfortune descended upon us. Having woken up from a long mental slumber, the Czech people, encouraged by their ... at that time ... still exclusively German-speaking nobility, demanded the right to an intellectual development in their own language; they demanded the establishment of a Czech university in Prague. A fever of fear and hope, a tension like before ... a thunderstorm after a long drought tortured all of Bohemia at that time, and although we children were raised as Germans, we felt the same fever.

To this day I remember the extreme excitement on the day when ... the decision about the Czech university was to fall. When my father was expected back from his session of parliament in Prague, we stopped reading, writing our homework or playing the piano ... finally ... we heard the coach ... [and] my father entered the hall.

Over his powerful-looking Russian fur collar ... his face shone triumphantly. "Victory!" he called. "Total victory!" The Czech university basically did not concern us, but we jumped with joy and asked for the next day off.

In the course of the evening, father still told us of the breathless feeling which had prevailed in Slav Prague the whole day, how people were coming together in ever changing groups in order to tell each other of the state of affairs in parliament ... and how finally wagons [in the street] stopped in order to let everyone listen undisturbed. ... With the dramatic instinct characteristic of the Czech people, a large number of listeners had equipped themselves with torches which were to be lowered and extinguished if things went wrong.

Then a window of the House of Parliament was opened, and the result of the voting was announced to the crowd. My father assured us that he would never in his life forget the solemn impression, when the deputies marched between the patriotic human lane with the ... raised torches … while again and again salvoes of sláva [glory] shook the air. It was a rejoicing which, as the Czech patriots expressed it, the martyrs of the Czech Battle on the White Mountain were bound to hear in their graves.

We shed tears of enthusiasm … We were not for nothing the children of a woman who had almost married Ladislav Rieger. …

There was something paradoxical about us … being raised in German, but identifying so much with the Czech cause, yet this is how it was at that time: one felt Slavic and one spoke German.

I am now an old woman … who has learned to love … great and noble Germany with her whole heart, has found her best friends there and lived her best days there, but I am still deeply moved when I recall the first great victory of the Czech national movement.

After my father had described the uplifting impression of the great historic episode, he … remarked: "Actually it was damned reckless of me to … spoil my relations with the Germans. After I cast my vote, I called to [an acquaintance]: "Are you also suicidal like myself?"

When setting up the extremely questionable brewery, my father had to borrow capital … Since the wealth of Bohemia, except for the real estate which belonged to the agrarians, was exclusively in German hands, he of course borrowed from Germans. A short time after he voted for the Czech university, all of his mortgages were cancelled … After a few painful attempts to get help … he had to go into bankruptcy in March 1866.

There were family gatherings … endless examinations of the business books by a cousin who was a lawyer. On my father's face there was a sentimental smile which disfigured him …

Again and again we heard him say during meals: "I was just an idealist."

When I asked my mother what that was, she answered …"somebody who places more trust in people than they deserve."

Since I had become an extremely bright child, this kind of idealism resulted in more impatience than sympathy with me. Already then it seemed to me as if trust was something very great and precious which one ought to handle cautiously.

In contrast to my father, who was totally exhausted by his misfortune, my mother behaved heroically. But finally she also broke down.

It was on a Sunday afternoon and her best friend, Pauline von Dormitzer, had come unexpectedly for a visit. It feels to me as if it had been yesterday.

The two friends sat on a sofa … in the salon … with my mother's youngest brother, Uncle Alexander. We three children were in the adjoining room, with the door open … suddenly we heard mother with a thin, shrieking voice: "Pauline, I am a beggar." And she staggered on her brother's arm past us to her bedroom, where she lay on her bed sobbing disconsolately.

The next day mother told us about our misfortune. We knew about it, but she called it by name for the first time: Stopped payments, bankruptcy.

We had to give up all our possessions to satisfy the creditors as much as possible. We would move to a city, any city … would live in two small rooms, father would look for a modest position and mother would give lessons.

Our hearts ached at the thought of our future … but we pretended to be heroic … My [heroism] broke down on a … ridiculous occasion.

Aunt Rosa … had invited us to come to Kamaik … until our situation would be clear. Our poor mother was to be spared at least the most painful impressions. … despite the bad situation, we were happily looking forward to Kamaik. …

As I already mentioned, since our return from Venice we had to be very economical. Mother had sacrificed one of her dresses every year, in order to make two for us. But … her supply did not last, and so the old rags had to be patched as decently as possible. The worst were the hats. We used to get them from the best milliner of Prague, but there was nothing left of them. Mother decided to make us some herself … she bought two black straw hats reminding one of the Salvation Army and tied cheap blue taffeta ribbons around them … I broke out … in tears, of which I am still ashamed today … Mother only looked sad and depressed at the Hallelujah hat.

[Their excitement about returning to Kamaik turned into disappointment.]

The first surprise was the wide highway from Leitmeritz … to Kamaik. But then came the real surprise. Kamaik did not exist anymore. The crazy house with its wonderful cozy old fashioned atmosphere had been swept from the face of the earth … in the midst of the dear … wildly blooming … garden there was a villa with shiny … windows, painted bright yellow, a suburban … villa in front of which a tiny fountain sent its meager stream of water in the air.

While Aunt Rosa was still explaining the many advantages to my mother, I sneaked away. I looked at the … yard, which the architect had not yet found the time to improve off the face of the earth, to see if anything was left of our dear old Kamaik … and cried … .

In the introduction to her novel Blanche,[5] *Schubin tells briefly about her childhood and then continues a little beyond it in time:*

For a time we were very badly off ... Since for the sake of economy we now stayed in the country all year, the expensive teachers were eliminated. Only the Irish Englishwoman remained ... whether she was half-paid ... or not at all at times made no difference to her ... She stayed until we began to travel around the world like gypsies ...

And now I would ... like to explain how my existence developed from the most anti-social one into an international one. ...

Our sudden poverty deprived us of all our friendships—with one solid-as-rock exception. Our estate was off the beaten track, travel was difficult, we could no longer offer the former generous hospitality to our guests, and nobody wanted to make sacrifices.

My sister grew up to become a very pretty girl and often stayed with friends or relatives in Vienna and Salzburg, who spoiled her very much. ... I always stayed at home, grew up lonely ... in the midst of an all-Slav population, between my mother and my governess.

When our conditions improved and I could have gone out, I was ... shy and did not want to. Instead we traveled here and there, but never as tourists. We always settled down for

Ossip Schubin

half a year ... or several months in Paris, Brussels, Rome, England or America. ...

We were just preparing to visit ... dear friends who lived in a charming castle, when the war broke out. Due to my international character I could not experience the war as other people. I had the same feeling of intensive, indescribable pity for all participants.

Thereby, I naturally came into conflict with many of my best friends. They criticized my lukewarmness, I often felt offended by their hardness. Later I also learned to have pity for this exaggerated hardness ... All the warring peoples suffered ... from [it].

[Here Schubin reports on the circumstances of her first published work].[6]

I was just fifteen years old when ... "Niklas Z." was finished. It was a short, very sad story about a schoolmaster's son who was a great genius and at the same time a clumsy fellow ... but a virtuoso on the piano. He fell in love with a countess ... who finally became engaged to a lieutenant of the hussars ... And then the poor, clumsy, warmhearted artist killed himself, and the countess cried bitterly. ... My first work ... was printed in *Bohemia* [a daily paper in Prague]. The style was clumsy and the editor corrected the spelling, but it contained a description of the Bohemian Forest which was praised highly ... . This is how my writing fever began, and my later attacks came in the same way—always a ... concentrated nervous excitement released an activity of the imagination ... .

Although I discovered shortly afterwards that I had a nice singing voice—which I destroyed by cultivating it too eagerly—I still had time to scribble down a novella here and there. Between my fifteenth and my twenty-fifth year I wrote a whole series, partly of drafts, partly of ... stories, in which only two provincial papers were interested ... Later the taste of the publishers changed, and they were glad to print the formerly rejected products of my pen ... .

At that time ... I almost would have given up if Fritz Mauthner, my countryman—whom I did not yet know at all personally—had not seen to it that the "Deutsche Lesehalle", a supplement of the *Berliner Tageblatt*, printed a little story of mine.

Meanwhile I had ... buried my beautiful voice for good, after having wandered with my mother and sister from one famous singing teacher to the other ... Tired and miserable, I moved back to dear old Lochkov, where I grew up. At that time my mother advised me to revise one of my novels, which had appeared in the *Prager Abendblatt*, and to try to publish it in book form.

I worked without the least enthusiasm, mechanically. Suddenly my imagination broke the old form, I built a different novel[7] on the same motif—only needing to copy the colorful pictures which glided through my soul.

I still remember how on the 17th of January 1883 we were sitting at breakfast ... I opened [the publisher] Minden's letter ... it contained a [three page printed review by Julius Rodenberg]. And what a review! It began with the words: "Whoever Ossip Schubin may be— we are sure that he can no longer be a young man!" I began to sob. From one moment to the next I had been raised to the rank of a ... writer ... . With a very serious face my mother quoted the famous words of Anna of Austria to Maria von Gonzaga: "Ah, ma pauvre fille! Te voilá reine de Pologne!"

From Schubin's cousin Hedda Sauer—the Wigsa of her childhood—we gain glimpses of Ossip in the years of which we know little. She seems to have been jealous of her more successful compatriot Marie-Ebner von Eschenbach and probably also of Rilke. In a letter to Hedwig Sauer, written in 1925, she said about him:[8]

I forgive him much, because he has written the charming Cornet *[The Lay about the Love and Death of Cornet Christoph Rilke]* and half a dozen lovely, lyrical poems. As for the rest—the greatest fake of the century spreads a mystical darkness over his bourgeois youth. That prince on the pea in the highest degree could not accept the invitation to Laučín, because Princess Taxis did not send a car to Paris for him, because the train trip would be unbearable, etc ... . He had large ears that stood out, a very ugly mouth under a petit bourgeois moustache, some kind of a nose and wonderfully beautiful blue eyes which did not fit in his face at all and lead one to suspect that he must have been a pretty child—along with shoulders like a champagne bottle and a purple overcoat ... to me he was an enormous disappointment.

Hedda commented:[9]

Ossip, led by an intelligent, but presumably autocratic mother, remained ... somewhat of an enfant terrible all her life ... Her human greatness lay in the fact that she easily made her peace with the vicissitudes of her material life. When the prosperity of her parental home broke down, Ossip and her sister Marie—in a life of hard work—again created an existence for themselves which seemed pleasant to them ... in hotels and in rented little castles, with coachmen and servants. ... Another financial misfortune came, yet when Ossip invited us by letter in 1925, she remarked with her characteristic, sarcastic humor that the time of coaches was unfortunately over ... .

In 1930, after her seventy-sixth birthday, she wrote:

Having outlived one's time is a miserable state ... Where is the Ossip Schubin whom everybody wanted to know, beginning with Austrian archduchesses and Russian Grand Princesses? ... like many has beens I have been sent from the "belle étage" to the attic ... sometimes when I lie down for my afternoon nap, I think it would be nice not to wake up. At other times I would like to throw myself at the inkwell and put down the many things which still bubble inside of me. Then I laugh about myself. In the present jazzy belles lettres there is no room for me any more.

In winter she often lived in the old Prague hotel Blue Star (on Příkopy) together with her sister. She died there in 1934. ... she was like a precocious child, to whom everything is a game. She was at her best in a rural environment ... We visited her a few times in the rented castle of Košatky ... She received us at the station in a tiny Czech village ... The castle would have been very appropriate as a [setting] for one of her novels ... [with] many ... Baroque Saints ... a draw bridge, a tower ... ivy ... a beautiful park. For dinner [Ossip and her sister] appeared in silk, with cobweb stockings and satin shoes, both with necklines like for a ball. ...

In the evening ... Ossip played melancholy melodies by Dvořák ... She often spoke about her childhood ... [it] was like a continuation of her memoirs ... . Her oral narrative talent was perhaps even greater than her writing. The mood it expressed seemed to be the last chords of Baroque.

Outwardly, Schubin may have seemed like an anachronism, but in a letter to a friend on the 18 of January, 1919 she expressed a sentiment which was ahead of her time as well as ours:[10]

The day must come when all peoples will extend their hands to each other and say: To understand everything is to forgive everything! On that day I shall also be forgiven for only having one fatherland, the world, and that I only know one nationality, humanity.

NOTES

1. The Habsburg Myth in Austrian Literature.
2. "Die Flucht aus dem Alltag. Erinnerungen einer Siebzigjährigen" in *Neue Freie Presse*, 19.5. 1914, p. 3.
3. An imaginary land of luxurious and idle living, better known in German as Schlaraffenland.
4. She grew up to become the poet Hedda Sauer.
5. In *Kürschners Bücherschatz*, Berlin–Leipzig, 1919 (unpaginated).
6. *Die Geschichte des Erstlingswerks*, ed. Karl Emil Franzos, pp. 259-267.
7. The novel *Ehre* (Honor) became a huge success.
8. In an unpublished letter, in the estate of Professor August Sauer, Hedwig's husband, in the archives of Charles University in Prague.
9. In Hedda Sauer's unpublished memoirs, *Begegnungen mit Zeitgenossen*, ibid.
10. From a collection of manuscripts in the Austrian National Library.

Chapter 5

BERTA FANTA

(1866–1918)

*A*mong all the women assembled in this book, there is only one whose life circumstances seem to have been close to perfect: Berta Fanta née Sohr. She was born into a well-to-do Jewish family in the small town of Libochowitz, near Prague, in 1866, but spent most of her life in the city. There, at the turn of the century, she was the hostess of a well known literary and philosophic salon.

The vivid but somewhat patchy reminiscences of her daughter, Else Bergmann, covering mainly the time of the salon, are our best source of information about her. Fanta supplies a more introspective view of herself in her own diary, but it only spans a few years, beginning in 1900.

Both Else and Berta were interested in their ancestry and share the belief that knowing more about their roots would help them to understand themselves better. This exploring was done more sympathetically by Else than by Berta, who clearly scorned the older, rather ordinary, non-intellectual relatives who were still living in her time. The fact that her carefree lifestyle was made possible by her hard-working parents seems to have been taken for granted. What unfortunately is missing is almost any information about Berta's childhood, about her decision to marry Max Fanta, and about the first years of her marriage, before she began to attend the philosophic circle named after its meeting place, the Café Louvre, and which later gathered at her house.

Her son writes:[1]

In the years before the war, a small circle of philosophically interested men used to gather to study idealistic philosophy. Hugo Bergmann was the intellectual head; my mother was the linking and enlivening element, Felix Weltsch was the analytic thinker, Max Brod always brought stimulating ideas ... Not only were Kant, Fichte and Hegel examined ... word by word, but some of the more speculative ideas and contemporary interests of the time became prevalent topics; these ranged from psychoanalysis to anthroposophy and even spiritism. Professor Marty introduced the group to Brentano … the physicist Freundlich lectured about quantum theory, and Professor Hopf [a friend of Einstein's who also attended those gatherings] spoke about the theory of relativity. The mathematician Kowalewski discussed Kantor's transfinite numbers, and the philosopher Christian von Ehrenfels, who was preoccupied with sexual morality, advocated polygamy in order to ward off the "yellow danger," a fear not uncommon at the time. For a while Indian philosophy was at the center of interest,at another time it was Nietzsche.

> *Some evenings were also devoted to music, art and sociability, the latter involving such activities as masquerades with literary themes, or parodies of literary works. The gatherings seem to have ended with the beginning of the First World War, perhaps when the Fantas' son-in-law, Hugo Bergmann, was drafted into the army.*
>
> *As we have pointed out, a deep gulf separated Czech and German culture in Prague. Berta Fanta and her friends read belletristic literature from Germany, Austria and non-German speaking countries, but almost surely no Czech literature. Music was the one exception. Fanta attended concerts of Smetana and Dvořák, and even seems to have had a special emotional affinity to them.*
>
> *Berta Fanta seems to have lead precisely the life she wanted to lead. Apart from one remark suggesting that she should not have married her husband (because he was no better at raising children than she was), she seemed content in her marriage and only sometimes expressed slight amusement about her husband. Nevertheless, she suffered from periodic depressions, though they may not have been too severe, and she seems to have accepted them as part of her mental makeup, and as fortunately just temporary.*
>
> *I shall let Else Bergmann[2] continue in her own words:*

Out of love for her son-in-law Hugo Bergmann[3] and disdain for the decaying social order in Europe she was determined to go to Palestine with us and to radically change her life. Quoting from her [undated] letter to Bergmann: "Dear Hugele, I am now very much occupied with your plans for Palestine. They also mean a chance for me to live according to my wishes, my longing. I imagine that everybody living in such a society [in Palestine] actually feels that their daily life is beneficial, that they have finally reached a solid foundation of doing their duty toward others without having to give up their individual striving.

I think it would be good to know how to cook properly and to understand gardening, so that in my old age I could still be useful to all of you as a cook or as an overseer.

I cannot tell you how unspeakably repulsive our social order is to me. I feel as if I were walking over swamps in which I seem to be drowning.

If one could live as a free person among free people, then nothing could keep me in Europe. Renouncing the pleasures of higher culture will be very easy for me, I think. So I now have a hope before me."

She died in her fifty-second year, evidently of a heart attack because she overexerted herself while making dough to acquire culinary skills.

Hugo Bergmann wrote in his diary as he was observing the traditional Jewish watch over Berta Fanta's dead body:

"From my diary, 18 December 1918, when I was alone with her dead body.

Mama, Mama, if only I could capture what you were! Oh, if only we humans would never lose our consciousness that every day can be the last!

If you remained who you were, don't you now, somewhere in heaven, discuss the strangeness of waking up in the morning as always, and now in the evening ... you have passed through that gate of which you were so often frightened! You feared it and you loved it and all your life you thought of nothing but this trip. To you life was nothing but an experiment for death, and the hour which you have now accomplished was the goal of your life.

We all have lost you and each of us bewails his mama. Life is so cold and we are freezing. With you there was always ready warmth, always praise, always love. And stimulation.

Like those Sunday walks before the war! One strove to have something prepared for the family holiday: ideas or essays to discuss. How eagerly you took everything in! Nothing was more pleasant than to teach you, because the gratitude of the learner spoke from every word.

Together with Else and you, we read Achad Haam[4] in the summer of 1914, and I was so happy about your interest in what until then had been strange to you. And you were immediately ready to draw the last consequences, you learned Hebrew ... and you were happy about every difficult new word.

How much, Mama, did we experience together in theosophy! At first I laughed at you. Then you won me over and we went [to lectures] together, and I defended the old view against your growing scepticism. Like a little bee you flew to all knowledge and collected delicacies.

We know that our marriage is your doing. How much goodness you gave to our young love, from the start when you beckoned me and said that you approved of my marrying Else—I myself had hardly thought of it—but that I should not walk around with her too much in town.

The Sunday evenings (in the gazebo) with fried fish or with cold cuts! You always knew how to organize evenings. You told of your youth, of your infinite longing for an education; you spoke of how you wasted your youth as a young woman, how late you found your road to education, and of the temptations of your life.

Your life was nothing but a sequence of tasks you assigned yourself. For months you once learned to recite poems backward to strengthen your memory; then there were mathematics lessons.

And this passionate search for interesting acquaintances: how many swindlers did you fall for, surely, but again and again you attracted people who were different than the masses! You visited soothsayers, spiritualists, you went to vegetarian kitchens ... Nothing was strange enough for you; you knew that the truth does not lie on the highways of mediocrity and ordinariness. It was always painful to you, that it all remained theory to you and that you did not find the strength to jump into the adventure. And yet in the end you wanted to go to Palestine with us.

Your introspection was truly great. You never lived the simple, naive life of those who don't reflect about themselves. You observed yourself and you reported about yourself. You were inclined to be vain, but you knew it, and checked yourself.

If only this war had not come! If only we had continued to lead our rich, beautiful life of 1914: now all that is over, and you, dear Mama, are leaving us, who knows, perhaps struck to death by your love and worry about me during this whole time. Stay with me, you luminous, pure, kind one!"

Else Bergmann's vivid narration of her family and especially her mother makes one wish that she had written much, much more:

For a long time my family has lived in the small towns of Raudnitz, Libochowitz and Budin, about half way between Karlsbad and Prague. There one finds our family names in all the cemeteries on the ... old tombstones which all look like Moses' tablets of the Law ...

Mama was a romantic, always sentimental and always terribly sad. She felt repelled by life in the family, and intensely loved her only sister Ida. The two emotional girls were under the supervision of French and English governesses; both were very gifted and very eager to learn.

My mother also went to live in Prague with Uncle Ludwig and Aunt Luise. She went to a school ... for daughters from "better" families, was an outstanding student and idolized her teacher, until one day ... my mother used the word "nebbich." The teacher told her that this was not a German word ... that it was Jewish and insisted that it not be used any more, whereupon my mother broke out in tears.

Ida painted, and my mother wrote poetry and played the piano very well. I often visited ... Libochowitz with my mother; I walked with her on all forest paths, there were storks parading in the meadows, and I have never seen as many violets in one place as there. In the distance the fine sound of a church bell could be heard, called.. the "Poppelser Bell." It was proverbial in our family that it always began chiming later than all the other bells. Later they referred to my father as the "Poppelser Bell," because he was always absorbed in thought, listened to conversations with half an ear, and then usually added a sentence to the discussion, which he ... had just heard from another person.

When my [maternal] grandparents still lived in Libochowitz, Grandmother bought a house with a pharmacy on the main square [in Prague]. She decided that my father should become a pharmacist, and later on take over this pharmacy. My father had actually hoped to have an academic career at the Prague technical university, and for a professorship in crystallography. But my grandmother's command beheaded these hopes, and so he became an ordinary pharmacist. This did not prevent him from fighting for my mother's hand, and in the ... gazebo at the far end of the garden he fell on his knees before her and begged her fervently to become his wife. My extremely romantic mother could do no more than give him both hands to kiss and to whisper "yes".

My parents first lived on Leihamtsstrasse before moving to Old Town Square.[5] Papa established a soap factory in the large, ancient yard adjoining the pharmacy, but he did not know much about it, lost a lot of money and so grandmother ... had to pay for a second dowry.

Unicorn house in Old Town Square

The unicorn on the facade of the Fanta's house

The Old Town Square

But as a pharmacist my father did well, and the pharmacy became one of the best in Prague. It was furnished in Biedermeier style with mahogany furniture, with a clock which had an unusual dial in the form of a semicircle, and with hands in the form of a winding snake ... Franz Kafka liked our winding staircase and said: "If one calls such a staircase one's own, one's whole life must be influenced by it."

Earlier inhabitants of the house were less fortunate. One, and the whole Czech intelligentsia and nobility along with him, was beheaded after the Thirty Years War [actually in 1620] ... in front of the Town Hall. The house had gigantic cellars, and during repairs a subterranean rococo hall was found.

In this ancient house with its large rooms my parents created a beautiful home for themselves. There were large parties, costume balls and "live pictures"; Aunt Ida and Mama and many friends of the family wrote plays, which they and their friends then performed. Most of the "live pictures" were humorous. I remember one which was supposed to represent Hero and Leander. Hero sat on a box in a Greek gown with a long blonde wig and with a burning candle in her hand. Leander lay on a chair on his stomach, likewise in Greek costume, and looked up to her with a desparate expression while pretending to be swimming. I remember Papa and Mama dressed as Hansel and Gretel and singing a children's song from Humperdinck's opera ... and my father as Cyrano de Bergerac with a huge illuminated nose and my mother as Roxanna ...

Once the philosophic circle produced a play on New Year's eve ... by the poet Franz Kafka and the art historian Oskar Pollak, at that time Kafka's best friend. It was a satire on Brentano's philosophy. The main character, Walter von Stolzing, was played by Oskar Pollak. This philosophic-poetic circle could be called the second stage in my mother's development. The first was characterized by the society whose members came from liberal German Prague. At that time the

Jews would never have guessed that anyone would ever question their German identity and they were on very friendly terms with other Germans. The focal point of German society at that time was the German Casino on the Graben [referred to in some texts by its Czech name Příkopy] where most of their social life took place. My father spent his afternoons in its reading room. Among the lectures held there, the one by Theodor Herzl was received with great astonishment. In the charming rococo hall, costume balls taking weeks to prepare were held ... To portray a pearl, Mama wore a pearl colored costume made of a veil and carried a kind of a parasol in the form of a sea shell. Another time the sisters were dressed as Egyptian princesses and pulled the figure of an African with an ostrich fan behind them.

My mother and my aunt were known as women of high intellect and were very ambitious. Among their friends were many writers who in daily life were lawyers, doctors, etc. One of them, Dr. Bondi, was an inveterate bachelor who insisted that no woman could impress him. My mother and my aunt decided to play him a trick and persuaded him to answer a newspaper advertisement which was signed "Nerilla," then the name of a well known mermaid. A correspondence developed which lasted for two years. Dr. Bondi, who was very much in love, read the letters which he thought so wonderful to his friends in the Casino. My father ... would quote sentences from the letters and say to my mother: "That is some woman, you could never write like that". Finally, when Dr. Bondi's urging had become extremely insistent and all of Prague society was already quoting Nerilla, the two women bet him, in front of a large group, that they would be able to provide him with the greatest surprise of his life. Dr. Bondi smiled sarcastically and bet a wonderful diamond ring. The women then told him, that they would introduce Nerilla to him in that very hour and told him the story. Dr. Bondi was so shocked, that he became ill. It disturbed their mutual friendship for a few years, but he remained a bachelor ...

My mother subscribed to a box in the German Theater—grandmother Emilie and grandfather Albert had subscriptions to seats in the orchestra—my mother and my aunt missed no Wagnerian production and also attended the famous May festival which brought together many celebrities. There one saw Sonnenthal, Kainz[6] and ... Mahler, as well as the Vienna Philharmonic Orchestra.

The plastic arts also played an important role in the life of this generation, which was totally oriented toward the enjoyment of art and life. They visited exhibitions, and an annual excursion to Munich to see the exhibitions in the Glass Palace was taken for granted. Together with some other artists my mother's sister founded the "Club of German Women Artists", which ... became the center of [German] artistic and intellectual Prague ... by providing free lunches and dinners for poor artists it was a great blessing to many. What my mother and my aunt learned during extensive travels they used in lectures for the "Club for Women's Progress," This club was founded for the advancement of women's emancipation ... and by inviting outstanding personalities greatly stimulated intellectual life. Mama was a frequent and popular speaker ... There were many more Christians than Jews in the audience. Only a few of the Jewish women of that time were interested in serious questions.[7] My mother's friends were therefore mostly Christian, and playing piano duets brought her together with some of the women from the best "Aryan" society. One of her best friends, the wife of a major industrialist and weapons manufacturer, Marie Roedel, once asked her: "Berta, we are such good friends, tell me the truth ... Do Jews need Christian blood for Passover?" This "Club for Women's Progress," which was Christian German and democratic, contrasted with the purely German Folklore Society, which was of course totally closed to Jews and which was notorious for creating the antisemitic scandals that frequently took place at the German University and Technical University and which caused many Jewish professors and the [Dozenten] sleepless nights. My aunt Ida Freund was able to create an impressive position for herself doing charitable work through this Club. She was a member of a number of committees, was acquainted with the wife of the governor and of the police president and other noble ladies, and finally was awarded the Order of Empress Elizabeth by the Emperor.

Every one of those evenings, which will remain unforgettable to me, had its own motto; on the Goethe evening, the participants had to wear costumes from his time and to represent ... personalities from Weimar court society and from Goethe's life and works. The evening was opened with a minuett. The ladies appeared in period costumes, the men ... in officers' uniforms, with high boots, white leather pants and red jackets with gold braid. The dances were taught by the ballet master of the Prague German Theater ... Among the Christian gentlemen were officials of the German Savings Bank. One of the bank officials was a tall, well built man who dressed up as Goethe, and all of Goethe's loves entered after him. My mother was dressed as Goethe's wife, Hugo Bergmann as Wagner ... Another evening was devoted to Spitzweg[8] and a third to Frans Hals. On the Goethe evening Max Brod and Franz Kafka came as diplomats in tails with lace inserts, Brod with a green ribbon and Kafka with a red ribbon across his chest.

Gradually there was a change in my mother's life. Her deep esteem for Wagner led to mystical and religious experiences and she became a fanatical Nietzschean. In daily conversation quotations from Nietzsche and Wagner dominated.

We children received a so-called free education which was very bad for us, because we had nothing firm to hold on to. In my family the Jewish tradition had already disappeared in our great-grandfather's time. My father was especially interested in Islam, and it took my mother a lot of effort to dissuade him from converting to that religion. He was influenced by the writings of Raschid Bey, a German writer who made Islam fashionable …. After this Nietzschean period Mama became acquainted with *Dozent* Kastil, who gave her and my aunt lessons in philosophy … . She became a hard-working … student at the university, and after a short time a student of professor Marty; she took all the examinations and won the friendship of that noble man.

Brentano's philosophy and attitude toward the problems of the world and toward other philosophic systems were … discussed in professor Marty's apartment, which was considered an inner sanctum in that philosophic circle named after the Café Louvre where its members congregated. Besides *Dozent* Kastil and *Dozent* Eisenmayer, Professor Ehrenfels, who was an interesting and original counter-pole to the cool and logically thinking Professor Marty, used to take part, and later also Professor Einstein. He was also a poet and a composer, and a play of his with mystical content was produced in Prague. In order to gain access to Professor Marty's seminar, he wrote a very interesting pamphlet trying to prove that Richard Wagner had taken his main motifs from Felix Mendelssohn.

Grandmother bought a villa in Podbaba, a small community of villas, and gave it to her two daughters. We always spent spring and part of summer there. The house was bought from the Zdekauers, a baptized family of Jewish notables. The garden and the staircase were adorned with copies of Greek statues … this house in Biedermeier style left a very strong impression on me. …

The Wild Šárka

We took beautiful walks through fields, groves and the so-called "wild Šárka", the most beautiful area near Prague. Boat trips as well as swimming in the Moldau alternated with large parties, family gatherings and walks through the *Baumgarten*[9] and through Troja, the park with statues from the time of Maria Theresa. The family also went on major bicycle excursions. Each bicycle had a name: my father's was called "Atlas the carrysome," my aunt's "Grane the runner," and mine was called "Mogli the frog" …

My mother and my aunt organized large-scale philanthropic activities in Podbaba. They applied to the community for money to support elderly women, and my mother and my aunt contributed much of their own money. The whole town changed its attitude toward Jews. When my family bought the villa, there was an unimaginable anti-Semitism among the population. When we appeared in the street, we were called names, and my grandfather Albert once insisted on running after the culprits and giving them a good beating.

Gradually the population gained great confidence in our family … . The wives came for advice with their marital problems, children who were mistreated by their parents were taken to institutions … Pregnant girls about to jump in the Moldau were placed with midwives until their children were born. I especially remember an unusual episode: a very beautiful girl had an affair with an officer and became pregnant. Her father, a high official, drove her out of the house. When she was about to commit suicide, she accidentally heard of the two charitable women and … came to our villa. My mother immediately took her in, checked on the facts, took her to a midwife and wrote the officer. He paid all expenses and we heard later that he married the girl. The … father likewise came to the villa and … kissed the hands of both women.

My mother's favorite place was a picturesque farm which belonged to a Christian German-Czech family. The Niessners were typical old Austrians. The property was a former flour mill, with a picturesque wheel, a brook, and a barn, on the roof of which the pale green moss glistened in the sun. There, surrounded by daisies and bluebells, by the song of nightingales, she devoted herself to her philosophic studies and to her poetry, while aunt Ida painted … There Mama wrote her diary and gave an account of all the important events of her life. Unfortunately my father took the liberty of excising passages from my copy, which in his opinion were offensive.

The next step in her development was to study the theosophy of Annie Besant as well as Indian wisdom. The two sisters lectured about their studies and experiences to large audiences, so that German intellectual Prague took part in their intellectual development. They also came in contact with anthroposophy. Rudolf Steiner's lectures stirred up the circle, and it was in the halls of my parents' home that the founding of a new anthroposophic lodge was celebrated. Our drawing room was emptied of furniture and along the walls were placed leafy plants interspaced with bouquets of red roses. There was also a mighty bouquet of red roses in front. Steiner named the lodge for the famous philosopher Bolzano, and also in honor of Hugo Bergmann who had just published his work on Bolzano. All intellectuals were electrified by Steiner's novel impulses. I remember noticing during the lectures, how Franz Kafka's eyes sparkled ... and a pleased smile lit up his face. For several years my mother's life was devoted to the strenuous study of philosophy and anthroposophy. Her Goethe courses, where she traced Goethe's intellectual development in a most original way, were famous.

My marriage to Hugo Bergmann was an incisive experience for my mother; it was the fulfillment of a strong wish. She wanted a son-in-law exactly like Hugo Bergmann. When the war broke out my mother's despair over Hugo Bergmann having to join the troops in Galicia in the very first days was indescribable. Day and night she thought of nothing but of how to remove him from danger. When a colleague of Bergmann's came to Prague at the end of the second year of war, she pleaded with him to make it possible for her to go to the front with his company, which at that time was in Hungary. The lieutenant succeeded in getting her permission to go along as a nurse. In the meantime she had completed a nursing course at the Jewish hospital in Prague, which gave her the right to report to the front as a Red Cross nurse. With heavy hearts we let her go. Unfortunately ... she came down with a kidney disease which had been latent before, but which became much worse due to the difficult conditions. Berta Fanta managed to get her son-in-law to Vienna and to safety, where much of the family was gathered and she availed herself of many cultural opportunities.

My mother often said Dr. Steiner turned out to be right when he once said that Hugo Bergmann would live safely through the war, and that he was destined for great tasks in Palestine. Unfortunately she did not experience the fulfillment of this second part of his prophecy.

Unfortunately, Berta Fanta's diary[10] which follows is very fragmentary:

14 November 1900 Today was a happy day for me ... in the morning, after a night of pleasant dreams, I got up feeling competent and stimulated. There are days when one perceives ... one's experiences as enjoyment, other days when one ignores all that's most beautiful and

most valuable, and perceives everything that requires a harmonious participation of our soul as hostile and disturbing. Such moods or inhibitions come to me regularly, always at certain times, and they are connected with a bodily exhaustion that prevents me from feeling healthy, and I am overtaken by an unpleasant indifference that is sometimes replaced by obstinate anger ... . Today I was receptive and proud of myself. I was very pleased to be able to follow Professor Ehrenfels' profound lecture on Wagner, Tolstoy and Ibsen with real understanding. I felt ... my whole body becoming warm, beginning with my brain, how whole chains of thought formed ... . Next to me sat Anna Tschinke, a beautiful, natural, independent girl. She always speaks about something unexpected.

[Sometimes] all the faces which I cannot stand ... disappear and I feel the beneficial proximity of my dear sister, a person who understands me and whom I love with all her good and bad characteristics ... . The voice of Ernst Wolzogen[11] whom I heard speak last week had a strange effect on me: was it a sensuous effect? I almost think so ... this ... voice could [seduce me] ... .

21 November 1900 There are climbing plants with stems growing like spirals. When an attempt [is] made to force them in the opposite direction the plant dies. People always want to change the spiral of our character; if the attempt succeeds, our personality dies too. ...

Only when you have peace does the "vital feeling" begin. Only when we feel satisfied are we king.

I am too rash in my judgment about people, books and works of art ...

26 November 1900 To my mind the Creator of the world is an ungraspable being that, due to an incomprehensible interest or wish, has prepared a mysterious script for us in the laws of nature. The signs are ... hard to decipher, but one day complete understanding will surely be achieved. However, those who succeed in this will never come closer to the character of the puzzle maker ... Even if a mosquito could recognize that I can kill him by the pressure of my finger ... it is still unimaginable to me that this mosquito could ... conclude anything about my thoughts and feelings ... and yet it would have at least seen a small part of my real person, while we only have a vague idea of an abstract will.

How subtly—uniquely—the greatest creator lets us all speak, act, express feelings, portray characters. We have to learn to give up trying to understand the sense of the lofty spectacle.

A scene at our house in the morning. My husband wakes up exclaiming: "Snake, snake." These words have a strange effect: Else

Charles Bridge.

calls out, pleasantly amused: "Aha, so Mama again kissed somebody in her dreams, did I guess right?" Answer: "Don't mix into things you don't understand!" Then, [her husband] turning to me in a strict, inquiring tone: "Do you know a Mr. Kraus?" I reply calmly: "I know six Krauses." "So describe them to me one after the other." "I can hardly do that, I would confuse one … with the other." "O.k. let's make it short: Do you know one with a red beard?" I laugh so hard, that my jealous spouse feels intimidated and decides to settle the matter for himself. With my inborn meanness, however, I cannot help saying: "Darling, let me at least be unfaithful in my dreams; in reality I don't have the courage." My pen refuses to put down what followed.

7 January 1901 Today my husband took me aside solemnly and said in a well-thought-out, sober tone: Now answer this question I am addressing to you, but you should be true and open. Is it possible that a woman who loved her husband can just as deeply love a second when she is a widow? "No", I said enthusiastically and he grinned most contentedly: "I think not only the second, but several more." I only heard a coarse laugh.

This was a terrific New Year's Eve. We experienced midnight on Charles Bridge. Goldbrunner took out that ceramic object so necessary for us civilized people [a chamber pot?] and brought forth twelve solemn sounds from the above-mentioned vessel with a wooden spoon.

10 January 1901 … How infinitely hard it is … to raise a child!

My Religion

1. Don't pray to the Creator as people do, who thereby degrade him. He is ungraspable in his infinite goodness.
2. Create for yourself a world of your own in His image where the laws of your character govern.
3. Treat your body and spirit with reason, so that you may live in good health on earth.

4. Try to find beauty and art everywhere; if you seek with all your senses, you are already in the realm of beauty.

5. Give the poor of your money, not of your charitable mind, and seek the rich in spirit, so that they give you of their coin.

How long will this remain my religion?

When we occupy ourselves with one of our fellow beings intensively, we live doubly ... .

16 January 1901 Yesterday was the fiftieth Bohemian chamber music concert ... An andante ... from a Smetana quartett moved me deeply. I felt as if the viola and the cello tried to embody the general fate floating over mankind ... in the form of a ... melancholy basic melody, while the two violins floating lightly above it sought to reproduce our better individual lots, our most personal experiences—sometimes trembling joyfully, as if with wings, sometimes convulsively ... then a quintet by Dvořák followed, sparkling with intelligence, an overabundance of musical thoughts in the sweetest form, with Slavic coloring ... .

12 February 1901 Today when I practiced the piano with Else ... I had the immensely disturbing consciousness of what all else might be going on in the world at that moment. I became dizzy thinking of life in all its height and depth ... all the emotion released at that moment in billions of creatures, all this striving and devotion, all the immense becoming and dying, all the color and ... beauty, all the pain and blissful illusion ... I directed my attention again to the playing fingers and thought: "Just do your duty of the moment quietly, you tiny creature of the moment, lower your eyes to the white keys ... the immeasurable playing of the strings of the world would only tear you away into an immense whirlpool, in the abyss."

14 May 1901 Ida, I and big Otto [her brother in-law] spent a few days in Libochowitz. We longed to see the places of our youth again ... Lost in dreaming, surrounded by memories, we sat on the pedestal of the rural saint in the market square ... With invisible steps all the experiences and persons of earlier times approached us ... the hunter's house ... glistened in the castle garden ... it was a fairy tale mood, but one which only adults can experience whose aesthetic understanding has been trained. This bluish gray steam ... which enveloped the beautiful groups of trees, this broad view over rich meadows and fields bordered by lightly rolling hills, the birds gracefully swaying from tree to tree and this overabundant wealth of flowers, all that was already there in our youth, but ... we only discovered it now, and we felt ... how thoughtlessly we then had bypassed what was the most valuable.

It would have destroyed the fairy tale mood for me, if treacherous imps and hobbling witches had not also expressed themselves next to the wonderful gifts of the radiant lakes of beauty. Naiveté without cruelty would be flat; it adds the necessary depth. ...

24 August 1901 My father-in-law visited me yesterday after fifteen years. It was as if a representative of a strange world would sit next to me. ... He sat in our little garden salon, took one book after the other in his hand. The fact that there could be three books lying on a table unused at the same time and costing so much was the most striking to him ... . Then came all the naive questions, why Else was going to university ... what we were doing in Podbaba, since we were not running a dairy farm. As a tree sinks in a thick forest, he will one day die without leaving a vacuum ... .

Today I was overcome by a deep sadness which always ends in a tired indifference ... At such times I am seized with such pity for myself and the lack of clarity in my world view, and with such painful sympathy for my child, a being which should be guided by a ... sure hand and not by a pair of parents who are totally unsuited for bringing up anybody. My husband has, to be sure ... definite views, but how are they founded? Here is a young girl, as if from a novel, like a flower, losing her pollen when she gives in to her sensuous stirrings. These sensuous stirrings don't pay attention to the pollen and appear when they have to—but that is impossible, the girl must remain a bud ... until the ideal fairy tale prince of a husband turns her into a rose in full bloom by a kiss.

My ... husband thinks like this, despite my revolutionary counter-current which would like to tear down the old dams in order to gain a new, true, open feeling—but then I lack a self-assured will and knowledge. So my poor children are in unsteady hands. I am only consoled by the thought that the self-government proper to every being, which we supply with good nourishment through example, together with stimulation to think and acquire varied knowledge, will go the right way, regardless of all the asinine education.

8 September 1901 A Sunday afternoon ... Father, Otto Freund and my husband sit in the gazebo; they are playing cards ... Mama and Mauthner are playing ... one game of chess after the other in the little salon; Else carries on an amusing conversation with her girl friend. There are other visitors, and I sit in the small room to capture this snapshot. Before me lies *Der grüne Heinrich* [Green Henry, by Gottfried Keller], which I enjoy very much, and a volume of Nietzsche ...

... I have a secret fear of boredom ... and when I read for entertainment, something inside tells me I must not devote myself to such

... pleasures long; you must continue to educate your mind through reading and understanding difficult philosophic thoughts. By writing down my own thoughts ... I often waste many hours of my life unconsciously. Some days it is hard for me to live up to the smallest obligation ... This inner depression is ... a treacherous enemy which I cannot defeat because I don't know its ... cause ... Do the opposite characteristics of my ancestors fight a desperate struggle for dominance in me? I hate my weak ... reason which lets itself be intimidated by every fog ... despite my longing for clarity ...

13 September 1901 I sit next to Grandmama on a sofa ...[the room] furnished with dark, plush furniture, an overly solid, giant table and a lamp with graceless decorations hanging over it, a piano which is turned into a mournful object by its large, dark green cover. Colorless family pictures in brown frames filled with the dull ... features of *nouveau riche* Jews.

... tired, sad leafy plants that seem to long to get out of this world of banished sunshine and non-nature. The aunt, the owner of this room, seems to have grown out of it. Body and soul ugly of form ... selfsatisfied and of broad build ... she asked me how I am. I replied, "As a human being can be, not well, not exactly doing badly." She: "You live in fortunate circumstances, with a good husband, children, how can you tell me ..." I repeat: "Perhaps I am unhappily in love or perhaps I suffer because I don't know why I live, or what purpose the world has." She, ironically: "Look here, a philosopher ..." My half hour's visit was over, I gave Grandmama a hearty kiss and went out, away from this boring banality.

25 September 1901 Again a summer passed and I left Podbaba. The children go to school ... Else ... refuses steadfastly to learn under Mr. Lederer [a tutor]. ... I am not going to influence her since I avoid force, if it is not absolutely necessary, as a matter of ... principle.

8 October 1901 I have tried to direct my attention to ... Mach's[12] ... comparison of the physical with the psychic; I began to read Brentano's philosophy—I didn't succeed in forming a chain of thoughts.

... this inability to concentrate is an immense weakness.

A novel, *Familie Ursleu*[13] by Ricarda Huch, again captivated me extraordinarily, through the vital tone of stormy passion ... Björnson's play *Beyond Strength*, claiming that everything which exceeds our ... strength is harmful, is ...convincing.

When I walk in the street with Else it is as if people wanted to say: "The mother is still a beautiful woman; the daughter already is beautiful ... ."

19 October 1901 Liszt's Faust symphony awakened all the feelings of horror and joy in me which until now only Wagner's music produced.

20 October 1901 Yesterday, Sunday, I totally devoted to the family ... I went [walking] with Else, and since I wore my reform dress[14] ... my husband, who grew up with the most solid principles, could not stand such an innovation and pretended that he didn't know me.

17 November 1901 Recently I have lost so much that is positive in life, that I still stand as if before a grave in which fate has submerged a piece of my innermost fervent feelings ... I associate with the same people, but their exterior seems like a familiar cover behind which there is a strange, cold person ... From this paralyzing feeling about reality, I was awakened by a lecture on the painter Böcklin. I came to life again in this wondrous world of many colors; the stimulating thoughts presented in charming form made all the strings of my spirit vibrate... . I came home transformed and was able to reproduce almost all the mighty impression for my husband and Else.

7 December 1901 ... I have to be content with my beloved sister; in her company I feel the joys of a kinship of souls ... In the company of the women of my acquaintance I feel deprived of dignity and raped ... by all these banal, untrue phrases I speak to them ... which don't come from my free self. I hate these empty larvae from which no butterfly flies, these puppets wound up by everybody's wisdom ... . In all these misfits a soul also lives, only it is condemned to dark captivity.

14 December 1901 Yesterday's seminar was particularly stimulating or actually exciting. It was a ... court trial. My noble, regal Nietzsche was the accused, a cool, rational show-off his public prosecutor ... listeners who did not know him were the judges. They took his diamond-studded tiara from his head and designated it pinchbeck gold ... his mind ... was called sick and worm-eaten and blasphemed. I forgot that I was in a seminar ... I took over the defense of my darling. Neither the cool, sceptical manner of Dr. Kastil, nor cool, benevolent ... Prof. Ehrenfels could intimidate me; I hurled my convincing, emotional arguments in their faces. I described the intoxication, the bliss Nietzsche gives me, the immense effect which his thoughts have on my views of life ... I think the two gentlemen felt rather uncomfortable.

21 December 1901 ... yesterday at the theater I was suddenly overcome by a deeply melancholy mood; I saw the whole, happy audience dead and buried, the girls now dressed in white, old and wrinkled ... I had to think of feelings, and only when the idea that all we see, hear and feel is the appearance of something essential which we can never grasp sank in totally ... could I again give myself to the sensuous magic of the music. An inner voice told me to accept the deception, that one can only live in that way ... .

18 March 1902 Only one's own innermost experiences … create values for ourselves. What we see outside … is only a reflection … of our emotional world.

21 March 1902 My husband said to me: "I would be happy if you could love me as much as I love you." I replied: "I would too."

10 April 1902 When I love somebody from the bottom of my heart, when near him/her I can forget myself, a fervent flood of gratitude pours over me, giving me the strength to do them only good … . Unfortunately few people have this … effect on me.

4 May 1902 Poem
    A thought of God works in us
    We are subjected to it powerlessly
    Law and Necessity are its motto
    We human beings call it "our own life"
    We can never grasp the high meaning

I read this poem to my husband and children at dinner; Else liked it extremely well … The quiet garden poured the most pleasant fragrance toward us, the firelilies gleamed in the moonlight secretly and half hidden, and the crickets chirped their happy song of sensuous joy … .

25 July 1902 Oh, how you look compared to these individuals full of character, you miserable "magnificent" palaces of the present, you types without personality![15] Else and I let the old magic sink into us … then my husband came and expertly named the year the buildings were built, the names of the masters … and the magic was gone … .

30 July 1902 I especially want to mention this day because it was filled with many good moments.
    … first thing in the morning I felt very comfortable and studied Marty's psychology in bed … then later, after I had done my housework, I read Eckermann's *Conversations with Goethe* … then in the afternoon a good dose of Beethoven and the consciousness of having done my duty, by which I mean playing all the scales, sharp and flat, in the opposite order. Now in the evening a swim in the river in the company of my … daughter, who just turned 16, writing this … in the garden, surrounded by … bluebells … What else can I ask for?

9 August 1902 [today] … I had the feeling of being in a safe harbor … while my fellow beings had to fight against all imaginable dangers … no day passes by for me without awareness … .

25 August 1902 I would like to live every hour of my life with a receptive mind, governed by the most intense feeling … [it] should not give me its content in sparse drops; no, its juice should pour from all pores … .

4 November 1902 I cannot aquire complete confidence in my views ... my actions and life's goals ... .

22 November 1902 When I am alone with Grandmama, I always direct our conversation to events of long ago. In her descriptions ... the dead arise ... who suffered so much in life ... work and misery were the basic tenor ... .

I have read *Jörn Uhl*,[16] Gorki's *Vagabonds*, and I empathized so strongly with Goethe's *Sufferings of Young Werther*, that it seemed Goethe was expressing my own feelings ... if only my self could have unfolded rather than be squeezed into a cardboard box full of false prejudices and limitations! I feel I would have been capable of a self-destructive passion if my drives and instincts had not been weakened and sidetracked ... in the Procrustean[17] bed of leveling banality.

Are there joys as powerful as the sorrow felt at the coffin of someone one loves? Who has the right to torment us human beings so inhumanely? I asked myself today at the funeral of little Richard ... The silvery shimmering coffin, the colorful ... wreaths with their white streamers; the atmosphere of the richly dressed priests with their serious, fairytale gestures and harmlessly conscientious farce formed a contrast to the faces of the mourners distorted with pain ... gnawing pity alternated in me with joy over the spectacle rich in forms and colors. I sit at the table in my harmoniously beautiful room in the evening. My husband is reading across from me, Otto has finally gone to bed, after endless warnings and threats. Finally it is quiet ... I feel as if there were dark veils waving over the heads of my dear children ... I see them far from the protective, cosy home of their parents on intricate paths ... in the restlessness of life, where the most varied dangers threaten. I feel tears in my eyes and wish I could pray.

14 January 1903 Yesterday I hurt a human heart. Being sometimes too quick, I told Mr. Kohn that he is superficial. This remark hurt and tortured him. I am totally open and honest with people I like ... that is why people ... are interested in me, i.e. those whom I consider worthy of seeing my true personality.

22 January 1903 Today there was a bright light shining in me, like sparks, many rainbows spread their colors over my soul ... Oh life, may it live!

26 January 1903 Yesterday I made the acquaintance of an interesting man, Dr. Horneffer, who hides the soul of an idealist and dreamer behind a pedantic schoolmasterly appearance ... He wants to transform Nietzsche's religion into a practical, usable ethic; he wants people to live Nietzschean instead of Christian or Jewish lives. While this

guest sat at our table … wide vistas opened up before me, my mental nearsightedness ended … My husband, who was very nice, however, is a master at making a grand idea small, so small that it is like an insignificant individual event, inhibiting any deeper penetration … .

11 February 1903 Last night we enjoyed fried carp; a small bone stuck in my throat … After it had been removed …—various ideas came up in the small group around the table—my husband said: "From this event, one is to draw the conclusion that one should never eat fish in a crowd." Otto replied: "That would be too bad … especially salmon … mmmm, I cannot say how good that is … ." Else added: "And salmon is so good, so decent, it doesn't even have bones that could hurt you." I replied: "The salmon is rewarded because it is so good: no other fish is caught, killed, stewed, fried as much. … It is similar with people; if somebody has a poisonous temperament, everybody fears his sting … and deals with him with the most loving gentleness. But if a human being is entirely without bones … that is to say, defenseless … in his … goodness, then his dear fellow humans … attack him … consume him spiritually … and then say he is a good, decent person. …"

7 March 1903 Last night Grandmama told me various things from the family chronicle … . She mainly spoke of her grandfather Lazar Taussig from Budin[18]. This old gentleman loved my grandmother very much, he appreciated her soul where only dark blossoms sprouted, for … love had never given it warmth … this learned grandfather once wrote my grandmother a beautiful Jewish letter … which she remembered … despite her eighty-six years: "Everybody should often think of another person whom he esteems. And with every action you undertake and with every step of your life you should think about what your grandfather would think of it … ."

I think that the value of a person can be seen by how long he can stand to be alone, without being nourished by other people's thoughts, e.g., books….

11 March 1903 To have a world view of one's own takes broad scientific and psychological knowledge … but I think that everybody can make a plan for life which he can follow with all his strength. My life's plan is to strengthen my judgment.

… Every day, every hour should be used to follow this plan. Now I divide my time in the following way: three hours a day are for my education … of course, I can stand such activity only for half an hour at a time; in between I rest or I practice the piano which I also consider necessary. The rest of the day I devote … to people I love or toward whom I have obligations … In summer I have a need … to spend time in nature. I am not a stoic ... I want to feel the whole world of beautiful appearances. In winter I like to have the impact of the theater, music or other works of art. An annual trip also finds its place in my carefully thought out life's plan. Outward hindrances or inward disturbances often destroy the ... plan ... but they pass ... .

... Until now I assumed that by making myself happy and contented I also brought joy and peace to those near me ... I also held on to a second principle, namely not to interfere with the thought and emotional processes of others ... but now I have learned that that [i.e. to interfere] is ... a strict obligation where the children are concerned.

> After this, the entries in Fanta's diary are few and laconic. She closes with the following notes:

26 June 1903 Everything we know, we know through our senses. Would God have taken so much trouble to deceive his creatures?

2 July 1903 I am only one person, one drop that forms the ocean of ... human beings and yet I am the total owner of a realm which seems to be without limits ... .

16 December 1904 Recently I have been occupied with the aesthetic issue of what is the form, and what the content of a work of art. ...

8 November 1908 The more knowledge, the more puzzles. ...

End of March, 1911 Meditation Exercises

Notes

1. Otto Fanta, "Die Handschrift" in: *Dichter, Denker, Helfer. Max Brod zum 50. Geburtstag*, Mährisch Ostrau, 1934, p.103.
2. In her unpublished manuscript, "Familiengeschichte", in the archives of the Leo Baeck Institute in New York.
3. Later head librarian, then rector of the Hebrew University in Jerusalem.
4. An East European Jewish thinker.
5. The central square of historic old Prague. Not only was the Fantas' pharmacy here, but also the old Town Hall and the Kinsky Palace, where Kafka's gymnasium and his father's store were located. The square remains today much as it has for generations, but, in 1992, when I asked the pharmacists who now work in the pharmacy about its history, they knew nothing about it.
6. Famous Viennese actors.
7. This impression is contradicted by Else's claim that Berta and her sister Ida limited the Jewish participants to one third of the total, indicating there were more Jewish interested women than participating.

8. Carl Spitzweg (1802–1885) a painter, best known for his humorous scenes from the every-day life of the petit bourgeoisie around 1830 and his portrayal of eccentrics.
9. A park in Prague.
10. Her unpublished diary (1900–1911), in the possession of her grandson, Dr. Martin Bergmann, New York.
11. A writer.
12. Ernst Mach, the Austrian philosopher.
13. Actually *Die Erinnerungen Ludolf Ursleus, des Jüngeren.*
14. This type of turn of the century dress was loosely cut, with simple lines, and above all comfortable and worn without a corset. It was generally worn by emancipated women who rejected the unhealthy, corseted styles of the day.
15. Fanta is writing after a two weeks trip to Goslar and Hildesheim.
16. A novel by Gustav Frenssen taken very seriously at the time.
17. From Procrustes: a legendary Greek brigand who used to lay travellers on a bed, and if they were too long for it, cut short their limbs; but if the bed was longer, strech them to make their length equal to it.
18. This Grandfather is mentioned by the German poet, Johann Gottfried Seume (1763–1810) in his travelogue *Spaziergang nach Syrakus*, 1803. He recalls his encounter in 1802: "In Budin, an isolated and desolate place, I discovered a good library at the Jew Lazar Taussig, and since he had lent Lessing's *Nathan* to a friend, I borrowed Kant … ."

Chapter 6

HERMINE HANEL

(1874-1944)

I first heard about Hermine Hanel from our late friend Hermann Wein, a philosophy professor at the University of Göttingen, many years ago when I was working on my book about The Jews of Bohemia and Moravia. *I was looking for descriptions of Jewish milieus in Prague and Hermann had told me that his relative Hermine, who was partly of Jewish descent and born in Prague, had written an autobiography. I borrowed it, but found little in it suitable for my purpose and sent the book back from America to Althöllmühle, the Weins' Bavarian country home. A few weeks later, the early sixteenth-century farm house burned to the ground, and with it Hermine Hanel's book.*

I remembered it again in connection with my search for memoirs of Prague women, and was fortunate to be able to borrow a copy of the very rare book from Hermine Hanel's son, Georg Deiglmayr. We know her chiefly from that book:

Hermine was the daughter of a Jewish mother and a Catholic father. As her mother died shortly after her birth, she was raised by her Jewish grandparents along with her nine aunts, her mother's younger sisters, in an imposing house in the New Town of Prague. The grandfather was very patriarchal, and although the family was well-to-do, there was something spartan about the household.

Like most of the German speaking women from Prague I was able to find, Hermine dwells a great deal on her relationships with famous men. They were generally much older than herself, as were Ludwig Deiglmayr, her husband of about twenty-five years, and the man to whom she was briefly married in her early twenties. Was there a possible connection between these choices on her part and the fact that her father had left her with the family of his in-laws where the man of the house had little time for her?

Like most of the Jewish women included in this volume, Hermine left Prague, first for Munich, then moved to Vienna and back again to Munich to live independently and to pursue a career as an artist and a writer.

With our other protagonists one looks in vain for role models, specifically named or just followed. However, Hermine Hanel, or Mizzi as she was called, clearly modeled herself after the heroines of the German young woman's novels of her time. At that time all young girls read Der Trotzkopf[1] (meaning literally spiteful head) and the like: stories of young women of marriageable age, pretty

*and spiteful, with dark, unmanageable curls (like Mizzi), tomboys whose
mothers and grandmothers watched with concern, amusement and mainly pride
as they teased their suitor—a man totally acceptable to the family, somewhat
older than the young woman and a good provider. In the end the young women
are "tamed" by the man and lead into the secure haven of marriage. Mizzi saw
herself, too, as a young filly that had to be tamed—although by the time she
entered her second and final marriage she was thirty-five years old and had lived
on her own for a long time.*

*It was then that Mizzi terminated her Bohemian existence and married into
an upper-middle class Munich family. She had three children. From her daughter, Lilli Deiglmayr, I learned that her parents each continued to pursue their
own interests. Mizzi wrote fiction and worked as an illustrator until the Nazi
racial laws put an end to her publications and public appearances. Her husband,
an architect, died in 1937, Mizzi herself died suddenly during the bombing of
Munich in 1944. Despite tragedies in her own life and in the world around her,
she seems to have been one of the rare people who are satisfied with life as it is,
with one important exception: the female role into which she was born. She neither had a high opinion of the grandmother who raised her nor of her nine aunts,
nor of any other woman she mentioned. She wrote a great deal about her male
friends—mostly much older than herself and in prominent positions—but she
had almost no women friends. She also felt that her own "generosity and cleanness of approach" were the masculine characteristics of a gentleman and kept her
from being happy as a woman. In fact, she even thought that Weininger, to
whom women were "only sexual creatures without character and with a mother
instinct" may "in many ways be right".*

*Her autobiography follows. For reasons of length I have had to omit detailed
descriptions and sometimes whole episodes as well as many flowery passages.*

My mother's father came from a very simple background. As a young
man he had come to the capital from a small Bohemian provincial
town, only trusting his own strength. There, thanks to the recom-
mendation of the rabbi back home, he was given free meals in well-
to-do families. On the other days he starved. Modest, of sturdy health
and great energy, intelligent and ambitious, he succeeded in making
his mark in the business he entered as an assistant, and ... soon
acquired it. ...

When he married a girl ten years younger than himself at the age of
thirty, he was already moderately prosperous, and increased his wealth
through this marriage.

Grandmama came from a respected, well-to-do Jewish family of
businessmen and had received a good education. She spoke English
and French well, read a great deal, although indiscriminately, played
the piano, made fine embroideries and was an excellent housewife.

Grandpapa was the despot and patriarch in the house. Nobody dared
to oppose his will. The energy with which he had worked his way up

from poverty stayed with him in old age. As a rich man, he held on to his simple habits, rising summer and winter at six in the morning, sleeping in an unheated room, taking a cold bath and working from morning until late at night in his large hops business. Unforgivingly strict toward himself, he demanded the same self discipline of his environment. He provided a counter weight to his wife's easy going tolerant attitude; it must not have been easy to rule a numerous family and to increase its prosperity in spite of the large expenditures.

Grandpapa was stocky and sturdy, his coloring was bright, his beard and hair were white, his eyes blue and sharp. Grandmother was small, lively, with sparkling dark eyes and quick movements. Childlike and full of humor, she subordinated herself to her husband's will. She was too modest to live her own life, and her thoughts circled around her husband and her children ... . Until her old age, she remained a harmless child in need of guidance. ...

She was kind toward servants and being generous toward all in need, she was often taken advantage of, which did not reduce her pleasure in giving. Although modest in her demands ... she worried forever about the quick disappearance of money which her little hands were not able to hold together ....

My grandparents had ten daughters and two sons ... the female majority prevailed over [my grandfather's] individual will. ...

My mother, the oldest child and her father's favorite, seems to have been different from her frivolous sisters. Thoughtful, nature-loving, gifted with a lively imagination and individualistic, she probably often felt lonely in the large, noisy house. At the age of seventeen, she was not a beauty, but attractive, with big beautiful brown eyes and fine features. When she met my father, who was ten years older, she fell in love with a deep passion. Papa came from a patrician family which was emphatically German and for generations had been one of the most respected in Prague. His brothers and sisters were handsome and so was he, the eldest ... . His noble face with the slender nose, his expressive mouth and high forehead framed by brown curls, his slender figure and his ... reserve made him seem to be her destiny.

Since my father was passive by nature, I have to assume that my mother's desire led toward the marriage. Although he loved her, because of the powerful hindrances standing in their way, he probably would not have taken the initiative. His family was strictly Catholic and marriage between Christians and Jews was very rare in those days. Grandfather, very self-assured about his riches and position, did not want to tolerate his daughter merely being accepted out of kindness into her husband's family, and energetically opposed the union.

But his eldest, who had inherited his iron will ... would not let go of the man of her choice. And she was so depressed by her father's refusal, that her health was in danger ... . So with a heavy heart her father gave in to his darling.

The young woman was declared without denomination. The marriage took place in ... City Hall, which created an immense sensation because it was the first interdenominational marriage in Prague.

Despite her passion ... she allegedly was still a virgin after the honeymoon ...

After a year, she bore a boy who died, however, after a few months of a throat ailment.

And again her womb was blessed and she brought a little boy into the world who followed his little brother after a few weeks into the Realm of Shadows.

And because fate is often merciless and piles up all the sorrow on one weak person, my father, who headed a large metal business, suffered considerable losses through no fault of his own which further darkened the house marked by death. Papa turned to his father-in-law for help, but it was not granted. And the estrangement of the two men which was to last until grandfather's death later presented me with a dilemma as well.

In the fourth year of their marriage, I was born on a mild September evening. The Jews celebrated the Day of Atonement ... Grandmama, who did not frequent synagogue often, was at services. When she received the news, regardless of the prohibition of riding [on that day,] she rode hurriedly to see her daughter.

So I, standing between two races, was born on the Evening of Atonement. Was it a good omen, that I was supposed to reconcile the two hostile tribes?

The birth was normal. I was a strong little child and there was hope that the young mother, who had suffered so much, would blossom again along with her little daughter, but she was infected by her nurse with puerperal fever. Hygiene was still very primitive, many women in childbed became victims of this insidious disease.

Mama was so exhausted by her suffering, that she longed to be delivered from it and with a gesture of her hand sent her ... child away, as if she wanted to say: "Don't tie me to life with fetters of love—let me sleep forever!" And so, while my mother hovered between life and death for three months, I was taken to the house of my grandparents, which was to be my home.

Toward Christmas, mama's suffering was over. She died as a heathen, without the consolations of baptism and of extreme unction which had been offered to her. Her last wish was:

"I want to rest next to my boys. May flowers and music accompany me to my grave!"

My mother died twenty-two years old. Her life died down like a melancholy song played on the cello. ...

[Her] longing to sleep next to her children clashed with clumsy worldly or rather ecclesiastical considerations. Since she died without having joined "the only church assuring salvation," the clergy denied her a funeral in the family tomb in the Catholic cemetery, where ... her baptized little boys were buried.

And only after upsetting, painful negotiations with the highest clerical authority in Rome, through dispensation by the Pope, was the burial of the "heretic" next to her children permitted.

The mob of Prague had gathered at the cemetery and behaved disgracefully. Papa's family showed no great sorrow about the loss of the young woman who had been too proud to force her way into their confidence ... .

Grandfather, mourning the death of his eldest daughter deeply, did not forget the humiliations. In his anger ... he decided that I was not to be baptized, and my father gave in to his wish. My father was so deeply hurt by the behavior of the clergy ... that he later became Protestant and raised the children of his second marriage in that faith.

My grandparents did not want to part with me ... . Papa ... could not take care of [a] little child and so ... I was raised by my aunts, the youngest of whom was only six years old.

Named "Hermine" after my mother, I was given the nickname "Mizzi" which stayed with me to my old age. Little dark-haired and dark-eyed Mizzi was a welcome but strong-willed toy for her aunts. In my first year, I was taken care of by a Czech wetnurse, a good natured, simple young peasant, and I developed well. Božena remained attached to our house. Every fall on my birthday, she came ... into the city and brought her "milk daughter" a gift ... .

The older I became, the greater became my embarrassment vis-à-vis [her]. The good-natured ... woman in the wide red skirt, puffed out over many starched petticoats, her red stockings, the black velvet bodice and the colorful handkerchief kissed the hem of my dress in embarrassment. Since she did not speak a word of German and I only few words of Czech, we could not communicate. The feeling that I owed her thanks only increased my discomfort about her submissiveness ... . After being served ample food in the kitchen, Božena used to leave with gifts of clothes ... and toys. She brought the gifts to her daughter ... The little ... girl whose mother I had taken away at a tender age often occupied my thoughts. I felt the injustice of a fate which forced a poor woman to leave her newborn child in order to nurse a stranger.

Later I was entrusted to a nursemaid, a good natured old woman who had already taken care of my younger aunts. "Little Aninka" was extremely popular ... she hardly knew how to read and write, but she told us wonderful fairy tales and stories, and sang me to sleep ... with melancholy and cheerful folk songs. I controlled her and loved her on condition that she obeyed me. ...

Grandfather, who witnessed a scene in which I stubbornly won [a victory over Aninka], put a sudden end to this mistress-and-slave relationship. He declared that it was time for me to learn strict discipline and forget my Czech-German gibberish. [From then on I had] a governess.

I did not like to play with dolls. When I was asked ... "What would you enjoy?" I replied: "Give me a horse." People shook their heads: She is not feminine. She has no feeling for motherhood ... .

Most of all I loved animals ... I envied the kittens which slept with their mother and also the downy little birds. A little bird that had fallen out of its nest and missed a mother's love, I would have liked to slip into a bed and to warm up beside a mother ... .

Our house on quiet Stefan Street, in New Town ... looked comfortable with its two stories, wide facade and gleaming windows with white lace curtains ... . The office was on first floor. On the right, there was a stately ... staircase covered with a red carpet leading to the social rooms where there was always the fragrance of hyacinths, lilac, lilies of the valley, and narcissus raised in our hot house.

The dining and social rooms faced the street. Partly separated by glass doors, they were furnished with damask furniture, high ... mirrors in golden frames, thick Persian rugs, beautiful vases and pictures. The largest salon, furnished golden yellow in baroque style was vaulted over by a blue sky; angels, birds, butterflies flew in the ... sky, rich wreaths of fruits and flowers covered the sides. In the smaller salons, black ebony chairs were covered with peacock blue silk. The dining room was kept dark by colorful bull's eye panes; on the large, carved oak credenza, there were huge tankards, pitchers and gleaming silver utensils ... .

In contrast to the social rooms, my grandparents' small bedrooms were extremely simple, and grandfather's study with its black leather furniture was also in keeping with his way of life: severe and almost bare.

From the front part of the house a long corridor lead to the rear wing ... sunny rooms [were] the realm of my aunts and my nursery ... . In the garden, the birds twittered ... in the rooms ... the bright laughter of girls was heard, a young virtuoso played on an untuned piano and accompanied her sister playing the violin. Girl-friends visited ... there was giggling and cakes were nibbled at. The bitter smell of hops … was mixed with the fragrance of the blooming linden trees.

The "Ten-daughters-house" as it was called, was roomy and comfortable, with many extra little rooms and cubbyholes, and yet built … impractically. The huge pantry contained … almonds, raisins and chocolate, canned fruit and … sweet liqueur, but that sanctuary remained locked. The kitchen, which was in charge of an artist who … had grown old in that position, was as large as a dance hall … .

What I have treasured most in my life is that I could grow up on our own property; I never would have felt so much at home in a rented apartment! … I also planted radishes, beans, corn, peas and lettuce and had the brave plan of increasing my meager pocket money by selling vegetables. …

Grandfather, whose way of life was spartan up to his old age, grumbled in vain about the rising expenditures [in the household]. The money spent on clothes angered him so much that … we [children] then wore smocks of hop sacks … He constantly tried in vain to hold the vanity and wastefulness of the female members of the family in check. …

The anniversary of my mother's death was around Christmas time. Grandmama never forgot to decorate mama's grave with flowers, and on All Souls Day, we placed a wreath on her resting place. I remember walking over to the family tomb, the paths overblown with leaves, and snow between the graves with crosses and wilted flowers … .

Many thoughtless words impress themselves on a child … . "The little one has no heart," they said, because I seemed to love nobody and remained a wildcat that went its own way. …

The feeling of being different and misunderstood has dominated me since my early childhood … I feel I am unique. I love people as personalities, but the masses have always remained strange to me. They called me selfish. Holy Scripture teaches us: "Love thy neighbor as thyself." Who doesn't love him/herself, remains indifferent towards others … .

When I became older and found out that my mother had died after my birth, I was tormented by the idea of my guilt.

Impressions in early youth are so strong, that one can hardly do enough to save a child from undesirable experiences … . A maid to whom I was entrusted at a tender age took me to a variety show, where I saw with horror the pale ghostlike heads of kings, artists and criminals. This view was so frightening to me, that I became sick from the smell of the wax. From then on my revulsion against wax was so insurmountable … that the light of a candle made me violently ill … . I also never ate honey again. …

My fine senses took in all impressions … my sense of smell was developed like that of an animal … Later my opponents used to say: "She has arrogant nostrils." …

My father's family was strict in observing religious duties without understanding the meaning of Christian love and didn't pay attention to the motherless child. Papa's parents were dead, and his stepmother and siblings were conceited and cold. I remember as a small girl visiting an old paralyzed woman in an easy chair, my step-grandmother of whom I was afraid. Papa's numerous brothers and sisters were beautiful and distinguished looking; the women played an important role in the German society of Prague. …

My father avoided social gatherings, worked hard, lived in a small apartment and visited us twice a week. He avoided seeing my grandfather … but the relationship between him and my grandmother always remained cordial. I was proud of my attractive papa. My sense of beauty which developed early took pleasure in his appearance; I liked him to touch me and felt related to him by blood. The secret sexual attraction between father and daughter … linked me to him … I was like him outwardly, but our characters were different. My stubbornness repelled him.

He was reserved … and I needed impulsive tenderness and warmth. Only love could tame me. Papa did not speak about my dead mother or let me attach myself to him by reminiscing lovingly with me. I think that my mother's unpliable character was difficult for him, and it was painful for him to find the same stubbornness in his little daughter … Since he only came to visit, he could not bring me up and influence me. We did not become close, he was not a steady part of my daily life.

When I was six years old, grandmama said: "Your father will marry again." I was afraid, because I thought of the bad stepmother in Snow White and in Cinderella. But when the tiny delicate young woman asked me modestly to call her mama, my fear disappeared.

She came from a Prague German family, and was well educated, kind, musical … She loved me and always tried to mediate between [Father] and me. [They] wanted me to live with them, but my grandparents did not want to part with [me].

Two stepsisters and a stepbrother were born. Hermine did not want to be a stepchild in that family and continued to go to her father's house as a guest and to play with the children.

No book of fairy tales is as magnificent as the living picture book of the city. At the shore of the Moldau the loud world disappears. Sixteen proud bridge piers support statues of saints donated by pious

The Old Town Square

families. Towering above all stands the patron saint of Bohemia, St. John of Nepomuk. Everyone goes on pilgrimage to him on St. Nepomuk's day in May. On that day … the city is full of colorful country people in … costume. Children and women say their prayers before the … silver tomb of the patron saint in the Cathedral which is surrounded by twenty-seven silver lamps and one golden one.

When I lean over the railing of the stone bridge, I see brave Roland, my favorite … .

On the other side of the river, on the Lesser Side, there is one palace next to the other in steeply rising streets. I decipher the words on the stone coats of arms above high portals, the coats of arms of old, influential families, which determined the fate of the country. Some palaces are empty and uninhabited, but in front of others there is a ... doorkeeper with golden tresses.

High up on the Hradschin, the closed windows of the castle flash ... in the sunlight ... Below the city rests with its hundred towers, the sparkling ... crosses and the profusion of roofs, framed by blooming hills ... . The ruin of the Daliborka[2] protrudes ghostlike in the blue sky ... .

I ... flee to the nearby street of the alchemists which seems like a child's toy with its ... colorful little houses. There in Emperor Rudolph's time the alchemists carried on their trade, shying the light of day and brewing noble gold in strangely shaped vessels according to secret recipes found on faded parchment. Now poor people live in the narrow little street. Women stand before wooden troughs and wash clothes, while pale children dance to the sounds of a mouth harmonica. The windows of these houses look into the depth of the rich wilderness of the Stag's Ditch. Now fire lilies, jasmine and raspberry bushes proliferate between apple trees in the overgrown grass. Where once noblemen hunted ... the bells of Loretto Church chime in honor of Easter ... I look ... at the chapel [decorated for the day] where many candles burn at the feet of the Mother of God and the altar is decorated with roses, jasmine and white snowbells. ... The crosswalk of the monastery ... is decorated with faded frescoes from the lives of the saints ... According to legend, a pious queen was tempted by a seducer and prayed to God to disfigure her, so that she would not fall prey to sin ... and a mighty beard grew on the beauty ... .

Another page in the inexhaustible picture book shows the old Jewish cemetery which lies like an oasis in the grey stone desert of the [former] ghetto ...

I had concluded my evening prayer with the words: "Dear God, give me a good governess!" ...

On a dull November evening Mademoiselle Claire Doucet came from Geneva. When she entered the room, pale, small, delicate, and tired from traveling and extended her hand to me smiling shyly, my child's instinct felt the weakness of her will. We became friends. She also kept quiet about my bad behavior. ...

After three years, I was to learn English and Miss Doucet sadly took leave of us. Her successor, Miss Evelyn Muff, a small, grouchy Englishwoman of uncertain age, with vague features, a washed-out complexion and grayish-brown hair ... spoke English through her nose. ...

I could not stand Miss Muff ... But she soon left the house and ... I was sent to the German girls' secondary school.

Nevertheless, another governess was hired for Hermine.

What did [her nine young aunts] do all day? They played the piano, the violin and the guitar, they sang, spoke English, French and Italian, they cooked and sewed, they painted on silk and on china, they read and wrote letters, they flirted, danced, exercised and skated, they chatted and laughed. They knew everything and yet nothing thoroughly and prepared for their future profession as housewives.

Grandfather was so little pleased about being blessed with so many girls, that once nobody dared to inform him about the ... birth of another girl. But then the desired son and heir came, followed by a second son. ... The young aunts often fell in love, were enthusiastic about actors and singers. Foolish virgins, warm-blooded, uncalculating. Grandfather, who worked hard from morning til night to finance the expensive household and to give his daughters a suitable dowry, disregarded the sentimentality of his daughters ... and chose his sons-in-law according to profession and income. If a girl was in love with her future husband, so much the better ... they subjected themselves to their lords and masters and became excellent wives and mothers.

Grandfather never let a younger daughter marry before an older one. Every year a daughter left the house. I hated to see the aunts leave ... but I had a wonderful time on the prenuptial eves and at the weddings, which were always celebrated with a large circle of friends ... The table was always set for guests.

Some aunts stayed in Prague, others moved elsewhere with their husbands ... On holidays daughters, sons-in-law and grandchildren gathered in the parents' house.

I am sorry that the Old Testament Holy Days which Heinrich Heine celebrates in his "Princess Sabbath" and other pious customs of religious families were not observed in our house. We did, to be sure, nibble at the unleavened bread which the Israelites ate in the desert, but we celebrated only the feast days of the Church. Saint Nicholas appeared with his bishop's mitre and distributed sweet gifts. In the evening one hung a stocking on the bed, and at dawn one reached for it filled ... .

On Christmas eve the pine tree sparkled with lights, long tables with generous gifts for us and the servants were lined up along the wall. [Once] after I became so tired over carp and roast geese, cake and wine, that I had to be carried to bed, I sneaked back to the Christmas room on tiptoe, in order to enjoy all the splendor again in the morning light ... I went back to bed and dreamed about the wonders of the Holy Night. ...

Death, which had taken the eldest daughter, came for the second time to the house blessed with life ... the son and heir ... died of typhoid fever at the age of eighteen. This treacherous disease was widespread in Prague in my youth, the bad drinking water may also have been at fault ... . My grandparents now doubled their love for the second son ... Hugo was the darling of all of us, and we were very sad to take leave of him when ... he went to England to become an expert in textiles. Grandfather ... continued in the hops business by himself and bought a spinning mill in Northern Bohemia where the young uncle found his ... livelihood.

Hermine felt uncomfortable about the factory, that mechanical monster manned by workers whom she viewed as slaves.

My feeling for social justice rebelled against the body search to which male and female workers were subjected ... But since there were frequent thefts of materials, it was necessary. In the factory there were five-to-six hundred workers, about a third of whom were Czechs. Grandpapa appreciated the latter because of their industriousness, but the presence of two hostile nations often led to serious friction. Once a drunken Czech worker wanted to smash our gate with an axe. There were such bloody fights, that during a few weeks we had state police quartered in the house for the protection of the female occupants ... The large garden ... led to the high forest, which ... was also part of our property. And this forest with its creatures, old pines and firs ... is the deepest experience of my childhood.

There, in Northern Bohemia, she also became fascinated with the products of the glass industry such as buttons and costume jewelry.

How small and poor the real jewelry which I inherited from my mother seemed to me ... in comparison with this oriental treasure reminiscent of Aladdin's wondrous lamp!

As my mother's only child I had inherited her fortune ... Grandpapa administered it, and with it my education was provided for ...

Monsieur Buonaparte Andrée Chapeau ... was an old Frenchman who was to teach us dancing and manners. Every Saturday evening a few children of friends and my cousins gathered in our salon, and were introduced to the waltz, the française, the quadrille à la cour, and the mazurka. We also ... learned national dances, to stand up straight, to walk gracefully and to bow, to enter a room correctly and to greet properly, to sit on a chair and to smile nicely. The thin, agile gentleman with the dyed goatee stood under the chandelier with his violin in his hand, in tails, starched lace shirt front, short pants, black silk stockings and buckle shoes ... .

Every winter toward the end of the carnival season we had a house ball. ...

I still think of my instruction in music with horror. Aloys Gutherz, whose name was in gross contrast to his cruelty, was a fat, bow legged old man with an unshaven face and a bald head, who constantly put snuff in his pig's nose over the bushy mustache. He sat so close to me, that ... I felt sick. He ... stuck his sharp pencil in my palm when I did not lift my hands high enough, which hurt very much. ...

Among the fossils which have died out in our time of economy and independence was the hairdresser, an important personality and reporter of the daily chronicle [of gossip]...

Grandfather never forgot his impoverished youth, and so needy German students or commercial apprentices, regardless of which confession, received meals at our house on two days a week. ...

Fashionable clothing played an important role in our house of ten daughters. The young ladies were attractive and always dressed in good taste.

With rich girls, linens amounted to a tenth of the dowry. In our hallway were high armoires, filled with my aunts' dowries. They were so plentiful, that generations inherited old-fashioned [underwear] and pants with gathers reaching down to the knees. There was lace bedding for childbed, made of silk and fine cotton and trimmed with lace in every dowry. Young mothers who stayed in bed for six weeks after the delivery received their friends in an elegantly dressed-up bed. When a woman remained unmarried, which was rare and considered a misfortune, she had to console herself with the unused elegant ... bedding. My poor aunt Olga, who was still single at the age of twenty-three ... perhaps agreed to her unfortunate marriage to avoid such a tragedy.... Our good grandmama was very vain, and because beauty was considered a girl's most important attribute, she took care of our looks ... . To avoid a goiter, I had to swim with a choking cloth around my neck. We slept on a hard surface, without a pillow, and because of an alleged tendency to develop a humped back, I had to sleep on the floor. "Stand (or sit) straight!" I heard all day ... Unfortunately I had freckles and so I was admonished again and again: "Don't expose yourself to the sun!" ... Because of so many abnormalities I considered myself a monster and was pleasantly surprised when ... a student at the gymnasium praised me as a heavenly creature—despite goiter, humped back, freckles, rough arms and rough hands. ...

Robinson [Crusoe], Don Quixotte, Gulliver's Travels and other masterworks of world literature were given us in watered down editions,

Hermine Hanel as a young girl

so that they lost much of their interest. I read the popular ... writings by Nieritz and Hoffmann,[3] was fascinated by the adventures of Jules Verne, the French genius who foresaw many wonders of technology, and nourished my imagination with the hypocritical literature [fashionable at that time for teenage girls.]

She also read German historical novels, and English and French children's stories in the original.

The Bible made a deep impression on me. On the ebony table in our salon lay luxurious editions of the Old and the New Testament illustrated by ... Doré ... The pictures impressed me even more than the words, as I have always learned the most through my senses.

Beside the Bible I loved the German heroic legends. [They] impressed me more than the sagas of classical antiquity ... To this day our German fairy tales, Irish stories of elves, Andersen and the ... world of the Romantics still are my most faithful friends. ... I have expressed my innermost being by writing and illustrating fairy tales.

The private instruction which I had for four years with my ... cousin Vally ... became boring to us, and we were glad to attend public school. The girls' "Lyzeum", the best German school, had excellent free-thinking teachers and was frequented by daughters of the upper classes ... .

The teachers soon realized that I was gifted, but somewhat mischievous. Subjects which interested me, like geography, history, mythology and literature were easy for me; my essays were original and imaginative, but in mathematics and grammar I was a total failure. Popular with my classmates, I took a leading role whenever mischief was involved.

Despite much cordial camaraderie I had no intimate girl friend ... I longed for a brother ... a male influence ... I felt sorry for all girls, and the great sorrow of my life was not being a boy.

Religion was taught separately by a Catholic, a Protestant and a Jewish clergyman. As the only child without confession, I remained in the classroom during religious instruction. Because of my status as a heathen, I had an exceptional position ... and my feeling of isolation was intensified. It is not good for the development of a child to be raised outside a religious community and to … feel … excluded. …

My self-assurance which developed early, my rich surroundings and the prestige of my family led me to see myself as a child of the upper class … but … a child also … needs … a faith. …

My clothing was in good taste and gave me prestige among my classmates. At noon … the … governess waited for me at the door of the school, and I had to speak English or French on the way home. … My grandparents made the mistake of always entrusting me to older ladies who had too little love for children, instead of giving me young, happy governesses as friends. I became increasingly stubborn and hard to manage.

Grandpapa had a heart condition for years, and had to be spared all excitement, but there were always fights [between me and those who were supposed to tame me]. "You are more trouble than your nine aunts," grandmama would say.

After my fourth year in school, the family decided to send "the arrogant brat" to boarding school. [Her father went to Dresden to look for a Protestant boarding school — since he and his other children were Protestant.] Apart from Prague I knew no large city and was charmed by … Dresden. Grandmama (and I) stayed at the elegant Hotel Bellevue … The next day she saw with horror how I … together with the piccolo of the hotel, slid down the banisters from the second floor to the lobby.

> Hermine and her grandmother were received in the petit bourgeois salon of the Schwarzes' pension by a chubby matron, and in the evening the grandmother went back to Prague. Food parcels from there were very welcome, because Hermine considered the food in Saxony unsatisfactory both in quality and in quantity.

And yet we were quite cheerful. Sixteen girls between the ages of fifteen and eighteen were given their final polish. Our instruction was mainly limited to art history, history, literature, languages, and music.

Unfortunately we were not taught any household subjects. As the youngest … I was spoiled. …

It was a matter of honor, not to speak to me about certain delicate subjects. I was not curious and did not ask. The honorable Saxon [matron] was disgusted with my short skirts. "Austrian frivolity" she said …

During my leisure time I devoured history books and read with glowing cheeks about the French Revolution, about Napoleon and about the German Wars of Liberation.

Art history classes also fascinated me. After classes, we went to the Art Gallery … . In Dresden my inborn love of art … was deepened … Theater, concerts … and opera enthused us so much, that we recited monologs ... until deep in the night ... We read dramas ... with divided roles. It was really a stimulating time, and I was passionately interested in learning.

On Sunday afternoons ... sometimes a tall slender young Englishman with a pale, expressive face came visiting. Mrs. Chamberlain, Mrs. Schwarze's sister, the wife of the writer who was yet to become famous, was ten years older than he ... She worked with her husband in the archives collecting ... material for his voluminous works. Their marriage was dissolved after decades, when Houston Chamberlain[4] ... married a daughter of [Richard Wagner]. ...

The head of the pension tried to interest me in her faith. But the long sermons, the sobriety of the [church] appealed to my southern temperament much less than the incense drenched mysticism of the Catholic cathedrals. My childhood impressions in the old city of the hundred church towers[5] and my descent were bound to lead me to the womb of the "only church assuring salvation."

Papa wrote: Now that you can judge for yourself, I would like you to become Protestant, but you would have to keep your conversion secret from grandpapa ... "I shall never lie to my grandfather," I replied and remained a heathen.

At the age of fifteen, I fell in love—with a dead person, but to me he was alive. I worshipped the brilliant, charming, unhappy Heinrich Heine. I felt as if his poems were directed to me. Heine dominated my imagination and my dreams. His *Book of Songs* became my bible, which I read before going to sleep. I kissed his picture with the sharp, intelligent profile and the sorrowful, sarcastic mouth. ...

After a year and a half, I left the pension in Dresden. ... I didn't like home as much as before. Grandfather had aged ... his heart condition had increased his irritability. ...

Of the fun-loving aunts, only the two youngest were left at home. Olga had married against her father's will ... .

I was not able to subordinate myself to a governess. Miss Amanda Stark ... was forty-five years old and as North German as possible, a pastor's daughter from Lübeck. ... She was terribly well educated, she knew everything ... but her dry way of teaching did not captivate me, and the books which she read with me were too advanced for me ... .

In the atmosphere of old grandparents, beside the ... [Fräulein] who had never been young, I felt miserable—like a young, strong animal locked in a cage.

As the art of cooking is considered particularly important in Bohemia, and especially in the house of my grandparents, I was also supposed to be introduced to it. Our servants, Mariánka, Katinka,

Aninka, Božena etc. were good, hard-working, modest Bohemian girls, devoted to their masters, polite, indeed humble and satisfied with their lot. They were treated well, had plenty to eat, did their duty and with natural tact respected the differences in social status … .

My talent for drawing was already obvious in my early childhood, painting was my favorite activity … but unfortunately the instruction of young girls was limited to dull copying … and so my talent was not developed.

[The grandfather's death was an incisive experience in Hermine's life].

Fully developed, almost voluptuous, but with fine joints … I attracted attention in my simple mourning clothes. I had an oval face, dark eyes under black eyebrows, a slender nose with mobile nostrils, fresh lips, firm, white teeth like those of an animal of prey and a peaches-and-cream complexion. My dark, thick, hard-to control hair was pressed into braids. Of sparkling temperament, like a wild purebred horse, natural, impulsive, uncalculating and without coquetry, I was overflowing with youth and strength. The indefinite clair-obscur of the mixture of races gave me a special charm, a certain something which attracted people to me. Why should I not now, thinking back on the spring of my life, take pleasure in my beauty of which I was never vain, but which I gratefully accepted and which gave happiness to me and others through this grace from God?

Mornings I had to have lessons with Miss Stark, afternoons I played the role of an admired young lady. Among my admirers was a manufacturer from Vienna, a man of thirty-eight … His interest in me was so great, that he asked me to marry him. I was not yet seventeen, and it flattered me to be loved by an older, experienced man. Grandmama would probably have consented, because she felt burdened by the responsibility of raising me.

> On a holiday in Hungary she met Géza, a nineteen-year old Hungarian who became a good friend and had a great influence on her. After Hermine's youngest aunt was married, her grandmother seemed old and the question arose of Hermine moving to her father's household, but he declined.

I asked: "Let me go to Dresden or to Munich and become a painter. Or let me go to a college in England; in that land of freedom one is not treated only as a girl, there are friendships between girls and boys … . I have such a great longing to learn and to see the world." As the heiress of my mother's fortune I could have paid for a stay abroad, even under the protection of a chaperone—but … it was thought improper to let a young woman study something seriously.

There I sat with my unused strength and did not know what to do. I became restless and tortured myself and my surroundings. I had little interest in the household, and so I read indiscriminately, practiced my languages, went for walks with the "Fräulein," strummed on the piano, painted according to floral patterns and thought of my … life as wasted. "She should get married soon", said relatives and friends, and grandmama also found this … the best solution.

And so in winter I was sent to visit my married aunt Minna in Vienna. They hoped that I would find a bridegroom … I visited the wonderful art galleries and theaters and admired the … busy, elegant city.

> *The man who had proposed to her repeated his proposal, and another older man asked her to marry him. She refused both, perhaps thinking of Géza. One night, when she came home from a ball in a cab, she found at her door a lieutenant whom she had met at the ball. He asked her to marry him, and she consented. From then on, she considered herself engaged to a man she didn't know, who shared none of her interests and who could not even spell correctly. She could not marry him and yet she had given him her word. She told her cousin Vally about her predicament and asked her to tell her what happened between married people.*

In spite of my lively mind, I had never thought about sexual relations. Vally, proud of my confidence and her knowledge, explained to me the facts of life. I was astonished, but not alarmed; with my healthy attitude I found nothing that was natural repulsive. And then I sent my fiancé a letter dripping with nobility … and bought myself … a few volumes of Ibsen: the emancipated Hedda Gabler was my model. …

Grandmama had inherited a considerable fortune … but she was one of those women who, always busy in the household and concerned about the smallest detail, never have an overview and think they are being economical while wasting money. She had a hard time getting along on her money as a widow, good-naturedly giving larger sums to her daughters and sons-in-law. She had … the cooks cook too much and indulged in many unnecessary expenditures.

The house … had become much too large … and was to be sold. The thought … was terrible to me … I felt as if I were being put out in the street … .

The house has been torn down long ago, but my longing rebuilds it.

We moved to an apartment in an elegant street in New Town, but I did not feel at home there. …

Grandmama, used to her husband's strict guidance, became more and more inconsistent. She forbade me in the evening what she had allowed me in the morning, and let herself be influenced in her attitude toward me by friends and relatives, so that our relationship became increasingly difficult … .

To alleviate her gout, she was ordered to take the baths in Wiesbaden. I was allowed to accompany her and saw a beautiful part of the world. My horizon was broadened in association with interesting foreigners, among whom I liked a white-haired lord, who had spent a great many years in India … I generally sought out … mature men, which did not prevent me from dancing … with the young gentlemen and officers in the pumproom … .

I enjoyed wearing elegant clothes, feeling young and wanted, dancing and playing tennis, but in the midst of all the sensations I asked myself: "Is this the sense of life?" One day God will demand an accounting from me … and I'll stand there with empty hands, because I wasted what was precious …

Grandmama went to Karlsbad. The doctor had stressed that she must not be upset during the cure, but since she could not leave me alone, she took me along, to the detriment of her gallbladder problem. The poor woman was upset about her foolish granddaughter who, instead of choosing a husband among her young admirers, amused herself with older aristocrats. The governor of Bohemia, Count Franz Thun-Hohenstein, associated with me so much, that … the proper citizens were concerned about my innocence, for the … gentleman was considered a dangerous man about town. But our relationship was … harmless. The man who was three decades older than I enjoyed a natural girl like me and said: "I wish I had such a nice daughter in my childless house …"

Karlsbad, 1896

Franz Thun ... was a member of one of the oldest families in Bohemia ... Conscious of the privileges of his rank, he knew how to keep his distance from obtrusive people, but was also popular with his political opponents and ruled the land with skill and energy ... His sentiments were pro-German, but he was an enthusiastic supporter of German-Czech equalization.

> *When there were anti-Habsburg demonstrations in Bohemia in 1893 by the young Czechs, Thun-Hohenstein declared a state of emergency and brought things under control. When he found out that Hermine was the daughter of a Catholic, but raised without a religion he was anxious to see her converted.*

He was not only interested in the beautiful girl, but also in the lonely human being. I responded with warm feelings and confided in him.

Since the Catholic faith and its mysticism slumbered in my blood, I wanted to seek refuge in ... that church. Thun promised to have me instructed by a ... clergyman ... He wanted to be my godfather. I longed for a faith, for the consolation and support of religion ... Robert Browning ... compares the Semitic race with a strong Spanish wine which does not taste good when drunken pure, but ... when a few drops are mixed in another wine, gives it aroma and flavor. Bismarck advised that an Arabian mare be crossed with a Pomeranian stallion. And indeed people of mixed race are often gifted and unusual, although they may sometimes lack harmony.

My dual descent had the advantage that I could choose my company here and there, as I pleased—and since I never judge people according to status, religion or nationality, but according to their true value, I have found friends in all camps. It concerned me little that the governor was much older than I and socially my superior, . In my appearance, my education and my way of life, I was equal to any countess. Youth and beauty are an "open Sesame", a tragic formula which breaks open ... prejudices ...

> *Through Thun Hermine met many other members of the high nobility, which annoyed her grandmother, especially since people gossiped.*

I told grandmother about my plan [of converting to Catholicism]. Since she ... considered my having been raised without a faith wrong and had merely given in to her husband, she had nothing against my religion. But papa said: "I advise you to wait. Your character is so difficult that ... you will perhaps want a divorce. A Catholic marriage cannot be dissolved in Austria, you cannot remarry. ... "

His arguments seemed plausible to me, and I decided to wait with becoming Catholic.

In winter, I was introduced to society and attended the ... German balls. I was very popular, but was disappointed that none of the young gentlemen aroused my interest. Prague society was too narrow for me. Czechs and Germans lived in two hostile camps, like the Montecchis and the Capulettis in Verona. One knew each other by sight, but one did not greet each other. More Germans walked on the Graben, more Czechs on Ferdinand Street.[6].

Even school children fought over the nationality question. Fights between German fraternity students, among whom there were also many Jews, and the Sokols[7] were the order of the day.

Czech society, more obliging than the German, was still new and liked to accept educated Germans in their midst. But Germans tolerant toward Czechs were treated like turncoats by their own people. I was never allowed to go to the Czech theater; my Czech admirers ... had to be satisfied to walk up and down under my windows and to send me flowers anonymously. A marriage between members of the two nationalities was almost out of the question.

When I visited grandmama many years later, she found a little book and said: "Here is the name and address of a professor of the Czech university who asked your father for your hand. He was of course turned down!"

The German inscriptions on the street signs and the black and yellow mail boxes were ... painted red, which resulted in tragicomic friction, until the Czech majority won. The population was Czech, but for the most part knew German, while we educated Germans, to be sure, learned French, English and Italian, but only a little "kitchen" Czech. Instead of sticking together in order to ... have power as a majority, German society split up into castes. The high nobility which, associating with the court in Vienna, tried to speak Viennese, lived on the Lesser Side like on an island ... .

In the theater, the nobles ... ignored the bourgeois public ... they all were on first name terms and related. They were well groomed, spoiled. Aristocrats did fall in love with beauties of lesser birth, but they did not marry them ... the children of an unequal marriage were not received at court! The nobles—attractive, tall people with good manners and a superficial education, convinced of the superiority of their race and the privilege of their birth—had that natural, negligent charm which gains sympathies for the Austrians in the whole world ... .

A large part of German society consisted of Jews, with the older, educated ones staying apart from the lesser ones. Officially there was anti-Semitism, but there was mixing socially and in business. And since gradually there also were mixed marriages, the races became mixed, and often the strong Jewish sense of family won the Christian spouse over … . Not only near, but also more distant relatives found protection and help in the common nest … I remember the family that took in the child of the oldest daughter with gratitude … .

The Prague atmosphere oppressed me. I felt myself to be a citizen of the world, standing as an individual above disputes of race and nationality. … This uncanny quality of the old city, the stuffy air, unhealthy, sultry and threatening, the burden of the past! This centuries-old crowding, inbreeding of old families, this looking backward of an old culture! There are inherited diseases, nervous diseases and insanity in tainted families. …

The upward striving Czech element now hurried loudly to transform Prague into a modern metropolis, to banish the secret horror of the past from the loud present … .

Rilke … was a true son of "the city with the heartbeat", as Gustav Meyrink—who succumbed to its charm and in his *Golem* created a symbol of old Prague—expressed it. Franz Werfel, whose cradle stood at the shore of the Moldau, was deeply influenced by the strange mystique of his native city.

Theater played on important role in the cultural life of the city. The Czech National Theater, a splendid modern building at the quay of the Moldau, was distinguished by its … ballet and operatic performances. We however went only to the German theater where we had a box for each season. In the Theater of the Estates … where Mozart's *Don Juan* was first performed … the nobility had hereditary boxes.

Despite the general enthusiasm for theater, Hermine was strictly forbidden by her grandfather to associate with actors and actresses. When Hermine was nineteen, she realized that under Austrian law she would have to wait five more years before being of age and wanted to get married—temporarily—to speed up the process.

For this reason and for another which was not clear to me, I chose among my suitors the most inferior one, to whom I felt inwardly the least close, in order to leave him again without burdening my conscience when the purpose of this fictitious marriage was fulfilled. This unusual step cannot only be explained by my stubborn nature, but also by my upbringing which had done little to develop me emotionally. … Romantic and idealistic, I thought that the dissolution of such a marriage would be easy. I didn't think about the relationship between husband and wife. I wasn't going to give the unloved husband any rights over my body and mind, and was naive enough to think that a woman could only get a child from a man she loved … .

Theater of the Estates, built 1781-1783

Mr. Stöhr [as she called him] was forty-one years old, had a broad and heavy body and an ordinary face. He had no hair, dressed elegantly ... his education was deficient. He was considered well-to-do, had no profession, administered his houses, could be seen in the Variety Theater ... and in other places of amusement ... and was a man about town.

He approached me at a ball. Since he came from a lesser family, he wanted to gain access to good society through marriage ... He promised to travel with me most of the year, I was to enjoy my freedom and have all the dogs, horses, anything I wanted ... in the new life he was going to begin. I was to "ennoble" him. He extorted my "yes" in a weak hour and I soon regretted it ... .

Grandmama cried ... Papa was unhappy. All tried to keep me from that unfortunate step ... . The true subconscious reason only became clear to me later: it was the desire for sorrow.

One does not sin with impunity against the holy spirit of love. When I linked myself to that man, whom I did not respect ... I fell from light into darkness. ...

Since I did not make a secret of my lack of sympathy, Mr. Stöhr feared I would dissolve the engagement and pressed for an early marriage which took place in autumn in city hall. We went to Italy for several weeks, to the Riviera and to Paris ... I stayed away from him as much as possible, and he did not bother me.

He had been spoiled by women early. Oversaturated, aged early and worn out at forty, he was bored by the unaccustomed association with an educated young lady ... It sufficed for him to be envied his apparent possession ... . I wrote ... a fantastic story in which the heroine, an unhappy young woman on her honeymoon, throws her hated husband in the crater of Vesuvius ... . If Stöhr, who had enjoyed life ... and was a parasite of society, had one day died peacefully, I would have thanked fate ... .

After two months, we returned home and I found an elegantly furnished apartment in City Park ... I considered it only a temporary residence and not a home. I did not think of sleeping with this stranger and ... made no secret of [it] ... He again took up his accustomed life ... while I forgot the world over a book in my charming boudoir. ... My emotional life remained that of a young girl, but I had the freedom ... of a woman and disposed over any sums I wanted.

Of course, I misused my ... freedom. ... I went walking alone to my heart's content and rode on horseback, although that was then still considered "emancipated." I was one of the first ladies who bicycled in Prague ... . I wrote an article for the *Prager Tagblatt* "Let's Get Rid of the Fishbone" in which I rejected the corset and the long skirts and suggested short hairdos. I did not have the courage to cut off my long, heavy hair ... but I sent the corset to the devil, wore picturesquely designed dresses in the evening and put my gloveless arms on the railing of the box in the theater ... I wore socks ... Once when my skirt caught while I was leaving a carriage, my crime was revealed ... I was considered extravagant. ...

I laughed, nobody should know how miserable I felt ... I also kept silent at grandmama's ... where the aunts who were married in Prague sat around the ... table and spoke about their households and news from the city. ...

My housewifely skills were meager, but the efficient Czech cook and a smart chambermaid took care of everything so well that I could entertain guests. ... I had no women friends and preferred to associate with gentlemen.

Hermine consoled herself with her dogs, ran around outdoors, cried and begged her husband to give her a divorce. But he was satisfied to be envied his beautiful wife, and refused steadfastly.

Count Thun was as surprised by her marriage as everybody else, but gave her moral support which again resulted in much gossip.

The Czech-German question excited people so much, that the ... demonstrations and incidents of violence made the streets of Prague unsafe and the population was threatened by the insurgents ... martial law was proclaimed ... stores with German signs were plundered, windows were broken, the rabble penetrated into the houses of the bourgeois. ...

In the depth of my being love slumbered, like the sunken fairy-tale city Vineta resting at the bottom of the ocean. ...

In June, I went with Stöhr to Budapest to the Millenium Exposition ... When Géza bent over my hand to kiss it, I had to control myself not to embrace him—He was unchanged, only more masculine, but his dark, gentle child's eyes ... rested ... lovingly on me ... .

She believed that Géza loved her, but she felt that as a medical student he could not, or did not want to, step into her life.

A sultry summer day ... I can hardly breathe. I come back from a walk, sit down on a chair exhausted. ... And I feel how the dark, which has threatened me for a long time, descends and ... is about to destroy me. Suddenly I am paralyzed by the feeling of deathly cold, my blood ... stiffens. I want to get up, but I cannot; my left shoulder and arm are paralyzed, my legs limp, breathing causes a piercing pain ... .

Did I wait for minutes or for hours? The maid found me ... and carried me to bed. The doctor spoke of a one-sided paralysis, of pneumonia, of a nervous crisis and could find nothing definite. I lay for a few days with a high fever, without pain but breathing with difficulty.

In those feverish-clear sultry summer nights the animal in me broke and my soul awoke; from the animalic subconscious rose the conscious being of the spirit.

She continues writing in this vein, ending with]: I recognize the Pentecostal miracle of those blessed hours of suffering. There was nothing accidental about my life any more, since I had seen the great connection between me and the universe.

After a week, the paralysis and fever went away. The doctors did not understand my illness. [Hermine mentioned several times that it was strange she only met Baron Chlumecky relatively late, although they both had spent many holidays in Aussee. His friendship became the most valuable relationship of her life. When she met him, she saw an older gentleman, rather short, intelligent looking and with gray hair. He was the president of the House of Deputies, and a confidant of the Emperor].

What are a few decades ... compared with ... eternity? The true age of a person is not determined by the number of his years ... . The well of his youth was his kind heart, the warmth with which he embraced all of life, his ability to become absorbed in others.

He was the son of an Italian mother and of a poor Austrian official and owed his career to his intelligence and to hard work.

He was ... modern and although he believed in tradition, he took the side of progress and of the intellectual liberation of women. Extremely interested in music and art, he not only saw the young woman in me, but ... had an idea of my struggle for a higher form of life. He took me seriously ... and found ... talent in my early work ... .

We had breakfast together daily ... and walked through the deep pine forest ... Although I didn't talk about my marriage, he guessed ... how unhappy I was ... I felt at home with him, sheltered ... .

Suing for divorce, Mizzi lost the first and second round in court while living with her grandmother who meant well, but did not understand her. One day in court she saw a crucifix gleaming in the sunshine, which she understood as a sign that she would win in the end.

In a pension in Dresden, where she stayed between court hearings, she met Helen, an American-Irish woman who was to become a close friend. By way of contrast she remarked that the women in her world did not interest her because they were petty and envious.

My lawsuits took fifteen months. During that time I went to Munich in order to fulfill my favorite wish, learning how to draw. The city on the Isar became my second home. I knew nobody in Munich ... but in those freer circles people were used to seeing ... women alone ... The state painting academy was still closed to women, but the Association of Women Artists made up for that completely ... .

In Munich, I carried out a decision of long ago and took up religious instruction with a kind, enlightened old clergyman ... who answered my ... questions ... with loving tolerance ... My civil marriage was invalid to the pious Catholic ... "All your sins are forgiven, you are as innocent as a newborn child."

I ... promised to begin a better life. I never became a true believer in the meaning of the Church, [for that] it was too late ... My pantheism was stronger than the dogmas of the Church, and- I remained a wild heathen child with a fairy tale heart.

In summer, while visiting one of her aunts in Berlin, she was advised to hire a detective to spy on her husband. This led to proof of his infidelity, and she was able to get her divorce.

The whole city rejoiced in my victory ... My room was like a field of flowers. Chlumecky, Géza, all the old friends were happy ... I decided to stay in Munich ... and to continue my study of drawing ... I escaped from the decaying air of my home town burdened by its past ... .

Three decades ago, it was a disgrace to be a divorced woman. For men, she was easy prey, for women an object of scorn and gossip ... .

One stood outside ... But I have never paid much attention to the opinions of people.

Art ... I took it seriously and did not want to squander time with other things.

And all who had prophesied to me, that I would get into untenable situations and debt, that I would lead the life of an adventuress and go to the dogs, were thoroughly wrong and came to realize it. My crime consisted in my being ahead of my age ... The thirst for knowledge and independence, the desire to unfold my powers and talents, all that women are allowed now was considered a sin against the hallowed order ... .

Fate had not granted me the man whose wife I would have been happy to be and who complemented me. Four decades older than I, he was already married ... .

From my friend Géza, I received warm letters. I did not give up hope that one day we would find each other ...

Besides my painting which took up the whole morning and often also the evening, I attended courses for women, taught by university professors. That was not enough for my ambition ... Since I had not attended a gymnasium ... the hallowed halls of the university were closed to me.

She attended lectures in art history by the art historian Furtwängler, the father of the conductor, and referred to him as "that well-built man of noble German race." In Munich, Hermine met many interesting and famous people, such as Ludwig Thoma, Theodor Heine, Franz Stuck, von Kaulbach, von Defregger and Franz Lenbach who painted a portrait of her.

I was young, life lay before me. I called myself "Frau," but my feelings were those of a young girl. Thanks to the efforts of the Bohemian governor Count Coudenhove, I also could use my maiden name again. I only lived for my work and thought that the artist in me was winning over the woman. But I knew myself too well not to suspect that I was lacking something basic, and that I could find the secret of creativity only in passion. ...

The sensitive instrument of my senses, which a clumsy hand had touched without awakening it, was waiting for the artist who would produce sounds from it. ... [But] none of the pleasant young men who admired me appealed to me. ...

Chlumecky, her grandmother and her father all wanted to see her married, but she was still hoping for Géza.

Géza was deeply concerned about me ... He had completed his doctorate and we would have been well enough off for a simple livelihood. His family was fond of me, although they must have consid-

Hermine Hanel, drawing by Franz Lenbach

ered me extravagant ... My two dearest friends liked each other. Chlumecky said this attractive young man loves you, but he is afraid that your character and views of life are too different for a lasting bond ... My common sense told me to give Géza up ... I could not forget about him without bleeding to death ... .

She went to the Black Forest to see Géza again. His life was much quieter than hers; he took care of his father and practiced his beloved profession.

The differences between our natures had increased ... I would have been glad to adjust to his good and noble character, but ... he feared that he was not healthy and strong enough to tame the wild stormy bird ... Perhaps his love was not strong enough to overcome all hindrances ... "I shall always love you," said Géza, "I worry about you, don't get lost, it would be a pity—it would hurt me! ... "

It is not my nature to worry about what has been lost ... Perhaps I would soon have considered a ... bourgeois home a prison.

Mizzi took a trip to Paris and then moved to Vienna, to be close to Chlumecky, although she missed the easy, tolerant atmosphere of Munich. Again she met many interesting people, such a Johann Strauss, commenting:

I neither had time nor money to frequent high society and to waste my precious hours with gossip at boring ladies teas ... .

She worked in the studio of a painting school, attended anatomy classes and had small gatherings at her house which] included more men than women, because I have always felt closer to men than to women ... Shortly before ten the gentlemen left (her apartment), in order not to endanger my reputation. ...

Mizzi became acquainted with Artur Schnitzler[8] and they became very good friends.

To him I was not a sweet young thing ... he did not know where to place me. "You look like a woman who has reconquered her girlhood ... . You want to be everything at once, Messalina[9] and Gretchen[10], heroine and child, Sibylle[11] and fool ... you are not a woman at all. Böcklin[12] should paint you as one of his fairytale beings." He returned one of my novellas to me with these words ... "a good idea, simply put down without the slightest attempt to characterize, to provide

motives, indeed to write decent German. Often some genuine emotion, on the whole a strange mixture of the style of women's novels.
Genius, delusions of grandeur and dilettantism ... I don't think that
you are a poetic genius. You are very clever and don't want to be a
dilettante ... you have a long way to go ... I don't even know if you
are quite capable of going that road."

I read the letter with the crushing judgment ... I was dead serious
about art, and not knowing if I should become a painter or a writer, I
wanted to combine the two sisterly arts.

After my first work, *Lola*,[13] which appeared in a second edition ...
I had just written ... *Frauen* [Women] and a number of reviews about
... art, essays, travelogues, fairy tales and novels which were published
in Viennese, Prague and Munich papers under my real name. I did a
reading of fairy-tales in Prague after my divorce; the critiques were
positive, but my dress, my exterior were emphasized more than my
artistic achievement.

Who took a woman ... seriously, especially in Austria? ... Theodor
Heine, to whom I brought articles ... asked with a smile: "If one looks
like you, *gnädige Frau*, one doesn't need to work." He wanted to flatter me and I felt it as an insult.

Nobody understood my doubts ... Only my old friend understood
[the organic link between my life and my art.]

*Through his, Chlumecky's, mediation Mizzi also came into the circles around
the emperor*

My relationship with my family was excellent. The time had passed,
when I was pointed out to young ladies as a deterrent against extrav-
agance, and when papa was afraid that my younger sisters would imi-
tate me. My serious striving, my artistic success, my cordial relations
with outstanding people, my simple life and my orderly finances had
won me respect. They let me be an exception.

Papas wish for domestic daughters was not fulfilled, since my
younger sister studied natural science and the older painting. My kind
stepmother, who had many interests, always made my time [with
them] very pleasant.

Since three of my aunts ... were married in Vienna, I associated
with them. I visited grandmama ... every year ... [but] I had become
... a stranger to the Prague atmosphere. [Grandmama] ... used to
repeat: "Before I die, I would like to see you happily married". ...

I also felt the danger of giving oneself up to drives, of being
enslaved to sex, and aware of the ... heredity in my blood, I was on
my guard. ...

When she went to Prague for her grandmother's funeral, it was a cold, cloudless winter day

I go over the stone bridge ... under its wide arcs the frozen Moldau rests in its winter dress. ... On the other side the magic of the old street surrounds me. Between gray palaces with coats of arms and high churches I reach the wide, worn-out stone steps leading to the Hradschin. On both sides ... are poor little houses, humbly bowing like vassals and looking shyly up to the royal castle ... .

The wrinkled old woman still sits there under her mended, faded umbrella selling her apples, colorful sugar canes, wax candles and figures of saints as she has for years. With his war medal on his chest, the old invalid plays his hurdy-gurdy with its thin, whining tone. ...

After a fairly serious illness, Hermine spent an extended vacation in Northern Italy, in the house of an Italian painter and archaeologist. After her return, when she was hoping for a reunion with Géza, whom she still loved, he told her of his engagement, but assured her that he did not want to lose her. Her first pain however was followed by a feeling of relief

As in a difficult operation, my vital nerve was cut—but then I recovered ... . [His fiancée] was broad minded enough not to take something away from him that would have impoverished him, and we remained faithful to the love of our youth.

Mizzi intensified her correspondence with her American friend Helen, whom she describes as becoming a leader in the American women's movement

She is romantic, full of ideas, not at all American and dry, matter of fact. Her Irish blood is stronger than her North American utilitarianism. ...

I neither had the inclination nor the time to tie myself down. My studies were fulfilling ... I was too individualistic and too accustomed to freedom to subject myself to another will. And yet, although I had good friends, I often felt lonely after I lost Géza, and the thought of giving my love, my knowledge and my experience to a husband and to children took on clearer contours. ... The men in Vienna, with all their charm, seemed too feminine to me. A woman should lose herself to somebody stronger and not rule, but be ruled. ...

Among the men of my acquaintance, Hieronymus S. was the closest to me. He was taller than life size ... the only son of a major industrialist and of a member of parliament, a jurist, he had a leading position in a large bank, and was kind, modest and quiet, well educated, of good character ... He was seven years older than I. ...

Hieronymus was the right man for me in every way. Chlumecky, who valued him, also thought so. ...

He wrote me from Naples that he would enjoy nature and art much more with me ... I longed so much for sunshine and wired Hieronymus about my arrival. I thought that perhaps fate had destined this man for me and didn't want to miss the opportunity of becoming closer to him. ...

> *However, the trip on which she had set out with such great hopes, ended in disappointment. The son of a mother who had committed suicide, her friend came down with a serious mental illness and committed suicide himself several months later.*
>
> *Mizzi had other suitors, some of whom she recalls with mocking irony. She had a nostalgic visit at the country home of Géza and his young wife.*
>
> *She summarized how she dealt with ideas which were in the air in her time, how she wanted to see herself and how she thought others saw her at this stage of her life:*

In his famous book, *Geschlecht und Charakter* [Gender and Character], [Otto] Weininger has described women as only sexual creatures without character and designated the mother instinct as low sensuality. He perished because of his theory which has been disproven long ago. In many cases, he may be right, and it is equalizing justice if the masters of creation [i.e. men] who are only looking for female sexuality, only find a being that accommodates itself to their desires, yet can never be a pal for them and destroys them while they are having their pleasure.

Friendship between man and woman, such as that to which modern education and marriage aspire and in part have realized, was an unachievable ideal in my youth. There were only mistresses, wives, mothers, and housewives. Friendship between man and woman was misunderstood, the erotic *fluidum* ... the delicate intermediate steps were not recognized by the dull senses. ...

I, a young, desired and temperamental woman, found sincere friends because of my naturalness and honesty, my lack of coquetry. I never made men half-promises. Disdaining the clever tricks of females, I did not waste my love-capital in small coin. Love is not a parlor game, but a constructive and destructive natural force. I respected the feelings of others, even though I did not share them, and left them in no doubt about mine.

And if, despite a certain directness which did not flatter the vanity of others, despite my uncompromising love of truth, I gained sympathies, I owe this to my unselfishness and to my lack of calculation. I never sought the least outward advantage in a relationship and always judged people according to their inner value and not according to their position ... Since I felt that I belonged to no caste but to nature, it was easier for me to associate with people of different social strata and nationalities ... There were women more beautiful than I and certainly also much more elegant and charming, but few who were as sincere and as trustworthy ... my impulsiveness and my generosity, a certain cleanness of approach, all the masculine characteristics of a gentleman kept me from being happy as a woman. I was deeply sorry not to walk around in the world as a man. And yet I was a female with all nerves and senses, just not a comfortable little woman. ...

The view proclaimed by Freud and his followers, that the driving force of all feeling and action is erotic, has done much harm, and has confused the senses. Eros is a powerful god who controls life and represses all other feelings. A healthy woman can exclude her drives from her work just as a man can. Only an idle, hysterical woman is always under the power of Eros.

Hermine felt that Vienna was too decadent, seductive, superficial, sloppy.

I was tired of Vienna, as one longs for a stronger, simple diet after too many sweets and decided to leave the city that had been home to me for a few years. I had achieved much that I had hoped for ... If I had been dependent on my earnings, I perhaps would have concentrated on a certain area, but I followed my inclinations. I wrote for daily papers ... art reviews, essays, fairy tales and novellas, travelogues and sketches; picture books with texts suited me best, I had an affinity for animals and flowers ... .

And how did my works come about? Who can say? The secret of intellectual conception is unknown to the person who conceives ... . Impressions from childhood are inextinguishable, like in old tapestries the golden threads of childhood shimmer in the worn tissue of the past. The homey visual image of Prague, the romantic spots of the Bohemian city with the thousand towers ... lives in my memory. ...

My divorce and my artist's existence placed me outside the bourgeois world. I knew no prejudices and no prudishness. I did not think of tying myself down in marriage, but my development, my fate and my nature pointed toward motherhood.

After two more long, serious illnesses, during which she had much time to think about life, particularly her own—and after the death of her father—she was very much aware of her loneliness and realized that her activities had removed her far from housework, which never attracted her. But freedom had lost its charm, and loneliness oppressed her.

It is natural for a woman to create life, to preserve the species ... the strongest drive of any creature ... awoke in me and won out over con-

Hermine Hanel with two of her children

siderations of reason … Does a woman not lack the ultimate without motherhood? …

Every morning I walked past the villa which aroused my attention with its elegant, simple empire architecture … One day I had received a bouquet. I enjoyed the roses, but did not investigate who the anonymous giver was. Ten years later I met him … He was an architect, I a painter, both of us loved forms and senses. He was calm, I restless-foolish, he had blue eyes, I had dark ones. Nothing was alike, but opposites complement each other.

I advised him strongly against the daring plan [of marrying her]. He replied stubbornly: Am I not an architect who is supposed to build a house with a firm foundation … ?

I entrusted the rudder of the shaky ship of my life to this reliable man of good character. And I was not sorry.

Through my marriage with a Bavarian, whose family has belonged to the old Munich Catholic bourgeoisie for generations, [I] was not transplanted into foreign soil … a Southern Italian grandmother of my husband's has mixed [Italian] grape juice into Bavarian beer; together with my Austrian racial mixture this results in a strangely aromatic drink.

And what came out of this unequal union?

A girl and two boys. Dark won out. My children look at the world with their mother's dark eyes.

A woman wants to be treated like a child, with strictness and kindness and tenderness. Commanded at the right time and fondled at the right time, with a strong will and delicate feeling, she wants to feel as the child of a man, to feel young and in need of protection is the highest fulfillment for a woman. ...

My beloved children are my greatest possession. I am happy [with them] and ... I experience my own youth with them. ...

The recent past has not only transformed my personal life, it has also overthrown tradition, social concepts and customs. ... The world has changed, as have values. War and its spiritual consequences ... darkened our existence.

I just would like to say one more thing before I break off the story of my life: marriage and motherhood are not enough for an artistic woman. Love and art spring from the same source and cannot be separated. ... Physical and spiritual fertility complement each other. I have created my best works as a mature woman ... My romantic-imaginative nature ... the racial mixture of my origin, the light and darkness of the old city where past and present are mysteriously interwoven influenced [my] character and fate ... . I look from the mountain of memory over the great valley ... of the landscape of my life ... the small uneven spots have disappeared ... .

NOTES

1. Emmy von Rhoden, *Der Trotzkopf; eine Pensionsgeschichte für junge Mädchen*, in numerous editions and still published today.
2. An ancient tower, associated with numerous legends.
3. Gustav Nieritz and Franz Hoffmann, popular writers of novels for young people.
4. Theorist of racism and an acknowledge precursor of Nazi ideology.
5. i.e. Prague.
6. More Germans on the Graben, which is Příkopy in Czech, and more Czechs on Ferdinand Street, which is Národní in Czech.
7. See the general introduction, footnote seven.
8. A Viennese writer (1862-1931).
9. A Roman Empress, wife of Emperor Claudius, known for her licentious life and greed.
10. The innocent heroine of Goethe's *Faust*.
11. A Roman prophetess.
12. Arnold Böcklin (1827-1901), a Swiss Romantic painter.
13. I have not been able to find this or any of her other published books in any reference works.

Chapter 7

GISA PICKOVÁ-SAUDKOVÁ

(1883–1944)

G isa Picková-Saudková, living at the heyday of the Czech-Jewish movement, emphatically identified with it. She is the only Czech-Jewish woman of her time who left a written record suitable for our purposes. Although this record, her diary, which is in the Kolín city archives, is somewhat fictionalized, I decided to base a chapter on it because it covers some essential concerns very clearly.

Gisa Picková-Saudková was born in Kolín in 1883 into the family of a Jewish businessman. She attended school there and audited classes in literature, philosophy, history and art history at the Czech university in Prague. In the Kolín town directory of 1934 she is listed, along with her daughter Jiřina and her son Pavel, as a writer and journalist. Kolín, with 455 Jews, was then the second largest Jewish community in Bohemia.

In 1929 Picková-Saudková published her conversations with Otakar Březina, the most famous Czech poet of the time[1]. In this book she notes: "I lived in Jaroměřice[2] from 1911 until 1925, when my husband died and I moved to Kolín. But I still traveled from there to continue visiting the Master in Jaroměřice ... only later did I begin to take down the whole flow of his speech, as I remembered it. My life circumstances were not always favorable to such tasks." What she wrote there about her husband constitutes all the information we have about him: "26 August 1914. The Master remembers my husband, who is doing war service at the front as a veterinary, and he says he is one of the best people he knows. `And one must value goodness as much as genius, it is equally a gift from God ... it is something absolute like musicality or a gift for painting. ... Wherever my husband sees any need, he helps, and he is sensitive to the primitive suffering of man.'"

Our only other source of information about Picková-Saudková's life was provided by the Kolín archives and will follow my condensation of her diary. I first learned about its existence from Helen Epstein, the author of Children of the Holocaust.[3] Her maternal grandmother grew up in Kolín and considered Gisa her best friend. We can only guess if she was the friend called Zdenka in the diary.

Kolín Cathedral

I have shortened this diary to about one-tenth its original length, omitting many lyrical passages about nature and also Picková-Saudková's descriptions of places and people which did not directly affect her life.

22 September 1896 My brother Vilém has brought me this little note-book and told me to write down what strikes me … what I think … . This fall I started going to middle school … . It's different than the Jewish school where we had twisted, wooden steps, and it was hot and dark. Here there are wide hallways, and huge, bright, clean rooms … .

28 September 1896 I like going to this school, there's more variety than in the Jewish school. Only that crucifix in the classroom makes

me uncomfortable, seeing Jesus Christ spread out his arms. Are the Jews really guilty of his death? … I'm so glad I don't have to go to Jewish school any more, or cross the street with school books on Sundays. When the boys saw us … they'd shout: "Jews, you killed Jesus Christ!" When I was little, our nursemaids took us past the monastery cross and we kissed it too … . If our ancestors had joined Christ in the beginning, I'd be shouting after the other children now. I once asked father about it, but he only said no one really knows anything about that time … . Before the first and last classes we pray, but we Jewish girls don't have to, and I don't even want to. I would like to go berry-picking with the other girls, but I wouldn't tell them for anything. In some subjects we don't really learn very much here, we Jewish girls already know it … . I would like to know things like how the people in the Middle Ages could have

Jewish school in Kolín

been given such cruel punishment, and why they put up with it … why it doesn't happen now … .

3 March 1897 … I think I could understand other people better if I had some daily contact with them, rather than just wondering about them and our differences … . I blame my parents for not mingling … .

21 April 1897 I like our garden, the smell after a rain, the butterflies … . I wonder how others experience nature. They say Jews have no feeling for nature. Yesterday Dad told us he was walking to the factory … when a woman stopped him and said: "Don't hurry so to your factory! Look around you at the beautiful spring!" … She didn't say that for nothing. I have to listen when my Catholic classmates are talking about nature and see if it sounds different from what I think.

It's strange, but every village I've seen has a single little store and it's Jewish, even our town has one Jewish store next to the other. I wouldn't have noticed it … but once our Sokol[4] had visitors and they were shown around town. The store signs in the town square were pointed out, the names pronounced one after the other, each a German, Jewish name. Did they [the Czechs] want things to be different? They don't want to be shopkeepers themselves, but they blame us for doing business. I would like my father to be something else, maybe a doctor, or a farmer, with only enough for ourselves and nothing to sell. The Jews should be pitied because they have to do this trading, but instead everybody laughs at them because they're smart and afraid of everybody. What would I become, if girls could study at the gymnasium?[5]

3 June 1897 I was at the Pivoňkas'[6] … When I came, Anča was scrubbing the floor. They don't have a maid and we have two. Barča wakes me up in the morning, passes me my underwear, brings me my breakfast. I'm sure Anča does it all herself … . Maybe this is why people don't like Jews … . I would like us to not be different. We let others do our work, but I'd like to kneel down and scrub too. Meanwhile Anča's mother sewed her a skirt … . I'd like to be able to iron and sew and not need anyone else. I don't even have a … mother tongue! Why don't my parents let us be Czech? Everything around us is Czech, but we … are Jews, and even … Germans! … I try to think in Czech, but I don't always manage.

8 June 1897 … When I look at my mother and other people, I see her isolated from them even though she mixes with them and does a fair amount for them … . But I don't want to be separate, I want to belong to "the people."

24 June 1897 I am often told: "You should have been a boy". I wish I were. Only a man's life is really a life. And we Jews? We're condemmed to being outsiders everywhere.

12 September 1897 Miss Skřivanová explained how a landscape creates people in harmony with itself … . Then why are we Jews different? We've lived here a long time … . The teacher Vedenková is nasty to me, to all of us Jewish girls. Today is Saturday. She asked me to pick up something from the floor, then immediately corrected herself … . "Forgive me, Dubová,[7] I always forget you don't do anything on Saturdays!" She has done that a number of times. I would like to write on Saturdays, but the other Jewish girls would think I'm a traitor. It's stupid for us to always be different … . I'll drill myself in Czech and learn to speak like a professor, or like a villager!

6 December 1897 St. Nicholas' day! … I wish I had a mother who sews for her children, cooks, irons and tells fairy-tales. I think the pure native language breathes on children from these fairy-tales … .

17 December 1897 … Vilém asked me if I believe in God. Of course I told him one cannot believe. Why should I believe what our rabbi preaches and not what the priest tells my classmates? "Then what do you believe?" I answered, "Nothing." He became very angry, I've never seen him so furious. "So it's nothing! The whole world is there for nothing!" Vilém is not burdened by Judaism. He does not pull at his roots as I do. He's so unshakeably firm.

27 December 1897 Christmas Eve is over. We don't have a tree, but the mood is solemn and special … . Only the girls in the kitchen received gifts … . Mother had found out what each one wanted, and she set the kitchen table for them with a table cloth and placed their gifts next to the Christmas pastry … .

People are afraid; father and the boys seem excited too, and I feel the stuffy atmosphere in the street. In Prague there is looting, martial law … and it seems to have something to do with us Jews. Father isn't involved in politics, he just reads about it. I don't understand. Why are we blamed when we just put up with what others do? We don't make the decisions.

Ota[8] asked father if he had always followed events from his sofa, even in his youth. "Don't you sometimes feel like having an influence on things?" he asked him. "No matter what a Jew does" father quoted from somewhere,[9] "the Jew is to be burned." … " Since we are always beaten, everybody should just take care of … his own business, his family." Ota did not agree: "It doesn't take much to stand aside." Father answered that the Czechs don't even want Jews to join them. They treat politics like … religion, and just as we don't like to see others in church [sic i.e. synagogue], … Czechs don't want Jews in their politics. Ota … then tried to convince father to join the Jewish national movement, but father became angry: "That's all we need, for us to claim we don't belong here! I belong here as much as anybody. Our family has lived here for over three hundred years. … " I know we Jews should renew our own national life, but I can't … go backward, and I don't want to. I must go where my heart draws me. I won't try to convince anybody to do the same, but I've already pledged my soul … .

Later Father complained about women and especially about mother paying so much attention to clothes. Mother defended herself, saying all women do so, the only differences between them are their means and taste. I think this is only partly true. When I go to market, the Jewish ladies are always dressed up … while the Christian women wear everyday clothes and carry big bags, and perhaps a goose under their arm. Jewish women take along maids and don't carry anything.

27 December 1897 So I'm going to be thirteen, and I still don't know anything. Are there people who can follow everything? That isn't possible. I'm going to amount to nothing, nothing at all. Imagine, I only have seven more years till I'm twenty. That's when Jewish girls marry. But I won't. I can't even imagine it … .

28 December 1897 … One day I'll have to read the Bible. I'll be glad to read the New Testament without any explanation from priests, glad nobody taught me about Christianity so I can explain it to myself. It will be as if I am living in the time of Jesus and listening to his teaching myself. It must have been beautiful to live then. To experience something great!

20 March 1898 Today I was at Miss Malátová's.[10] She is sick and wasn't at school. I bought her roses … . I wondered if she would be annoyed, but I had to know if she was very sick. I stood on her porch a long time before I dared knock. She opened up … all wrapped in shawls … . It was not the Miss Malátová whom I had imagined living in a beautiful … room. Her place looks poor, there's only a music corner with a piano, a violin, and a lot of sheet music. Still she is wonderful and I shall love her to the day I die.

15 June 1898 Now I know, it is terrible. How is it possible? If it is true, then I don't know what life is about and what it means for a man and woman to love each other. Does this go with "love"? No matter how much I loved a man, I still couldn't … no. And if he loved me, could he ask that of me? There must be something about it all I don't understand. Who will explain it to me?

Poor Růženka Malátová! They say there is going to be a disciplinary investigation. And men to investigate that! Perhaps it can't be true, they say a state policeman used … to visit her. My beautiful, golden-haired, blue-eyed Růženka Malátová, and a policeman who deals with thieves … . Surely she won't marry a policeman, yet another won't marry her … after this! And she is not to be allowed back in school because she could be a bad influence on us … . It is terrible … . I shall go right now and kiss her hand so that she knows I'm on her side. But where can I see her? My golden, dear, beloved. Such a pity! …

15 June 1899 Miss Skřivanová … asked me … what I'm going to do when I finish school. I don't know yet. Recently Mother mentioned they might hire a German governess for me. I shall really fight that! I told Miss Skřivanová, I'd like to continue studying all subjects, especially physics and chemistry. But I also want to study literature. First I'd read the main works of all nations and then Czech literature to see how it fits in with the others. Miss Skřivanová only shook her head and said: "It's a shame about you, you're gifted." Why is it a shame? It seemed as if she wanted to say: "There is an immovable rock here." … It bothers me … .

30 June 1899 There *is* a girls' gymnasium … . It would be wonderful to go there, but my parents won't let me. We … only have one student: Vilém. They won't let me, a girl, be a student as well.

5 July 1899 Last night I heard shouting in [my parents'] bedroom. First mother: "You can't order the kind of children you want, you have to take them as they come." That means me. And father: "A man hasn't been born yet who wants a wife smarter than himself." The result is, I can forget about Minerva.[11] …

This morning mother told me Minerva is only an experiment and all humoristic magazines make fun of women who are "blue stockings". They want me to be a well educated girl, able some day to be in charge of a nice household, able to understand her husband's profession a bit … . I'm supposed to be educated for some man I don't even know, God only knows what he'll be like … . Where would I find a man meant just for me, a man I could say was born … just

Elbe river near Kolín

for me … that I grew up just for him? What a miracle it would be for me to meet just this man in this wide world!

In the book by Sienkiewicz Ervín gave me, it says: "I am even sceptical of my scepticism." I like that idea, to hesitate about one's judgement … . In the end I agreed to stay home and take lessons … .

5 August 1899 Today I was all alone in the water. I swam far out into the current, the whole island stayed behind me. The birds flew over the water, dipped down and drank while flying, then rose up high again and the air shone with silver. I felt wonderful alone in the water.

In the afternoon I often sit in a canoe on the river, or alone with Zdenka Samková. Zdenka is Jewish, but she never went to Jewish school. I don't even think she knows German … . In the evening I can't stand being home. Zdenka picks me up and we go … out.

15 November 1899 Well, I've been having private lessons now for several months, but I question their worth. The lessons are always the same tight, closed circle I sought to escape, always science for every-day use, while I yearn for something beyond, a real science I suspect behind what I'm learning, but which … I can't find by myself. What do I need mythology for? …

The classes where I meet the boys are the best … . Sometimes they speak to me like to a serious, adult person, or as if I were a boy, and I like that best. They tell me about books … pictures, events. They're Jewish boys, I would like to know what Christian boys are like. Viktor Weiss is already a law student. Ervín Fuchs lends me books. He brought me Hamsun's *Good Earth*, Viktor brought me *The Strong Man* by Przybyczewski. Both … deal with artists and the … fall and ruin of pure girls, and each time a writer is guilty. Did the boys guess that from the depth of my soul I long to know … people who create? Actually nothing interests me except what takes place in man. It always seems to me that we can only ever understand ourselves … we try to capture the other in vain … .

21 February 1905 Today I'll start writing again, on my 19th birthday … . I'm curious to know what will become of me.

Sometimes I imagine myself conversing with a stranger, well, not a complete stranger, a young man I meet out in the street. From the very beginning … our glances merged meaningfully, an unforgetable, beautiful glance. Blue eyes—the miracle of blue eyes! The last time he greeted me … his eyes drowned in mine, it captured my heart and my hands … trembled … . Was that ecstasy? … But it's more like a pain I would like to feel … constantly! … I don't even wish to … know him better … I only want to gaze into those blue eyes.

At noon today I was on the ice, alone. The river was frozen and I went skating on it. The ice was like a mirror, the sun warm. The frost sparkled on the trees, and I, completely alone in this ... white world. What sweet quiet loneliness! Not to be mirrored in anyone ... . What freedom! Sliding on the ice limited only by the rhythm of my own breath. Thus I would wish to glide through life, carried along by the current of public life, in harmony with it, free and yet part of the whole.

28 February 1905 Will I ever find peace in the womb of that nation ... greeting me, calling me, welcoming me from those blue eyes of that stranger?

28 May 1905 That Ervín Fuchs! He wants to give up the Jewish religion, even change his ... name. He's an enthusiastic Czech nationalist ... . I almost envy him his determination, but I cannot agree with him ... . There is something unhealthy, forced, extreme about it ... . To love one's country, that's alright. But why with passion? We love our native country naturally, as one loves siblings ... simply. Ervín does seem strange to me, always so dissatisfied ... . I couldn't live if I did not believe in man ... . It's not enough for him to leave the Jewish community and to change his name, he also wants to be baptized. I shivered at the thought of accepting baptism and not believing ... . "Do you think it's going to help you to merge with the others?" I asked. "For that you'd have to be imbued with Catholicism, experience what ... the others have experienced since childhood ... . I don't believe in our religion any more either, but I'll stay a Jew. Our Ota says there's such beauty in Jewish history and literature that a Jew who renounces it is a fool. It's our duty ... to learn about it before we renounce it."

I cannot get used to not thinking ... in German.

23 November 1905 A little crowd of boys, students and young doctors were discussing the demonstrations for universal suffrage. Viktor saw me and shouted: "Here is Miss Dubová, she surely will go with us, she's a great admirer of Masaryk!" ...

He has no idea how I hate to expose myself!

28 November 1905 The demonstrations are over ... . Of the well-to-do, only the young joined the march. I walked with my blond friend Zdenka ... so we were not too noticeable. Two black haired Jews would have been conspicuous ... .

Suddenly after the last speaker had spoken ... and the lines began thinning out, a woman's voice ... shouted out right behind me: " ... Let's attack the Jews!" My heart stopped ... more and more voices joined in ... . Wild glances, furious gestures. Why go after the Jews?

A fair number were even in the demonstration! ... I was terribly sad. Zdenka ... wanted to disappear. I held her back, let them see we are a part of them! ... Who will convince the people that we're not their enemies? ... I have to become involved, but I don't have any concrete idea how ... .

18 December 1905 Mother was not well today. Since Dr. Stern wasn't home, Dr. Šimůnek ... took his place. I told him I had heard him speak in front of City Hall, and he invited me to come to the Realistic Club, offering to introduce me. The Realists in our town, as far as I can tell, are not exactly "the people," but they will be good for a start. Once in a while Dr. Šimůnek used the expression "detailed work, Masaryk demands detailed work." ... Perhaps I'll meet "the people" in "detailed work" ... . In myself I find little that would be of use.

18 December 1905 They say a "single"[12] girl. That I am, but with very little freedom. Viktor Weiss stopped me on the promenade this evening, and laughed when I told him I have to be at supper at six. So I stayed, and it resulted in a terrible fuss at home ... .

20 February 1906 Twenty years old. I have no romantic feeling for dates, but that date reminds me I must create my life more clearly. Will I succeed this year? ...

21 February 1906 The first to congratulate me were our two girls. They also brought me a bouquet ... and could think of no better wish than that I should become a bride this year ... .

I celebrated my birthday by taking a beautiful, long walk across the Elbe into the quiet, wintery forest ... . I remembered walking there last with Viktor Weiss. Could I marry Viktor or Ervín? Never! Viktor and I have been friends since childhood ... . I know him too well to love him. Dark-haired, dark-eyed! Impossible ... .

He is even considering becoming a partner in the Kraus margarine factory on the condition he marry the boss's daughter ... . "Do you need to sell yourself? Is that why you went to university?" I actually screamed ... . And Ervín! Our maids think I could marry him ... a man who does not believe in mankind. Ervín was pleased I had asked for the books he recommended ... and so enthusiastic about Meier-Graefe's study of van Gogh ... .

I want to be liked, but not by everybody. When I notice the glance of a man in the street, I want ... to be invisible ... I want to be loved for what I am, not for how I look ... .

I always hope the days will not go by without something happening ... . My birthday was full of events and full of thoughts ... but it did not end happily. I feel sad. The problem of what to make of my life is overwhelming. What should I live for?

24 February 1906 I was at the funeral of old Dr. Stern, and saw his son there. I cannot forget the sight of that grief stricken young man. That broken figure seemed like a tomb stone—the symbol of Jewish mourning—his oval face greenish and bloodless, the eyes like black almonds and thick, red lips ... I wrote him ... Why do I feel so sorry for a man I only saw once?

5 March 1906 Today docent Dr. Stern came to see us ... to thank my mother for having cared for his father in his illness, and to thank me as well for my letter which "was very precious to him" ... .

He told me he was writing a work on the essential character of the Jewish nation ... about what remains after the influence of neighboring nations, occupation, climate, etc. are discarded, about what has always distinguished us from the surrounding nations and will eternally distinguish us. How many thoughts ... popped into my head! I showered him with questions ... . Did he mean physical and mental characteristics? How can one determine if the two are connected? "You are working on a difficult, complicated problem," I said. "There will have to be a poet at work beside the scholar, although of course only a scientific treatment can have real value."

He answered: "What you have just said is itself a valuable document for me! Look, by chance I meet a girl and in one sentence I tell her what I'm working on ... . I don't know many Christian girls, only a few Viennese, and no Czech ones, but I can't imagine a single one of them reacting just as you did. To us Jews, thinking is not suffering ... it's a need and it delights us." When I asked about his colleagues, he answered: "I have lost my best collaborator, my father ... ."

I never felt such pity for anyone ... To my own surprise I suddenly put my hand on his thin, pale fingers. He looked at me in surprise and I, shocked by my own boldness, quickly withdrew my hand. We both blushed ... .

"One single collaborator would be enough for me," he said, looking into my eyes, "you would be better than any ... ."

"Would it be possible for me to work here while you are in Vienna?" ...

"I know", he continued, "I cannot hope for you to return with me, although I shall long for it. But I will write ... thinking of you." ...

"I would be very grateful if you would teach me to work scientifically," I answered.

It seems he fell in love ... so I should really distance myself ... but instead I agreed to correspond ... come what may. Even suffering. At least I will be living—finally living!

God, how oppressive four walls are! I have to get out, as mother does, and walk in the fields ... where the snow has thawed.

5 March 1906 As soon as I went outside, I could not for the life of me recall Dr. Stern's face ... . I turned the corner and suddenly "my blue eyes" appeared ... as always he immersed his glance deeply into my eyes, and I responded by bowing equally seriously. I know we shall never be introduced ... .

In the evening on the promenade, I met Ervín Fuchs: " ... So they picked Dr. Stern to be your husband? ... That's not your world! A sight from the ghetto."

"A noble sight," I interrupted, although I knew that he was right ... .

"But we, you and I, have left it. Our world is elsewhere. I need you, Selma, next to me!"

My God, what do I do with this love, too? I do not want it. I wanted so much to be loved ... . Where in the world is someone who corresponds to my need? ... Stern and Ervín both think I am their other pole, but what do I feel? Ervín said: "You must not stay in the narrow ... Jewish environment. You need to go out into the world. I often think even the Czech environment is too narrow for you, that you should go farther, perhaps to Paris." My friend understands me pretty well, but I could never convince father ... . His daughter must get married, have children, obey her husband ... .

13 March 1906 Today Dr. Stern came to say good-bye. It seems he has understood ... I am only interested in the work ... .

When he said "Just think about how many languages our nation has passed through! ... " something stirred in my heart at the words "our nation." Where are you leading me, Dr. Stern? ... Backwards, to where I came from? ... If I come to feel the Jewish nation is mine, will I stop longing for my "blue eyes?"

The idea of innate characteristics only seemed possible to me if one believed in a theory of race ... . "I don't know if the Jewish nation is a race," he said, "but they are a nation ... . Through thousands of years of association with God this nation has arrived at a code to live by ... ." I was so afraid of Jehova as a child. Something petrified, cold rose up before me, while at the same time I realized that this young Jewish scholar, my new friend, feels this thousand-year-old process in his veins. I should tell him ... "I cannot work with you ... your spirit is foreign to me." But I did not ... . "Don't you sometimes go to

Vienna?" he asked. I have an invitation from my aunt ... and would like to see Vienna, but I find my aunt and uncle hard to take.

22 March 1906 Dr. Stern demonstrates his types by several historic personalities who have ... spoken sincerely about their ... inclinations ... . It is too bad my friend only applies his theories to the intellectual history of the Jews. Those sentimental and melancholy Jewish figures! Others ... go through life militantly, Havlíček with humor, Palacký and Masaryk with realism! ... The Jews lack everything I like in the Czechs ... .

I am looking forward to Vienna, to Dr. Stern, to Vilém.

30 March 1906 Mother wants me to be a lady ... . It is better to remain a modest girl ... simply dressed ... and to become a thinking, acting individual ... . Despite all my striving for genuineness I am not without ambiguity.

In Vienna, 6 April 1906 Vilém was impressed that a scholar of such reputation, the pride of the Jews of Vienna, came to see me ... Wherever a Jew becomes famous, all of Jewry declares him as its son ... Wherever a Jewish scoundrel appears, we are all forced to adopt him.

"Do you love him?" Vilém asked me suddenly. "No!" I replied ... . "Then you shouldn't have become involved." I felt he was right ... . We sent Dr. Stern a card and invited him to Vilém's for the next day ... .

When I get older, I fear I won't be very different than Mother. I see more and more things in myself that I criticize in her.

Being the hostess, I couldn't really follow the men's conversation ... . They talked about Freud, Vilém applying his theories to the diseases of whole nations.

I don't know what got into me: when Dr. Stern was taking leave, I handed him the flower from his place setting. He blushed in surprise and I did also ... . When we reached my relatives' house ... his lips remained on my hand longer than politeness required. I don't recognize myself, I am flirting ... .

13 April 1906 I cannot walk into a Catholic church without feeling that I am desecrating something. The consciousness that ... I am not putting my finger in the holy water, don't kneel down, don't make the sign of the cross ... depresses me ... .

Uncle, that stupid, dirty old man, is he crazy? He came to see me this morning ... . He looked so strange and suddenly he reached into the neck opening of my housecoat. It was so terrible I sometimes think it didn't happen. What am I going to do? I cannot stay here, but how am I going to explain leaving to my aunt? ... I cannot tell my parents either ... . Only the Elbe could wash off that dirt ... . Father complains when I go out with my "boys." He is afraid that I may be corrupted, and sends me to be brought up by my old relatives ... .

17 April 1906 When I go for a walk with Vilém, with Stern, I like to window-shop, to see Klimt's pictures with their soft lines and sweet colors, or Copenhagen china ... . But today I feel a revulsion for it all, everything in this frivolous city is mere vanity ... for play, for sin, and sounds like an uncouth hit song for that red-cheeked old man with the shiny bald head ... . I never knew how nice and clean home is!

In Vienna, 19 April 1906 The improbable has happened. We were together in Schönbrunn. I realized that my own fate was being decided, that I could not escape ... . Was it because he freed me from the oppressive environment ... of my relatives? I gave in to my fate like a weak blade of grass swimming on the river.

"You say you will not stay in Vienna much longer," he said. "Therefore I am going to risk everything and ask if the idea of becoming my wife would be terrible for you?" "Terrible surely not" I said with conviction ... . I did not dare to look at his unusual, asymetrical face, afraid of feeling the extreme distance which separates me from every man and from this one especially ... . I wanted to hold on to the illusion that I had found ... a man for life, a task for myself, and a love that would eventually come. In the corner of my heart I suddenly heard protest ... . I said: " ... Doctor ... I do not live a Jewish life, but I could work with you. For years I have been preparing to live with the Czech nation." ... To my amazement he did not try to argue and said he would put no obstacles in my way. "You can work for the Czech cause in Vienna, I myself can introduce you to Czech intellectuals ... . Only one thing would be necessary: that you be fond of me." ... Again I felt sorry for him, and I knew that I would lose him forever if I now said no.

"I am fond of you, Doctor." "So, do I get a kiss, Miss Selma?"— "Rather my word, Doctor," I stuttered. I took his hand, I pressed it to my heart ... .

I am no longer alone, I have found my other. Why do I doubt it? ... Is he not a scholar, a philosopher? And he loves me ... . What more ... could I ask for? ...

The day after tomorrow I am going home ... . My fiancé, Rafael— I shall have to get used to that high-class name—will join me on Sunday ... . I am not looking forward to it, but my parents will be happy ... . Father will say: "I have betrothed my daughter." Somebody, a force beyond myself betrothed this daughter, not I.

22 April 1906 He kissed me in front of my aunt and uncle and Vilém ... long and violently on my mouth. His beard was damp and both-

ered me. What does such a man think? That he has ... a humble little Jewish fiancée? ...

He obeyed my request and said nothing to my uncle and aunt, but one could see it on him a hundred miles away. He brought me beautiful red roses, white ones for my aunt ... . It seems to me that ... a little pink now shines through his olive skin ... . To know I caused that makes me proud and happy. Does he know, do I know what is in store for us? ...

I took a two-hour walk with my fiancé, and yet we came no closer to each other ... .

Estranged, I take a walk in the fields back home ... my soul uprooted ... the blue-eyes have come to me, but too late.

In Brno, a traveler entered my train compartment, my other pole, the man destined for me since eternity. It was as if we had known each other forever, that we belonged to each other. His first words, in a pleasing, soft voice opened my heart wide ... . He is a poet, I know his modern, sweet lyrical poetry ... . We have promised each other to meet in Prague ... . When we parted he embraced me ... kissed me sweetly, it seemed so natural.

I asked him for a photograph. And then, quietly and looking guilty, he said: I cannot ... child, I am married ... .

Dr. Stern is coming on Sunday ... . I never knew life could be so difficult ... . Or does fate adapt to us? Do simple people experience simple, transparent happiness, and only we complicated people have nothing but knots to untie? The spade has dug deep under my roots and I am staggering ... uprooted. I constantly hear my blond, blue eyed song of spring in my heart ... .

My parents buy me clothes, complete my dowry, are burning to set the date. They do not suspect how far I am from marriage ... . I am actually happy, I even spent a beautiful day with Rafael ... . How sensitive he is! He does not ask me about anything ... . I would never have thought it possible to love someone while tolerating the love of another ... . Driven by wind and storms, we yearn to take root firmly and grow into heaven ... .

Whenever I used to meet a new person, the most important thing to me were the insights he gave me. My only memory of Jaromír is his appearance, the tone of his voice, how sweetly he spoke to me, and his embrace. I hope it never evaporates from my senses, sometimes I fear it won't last ... .

6 May 1906 Is it possible that he does not remember me? ... He is married, but he could still write ... . A letter comes from Rafael every day

... . The longing cannot be stifled ... Jaromír ... . I am going to Prague ... . He is not free, but that is no reason to avoid each other for the rest of our life!

8 May 1906 There is nothing but love! I love him, Jaromír loves me! ...

ll May 1906 I went to Prague to gain clarity. I have brought back even more confusion. Extreme happiness ... and pain ... .

Tomorrow Rafael wants to come ... . If his love could only evaporate! ... And my parents ... what will they say? It will be unbearable. Jaromír does not write ... . We sat together on the Nebozízek[12]and I saw him whispering something to the waiter. Then he asked me to go inside ... to a nice little room there ... . Something in me said not to go. He could not have had bad intentions and he did not press further. Perhaps he was afraid of being recognized ... and just wanted to be alone with me. If I could look into his soul and gain certainty! ... I believe he feels he has met his fate in me ... . But why does he not write?

When he accompanied me to the station, I suddenly realized I had to tell him I am going to be married and will move to Vienna. He said: "So we won't be loving each other long." It was not the answer I had expected.

13 May 1906 I allowed Rafael to come. He brought me a beautiful gift, an old Vienna set of coffee silver ... . I was sad ... . I am fond of Rafael as of a dear brother and I don't want to hurt him ... . I torture myself with the question ... of my guilt ... . I first wrote to him ... so that my days would not be empty ... . If Rafael were poor and miserable, I would feel obliged to stay with him ... . Loving Jaromír, I simply cannot marry Rafael ... . I look ahead ... I do not want to collect the fruits of an ancient tree [Jewry] ... . There is only one fidelity, to oneself.

14 May 1906 Rafael suspects something. He writes of a shadow between us ... . How will I tell him?

My mission in life, to console, to strengthen, to work beside a creative man, what is happening to it? My heart aches ... .

20 May 1906 I had a talk with mother ... . I told her ... there won't be a wedding. Poor mother believes I am throwing away my happiness. I told her only half the truth, I could not tell her the other half, Jaromír, a Catholic, married, a Czech poet! I could be unhappy with anybody else, but Dr. Stern has the right to make a woman happy. Mother sensed something and said several times ... "except if you love somebody else ... ." She promised to fix everything with father ... . "We have to avoid a scandal." Selma stays engaged, but to somebody else! To her ... father and his feelings remain uppermost. Why

are we tied to parents, why do they feel our lives are theirs? ... Sunday, 26 May 1906 Rafael left ... . To see a man cry is unbearable! I cannot listen to him without pain ... . He is closer to me at this moment than Jaromír. What do I know of him? He insults me, I do not hear from him ... .

Monday, 27 May 1906 The worst moment was when Rafael asked for forgiveness ... . He said he should have given me up ... . My heart aches for him as well, I shall never forget him, I hope some time in my life I can do something for him ... . He asked if we have to part. [she answered] "If, my dear, you could modify your present feelings into friendship ... if you can do that, then come!" ... He has been good for my life. I don't know if the other one will be ... .

27 May 1906, evening Jaromír advised me to register at the Philosophy Department ... as an auditor ... . He would never understand my father's views ... . A girl is in the world to get married! Father's hair is standing up on end in horror that people will talk about me, or, as he says, about him ... .

I have finally decided to prepare systematically for the profession of a literary critic ... . The boys tell me my logic is like a man's ... . I must study psychology. Can Jaromír help it, that he does not experience meeting me as I imagined? The Slavs wait until one appproaches them, they don't run after people as we do ... .

My education is so hopelessly narrow ... . But I am looking forward to my studies ... . It's a good thing there won't be much time for love!

Sometimes I wish father would not let me go, that I need not experience my difficult love to its end, that the only obstacles to our love do not have to come from me ... .

29 May 1906. I have never experienced such painful loneliness as now when I have lost that sweet certainty that someone is thinking of me every day ... .

How many letters have I written to Jaromír ... and burned! ... I cannot stay here, I cannot stand the reproachful faces ... .

31 May 1906 I wrote [Jaromír] a letter, not as a woman who loves him, but as a young friend asking an experienced friend how to live her life ... . How did he answer? "Come, my Rose of Sharon!" I feel such shame.[13]

4 June 1906 We met in the little park in front of the Rudolfinum. When he saw me, he ran toward me with light steps ... . The heavy burden suddenly fell from me, ... my whole being opened up to him ... . It was enough to look into that clear ... round, blue eyed Czech

face ... . "Was the little girl sad?", he asked. "I know that she loves me." Not a word about having missed me.

I had to tell him about Rafael, that noble, refined, tactful man of penetrating intelligence, cultivated in all areas of art. He listened in amazement ... . "And why then ... " He stopped, but I understood him only too well. What you exchanged for him ... was not worth it. To me Rafael appeared as the most valuable gift life had given me. He also asked about Rafael's looks. " ... . He is not unattractive. His face even seems beautiful ... . And yet, if I had the chance again, my decision would be the same."

Jaromír's amazement means: You exchanged a great love for a little flirt. Does it mean Jaromír does not love you ... is not your "Blue Eyes" destined for you since eternity? Or is it just not clear to him yet, but one day will be?

He began to tell me about his wife ... no older than I. He married her as a seventeen-year old. He longed to awaken the woman in the child ... . Sadly he realized too late that to those wide-open eyes the world is closed ... . His little wife remains unaware, stupid, mentally and physically sterile ... .

What would a son of ours be like? I could scream to think it might have been ... . He kisses me, but does not say he would like to untie that nonsensical, sinful union.

16 June 1906 Every time Dr. Šimůnek has met me, he reminded me of my promise to join the Realistic Club ... . I have ... been there several times ... . It seems to me they have organized just to oppose the State Rights Party, not a very constructive goal. They are mostly Protestants, some Jews, very few Catholics ... almost all older gentlemen ... . There is something proud, aristocratic in the very way our Protestants hold their bodies ... . Masaryk is their authority ... .

I don't always like it at the club. I wish they would only deal with big time politics ... . Why do political struggles drag people down, when the struggles are about ideals, the common good and the security of the nation?

They elected me secretary, but I don't understand those things ... . I looked at earlier minutes, and I try to follow the usual tone ... . I have to overcome my shyness and uncertainty.

3 July 1906 I had not seen Ervín Fuchs for a long time ... . He stopped me in front of our house. I told him I was going to university ... . He was surprised that I had had my way with my parents ... . No use telling him how ... father whipped me repeatedly with the sentence: "We are only business Jews." ...

I did not dare to speak about Prague yet. My parents would suspect something, not understanding why I prefer Prague to the ... international world. Prague seems a small provincial town to them ... .

10 August 1906 I have already rented myself a place. Father was beside himself to find I live in the family of a small turner in Smíchov ... . He was sure I would live with a "better" Jewish family, and be considered part of it.

But I am glad to be with modest people ... where I can find "the people." It is a nice room ... near the lecture hall where most of my new professsors will lecture ... .

Of course I also met Jaromír ... . He has a beautiful head, turning a little gray at the temples ... perhaps his legs are a little shorter than they should be for his wide shoulders ... .

I love him because I came to know love through him ... . He said that he was so happy I would be in Prague permanently ... . I told him my parents hope ... I'll soon return remorsefully to the ... family. With a special emphasis, he said he also hoped I would have some sense ... . When we parted, he pressed a slip of paper into my hand ... a poem written in his tiny, but clear hand.

2 October 1906 I have fixed up my place at the Malinas'. I hung up a few pictures ... arranged my little library, and then went to see my land-lord's family ... . The Malinas have rented their only room to me, large and with a view into the ... gardens next to the Moldau, and they, the parents and two children, are crowded together in the kitchen ... .

Monday, 5 October 1906 For the first time a few girls are in the lecture hall.

7 October 1906 I announced my arrival to Jaromír with a card I sent to the library [where he works as an archivist]. He does not answer ... . It is humiliating ... . I have to be satisfied with crumbs while I give my whole self ... . Why does it not occur to that man that I might need some advice? ...

View of Prague

11 October 1906 Jaromír introduced me to his friends at Slavia, his social club. They are journalists or writers, everyone something, only I am nothing.

I was interested to see Jaromír in a circle of people … . "I am also a nationalist," he said "because my people suffers. If I have children, they will have to learn German, but not perfectly." … Bravo, Jaromír, I told myself, only those children will not be our children … .

He invited me to join them for supper … . Some of the wives will come, also Jaromír's … . I do not want to know her … .

22 October 1906 We take walks around Prague with Professor Matejka and look at churches, palaces etc.; on one of those walks I met a fellow student, Sklenářová … .

Yesterday Věra Sklenářová came to see me in my apartment … . She is already twenty-six … with beautiful features. She said she would never get married … . She laughed at me when I said nothing could be more beautiful than a happy marriage. "A man wants to feel good, and we are there to help him … . A man always wants something, either "that" or something else. But love us? Ridiculous! … His wife is himself, his property, his prestige, she belongs to him … I hate them all!"

Could it be possible that to Jaromír even his insignificant and, as he assures me, unloved wife, would be more important than I?

2 November 1906 Věra asked me to help her pick out material for a dress. I liked some … in the window of Wolf and Schleim … but she said, "I certainly would not buy from a Jew!" …

Should I tell her I am Jewish? Věra would assure me her anti-Semitism does not refer to me. Almost every Jew is such an exception … . Too bad, I would have liked to know her better. She is so strong … unsentimental … . She has the independence I can only dream of … .

4 November 1906 Today we were at the Waldstein Palace with Matějka's seminar. Suddenly Ervín Fuchs joined us … . He asked if I knew that Dr. Rafael Stern was going to lecture in Prague … . I would like to see and hear him, my friend Rafael Stern … . If he knew how deeply I have sunk! …

4 December 1906 … I have also begun studying Russian … . Jaromír's friend, editor Hejduk asked me what I am studying [and then said] "What good will all this do you? Your task is elsewhere."

"I would not know."

"You know very well." And he laughed again. His laugh insulted me more than his words.

Then Jaromír asked me to take a walk. He put his arm under mine. When somebody greeted him, I saw how he bit his lip and let me go.

Where am I, if the man I love has to deny me? ... He took me to a bench under old willow trees ... .

"Did you understand today how cruel you are to me?" ... he said. I did not understand. I could have cried. "Don't you see, things cannot go on this way?" ... I saw a glimmer of hope; he wants me for his wife!

"I'll come see you tomorrow." I almost consented, but there was something in his eyes that prevented me. "It is not possible." He was irritated, wanted to know why. "What would my landlords think?" ... "You are wasting your youth!" In his eyes there was an evil fire ... . I shook my head. "You fool," he said and left.

My head, my whole body ached ... . I lay down in my cold room ... . In the morning my limbs felt broken, and on top of that my mother came ... . She was horrified at how I looked and insisted I go home before Christmas vacation. I'll go and avoid meeting Jaromír. I cannot forget his mean face.

7 December 1906 I had no idea what a thunderstorm there would be at home because of my stay in Prague, that father would scream I was ruining my reputation ... . I don't know if my parents know or suspect something about Jaromír ... . Worn out by the scene with them, I had to receive Viktor. I noticed a special expression in his face. I wondered what was the matter ... . Then he said: "By the way, I met your poet. Yes, we spent a night out together. That poet of yours was one of the wildest ... . I had to promise to bring you to him, and he said another time he'd bring you to me, that nothing is eternal, and love certainly is not ... . We were drunk ... ."

Poor Jaromír ... he drowns his sorrow in wine ... . I must speak to him. It would be hard for me to live without people's esteem ... .

In Prague, 7 January 1907 He was in my apartment during my absence and left a note—I'll be at the Club Saturday after Twelfth Night at six in the evening.—Nothing more ... . The gentleman need only command ... . If I did not know he is suffering, I would not go. God, how I look forward to it ... and I am afraid! ... May he be nice ... and happy when we are together! ... Two lectures in the morning, two in the afternoon ... in the free hour between I'll go to Matějka's monuments. I am alive! ...

8 January 1907 When I came, Jaromír was already sitting in our corner ... . He took me violently by my elbow. "Come!" We walked aimlessly ... . "I did not want to love you, I fought it for a long time. I wanted to play, to pick the strange, foreign flower and enjoy it for a while. I am no longer the cat and you the cute velvety little mouse, rather you are playing with me ... . I had made up my mind to end it,

but can I? I am possessed with you!" ... Foolish Jaromír! But it is better this way, than for me to be a poor little girl raped by a man!— "I'll go crazy!", he suddenly said with his mouth all crooked. Why should he go crazy? Everything depends on him! "Everything in life can be solved somehow", I said. "Then solve it"—"Only with you. I cannot by myself." Will he finally understand? My eyes hang on him ... . He wants me to suffer for us both.

"You know it isn't posssible." "Because you don't love me", he answered ... . He embraced me violently, and bit my lips until they bled. 14 January 1907 He waited for me at Charles Bridge. Now at least I know he loves me.

"I was nasty to you, I know", he said. "Forgive me. If you knew what torture this is for me, you could not be angry. When I left you the other day ... I considered breaking off everything and beginning again ... . It is not possible ... . My mother is living with me, I cannot drive her away." ... I really could not live with an old person ... but how does he know?

She is a poor, simple woman. They had a cottage in the village ... . I have always wanted to come closer to the people ... what could be more beautiful than having a simple Czech grandmother for my blue-eyed Czech children? ... Why could I not? I would want to be alone with Jaromír ... . "Also, my wife does not suspect I suffer in our marriage." ... But me, he can hurt me ... .

"So, my dearest, we are not going to be seeing each other any more." My mouth says it, but I grasp his hand for fear he might agree. "I can't liberate myself any more ... . You have even reshaped ... my creative work ... . By opposing some things in me, you make me discover myself more fully. The world appears full of conflict to me ... . I know I am selfish ... . We only truly love the woman in whom we can live selfishly." ... In me there is calm; Jaromír is my only way.

Věra Sklenářová invited me to her place ... . I told her I am Jewish ... . It did not embarrass her in the least. "So what", she said. "You made me think Jews are repulsive to you." "That has nothing to do with you." ... Věra began to feel uncomfortable. "You are not like the rest, but also not like us. In short, I like you, come and see me tonight, it's an anniversary for me." I asked her to tell me what it was. I had no idea she had experienced the hardest thing there is.

She had a love, a young country doctor back home. It never occured to her they might not marry. One day she realized she was going to have a child. She was not frightened as I would have been, she hurried innocently to tell him. But he had not thought of marriage, he would perform an abortion. She felt horror, revulsion, left her position and parents. A little girl was born and lived only four months. Yesterday it was two years since her little girl had died.

4 May 1907 Today I met [Jaromír] with his friends on the way to the club, and they asked me to go along. I had never been at such a simple ... cheerful gathering ... . I was amazed how much beer they could hold, including my poet ... . When we went home, he took my arm ... . I came to know new sides of Jaromír, one quite nice ... one I'd like to forget.

6 June 1907 Today I met Jaromír with his wife. He walked arm in arm with her, as he does with me. A pretty little blonde in a blue suit ... . He greeted me ... . My heart stopped ... . I have a terrible feeling of ... shame that my life is founded on something false ... . I feel sorry for her and for myself. Neither of us has him ... . Oh, for the strength to give him up! ...

22 June 1907 He feels as I that something has changed in our relationship. "In you there is everything I love and hate in a woman." What does he hate about me?

In domestic prison, summer holidays, 5 July 1907 Father is terrribly angry at me ... . I had not expected him to carry on like this. He said my studies are over ... . In his eyes I am a lost soul ... .

At home, 10 July 1907 I wait, and nothing comes. Jaromír promised he would write.

At home, 3 August 1907 [Yesterday] we rented two canoes, I went with Viktor, Zdenka with Ota. I had never experienced such an evening ... on the water, the sky full of stars and the moon fiery as the sun.

Viktor rowed quietly, one could only hear the splashing of the water ... . We sat down on a park bench. There was such a strange mood in the air ... and the fragrant linden trees above us ... . My heart melted and turned toward Viktor ... . Today everything merges in my mind ... the enchanted kisses, his dark head ... ruby fires in dark eyes ... a dream which ends in the painful sweetness of lips, a mist of the head and of the senses. I never felt as well as last night. But it wasn't Jaromír! I feel neither sorry nor guilty ... . There is only a tenderness in me and a longing for Viktor.

Evening, 3 August 1907 But this is not my character! ... Who knows where Viktor's thoughts are today ... . Am I no longer faithful?

4 August 1907 I didn't go out of the house today. I do not want to meet Viktor.

4 August, afternoon How fortuitous! Vilém is moving to Brno and

invited me to help him furnish his office and apartment … . I need some distance from myself, perhaps then I'll see … clearly.

Brno, 8 August 1907. There are two Brnos: German and Czech … . But Vilém … had himself registered in the Czech Chamber of Commerce … . He simply ignores conditions … . I am afraid he will suffer for it. He has many colleagues here whom he knows from Vienna … . He, a Czech doctor, speaks German to them in the street … in the coffee house.

10 August 1907 The memory of that evening with Viktor Weiss accompanies me like a discordant undertone … . I do not love him … but I would not like to wipe anything … out of my life.

The worst part is, Jaromír is somehow disappearing … . I know he will reappear, more real than ever, and forever! …

Jaromír has been silent for a long time … . He does not love me enough … . And what has become of the love fate intended for me?

15 August 1907 … I am home again and as I step out … I meet Viktor … . I wait for a question, and wonder how I am going to explain my sudden departure. But he acts as if nothing happened … . Does the whole episode have no meaning for him? …

24 August 1907 Jaromír invited me to Prague. He writes briefly: "I ask you to meet me. In the next few days I shall be at the club from five to seven." I'll go tomorrow. But I feel dead inside … .

26 August 1907 Jaromír was determined to end his marriage and to marry me. The fulfillment of all my dreams! … To have a child with him, a blue-eyed boy with golden hair! … Surely he expected expressions of bliss, of thanks. How much it cost him! … And instead of bliss—emptiness, death! I don't understand myself; how could Jaromír understand me! … Was it because he had waited so long? I only see his frightened eyes. I shall never forget his voice. "So you enticed me out of my corner and I crawled out like a trained little bear." It was terrible. I tremble to think of it. He is completely right. But I cannot help it … . My love has evaporated.[14] …

I cannot marry my great love without love … . But have I not experienced it all … with Rafael? … It almost merges into one … I cannot love simply, absolutely … . I can't even say life treats me poorly … but I don't know how to live!

6 September 1907 Viktor … sometimes goes walking with the girls and … greets me like a stranger.

14 September 1907 I hadn't seen Viktor for a week, him who ruined my happiness. No, I must not blame anyone else … .

30 September 1907 Father is not letting me return to Prague to study. Since I broke my engagement to Rafael he sees me as a lost soul. He dislikes every word I say … . It is terrible at home. I feel guilty about Jaromír … . I torture myself seeking an explanation. Yesterday I read in Nietzsche's *Beyond Good and Evil* about the fear of eternal misunderstanding … . Could that have been my motivation?

2 November 1907 I must get used to appearing in public without embarrasment. The men [at the Realistic Club] asked me to speak at the … meeting on behalf of youth. But can I speak for freedom of thought … against the Catholic clergy, I, a Jew?

12 December 1907 Vojan[13] played in *The Merchant of Venice*. Never before did I have such a live impression of theater … .

I am a dilletante flirting with life, with ideas and life's mission … . Fighting my way to a mission … . Perhaps a woman only finds enough strength for her task next to a man, with him … . Is it weakness to need a man beside you?

When I understand a thought, I absorb it … instead of keeping it a part of my knowledge … . I am not capable of scientific work … . Perhaps it would be easier for Ervín to go through life with me at his side … . Why can I not love Ervín?

28 December 1907 Viktor joined me in the street … . As soon as the last houses were behind us, he pulled me over to himself and violently kissed my mouth, eyes, every part of my face … making up for the time when he was distant."How I loved you, how I longed for you! … Evenings … I watched til you turned off the light."

He often says he is disgusted with life … . I don't know why … .

5 January 1908 Masaryk lectured here. Why was I somehow disappointed? … I enjoy understanding an idea, putting it into practice does not interest me … . I should finally realize that … thought is only valuable when it serves life … . When he spoke about philosophy at the university … it was philosophy interwoven with life, it was politics interwoven with philosophy. The theoretical abstract idea was not always apparent in yesterday's speech … .

8 January 1908 … My parents want to marry me off … . They haven't understood yet that I'm not suited for that kind of deal.

Mother was married off in the same way, is perhaps not deliriously happy with my tyrannical father, but her life was, after all, bearable … .

[Mother says] they had not expected another chance for me after that scandal … but now there is this manager of a spinning factory, engineer Klein, a wonderful man … .

9 January 1908 Is there no-one to free me? … Viktor? … I wanted my

life to be a monument, but what kind of foundation can I be thinking of now? A cement that crumbles … . If the two of us married … our house could become the intellectual center for the town youth … where all the threads of life, national, political, artistic came together … . In time even Ervín would become reconciled. Life could be beautiful even with Viktor … .

I am an incurable optimist! … To believe that at Viktor Weiss's side it would be possible to think of anything but holding on to him … . Wouldn't this be prostitution? … To be just an object of pleasure … .

22 January 1908 … I told Viktor about my troubles. "You are an obedient daughter" he answered with an impertinent smile … . Maybe he says to himself: "Too bad I didn't go further with that girl." Was he prevented by his Jewish boy's concern for a Jewish girl from a family of friends?

15 June 1908. How difficult to find a firm foundation for living! A child could save my heart and spirit. How easy to heap life's tasks onto one's unborn children! Do we know what they will be like, do we have that right?

28 June 1908 The Realistic Club meeting was unusually lively today. The Hus celebration is approaching … . Dr. Šimůnek … talked to me about it on the way home.

8 July 1908 When the masses moved to the Elbe from the town square I was with them, as a limb of a living body … . I no longer dwelled on the fact that there was once a real stake with a live person burning on it … . It was a joyful celebration and foolish as I am, I joined in.

"How your eyes shine", Dr. Šimůnek said as he walked up to me. It was a beautiful, starry, warm night … . He sometimes has such a boyish laugh! … He has beautifully constructed hands … .My mother stood in front of the house in her housecoat … . "Where have you been, for heaven's sake?", she said in German … . [Dr.Šimůnek] was embarrassed and quickly left … . I'll run away, if they limit me like this.

9 July 1908 … Viktor saw me with Dr. Šimůnek at the Hus celebration … . It's foolish, but when I saw him from a distance, I felt a sting in my heart … . And today he sent me potted flowers. The room is full of them … .

3 October 1908 It is always the same. Whenever I am near a goal, I step back, I hesitate, I become afraid.

19 October 1908 Without asking me, my parents invited that engineer Klein, whom they had picked for me to marry … . I had promised to be at the exhibition in the afternoon … . The guest actually came in

the morning, the hours dragged on like geography lessons ... . He acted ... as if he had never been young ... . I didn't feel like talking to this strange, bearded gentleman ... . Mother watched me fondly and encouragingly, father sternly ... . The gentleman ... seemed moderately in love ... . When I joined the conversation about politics, father rolled his eyes furiously. A girl and politics!

At dinner I announced that I was on duty at the ... exhibition. My parents were shocked, but thought I was only going to explain I could not stay ... . They showed up at the exhibition with the director [Klein] ... . I could not leave the desk ... and when he was leaving he even said he liked my being so active ... . He and my parents assumed I would come home at five when the exhibition closed, but I showed the visitors from Hradec[14] the town and stayed with them while they had supper. I came home at nine, the gentleman had left, evidently insulted ... . Father got up from bed, ran around the house in his underwear shouting ... . They said I had embarrassed them terribly ... . They had been looking for me in all the better restaurants ... . Vilém will have to explain to them that I am going to have nothing to do with these tried ... and true, venerable methods.

20 December 1908 Why don't they let me leave? ... If I were poor, I would go out into the world as a servant. What repelled me most about that gentleman was the thought of spending my whole life as a rich and idle lady, in comfort and luxury ... . If I went abroad, how would I support myself? ... Meanwhile the years pass.

8 March 1909 ... I do all I can to help the work of others become known, but I myself will never create anything ... . There will be nothing more. I didn't have the courage to be a poet's mistress when he needed me; I couldn't even do what every stupid girl could have done.

6 July 1909 My parents went to Marienbad. They wanted to take me along, but I didn't go ... . I cannot take part in my parents' problems, their business or their petty quarrels. I only want to live MY life!

28 November 1909 Several times now I have met old Mrs. Weissenstein, the matchmaker, at our house ... . She was not deterred by my ironic greeting ... .

I had a terrible scene with mother. To her too I am evidently already inferior goods. Everything significant one experiences in life seems to lower one's value. I want to go through life without their halo ... .

Gisa Picková-Saudková is mentioned in connection with the transport of Jews from Kolín to Terezín7[15] in 1942. In Rabbi Richard Feder's book Židovská tragedie [The Jewish Tragedy] Dr. Erwin Winternitz recalls that in December of 1943 a transport went from Terezín to Auschwitz-Birkenau, and that it included Picková-Saudková and her son Pavel. In the same book there is a memorial to her by Dr. Feder:

"To you, Mrs. Gisa Picková-Saudková, I devote a sorrowful memorial, to you, an enthusiastic admirer of Březina, and a great cultural worker! Even in Terezín your pen did not rust. You wrote a play for the Jewish children. You had already assigned the roles, you had held the first rehearsals, had invited me to the premiere when you were called from your fruitful activity and sent to the Polish torture chambers … . Your admirers … honor your memory."

NOTES

1. In Gisa Picková-Saudková: *Hovory s Otakarem Březinou* [Conversations with Otakar Březina], Prague, 1929.
2. A town in Moravia.
3. (New York, 1979)
4. See footnote number seven in the introduction.
5. A gymnasium was a secondary school which prepared for university.
6. The family of a teacher whose daughter was a classmate of Gisa's.
7. Selma Dubová is the name Picková-Saudková gave herself in this diary.
8. The narrator's other brother.
9. Actually this is a quote from G.E. Lessing's *Nathan the Wise* (1779).
10. The narrator's teacher.
11. The Czech women's gymnasium in Prague, see the General Introduction.
12. In Czech the word "single" is the same word as "free".
13. A famous Czech character actor of the time.
14. Hradec Králové, a town in Bohemia.
15. This North Bohemian fortress town, known also by its German name Theresienstadt, was a Nazi concentration camp from 1941–45. Designed to appear as a model camp to dispel international criticism of Nazi policies, it was displayed to members of the International Red Cross and a propaganda movie was made of it. Although not an extermination camp, conditions were still cramped and dirty and tens of thousands died there.

Chapter 8

GRETE FISCHER

(1893–1977)

Grete Fischer was born in Prague in 1893 as the daughter of a Jewish manufacturer. She studied music and literature at the university, and during the war worked with Galician refugees. In 1917 she moved to Berlin where she became an editor in Paul Cassirer's publishing company, and later with Ullstein. She also reviewed concerts for the Berliner Börsen-Kurier from 1922–1931 as well as for other Berlin newspapers. In 1933 she lost her position as editor. The pages of her diary are not dated, but we can assume that the entries about supporting herself by teaching in a music school may refer to that time. In 1934, after a trip to Palestine, she emigrated to London, England where she did various kinds of work, including broadcasting in German for the BBC. Later, without ever having had any formal training in the field, she became very successful as a teacher of children who were brain damaged or had psychological problems. She died of cancer in 1977.

Her publications included Palästina, das erlaubte Land, [Palestine, the sanctioned Country], Paris, 1934 under the pseudonym, Josef Amiel, and several children's books, articles and pamphlets. Her autobiographical book Dienstboten, Brecht und andere Zeitgenossen in Prag, Berlin, London [Servants, Brecht and other contemporaries] was published in Freiburg/Br. in 1966, her volume of poetry, Schuld der Gerechten [The Guilt of the Just] in Darmstadt in 1974.

As Grete Fischer says in her autobiography, our main source, her aim was not to tell the story of her life, but to tell of people who passed through her life, to offer a document of her time. The story of her own life as it emerges in the book is indeed incomplete; important facts and dates are missing. Nevertheless, it supplies us with what seems to be a fairly accurate picture of Grete as she developed from childhood until her seventies.

However, I still went to London to fill in some information from her literary estate and from people who knew her. What I encountered there was a room full of boxes with manuscripts of Grete's published and unpublished writings. By far *the most important, however, were the loose, partly illegible and mostly undated pages, letters, notes, poems. In the short time available I selected and xeroxed portions of that material and then spoke to people who had known her in London, especially in Club 43, the apolitical cultural organization of refugees in which Grete had been active, and in the Pen Club of German authors abroad. I also spoke to her niece in Northern England and to two men, now in their forties, who were children when they knew Grete.*

I left England with a clearer image. It was not that in the book she had painted a smoothed-out, idealized picture of herself for public consumption, but rather that the reports of her friends, and even more her private writings, revealed additional dimensions. Grete wavered from childhood on between the feeling that she was capable of the best work in various areas, and feelings of inadequacy. She turned into a highly competent, and, if we can trust her own writings, a serene woman, although circumstances, the Nazi period in Germany and existence as a refugee in England, and the handicaps she encountered as a Jew kept her from reaching her true potential.

The major part of this chapter is a condensation of Grete's autobiography.[1] As I would at best be able to date the entries in her private diary approximately, I have arranged the sections from it by topic. The most extensive of them will deal with two interwoven themes: her personal insecurity, especially in regard to her relationships with men and specifically her relationship with the director of the music school where she taught.

Although none of the persons or printed sources I consulted could give me any information about the man, and indeed there is no mention in her book about her activity in the music school, the material is important because it reveals additional facets of her personality.

I am beginning this chapter with those portions of her autobiographical book which deal with her self, her environment and her concerns, and omitting for the most part those which deal with people to whom she was not particularly close, either privately or as an editor.

Mama—I still don't see her faults. She was probably an average person of her time and environment. A lack of nerve, especially vis-à-vis her husband, was probably due to her upbringing which had also deprived her of her natural cheerfulness. Only under the pressure of sorrow and compassion did she forget herself to such a point that her real character became obvious. I understood and loved her independently of all judgment when I was more mature. My love was great enough to think of her always, but not to stay with her. I let her go to her death alone.

We could argue with Papa ... and I fought furiously against his shallow pessimism. He sensed the coming misfortune, and rallied against everything that seemed to lead to it. At the age of twenty, however, I wanted an active, successful future, and we could not agree ...

At fifteen, in 1908, I experienced periods of childish depression and wrote in my diary ... "all praise is proof to me that I shall not deserve any higher praise ... but plenty of criticism ... Why does my father have such high hopes for me? Does he have the right? I cannot do what I, what he, strives for. He never expresses it, and yet I know it. He loves me very much and I am attached to him, respect and appreciate him. I fear what he asks of me more than I can say. His wishes are the demands of someone who could not fulfill his own wishes, and wants to see them fulfilled in his children. I don't have the courage any more to satisfy him … .

All this, although nothing was further from the good man's mind than expecting me to perform like a genius! All he wanted was for me to practice the violin regularly … and to play well for him …

Papa was of medium height, medium slender, medium rich, medium smart—we were middle class in everything. All of my life I have disliked and feared mediocrity.

We lived in a household where everybody got his due. We were entitled to coffee with milk and rolls with butter in the morning, in the afternoon to croissants without butter, on Sundays to honey and at Christmas to Striezel [braided Christmas bread with raisins] … We did not think about the fact that other people were entitled to different things … that we went by train and took our summer vacation third class, while the girl who sat next to me in school … had a car and went first class; or that Father's workers had a quarter of an hour off for second breakfast, or that the man who delivered our coal got coffee and pastry from our lunch. This was how things were.

I always took my upbringing too literally. Since we were taught not to lie, I didn't lie. Since I was told that a decent girl didn't get involved with men, whatever that meant, I remained a decent girl …

We had learned to take care of ourselves and to avoid dangers and unpleasantness, and we followed these rules faithfully. But neither our teachers nor our own life force taught us when one has to ignore rules. We were ready to pass life by. …

I never became reconciled to the fact that Father never kept Sunday afternoon for us, but that he had to pay a visit to his aunt and uncle right after an early coffee. We children had to go along. We sat in the dining room, at the table with the fringed plush table cloth, which was not taken off, but was protected instead by embroidered doilies when the little plates for stale cookies were put on it. The conversation of the bored adults dragged through the afternoon … We were given a mountain of magazines … Our aunt assured my mother that her vanilla crescents would be just as good if she used only two thirds of the prescribed amount of almonds and put in flour instead … She was on the executive of two Jewish girls' orphanages and uncle had such functions at equivalent boys' institutions … my social conscience got its first object lesson there. And I was hardly thirteen, when I invented the expression "charity hyenas" for my aunt and her ladies.

... We were allowed to go with Toni to the Christmas market. The Prague Christmas Market, in the Old Town Square, before the ugly art nouveau buildings on its north side disfigured it, the Old Town Square without the clumsy statue of Hus, but with the slender St. Mary's column in its middle—what did we know about the cruelty of the executions [in 1620], the suppression of the Czech uprising? Toni bought us a wooden butter tub from a Slovak, and wooden plates, Turkish honey and Sutschuk, that wonderful sticky stuff ...

At home we never had a Christmas tree. My mother considered it wrong for Jews to celebrate Christian holidays—only the maids received gifts, and on Christmas Eve, the kitchen table was set for their festive meal and the Christmas plates were filled with fruit and sweets ...

We ... felt disadvantaged, and in my eighth year, I decided to decorate a tree of our own with Marianne [my sister] and to surprise our parents with it. We had just enough money for a tiny crippled fir tree and a few candles. This pitiful tree moved and annoyed my father who did not like to be petty. From then on, we were allowed to decorate just a little tree: concessions must not go too far.

But I fear that the pettiness was in part mine ...

Among my fellow pupils I only had a few friends. The other children did not like me. I was too little, too articulate, only seemingly quick (it is astonishing how often restlessness is confused with speed,

The Christmas Market in the Old Town Square

for instance in music), lazy in gymnastics—and sulked easily when I didn't do well. I could read better than any of them, had a terrible handwriting and was poor in math; I asked too many questions and always preferred to do something different than what I was supposed to do—so the teachers didn't like me either. I was considered precocious, smart, well read and behaved accordingly.

The only teacher I valued was the teacher of religion, David Löwy. He was shorter than me and very ugly, a very deformed hunchback with a big nose which was covered with pink bumps, and tiny eyes. But he was good. We all tried to annoy him, but he did not take us seriously, he was simply fond of us. For five years, he told us the biblical stories in our text book better than I have ever heard since. These old Austrian school books were so true in their simplicity that when I read Thomas Mann's *Joseph and his Brethren* thirty years later, the story of Joseph from this school book stood brightly in my way ... .

What was most striking about me was my language. From the age of two on I spoke clearly and used well-chosen expressions—compulsively. Words fascinated me ... Both parents spoke the careful Prague High German more or less without any accent, and considered it very important ... "Fischer is affected" said the girls in school. "Can't you speak naturally?" said aunts and teachers. But what was called "natural" was either the dialect from the Lesser Side, the hard Sudeten German with its confusion of B and P, and G and K and the unaspirated Slavic K, or it was the jargon, mixed with Jewish expressions ... The children from "better" families tried for pure *umlauts*. These language problems were typical of Prague, that city of two languages which was always embroiled in battles about their use.

By the way, we were made to avoid "Jewish jargon". ...

When we got a new teacher for German ... I criticized that she was unsure of herself ... But she won me over as I won her over. She was enthusiastic about my essays and my oral interpretations of readings, and gave me special attention. And when, in the course of my last two years in school, she offered and accepted more and more friendship, even outside of class, a strange relationship developed. It was strange in so far as I ... let an "adult" admire me and, although I was also fond of her, I assigned her a wooing and giving role. She wrote me little letters with the heading "Comfort for my eyes" and often delivered them in the evening at our door. However, I did not have a crush on her.

Mîne[2] offered to tutor me in Italian. So afternoons I went to her pretty apartment, she treated me to honey, fresh black bread and nuts, and we read Dante. Without knowing a word of the language, I understood enough to feel the greatness of the work. Looking back I realize how distrustful we have become. Today nobody would doubt that dear Mîne had lesbian tendencies, but I am sure she was as little aware of it as I, and except for the immodesty with which I tolerated her excessive feelings and my cool response, the relationship remained innocent ...

Nothing is as difficult as holding on to the person one has perhaps loved the most and for whose sake one has suffered the most. Hardly a day passed without me thinking of [my brother Walter]. Walter was born in the most sensitive period of my development, in my fourteenth year. He was "my" child ... the little brother I had always wanted ... I remember exactly how one evening, while I was reading, Mother stepped behind my chair and said: "you always wanted a little brother. Would you be glad if you got one now?" Without reflecting for a second, stooped far over my book, I said: "Glad? No! Now I have been the youngest for so long, we won't change it any more." That same moment I understood my rudeness, turned around and saw Mama's eyes full of tears. "Naturally I'll be glad", I cried, "that would be wonderful!" But it was too late. My shy mother, who was strangely depressed by her late pregnancy, already had received the blow.[3]

The Prague German identity to which we were raised seemed a matter of course to us as long as we had no contact with the outside world. Grade schools and gymnasia were Habsburg institutions, German because the official language was German. The teachers of the secondary schools came from the whole monarchy, they were Tyrolians, Styrians and natives of Trieste, Croatians and Slovaks, but the Sudeten Germans were the real German nationalists ... .

Children of my generation first learned to pray for the good Emperor Francis Joseph, then learned the history and the glory of the empire along with a foolish contempt for all other nations. It took me a long time to realize that seventy percent of these Prague "Germans" were Jews or Czechs. The Czechs were German officials because otherwise they could not get any positions. The Jews were Germans because their desire to educate their children was satisfied best in the German schools; besides, the Jews had engaged in venerating the German "Geist" since emancipation ... . In my world Czechs were servants, small tradesmen, Papa's laborers, but not office employees. The first cultured Czech, with whom I came in contact, was my violin teacher Baštař, but he spoke a somewhat unnatural, though correct German. I got my first impression of Czech literature in Berlin in 1918. My contemporaries, of course, were somewhat smarter; already before the war R. Fuchs translated Petr Bezruč's *Silesian Songs* into German, and Otokar Fischer Goethe into Czech.

I loved the language so early and so passionately, that it was easy to make me a blind nationalist. My first published poem was called "Deutscher Frühling" (German Spring) and appeared in *Deutsche Arbeit*[4], when I was thirteen years old. Professor August Sauer, to whom my father had sent the poem, wrote: "If you can change the unfortunate rhyme Maie—Freie, I'll print it in the next number." I changed it easily, and the ... next mailman brought me six Austrian crowns as an honorarium, two new silver coins which I am still saving, wrapped in pink tissue paper.

Deutsche Arbeit printed a poem by me in every successive year until the last one, a love poem, aroused sarcasm and gossip in the circle of "aesthetic teas"—sarcasm because "one" didn't publish one's poems in journals (Werfel's first volume of poetry was just completed)—gossip because they wanted to guess, to which youth it was addressed; I had meant none. ...

At least two thirds ... of my fellow pupils were Jewish, half of the Christians had Jewish relatives and the rest were Czech. The "semi-official" girls' *lyzeum* which was under state supervision, was mostly financed by Jewish money, as was the German Theater, the German vacation camps, the German Pulmonary Aid Society and the Institute for the Blind—everybody, including myself at the age of eighteen, was a member of about twenty German institutions, including the Reading- and Speaking Hall of German Students, the singing association, the theater association, the association for social aid whose youth group I had founded. As a delegate of the association of former students of the *lyzeum*, I participated in the plenary session of German associations in the mirror hall of the German Casino.

But there, in the shabby splendor of red plush and gold-framed mirrors, right after a talk by the wise poet Friedrich Adler, the leader of the German nationalists spoke, the delegate Karl Hermann Wolf. He sounded like a Hitler of 1912. I listened to the anti-Semitic bombardment and was silent during the first and second instance of name calling, but then I began to respond to the salvoes of stupid, cocky hate with booing ...

Then I went home, canceled my memberships in all organizations and swore that I would never again belong to one. I kept that oath until 1943 ...

[I wanted to get out of Prague, and had already written in 1909] "If I could only get away from Prague, from these ugly, indifferent people, so few of whom love me, since they all remember the intolerable child ... I would like to fight for a new love elsewhere—for sympathy—... to know others that I can think about, so I don't

always think and write about myself" ... I wanted personal friendships, not just a social circle. I rejected every kind of conventional
relationship ... I probably imitated my father's attitude. He did not
socialize and kept my mother from it, although she probably would
have liked it ... When I, at the age of seven, wanted to visit Pepi, the
daughter of a bank official, Papa said: "Her mother uses makeup, I
don't want you to associate with her." When I told him of a new
friend, Papa might say: "What does she want of you?" ... I slowly
built up my friendships [anyway].

I had two or three (girls) in every class with whom I could talk ...
At the age of thirteen ... I read literature for the first time ... I quickly
read all the Romantics ... then we decided to found a magazine. We
had an editorial staff, authors, illustrators and printers; the sheet
appeared monthly—one copy which we took turns copying neatly. It
was called *Der Pfifficus* [The Smarty]. We had news, articles, critiques,
announcements, verses and pictures. When the magazine was finished,
it was handed from one to the other, sometimes it was shown to parents and friends ... I already thought of myself as a writer, but I was
not the best—Anni was witty and original, Ilse was formally better.
This lasted about a year, then music became more important ... .

I had ... become addicted to the Romantics. I liked Hoffmann's
satires ... very much ... Most of our group[5] were already active in literature: Franz Werfel, Paul Kornfeld, Willy Haas and, as a rare guest,
Egon Erwin Kisch ... The "aesthetic tea" was to concern itself with
higher things rather than with banal conversations, and we were going
to read to each other from our own works ... . I remember that ...
when my turn came, I was too shy to show something of my own, and
instead read a piece by Hermann Hesse from a ... literary almanach ...
In this circle I was considered old-fashioned, romantic, backward.

In discussions I might have been aggressive, but I held my own and
was treated with respect rather than with fondness; once Willy Haas
and Paul Kornfeld came for tea to conclude a discussion ... it ended
in an argument, and in the end I became so ungracious and dogmatic
that my guests took leave and never came back ... .

I often toyed with the idea of writing a subjective literary history ... .
every critic [should be] clear about what impressions determine his
original judgment ... . One cannot eliminate the personal element.
Even historians are beginning to see that. We are too intent on shedding or denying prejudices before having understood where they came
from, and how deeply they are rooted.

My critical ability rested on a natural sense of form, mainly on a
sure ability to distinguish between genuineness and pose. I was fanat-

ical about the truth in everything … . This of course placed me in
opposition to all professional literati who praise each other in order to
be praised. That is how all of literary history came about, after all …
whoever did not belong to a circle was dead like Kleist … . I criticized everyone unsparingly. My real desire was enthusiasm—and my
constant fear was of seeing people smile about my enthusiasm … My
sister felt the same.

I have often reflected on the educational condition of this Prague
society. We were about the third or fourth generation of country Jews
who had come from villages and market towns to the capital and
become prosperous in trade and industry. To be sure, my grandfather
did have his daughter taught by good tutors in Raudnitz, but at best
that generation had some years of a girls' finishing or boarding school.
The Habsburg state schools which our fathers attended were probably
somewhat better than those in Germany, but a university education
only became a matter of course for their children. Undoubtedly
though, intellectual interests were common, whether genuine or not.
Apart from music and theater, classical literature was taken for granted
and a fair amount of good quality modern literature was read. The liberal education, of which I was later skeptical in Germany … was a link
which still existed … Even people who didn't read books, such as my
father, were well informed, and I now believe that this was due to the
papers which everybody subscribed to and valued. …

For my father, the [Prager] *Tagblatt* was too Jewish and here something must be said about the anti-Semitism of this voluntary ghetto.
We did not really suffer from the anti-Semitism of the nineteenth
century. We did not expose ourselves to it. One lived among one's
own … . One was, to be sure, a member of German clubs, but hardly
tried to play a role in them, and one was reconciled to the fact, for
example, that as a Jew one had little chance of a university professorship, so that important scholars were at best admitted as Dozenten. At
any rate in Old Austria one could become an officer without converting to Christianity … .

An educated Jew was essentially assimilated. My father argued passionately against the Catholic Clergy which really seems to have been
the evil spirit of reaction—but he also found stagnation and narrow-
ness among the Jewish religious leaders. While consciously Jewish, he
kept apart from the religious community. He went to synagogue only
on the eve of the Day of Atonement and only, as he explained to me,
because it was the anniversary of his father's death. He fasted and took
me along to evening services, which made a big impression on me.
The holidays were not actually observed, but we ate chicken and

sometimes had wine or traditional pastry. We were allowed to light candles on Chanukah, colorful Christmas candles which were glued to a log of fire wood … .

One went to religious class because it was compulsory. We were as non-Jewish as the others were non-Christian.

There were Zionists, the circle around Hugo Bergmann, Max Brod and the Weltsch cousins … the only thing that attracted me to it was the social side … the pioneers were anything but religious, rather socialist, nationalist, idealistic. We were not part of it. We were good Germans.

The generation of our fathers had participated in the destruction of Old Austria as well as in the destruction of Judaism. Now it is obvious that one can destroy a state but not a people. In our mortal fear, the bond among us non-believing, alienated brothers proved to be stronger than we would ever have thought possible. One … felt understanding … We found warmth and shelteredness again only when we were expellees.

Music played an important role at home. At the age of three or four I sang second voice … . When I was ten, I thought that I would become a great violinist, and had lessons … . But I lacked, as I did generally, the urge, the absolute necessity to devote myself to [it] totally … . I did not become a musician. After 1933 I excluded music from my life for almost twenty years, and never quite returned to it—no genuine musician could have done that, although my reasons could be considered justified. Music was my father, and after he was murdered, I didn't want it any more. But careful! To what extent is my mourning for the dead a valid reason for self deprivation? In other areas I improved as I was severed from my roots. My language was forbidden, all my activity in German was taken away, but my relationship to the German language did not change. The horror at the moral collapse of the world in which I was at home did not paralyze my will to live. And although I almost never forget when I eat that they let my father starve to death, I shall still eat …

I owe more to books than to teachers because I am a bad listener. As soon as a point in a lecture captivated me, I was sidetracked by my own thinking instead of listening.

I mainly studied with August Sauer, professor of modern literature who I found stimulating. …

Paul Wiegler was the theater critic for [the newspaper] *Bohemia*. I met him … with the manuscript of a play I had written under the influence of Hauptmann and Ibsen when I was seventeen. It dealt with a young man who died before he had reached fulfillment … . My German teacher Míne Ohnesorg, had arranged for Wiegler to read it. He sent me the message that I should come and he said that I had tal-

Building where the newspaper Bohemia *was printed*

ent … that I was gifted … but that I was too young to write a play for the stage … that I should write little stories for the cultural supplement … I can't promise that, I said coldly … .

On that occasion I evidently displayed one of the qualities which has prevented me all my life from making a mark. An uncanny ability to save myself from pain, especially from disappointment or rather shame. The first effect of every failure was shame. I have always demanded of myself to be able to stand criticism, but could do it only by sharpening my self criticism so mercilessly that nobody would say more against me than I myself.

Nothing and nobody was to hurt me. I leave the … implications to the psychoanalysts … certainly there is a connection to the overestimation of virginity in our upbringing. It is quite certain that my behavior hindered the development of my abilities very much. The desire to do everything by myself, without the help or influence of others, was disastrous. I thereby excluded myself from the glasshouse of Prague talent … People praised, encouraged, criticized, I did not praise … and was not praised … What was important is that I withdrew myself from that echo which enhances creativity. I … did not believe in growth—either I was great or small.

Later I worked with Wiegler, and came to know the kindness which, next to his stupendous knowledge and industry, was his strongest quality. While still half a child I did not realize it.

I resisted the storm and stress of the young generation. I skipped the beginning of expressionism. I rejected, then as always, everything that was fashionable … as soon as a book was a world wide success, I did not want to read it. I did not read Spengler in 1919, nor the *Magic Mountain* in 1926.

So I remained alone, and only secretly considered myself a genius … . All professional activity stayed in the middle, serving and criticizing. Wiegler also did not have the courage to try personal creativity, and rather worked himself to death than admit it … .

No matter how much people have meant to me, landscape was equally decisive. Prague at that time only consisted of the core of the city, ancient, beautiful, dirty, grey … when one looked down from the hills, grey steam always hung over the city like a cat … In the center, Prague was the most beautiful. I loved it so much that I do not dare to see it again.

But happiness was to get out of the city. We counted the years according to the places where we went summers … .

When later, in analysis, the analyst always wanted to insist on penis envy, it seemed to me that our envy of boys, our fervent desire not to be a girl, had very real causes. Along with all his insights, Freud was also tied to his time; in our narrow, constantly deprived generation every girl envied every boy. We were not allowed to climb on trees, because we wore skirts, but we were not allowed to wear pants. Studies had to be fought for; when Marianne wanted to go to university, she was fortunate that my Vienna cousin married a Miss Meitner, who was a physician. Her sister Lise visited us in Prague, and my mother only objected to the cut of her reform dress.[6] My problem was my chosen profession, "opera directress"—that did not exist! …

Much in my later behavior may be connected with the fact that all the young men of my generation were soldiers when I was growing up. One whom I liked had tuberculosis, was nevertheless sent in the trenches, and returned dying to the emergency hospital where my sister worked. Hermann Beck, a pediatrician and our good violist, died in Serbia while treating patients with spotted fever. Three others fell. The son of my father's cousin died in Serbia and they sent his father his watch and an uncensored notebook. The last entry was: "We are standing at the river, the Serbs sit on the other side of the bridge, under cover. The lieutenant has commanded us to go over the bridge, singly … each one on the bridge is shot in the head … I am next—" ! …

War, 1914, meant helplessness for us, because there was no role for us. I was old enough to feel the insanity, but … nevertheless, we had a feeling of duty to participate … I chose the "Club for Social Aid", a model women's organization which was concerned with the poor … In 1914 Prague had relatively few poor Germans. But the association was strictly limited to Germans, Czech cases had to be passed on to Czech organizations, because otherwise we would have been accused of fraternizing ... . I passed Czech applications on to Dr. Alice Masaryk,[7] although she must have had more problems than we.

At that time I first became acquainted with the Jewish refugees from Galicia, a kind of people I had never known. The Russian invasion of Galicia had made hundreds [sic] homeless. I was shocked to find that the women and girls were working, while the men and boys were studying the Talmud.

When I told my mother [that the opera director Lothar Wallerstein had invited me to work with him in Posen] she became totally desperate. The stage, abroad, at the opera, entrusted to a young lady-killer, and I not even twenty! If I absolutely must go away, she would give in, but not *that*!

I noted down then: It is interesting to see how the love of parents is actually transferred, excused selfishness.

When my mother saw how miserable I was, she showed the magnanimity of a victor, and promised not to stand in my way at the next opportunity ...

When I came to Berlin [several years later], I was lucky to meet Leo Kestenberg[8] right in the beginning ... . Without him I would have failed in the difficult, ironic atmosphere of the publishing house. Even as it was, I seem to have rubbed everybody the wrong way ... the book-keeper complained that I did not greet him first ... the producer ... was insulted because I contradicted him, the secretary because she had to take dictation from a lady. The sales manager, a Saxon ... with a small brain and bad manners, disliked me at first sight as I did him and ... Cassirer's ... physically and intellectually filigree partner did not ... take me seriously, which for me, aged 23, was of course the worst. ... the first book I had the opportunity to help edit was *The Dead Day* by Barlach ... .

In my life there was only one man who was home to me. B. came to Berlin in shorter or longer intervals. We never wrote each other. He had an apartment in Weimar, but worked in Erfurt in a big business to support his wife and child. He was still working on a great drama "Saul" which he had planned as a young man.

There never was a person without whom I could not live. I demanded that of myself and it was my fate. Often I did not think of B. for months. Then one night I would dream of him or suddenly think of him when I woke up. Then, when I came to the office, there would be a letter announcing his arrival. ...

We did nothing, went to eat, met in the evening, talked. He never pressed me ... .

Bernstein worked on a new edition of Lassalle's collected works, and I was assigned to him.

I had already been with the firm for almost a year, when Paul Cassirer came back from Switzerland, and it still took some time before I met him. I was introduced to him, he shook my hand limply, and I didn't like him. His elegance intimidated me, his arrogance outraged me, and I had an insurmountable resistance against anything that was boss ... . I never understood him ...

I overestimated everybody who was my superior, childishly thinking that he was clever, more powerful, freer than I, had everything and could afford everything. ...

Kestenberg asked me a number of times ... what I had written ... I was able to show him a short, fantastic piece of prose ... It was the story of the descendants of a man who had impregnated an ape in the jungle ... My idea of love was as indirect as my idea of the jungle ... Kestenberg had obviously passed on the manuscript. "I have read your piece of fiction," P. C. said in passing. "It can't, of course, be printed." ... So that was that.

The next time I was called to the boss, he involved me in a conversation. I liked that very much, a few inhibitions disappeared, then my boss got up and kissed me on the mouth. I jumped up and left the room, with red cheeks and confused. I considered myself a modern girl, free of any prudishness, emancipated, a rebel against the family. But I reacted like a young lady from boarding school. I went home, trembling with excitement, and wrote him a letter. I sent it off, but I wrote him another a few weeks later which I did not send off ... any of Marlitt's[9] heroines could have written it. I went to the boss when he called me ... "I received your letter, it's o.k., I understand." Whereupon we went to work. Was I sorry? Yes, I was sorry. But my basic attitude was the same. A boss who kisses his assistant is disgusting, and that can't be done with me. If I want a man, I'll pick him out myself. As usual I debated about that with myself for hours ... A few days later the conversation again ended with a kiss ... I began to negotiate, which may really have been fun for P. C ... . We talked ... about people, about politics ... even Einstein's theory of relativity which had recently become known. The enrichment I derived from these discussions was a lift; only sometimes he took me in his arms ... What I do not understand,—is that I knew so little what I wanted. If the "seduction" had seemed so wrong to me, as I firmly believed at the time, I could have left. ...

I thought I was one of the many girls whom he stroked for his amusement. I absolutely didn't want to sleep with him, but was much too conceited to strictly oppose the petting. P. C. became more insistent. ...

I loved my job, the work was easy for me, versatile and always new ... Bernstein let me make the index for the edition of Lassalle ... . Lasker-Schüler[10] ... was as stimulating as she was difficult.

P.C. came one late afternoon ... The boss was absent minded ... suddenly he asked: "Am I physically repulsive to you?" I honestly said "No." Now he lost his patience, the great patience he had shown, and tried to use force ... . I struck out in all directions like a little animal ... "you are stingy, petty, narrow. You will always be happy." I believed every word. Only my happiness was gone for years.

When I left after a few bad months, I took leave politely ... "Do you have another job?" he asked. "No" I said. "But don't worry about me. I am young, I can begin anything." ...

I lived in a furnished room, ate in the canteen and thought three times before I bought myself a pair of shoes.

I did not then, nor do I now, own a single object of art of even modest value. I love beautiful things, but I do not need to own them. That was a great advantage in the following years of poverty, I never felt deprivations ... I didn't buy a book for twenty years, no concert—or theater ticket ... There are people who are impressed by my strict economy. There are many more who value me less because I live as I do ... .

"How many evenings a week do you play chamber music?" Faktor[11] asked me. I counted five. "Do you play well?" "No." "Then you can just as well write critiques of concerts for me." So I became a critic for the *Berliner Börsenkurier*.

At that time, I still had a great opinion of myself ... the reviewer only had to be one step ahead [of the listener] and mainly be able to express what they perhaps did not quite grasp. The stylistic aspect was easy for me ...

[Paul Robiczek from Prague who had started out in Berlin somewhat parallel to me] did not fritter away his time with journalistic activities ... Kant, Marx, Goethe, Tolstoy became his witnesses, while I, with my lack of academic talent, could only start from my observations and use a certain ability to synthesize. But what we had in common in those early Berlin years was the sad premonition of evil, which was not yet confirmed, but many aspects of which we felt and saw. The political development did not seem as threatening to us as the increased indifference and brutality all around, in public utterances, in the press. They were coarse, clumsy, dishonest in language and some of them were so stupid in their attitude that a decent person stood there totally helpless, and I remember exactly, how I ... suddenly exclaimed: "We'll all die of stupidity"—indeed it is only by chance that we did not all die of it. Neither then nor later was Nazism for me a matter of a political party, rather a basic attitude, the most dangerous aspect of a narrow minded petit bourgeois, prepared to give up his moral ambitions, because a little flag in his lapel relieved him of any moral responsibility. ...

I had been unemployed for a year—my attempts to freelance had lead to nothing, I was not getting ahead with the book I was trying to write, and all I had was the minor position as music critic with the *Börsenkurier*—when Julius Elias[12] invited me to come see him.

"Actually I have never been able to stand you," he said cordially. "You are a contrary person. But then, you are quite a hardy girl." He then proposed I come to work for the Propyläen publishing house, the directorship of which he had just taken over ... .

I again proved to be a "contrary" person from the start. First of all I had arguments with the chief of personnel ... a major Kobiletzky, who considered it his job to give new employees unimportant jobs, and to get them cheaply. He said "ladies" did not exist as editors in the company, he would let me do what he wanted ... I was a secretary, i.e. with half the pay of a young editor, obliged to be there during all business hours.

At P.C.'s I had been independent, worked as an equal, and was glad to take advice from Kestenberg about things he knew better ... Dr. Reinhold asked me ... to find a good text of *Gulliver's Travels* ... I made a new translation. When I found out that Dr. Reinhold was getting all the recognition for the text, without even mentioning me, I was silent and worked without enthusiasm. ...

I loved *The Three Penny Opera* from the beginning of the book edition, in which I played a part. I also accepted Brecht's attitude, that it was his right to use other authors' subject matter ... In world literature there was always only a limited number of themes ... Originality is in the author's personality, in the way the subject matter is treated. I had always planned to write a study of these motives one day, and of their treatment in world literature –one of the many projects I did not carry out ...

Brecht's *Hauspostille* [Family Book of Devotions] appeared ... he had five copies bound in black calico with red edges and gave me one dedicated "to the creator of this book, comrade in arms Grete Fischer, cordially Bert Brecht, Berlin 1927". This was ambiguous in a way which could have cost me my life under the Nazis if they had caught me.

In the following years Brecht disappeared ... from my sight ... the next time was London, 1934 ... . from the doorway [of a house where there was a room to rent] his voice came: "It's all right to live here Miss Fischer, I do too." ...

Professor Korsch, a historian and a Communist, roomed with Brecht, they were the only prominent people. In the remaining rooms German Jews lived, young and old of both sexes, a dentist, a graphic artist and others. Brecht took time for me, and I was very grateful. I remember ... an oat meal soup I cooked for him in the landlady's kitchen, because he had a stomach ache and was afraid. I remember especially one or two evenings when he sat in my room and seriously tried to convert me ... The Communists seemed to be the only people actively fighting against Hitler. It was easy to feel a coward if one did not want to participate—narrow, selfish, lazy. To this day I cannot say if my stubbornness was just as wrong as his. Brecht was a splendid dialectician, very clever, and ready for any counter argument. But it is always harder to convince half an opponent than a whole one ... The basic idea of Socialism corresponded to my own ideal of human justice; what I opposed was the absoluteness of the party. I refused to fight for freedom by taking it away from others and giving it up myself. Brecht wanted to prove that the goal could only be reached that way—the freedom of the individual had to be sacrificed for the masses. We never reached an agreement because Brecht was absolute and I remained relativistic. There is nothing I appreciated more about him than that he admitted in the end I was inconvertible—but that our friendship did not need to suffer. A little later Brecht went to Denmark and I never saw him again.

A long time from now biographies will have to judge to what extent he eventually submitted to the party ... there are many indications that he reserved for himself the freedom to be, although not to proclaim, what he was—an individual.

I always had ideas in my head which I could easily write about. Since Jarcho [a friend] needed money, I decided to fabricate one [story] for the *Berliner Allgemeine*, the cheapest Ullstein paper ... the story became better and better ... until Korff of the *Berliner Illustrierte* bought my "Strange Little Girl" [for] 300 Marks.

I received a lot of praise for the story, was invited to contribute to magazines, to read from my works, etc. But I did not write more than before and was not able to muster the energy for more serious work. I only dictated a light, short novel on the following evenings ... which could not appear with Ullstein any more, because I wasn't racially pure enough for Mr. Goebbels ... The *Berliner Börsenkurier* printed it ... and people told me how comforting it was to read ... my title ... *Nicht traurig sein* (Don't be Sad) after reading the depressing news on the front pages.

For me the answer to the question of emigration was relatively simple. I didn't want to go back to Prague, despite all my love, although I was advised to apply for a free position as a music critic. In England I had friends ... and as a Czech ... I could emigrate without a visa. ...

Paul Robiczek, who had started a publishing company in Paris, asked me to write ... a volume about Palestine. In Athens [on the way to Palestine] I saw a ring of tin-covered huts around the city. "What is that?" I asked. "Refugees—two million homeless after their expulsion from Asia Minor." Sometimes it is good to remember one is not the only one.

I was never a Zionist ... but ... had a definite attitude toward the problem of many German Jews, who still understood their situation so little that they looked for a refuge in the whole world and only chose Palestine if worst came to worst ... I called my book *Palästina, das erlaubte Land*, and thereby wanted to express my respect for the pioneers ... .

[In England after the Munich conference] I gave a talk to a Rotary Club about Czechoslovakia. The vicar who concluded the discussion asked me ... "Aren't you also happy that your country was spared a war?" "No" I shouted. "And those who sell their friends will have to pay for it!" ...

I returned shaken and sick from Prague ... These trips to Prague between 1933 and 1939 became harder and harder. In Paris, I studied the situation of the refugees.

In London I found the atmosphere in Woburn House [a refuge for refugees] oppressive ... . I was almost prepared to agree with the critics who found the arguing, sadly passive seekers of help unattractive. Then I ... took a closer look at the people who still were well off, and who derived their upright gait from their undisturbed bourgeois existence. How would they look ... if the ground were pulled out from under their feet?

At that time I proposed that an inscription be placed on the door of such shelters: "Security is the basis of charm. The hunted are not charming" ...

Who can ask that those suffering be good or kind? Marie Schmolka, the best known Czech Jewish helper of people in need at that time, laughed:

"Naturally they cheat. What [else] should they do? They have been taken outside of the law, how can they live according to [it]? ... I am quite fond of the little criminals."

We laughed a lot, and I cried secretly. There was no point telling each other our woes ... .

The lawyer, who ... convinced me, rather against my conviction, to apply for restitution from Germany said: "You are unique. How could someone who is so well qualified, has had such good positions, never make more than a minimal income?" Why? Because [that] was all I expected. Compared with our real sorrow, poverty was almost pleasant ...

The house on Garden Square was a haven for all who spent their mornings in the reading room of the British Museum. I sat in this wonderful ... rotunda day after day for months and tried to collect material for a history of involuntary migration in the twentieth century ... I had the idea that political reasons and even wars are not so much the real causes of mass movement, but that a deeper impulse ... initiated them. It soon became clear to me, that [this] would be a life-long task, for which I didn't have time. But it is too bad that I gave it up too soon.

My excuse for my failure to carry out my ideas consistently was, in fact, that I had to eat; that meant first of all, looking for German lessons and placing articles in the few German language papers in Switzerland, Czechoslovakia, and the Jewish ones in Germany. ...

In the last year of the war one had to ask oneself seriously if one should continue living. It's not that I ever thought of suicide. I was always conscious how little time is allotted us, and that we can always wait for the end. I also did not think that I had a moral right not to endure. Suffering and destruction were general, the misfortune was not personal, we were only crumbs in the collapse.

The probability of dying from natural causes was diminished everywhere. There was fear in varying degrees. The question was different. Could I and did I want—the I with which I had lived so long—to still maintain myself? Although the details were not confirmed, I already knew that my parents and my brother had perished. That meant ... the loss of the people who loved me most and who would have missed me ... all my activity was ... without a nucleus.

My disturbed state manifested itself in difficulties with my work and with my employers, at first with the broadcasting company, then with pupils, or rather with their parents, then with the people who gave me literary assignments.

My flight from work developed into a senseless drive toward activity, from inventing recipes to making clothes ... or dolls which I tried to sell. In those years I learned to make hats, to do electrical repairs, to mend water pipes, to paint and to work as a cabinet maker ... .

My poverty never bothered me ... I was never physically sick. Therefore, I disliked the idea of psychoanalysis which somebody

Grete Fischer

suggested because of my inability to work ... . I consider my analysis a failure, although certain of its insights proved beneficial years later ... . I resisted so strongly, that for years I was regularly one half hour late. Anyway, I went ... At most, I appreciated in these desperate years that I could burden Frau Doktor with things with which one could not burden fellow sufferers ... . She admitted that I had fortified my inhibitions so solidly, that one could no longer get at their roots ... .

However that may be, I overcame the crisis for the most part. Today the elements of my original serenity and joie de vivre are released, I live because I consider existence the meaning of life. Existence means to feel and think as alertly as possible, to perceive, to take part. I was born with a gift for that, and I developed it consciously. That is the only thing I try to teach. I have never ... tried to fool myself. I demand that one confronts one's sufferings ... one can live with one's pain ... .

Too many people drag their misery behind them like a bag of potatoes ... and thereby neither help the dead nor the living ... just because I have no illusions about the individual's moral ability to resist, I have been able to see the positive in everyone ... the really good are as rare as the really bad, one must only try to strengthen those who are better. I am more critical than ever, tougher but hopefully kinder ...

I am tired of literature. Every year of my life I become angrier, more hostile toward phrases. The beautiful word which can express lofty thoughts is so pitifully misused, emptied by idle chatter ... I am not insensitive toward genuine joys, I enjoy a good sentence ... But what belongs on the dung heap I leave there.

Of course, my attitude is probably also determined by landscape: it was Prague, the glasshouse of intellectual-linguistic efforts which has disappeared forever since Hitler, the Prague of Fritz Mauthner and the clever German Jews down to Franz Kafka. We are related. Even the last generation still made its contribution to German culture. ...

I have encountered loneliness in all forms, except the last, most terrible one, the feeling of being abandoned in real despair ... when dying.

Loneliness has almost nothing to do with being alone. I was never lonelier than in a crowd. The feeling of not belonging ... is much more painful than being alone. It probably comes from a sexual root, from the desire for more intimate union ... . More than anything else it is the desire to have, although the desire to share oneself is contained in it too ... but two lonelinesses don't make togetherness. In the last analysis the root of most interpersonal conflicts is that our desire for love is so much greater than our ability to love ... .

NOTES

1. The following excerpts are from the autobiography already mentioned, *Dienstboten, Brecht, und andere Zeitgenossen in Prag,* Berlin, London.
2. The teacher's nickname Mîne, derived from Wilhelmine, means love in Middle High German.
3. The little brother was very important to Grete, from the time before his birth on. When she left home, she felt she could do so because there still was "a child in the nest". About seven years later, after Grete had left for Berlin, her brother Walter was struck with encephalitis from which he developed the crippling Parkinson's disease.
4. The monthly publication of the association for the culture of the Germans in Bohemia.
5. Grete and some of her friends founded a literary circle named the "aesthetic tea".
6. Lise Meitner, the famous nuclear physicist.
7. President Masaryk's daughter.
8. He was organizing a publishing company for Paul Cassirer.
9. Eugenie Marlitt was a writer of kitsch novels at the turn of the century.
10. Else Lasker-Schüler (1869-1945) was a great German lyric poet with whom Grete worked extensively.
11. Emil Faktor, the editor in chief of the *Berliner Börsenkurier,* whom she knew from Prague. He and his wife were personal friends of hers.
12. A former coworker at Cassirer's.

Chapter 9

MILENA JESENSKÁ
(1896–1944)

O*f all the women I considered for inclusion in this volume, Milena is the only one whose sympathies and friendships unreservedly transcended national, religious and ideological boundaries: her circle included Jews, Germans, Austrians, Marxists of various shades, social democrats, totally apolitical people and last but not least her nationalistic father. Milena had a very difficult life, but, given her character, there was probably no alternative. As she grew older, her life became increasingly rich and complex. She was generous, imaginative, loving, intelligent and reckless. She grew from Bürgerschreck to heroine and martyr, but what was the road in between?*

Milena Jesenská was born in Prague in 1896, into the family of a dentist who later became a professor of dentistry. Her mother died after a long illness when Milena was thirteen; her relationship with her father has been described as one of love-hate. After graduating from the prestigious women's gymnasium, Minerva, she took up the study of music, then of medicine, but gave both up. To break up her relationship with Ernst Polak, a non-writing member of the circle of the German, mostly Jewish writers centered around the Café Arco, her father had Milena confined to a mental hospital. She was able to leave it only by marrying Polak and moving with him to Vienna.

From the beginning, Polak had affairs with other women, failed to contribute to the household, and incurred debts. Milena earned some money by teaching Czech, as a porter based in the railroad station, as a housekeeper, and finally by writing articles for Prague newspapers. While in Vienna, she was twice convicted of stealing. Among her friends were several well-known writers, including Franz Werfel and Hermann Broch.

As a consequence of her translations of some of Kafka's stories, she met him in 1920. Kafka's love for her played a unique role in his life. To her, he was the most valuable person she ever met.

Her divorce from Polak was finalized in 1924. With the communist Count Schaffgotsch, she left for Buchholz, near Dresden, where they stayed with Alice Rühle-Gerstl for nearly a year. From 1925 on she was back in Prague, writing and translating. In 1926 she married the successful avant-garde architect Jaromír Krejcar.

After a serious skiing accident in 1928, she gave birth to a daughter, Jana, whom she called Honza. The severe and constant pain in her leg turned her into a morphine addict. The Krejcars' marriage deteriorated, and they were divorced in 1932. There is some disagreement as to when she joined the Communist Party, but in any case she began writing for communist newspapers and lived with Evžen Klinger, who shared her journalistic and political interests. From 1937 on she wrote for Přítomnost, the most prestigious liberal Czech weekly, and later became its editor-in-chief. By then she was very critical of communism.

Milena turned her apartment into a gathering place for German and Austrian refugees. After the occupation by the German army 15 March 1939 she became active in the resistance, was arrested in 1939, and died in Ravensbrück concentration camp in May of 1944.

Western—especially female—readers will probably read Milena's texts approvingly—until they reach the passages dealing with women's emancipation and the infidelity of men, and with the purported differences between men and women. On these subjects Milena seems very conservative, in fact even more so than my first protagonist, Magdalena Dobromila Rettigová, who, a hundred years earlier, had the reputation of identifying with the status quo.

Here we are touching on a complex subject. We should first of all keep in mind that all of the relevant articles were written before Milena was thirty-three, and that perhaps her most striking characteristic was the extent to which she continued evolving throughout her life. I do not share the view of František Kautman, writing in his introduction to the Czech edition of Kafka's letters to Milena, that she agreed with the old Czech housemaids' song: "Men, they're not people." There are too many facts proving the contrary. However, in this connection one should consider the early claims about Milena's alleged Lesbian tendencies, her love letter to her friend Slávka [Jaroslava] Vondráčková, and her relationship with Grete Buber-Neumann, which—if we believe Buber-Neumann, our only source on the subject—was homoerotic. It seems that with the possible exception of Jaromír, the men in her life were sick or in some way weak. Like my second protagonist, Božena Němcová, Milena looked all her life for her true love, perhaps not necessarily in a man.

There is no dearth of testimonies about what Milena was like throughout her life. However, in several of them—those of Kafka, Buber-Neumann, and others—she was seen through the eyes of love, and Jana Černá, her daughter, had a child's memories of her. But there is no essential conflict either among these witnesses, or with Slávka Vondráčková, another major witness whose objectivity and wisdom impress the reader strongly. In addition, we have not only Milena's published writings, but also a few of her letters, which reveal additional aspects of her personality.

Since the publication of Kafka's letters to her, something of an international cult of Milena has developed, a cult which has gathered momentum in recent years. I am watching it with mixed feelings. Many of its proponents have neither adequate knowledge of the culture from which Milena came nor a real interest in understanding her. The makers of a feature film and of an "artistic" personality sketch about Milena are particularly to be faulted.

Slávka Vondráčková (1894–1986) who knew Milena from her childhood on—though not always closely—was an original and successful artist, particularly in textiles. During Czechoslovak Communist rule, she wrote her memoir of Milena, which has only now been published after the "velvet revolution" in 1991. The manuscript had been deposited with and was later edited by Dr. Marie Jirásková, who kindly allowed me to use it before either of us dared to hope it would one day be published. My condensed translation of selections from it follows, alternating with other documents:

When little Milena was growing up, her father sent her to Sokol.[1] She enjoyed and excelled at physical exercises. Every Sunday, her father took her, along with a group of his friends, on long tours of the hills around Prague. It was there that she began to like hiking on highways.

Milena Jesenská

"When your heart aches, the highway will heal everything." She still recommended it to her readers years later.

When Milena was thirteen … Mrs. Jesenská died slowly and painfully. The end was difficult for her and her environment. When she lost consciousness, the doctor tried to bring her back to life through an injection. Milena tore the needle out of his hand and threw it violently onto the floor so that the broken pieces flew in all directions. When the end finally came, she realized with horror that the only feeling of which she was capable was relief.

Through the mediation of our mothers and older sisters, we entered our first Russian phase. Milena became acquainted with Dostoevsky at the Minerva gymnasium. She also began to go to the theater. She admired the singers and actors, showering them with flowers bought with her pocket money. She went to all of their performances and waited at the actors' entrance with bouquets. She also sent an armful of flowers to the love of her early youth, the [student/doctor] of medicine Fousek … . When Milena did not have the money to buy flowers, she picked them in the gardens of Bubeneč, in cemeteries and in city parks.

In summer, Milena went swimming daily on Sophie's Island, raced in the Moldau, ran around with good-looking trainers in the tennis courts, and experienced her first loves.

While a student at the gymnasium, Milena wrote to her teacher, Dr. Albína Honzáková, a well known feminist.[2] Some excerpts from these letters follow:

How I used to look forward to your classes, and how full of joy I used to be after them! ...

You have gone so far away from me that I can no longer go and talk to you about everything. But if there is anything special about me, striving to be realized—and with God's help that is the case—I hope and believe that I shall finally overcome my faults, such as my impudence and my partial laziness ... .

Prague, 7 May 1912 ... I promised to write to you about it all—I have written about a hundred pages ... . They are lying next to me. But now I feel I cannot send them. It's an ordinary story, and a few words are enough. I loved somebody, and when I was so very happy, I got his wedding announcement. There were several days and two nights; they were beautiful and they were mine. Now I hear gossip in Prague about my fairy tale.

[undated] ... I want to fulfill your wish and behave as one should in school ... . I shall be proper, calm, polite and distant ... like all those model schoolgirls. I didn't know that you also judge people in that way.

P.S.: The acacias are no longer blooming—only those around Loreta still are, and perhaps you don't know.

Gymnasium Minverva, 1890

[undated] ... I am taking so many nice books with me [on vacation] ... Zarathustra[3] ... another book which I know almost by heart—Andersen's fairy tales. They are the most beautiful fairy tales in the world, although they are not even real fairy tales. I have begun a little library for myself—I already have 150 books. And I love them all. I had them bound differently than usual, in tough Japanese paper and in soft leather which is so nice to stroke, and some in linen. I have almost all of Maeterlinck—I'll tell you a sentence from him: "I saw tears the source of which was deeper than eyes." Well, isn't this ... beautiful? And Ibsen, Björnsen, Wilde, Březina, Nietzsche, and Hardt [Hardy?], and many other people I love so much, and Hamsun, my God, how could I forget about him? They are very much mine ... .

[undated] Today I sat in church and cried with you. I don't know what would please you, and yet I have thought about it the whole day. I promise this year to be your most industrious and your nicest student, and I'll ask all the others to be quiet. I know this is not much. I would like to tell you about Hus, about Wiklif [sic] ... and all about Hussitism. I am so fond of that period, and mainly of Wiklif and Hus. I am hoping very much that you will ask me about him ... .

[postmarked 14 September 1914] ... You are such a precious person ... "May a great age not find you small." [Honzáková had said this to her.] No, surely not. I want to use all my strength not to remain little. I want to go far in life. I am looking forward to showing you the results of my work one day. They won't be small.

I am now on the foundation of a sober and clear life, and I feel good about myself—in so far as one can feel good today.

[28 October 1914] I love and have loved one person in the world, enough to give him my soul. Today I read in the paper that both his legs are shot—just a few words written here!

I am studying history for tomorrow, for a grade—O God, and in my head roars that one word lame, lame. Oh no, it isn't nice to be in this world.

Vondráčková recalls the interests and spirit of the time when they graduated from the gymnasium.

Milena graduated from Minerva and then threw herself into life.

At that time, we lived with Kropotkin and Herzen, and read Dostoevsky and Turgenev. We learned Russian, and also became involved with anthropology. We also took notes in the salon of Mrs. Topičová, the wife of the publisher and bookseller ... where anthroposophy is served after tea ... . At the Englishwoman's, Miss Trambeth's, the conversations are more intimate, more scholarly, with a touch of mysticism. Miss Trambeth taught us English. She also instructed the Prague German anthroposophists [at the Fantas'; see Chapter 6].

At that time, some romantically inclined young women used to meet in Růžena Svobodová's[4]beautiful apartment under the castle steps. They were fascinated by that woman, and even more so by her friend, the great F. X. Šalda,[5] and learned to debate in a scholarly fashion. Some young women, including Milena, frequented the Holandská, now Pařížská, coffee house on Nicholas Street ... which was then considered intellectual and Bohemian.

Café Arco where the Prague German writers met and where Kafka first met Milena.

Several groups met there at several tables ... Sometimes the Čapek brothers[6] also came ... the architects ... the painters ... and Professor Jesenský. And sometimes his slender, blond daughter came to see him. Hanuš Jelínek recalls in his memoirs: "At their table, I was struck by the painter Scheiner, an elegant man about town ... . He quickly noticed Milena's well-trained ... young ... body ... and she became his model. Her father didn't know about it." Later Milena exchanged the Holandská coffee house and the painters' studios for the catacombs of Café Arco.[7]

After graduating from the gymnasium, Milena wanted to study music, but lacked discipline and patience. So what about medicine? Again, there was the problem of discipline, but now also the terrible smell of the corpses. She heard Kierkegaard lecturing, and ... at the Arco, a lecture by Thomas Mann introduced by Johannes Urzidil ... new things that were unknown on the Czech promenade on Ferdinand Street[8] were presented there.

Passersby noticed two (later three) slender Czech women, sensationally elegant. All kinds of things were said about them.

For their final examinations [at the gymnasium], they arrived strangely dressed in light pinkish Greek-style robes. Milena set the tone, ordering clothes for all three from expensive dressmakers, but not paying the bills. The suppliers sought payment from Professor Jesenský! Are the young women lesbians?

They had perfect style. Their hairstyles were Pre-Raphaelite. There was nothing petit bourgeois about them. They were the first Czech girls to broaden their outlook through contacts with the younger generation of Germans ... . It was obvious that Milena was the leader.

Milena was arrested at five in the morning for picking state-owned magnolias. She knew no limits to her demands and to the gifts she gave. She burned her candle at both ends ... . Milena went through the artists' studios, stylizing herself consciously according to the paintings of Jan Preisler and Gustav Klimt.

Willy Haas (later the husband of Milena's friend Jarmila)[9] has commented on these Prague promenades: "Nearby began a world of mystery or at least of strangeness, of adventure ... the place where pretty Czech ladies and girls strolled [seemed] farther from this continent than Paraguay."[10]

Around this time, Ernst Polak showed up from somewhere. Father Jesenský and the students on the promenade described him as "some kind of paper-pusher in a bank." ...

A bank plenipotentiary, he had moved to Prague from his native Jičín and wished to complete his studies on the side. He lived on Smetana Quay 12, in ... a Gothic apartment house with a beautiful view of the Moldau and Hradčany. ...

Ernst Polak ... was very clever, and knowledgeable about literature; he knew languages, read English and French, associated with writers, adored Werfel and quoted his verses. He himself did not write.

Vondráčková here quotes Johannes Urzidil writing in his Prager Triptychon[11].

"There was an inexplicable magic about that small and insignificant-looking man which drove women irresistibly into his arms."

She also recalls that Milena wrote in the scrapbook of little Mařenka, Polak's housekeeper's daughter:

If I am to wish you anything, it is that you should remain a child for a long time ... When you understand this, you will no longer be a child. 19 September 1916.

Vondráčková continues:

Years later, Mařenka told me that as a child she had loved Milena and didn't know what her mother meant when she would say she couldn't understand how Milena, coming from such a fine family, could stoop so low ... .

Milena Jesenská

During her affair with Polak, Milena had a second abortion. [The first was allegedly at the age of 16.] Her father was very supportive, but when her longing for Ernst came back along with her strength, her father had had enough. Her forged checks had resulted in a scandal which he was able to mitigate only with the greatest difficulty. It horrified Prague society to see his daughter arm in arm with a Jew. He put up reluctantly with Milena's secret departures from home day and night, and her attempted suicide with morphine from his office. But to contemplate a half-Jew as a descendant of his blood, of which he was so proud: that was too much.

In June of 1917, with his authority as a doctor, he committed Milena to the mental hospital in Veleslavín ... . He was convinced that his daughter was simply crazy ... .

She could not live without Ernst's love. With the help of her friend Staša and the Veleslavín social worker, she got the keys to the gate of the sanitarium. But Milena could not go with empty hands. Jewelry was stolen from a rich patient. After an investigation, Milena's father was forced to pay bribes.

In 1920 Milena was to write to Max Brod:

Psychiatry is a terrible thing when it is misused. Anything can be considered abnormal, and every word can be used as a weapon by the torturer.

Milena's daughter Jana Černá wrote in her biography of Milena:[12]

When Milena left Veleslavín, her father agreed that she could marry Ernst. She was even promised a dowry, on condition that she would not meet him alone until the marriage, and that they would go to live in Vienna ... . She and Ernst married and left for Vienna.

It was ... Franz Werfel[13] who lured Ernst to bankrupt Vienna. He also invited Milena, whom he had always admired … seeing her as part of his "Sweetheart Prague."

Vienna meant failure after failure. The collapse of … currency values, winter without fuel, a shortage of potatoes, and the smell of sauerkraut in the houses everywhere. Values were turned upside down in the banks, in the stock exchange, in the shops and in literature … . Couples there lent each other money, food, wives, newspapers and coal.

In the poverty of Vienna, Milena's dowry was soon gone, and her household goods were gradually sold. Ernst became inconsiderate and arrogant. He studied neopositive philosophy with Professor Schlick, and women again surrounded him. In Vienna, he again played an important role in the coffee houses and among the literati … .

Milena taught children while their mothers scrounged for food … . Later, she wrote about this in the newspaper *Tribuna*. She gave lessons in Czech, also to Hermann Broch, whom she also helped to transcribe manuscripts. In addition, she translated into Czech for Sigmund Freud.

But Milena's most secure income came from carrying suitcases to hotels from the Western Station, an opportunity she learned of from the former Austrian officer, Count Xaver von Schaffgotsch.

Again there were loans, debts, and scandals about thefts. Again her father … helped. And again there was … morphine. She decided to poison herself to escape it all. But Mrs. Köhler, a kind and clever housekeeper, saved her. [Köhler] took care of the people who sometimes spent the night, writing intellectuals and friends of Polak's, but most often Werfel. Milena wrote in *Tribuna* in 1921: "This uneducated woman of the people from the last generation has the best heart of all the people in the world, and I love her with deep love and gentleness. I am always sentimental when I think of her."

Sometimes there was literally nothing to eat … .

At that time … Franz Blei[14] said: "What is the matter with Milena? She looks worn with care like six volumes of Dostoevsky."

She sent her articles to Prague, and became the social and fashion reporter for *Tribuna*, the liberal Jewish daily. She began: "Nothing in the world is external. Everything about you, your nose, hands … all has a relationship to your soul, and if you think that the phrase about the unpolished diamond … has anything to do with the truth, you are wrong … . One is profoundly responsible for one's facial expression, gait, and the way one dresses." (*Tribuna* 1920) … . The female readers agreed about the great importance of daily exercise, hygiene, a bathroom, an American kitchen. From Vienna … she reported about anything that … entered her consciousness.

Misery, hunger, the luxurious life of black marketeers, community kitchens, the *nouveaux riches*, cabarets, eroticism, thefts, ruined marriages … she mixed all of that with the cut of a fall coat, with the fashionable spring colors, with hairdos, gloves, stockings … prostitutes, brothels, cheap taverns, and post-war black marketeering … .

Ernst's extramarital affairs affected their … budget. There were violent explosions … . The vials of cocaine … calmed and intoxicated her … but the intoxication evaporated and she again fell into misery.

Lerchenfelderstraße! There she gave lessons, translated, argued with Ernst, wrote those chatty articles about fashion and the soul which Kafka liked so much, and which Ernst ridiculed. There she slept with Schaffgotsch, from there she went out to scrounge up money or to forget about her sadness, and there she devoured detective stories.

"Movies are something other than entertainment," she wrote. "One can compare them with alcohol, with opium … . How sweet it is to think for a while with the brains of the people on the screen, with the strong, direct, unproblematic, uncomplicated hearts of all the figures moving before us in beautiful clothes—although one doesn't have anything to eat."

Despite everything, Milena began to find herself in Vienna. Her journalistic writings led her to

Lerchenfelderstraße, where Milena lived in Vienna.

realize that her observations were relevant, and that she was able to express them well. Her experience of bitter poverty there also contributed to her temporary identification with communism.

She translated Kafka, whom she knew a little from the Arco … . [Eventually] they wrote each other daily, and the collegial correspondence turned into love. Kafka read her letters, and her articles in *Tribuna*, impatiently … And she wrote, for herself, for money, and now also for him—under the initials P. M. P., Mj., M. J., and F. X. Nessey.

Franz knew one musical style in Czech, the sweet language of Božena Němcová. Milena used this style, and added to it courage and passion. …

Both [Milena and Božena] longed to meet a good human being and searched for the right, simple life. Both broke through bourgeois morality. They loved unhesitatingly, impulsively, and were always disappointed. Both declared war against the social politics of their time. [I would, however, say that though they lived unconventionally, it was without a program of political opposition.]

Milena wrote to Max Brod about Kafka: "Those books of his are amazing, and he is even more so."

And Kafka: "My sleeplessness probably has various causes, one of which may be my correspondence with Vienna. She is a live fire, the likes of which I have never seen. A fire, by the way, which burns only for him. At the same time extremely sensitive, courageous, smart ... ."

How did he come to transform her into the Frieda of his *Castle*?

In those days, there was much correspondence: long letters and telegrams, communications by tube mail and by messengers. Kafka finally went to visit her in Vienna—he wanted to see the reality she had sketched for him ... .

"He walked up and down in the sun, he didn't cough once, ate a lot and slept like a baby, he was simply well, and his disease ... seemed ... like a little cold," Milena wrote to Max Brod. But in the same letter she remarked, " ... He will never be well, Frank will die soon."

According to her daughter Jana Černá, Milena was convinced that Kafka's sickness was his disgust and inability to live in the world that surrounded him.

"I know for sure that no sanitarium will succeed in curing him ... as long as he has this anxiety ... which concerns not only me, but everything that lives without shame, even meat, for instance. Meat is too bare, Frank cannot stand looking at it. I wasn't able to free him from that."

Milena and Ernst were always on the verge of separating ... . Milena wrote in *Tribuna* in the style of Kafka: "When you are worst off, when all exits are blocked, when your pain reaches its peak ... then the fast train hope emerges in your mind."

Kafka only sighs: "In the atmosphere of your life with him, I am really only a mouse in a large household which is allowed once a year at most to run across the carpet. How your letters dazzle me, Milena. I love you, as the ocean loves a tiny pebble at its bottom."

To her, these letters at first meant a great deal. They were like a salve for all her wounds. For the most part, their love expressed itself in letters. Milena knew from the beginning that Kafka was a great writer.

He suggested to her a stay in the country , in a nice Czech area, where she would not be dependent on her husband, because he, Kafka, would send her money to last long enough for her to get her health and nerves in order. In all of his letters, one feels concern, care, a desire to help, to respect and to love.

Milena again became beautiful, regained her self-confidence. Her articles were popular, and people reacted positively to them.

[But then came small instances of disillusionment.]

There is her description [in a letter to Brod] of Kafka sending a telegram from the post office: how he first looks for a window he likes, then slowly fills out the form, pays the amount the lady at the window asks for, counts and sees that she has returned more money to him than she should have, goes back to the window and returns the money paid in excess—then again she describes him counting the money. Frank realizes that he was actually cheated, and doesn't know what to do. She is repelled by everything she considers petty, she who is unable to count hundreds, let alone pennies. ...

Milena's articles at this time are so personal ... that they seem rather like letters. In an article in *Národní listy* there is even an apology addressed directly to Kafka—for the suffering she has caused him.

Milena passed Kafka's letters on to ... Max Brod, and she and Kafka reverted again to the formal term of address ... .

Between her and Kafka there were still indirect dialogs in the news-papers, but there were no successful visits with him any more, although they met a few more times ... .

The articles Milena Jesenská wrote in Vienna for various Prague newspapers increasingly reveal her journalistic talents which came to maturity in the 1930s. In several of these she describes the post-war atmosphere in Vienna which she saw as especially bleak.[15]

Can one be surprised if everyone says that life has to be paid for too dearly, and that everybody is in a kind of pathological suspense, which finds the most varied outlets? People who formerly didn't drink now get drunk or sniff cocaine every day, and the use of morphine is becoming a dangerous epidemic. Money is spent madly; gambling casinos and similar businesses show their terrible strength before the eyes of all. The general fatigue, depression and under-nourishment have, of course, brought about the desire for refreshment, for relax-ation, and because many years of a different life would be necessary before people could be refreshed naturally, everybody procures refreshment as best he can, even by the strongest means ... .

Since a day only has twenty-four hours, and only twelve for work, and since the wife takes care of everything at home and ages day by day and walks around dragged out and worn out, sickness is a luxury. How is one to pay for what a sick person needs urgently? Is it possible to punish the drunkard, the murderer, the addict with normal punish-ments, if in that person's whole life there is not a single normal day?

An empty stomach and shaken nerves absorb one's whole existence, and there is neither time nor strength nor hope for the soul.

When, during the celebrated trial of Georg Kaiser, Milena took his side, she must have thought of parallel situations in which she had found herself:[16]

Georg Kaiser, the German dramatist, was arrested. The accusation: theft ... Georg Kaiser was sentenced to a year of hard labor, his plays disappeared from the shelves ... . Georg Kaiser, after years of starving with his wife and three children, had a villa put at his disposal ... . The considerable income from his works ... was suddenly not enough for him. His expenditures in recent months rose to thousands of marks. Persian rugs and silver household utensils were taken from the villa, some to be pawned, some to be sold ... . The moral question of right and wrong for an outstanding person ... is surely one of the most painful.

Kaiser is a man who penetrated the human soul with great dignity. What happened to him are the grotesque realities of the world, before which one must silence one's brain and open one's heart. But ... journalistic stupidity ... poured its chatter over this case with gestures of such ... insensitivity, with such an ... absolute lack of the most primitive human goodness ... . They were like little hammers with barbed wire on them, which tear out a piece of flesh with every blow.

The press reproached Georg Kaiser because—with the money he had wrongfully acquired—he did not get himself bread, but oysters ... that he was not satisfied with two rooms, but wanted a palace. They forget ... that life is not logical. A person who has starved for months can't stand bread and beef, [but wants] caviar, pineapples, and salmon with mayonnaise. Hunger is not terrible by itself, but what hunger causes is terrible. It ... twists not only [people's] stomachs, but also their souls, hearts, and minds. It is perhaps an impossible task to satisfy a person who has once really looked misery in the face. The most terrible despair is rooted in misery, which results in conceit ... overeating, drunkenness ... . The person who has never starved cannot understand how close the pavement can be, when one looks at it for three days from the sixth floor, with an empty stomach. ...

Georg Kaiser ... cries to the judge: "I am a great poet who is allowed everything. Not because of current hunger, but because of hunger years ago." May he forgive me if I use his well-known name instead of all the unknown names ... . His battles, sins ... pains and atonements are his and God's affair. I don't dare to say a word of judgment either about him or about anybody else in the world.

I only wanted to write newspaper stories about the coarse, stupid newspaper stories at fifty dollars a line … . I only wanted to say that psychology is a lie, a poison, and the crime of our time … .

Milena frequently sympathized with unconventional views:[17]

The modern literature of the educated is obviously and oppressively immoral. Books of the most horrible pessimism are part of our daily diet. We attribute suicides … to the influence of bad literature, while [maintaining that] our good books seriously attempt to solve the question whether life is worth living. We point to the immorality [of bad literatures], while we philosophize over the question whether morality exists. We defend the principle of bigamy, of suicide and of perversity by the word "freedom." If one of those [allegedly vulgar] books contained half of what was in the books of good literature, they would have been confiscated long ago. The great masses … don't doubt that bravery is beautiful, and that work is noble … . Hopelessness has always been a specialty of the educated, like liqueurs and easy chairs.

Here Milena, who did not always practice what she preached, expresses some very traditional views about the role of women:[18]

Some very antiquated remarks about that female emancipation: for equal … rights, equal performance is necessary. If equal performance is to be possible, equal abilities are necessary [which in Milena's opinion do not exist]. … I don't know if God knew what nonsense he was engaging in when he created man: he did not create one man, but two people. But all these occupations … remain merely occupations with a woman … . The right kind of woman does not become a professional. At the bottom of her heart, a woman remains as God created her: a wife and a mother … fortunately, in spite of all the banners of the so-called women's movement … and that is her greatest value.

I tell all who are of the opinion that for these modest lines I deserve a beating, that I am usually at home on Saturday from two to five … .

Far from seeming indignant, Milena, who had suffered so much because of an unfaithful and irresponsible husband, actually advocated tolerance toward such men:[19]

After my article about the infidelity of men … I received many letters from angry women. How can I excuse something like [the infidelity of men]? … In reality, there is no life together without such conflicts. Every marriage is shaken by them, as a forest in a thunderstorm … . How bottomless would my insincerity have to be if I would use [both] phrases about duty and [the words] "I won't put up with that!" … Well, look attentively into his face, listen carefully to what he says—and understand him. Realize what he can and what he

cannot do. And live next to him with praise for what he can do. ...
To ask bravery of a coward is like asking a tomcat to bark. But it is
also possible to love a coward with one's whole soul. One must help
the coward, the liar ... .

Overestimating the importance of one's own feelings puts blinders
on one's eyes ... . Realize that he is as powerless, miserable and
lonely as you.

*In an undated letter of 1924 to the editor of Narodní listy, in response to his
inquiry as to how the paper should change, Milena writes that it is too full of dignity and pathos, that it sounds too bureaucratic and deadly boring. She continues:*

Forgive me, but perhaps *Národní listy* could use a few Jews—this is
half a joke and half the truth. The Jews have an immense, living sense
for newspapers ... . What is good in newspapers is certainly written by
Jews. You need new people ... more life and less politics."

*Then she suggests, among other things, that there be a section on books, targeted
toward women and children. The paper, in her opinion, should be entertaining,
the writing should be illustrated, and should come from many people.*

*There should be questions put to the readers, and answers from them, and
elements of surprise. Now that the paper has survived the revolution [of 1918],
it should get down from its high horse and build good things in the new state.
One cannot be a survivor every day, that gets on people's nerves ... .[20]*

*In a letter of August 1924, Milena writes about the malaise in her life
in Vienna.[21]*

Dear Doctor ... I expect to have left Vienna in a month. Divorce is
such torture ... and I slowly begin to understand that this could be a
reason never to split up ... . It sometimes feels as if they were cutting
flesh out of one's body, and there are moments when I think I'll die
of my infinite fear of life ... . That ocean of the unknown sometimes
frightens me so that I can hardly breathe ... . It is absolutely terrible
how alone one is in the world. I am giving up my apartment and selling my furniture—my husband has terrible debts, and I want to see
them paid up before I leave. So I'll be there in the street with a few
rags in a suitcase—after years of such desperate effort and tension.
Sometimes I think that I can't stand ... to get up from my bed and to
comb my hair ... My husband is also terribly alone, without money,
with debts, and he is devastated because he didn't get that other
woman. It is quite terrible not to be able to help him, when one has
been doing nothing for eight years but trying to help. I would like to
sell the contents of my apartment, my furniture and everything, and
with the money I would receive for vacating the apartment I would
pay my husband's debts so as not to leave him in such a situation, and

then I would leave. There is another girl expecting a child from him, and this somehow was the last straw.

In another letter of 20 November 1924, she writes to her editor that she finds the divorce proceedings extremely painful. Her father wants her to move to Prague and live with him, but she cannot do that—her whole marriage was an escape from her father.

In another letter to the same addressee, Milena outlines how she envisions her future work for Národní listy, stating that she would like to live in Paris, London, Rome or Moscow, and that what she would learn through her travels would surely benefit the newspaper.

A friend from Vienna days, Gina Kaus, remembers Milena in her book of reminiscences:[22]

And as much as I liked to talk to Ernst Polak [sic], it seemed incomprehensible to me that one could love him. I was wrong about that. Twenty years later, when he had to emigrate and went to England, a rich Englishwoman fell in love with him and married him ... .

Milena was the most colorful friend I have ever had. Since Ernst had an affair publicly, nobody had the right to reproach her with infidelity ... . Years after his death, she became famous because of the letters Franz Kafka wrote to her. She only once mentioned his name [to her], but did admit her affair with Broch.

It was certainly not that she was indifferent to Polak. He once spent a night explaining to her how much more she meant to him than she could ever mean to Broch. Full of pride, she told this to me. Polak remained the man in her life for many more years.

It must have been about this time that she stole something from me ... . One day I noticed that I was missing an old brooch with rather large emeralds. I knew immediately that Milena had taken it. A few days before, Milena and Werfel's sister Marianne had visited me, and Marianne had asked to see my jewelry ... . I spread it out on the table. At that moment the servant came and reported that another visitor had come ... . I went to the salon with the two ladies. And I knew ... that Milena had been the last to leave the room ... .

About a year later, she took a position keeping house for a couple of actors and was arrested after only two weeks. She had taken cash out of a drawer. We hired a lawyer for her ... During the hearing she said that she had taken the money to buy herself nice clothes. (In her Czech German, she said, "Was I in erotic crisis.")

She was given a short jail sentence, and then again lived among us: none of us held her misdemeanor against her.

On 6 June 1924, two days after Kafka's death, Milena wrote an eulogy of him in Národní listy:

The day before yesterday, Franz Kafka, a German writer who lived in Prague, died in a sanitarium in Kierling near Klosterneuburg, outside of Vienna. Few people knew him here because he was a loner, a wise person frightened by life; for years he suffered from a lung disease, and although he [outwardly] took care of it, he also consciously nourished it and encouraged it with his thoughts ... . "When the heart and soul cannot bear a burden any more, the lungs take over half the burden, so that the weight is at least somewhat equally distributed," he once wrote in a letter, and such was his illness ... . It made him almost impossibly delicate and intellectually refined, and terribly uncompromising. He put almost all the burden of his intellectual fear [angst] onto the back of his illness. He was shy, anxious, gentle, and good, but he wrote cruel and painful books. He viewed the world as one full of invisible demons who fight and destroy unprotected people. He saw too clearly and was too wise to be able to live, [and] too weak to fight, since he had the weakness of those noble, beautiful people who are unable to undergo a struggle for fear of misunderstandings, unkindness, and intellectual lies, knowing ahead of time that they are powerless, and who are defeated in such a way that they shame the victor. He knew people as only people of very sensitive nerves can know them, people who are alone and see them prophetically from a momentary lighting up of a face. He knew the world in an unusual and deep way, and he himself was an unusual and deep world. He wrote the most significant books of recent German literature; the struggle of today's generation in the world is in them, although without [the usual] tendentious words. [The books] are truthful, naked and painful in such a way that even where they are symbolic they are actually naturalistic. They are full of dry ridicule and the sensitive gaze of a man who saw the world so clearly that he could not bear it and had to die, not wanting to save himself, like the rest, by surrendering to any unconscious intellectual errors, no matter how noble. Dr. Franz Kafka wrote the fragment *The Stoker*, published in Czech in [S. K.] Neumann's *Cerven;*[23] the first chapter of a beautiful novel, which has not been published yet, *The Judgment;* *Metamorphosis*, about the conflict of two generations; the strongest book in modern German literature, *The Penal Colony;* and the sketches *Observation* and *A Country Doctor*. His last novel, *At Court* [The Trial], is in manuscript, having waited for years to be printed. These are the kind of books that leave the impression that they contain the whole world, that not a word needs to be added. All of his books describe the horrors of mysterious misunderstandings of guilt among people who are not guilty. He was a human being and an artist of such a meticulous conscience that he heard where others, being deaf, felt safe.

Vondráčková tells about how Milena saw Prague on her return and how her Prague friends viewed her:

Milena tried to feel at home again in Prague, but, after Vienna, she sensed a certain provincialism. "There is still straw sticking out of the Praguers' shoes," she said. We seemed inexperienced to her in the first red-and-white[24] decade, when we were shaking off the hated Austrian past.

From her stay with her friend Alice Rühle-Gerstl in Buchholz near Dresden, she came back elegant, well-read … . She knew Austrian literature, Freud, psychology. She manipulated with her personal charm, and wanted to put together a team, consisting mainly of [women] who knew the rest of the world. Her articles became lighter, not weighted down by a tragic mood, as the earlier ones were. She wrote about travel, mountains, dancing lessons. She went to Italy and wrote a well-informed article about cocaine. We[25] wrote about architecture, furniture, modern textiles, housing.

František Kautman wrote in his introduction to the Czech edition of Kafka's letters to Milena:[26]

During those years, ideas about lifestyles began to change radically. The new generation began to struggle for a clean, constructivist, functional style, with clean colors, and rejected everything fussy, superfluous, petit bourgeois in clothes, hygiene, sports and living quarters. Left-wing intellectuals, among them the fashion journalists Milena Jesenská and Staša Jílovská, and the graphic artist Slávka Vondráčková, discussed these issues in the daily papers. Milena writes about beauty, sports, jazz, joy in simple things, healthy tiredness, and hardiness in the face of pain. Women should educate people to appreciate beauty; near a woman there should always be a flower. But some of her articles are about social pity. She stoops sympathetically to beggars, prostitutes, poor mountaineers, and appeals to people's conscience. She admires Andersen's fairy tales, Chaplin's films, and Dostoevsky for his pity for the humiliated … . "Suffering makes people dirty, nasty, untrusting, twisted, but joy washes, strengthens, saves all."

At this time, Vondráčková could observe Milena closely:

She went to classical concerts, to the National Theater, and did not miss any of the performances of our little theaters … . Milena said to me: "How glad I am that I returned from that sorrowful Vienna. I do belong here … . "

At that time "literate" women met in groups ... . A smaller group fluctuated around Milena and her editorial office.[27] But with her nothing was permanent. Milena was not able to hold on to lasting, lifelong female friendships ... .

She was full of ideas. She helped her readers find inexpensive places to go on vacation with their children; she wanted to arrange community meals for married women with children, and she organized a poll about playgrounds in Prague.

Our generation, even the younger segment, remembers her articles to this day. How people waited for them! What will Milena say? How she was able to clear the still musty Austrian atmosphere! Did she form us? People felt she did.

Jana Černá, who knew about that period in her mother's life from hearsay, reports:

She translated *Peter Pan and Wendy*, which was to be the first volume of a series of children's books. Then *Mileniny recepty* [Milena's Recipes][28] appeared, and was immediately sold out ... .

I never saw her cook without a calamity ... . Milena ... usually ... put salami and a ready-made salad in the buffet for supper, and we each took a helping when we were hungry. ...

In 1926 another book of hers was published, *Cesta k jednoduchosti* [The Road to Simplicity] which she dedicated to her father ... .

Her work with the magazine *Pestrý týden* (The Colorful Week) did not last long, but she remembered it fondly. There she used to sit in the editorial offices with Staša Jílovská and with the caricaturist V. H. Brunner ... Milena had lots of people around her who needed to draw the strength of life from her. She was practically created to carry baggage which was too heavy for its owners ... . She enjoyed giving pleasure, but often people expected her to do things which were not humanly possible.

This letter from Milena, which Vondráčková reprinted in her reminiscences, contains, side-by-side, a confession of love and a request for money:

Prague, 26 October 1926 Dear Sláva, I have been torturing myself with the pencil in my hand all day ... .

I don't know how it is with you, I don't know if you loved me, what love between women is ... . Once I perhaps did, but it was too late ... . I am somehow only passionate for myself and would be awfully glad to find somebody who would untie my ability to be passionate and would make me able to bear it. Perhaps men don't know how, perhaps I am not brave enough ... . I don't know what it is to be honorable and faithful and what duty means ... .

I need to borrow money, about 6000–7000 crowns, but I won't be able to return them until next spring. I have debts ... . Jaromír is also just starting out ... . I feel awfully badly about it.[29]

Here is typical advice from Milena to women on how to care for their appearance:[30]

I am a broad-shouldered Slav and am therefore never going to wear little French dresses made for small French figures. I have a round Czech face and I am therefore never going to curl my hair. I have heavy calves and I am therefore not going to sit as if I had beautiful ones ... .

This reply to a letter by a woman whose husband is unfaithful continues in the same vein as the earlier article on the same subject. Milena not only expects infinitely more of women than of men, but she even reproaches women for crying:[31]

First of all, it is necessary to realize that the husband's infidelity and the wife's are not guilt on the same level ... . A woman has ... different responsibilities than a man. She can become a mother, motherhood is her mission and a task which obliges her to be pure and strict in her sex life even when it is difficult. A man is free ... physiologically ... . For him sex is a mixture of delight and obligation or deprivation, but for a woman it has serious physiological consequences. The man has no physiological obligations. ...

Try to remember what happened before. Perhaps you were not attentive, patient, friendly enough? Perhaps you were not sufficiently interested in his little wishes and ... worries ... or in a hurry, so that with worries and work you forgot to be pretty and charming? Men in reality are big boys ... and ... only understand themselves ... . The dearest and most beloved wife loses value if her eyes are red from crying ... if she spreads an atmosphere of pain ... . Be more pleasant than his mistress ... . You love him ... . Be brave. A conciliatory smile and patience would soon cure [him]. A tragic gesture, scenes, reproaches, threats make a mountain out of a molehill.

In her book of the following year, Milena continues to add to the obligations she sees for women:[32]

Nothing is as good for the skin as brave exposure to sun, air and water ... .

For a girl, having to stand on her own feet does not mean having to become independent of men; this is humbug, against which nature speaks volumes ... .

She does not wait until somebody carries her over a brook, but jumps herself, helps to support herself and her family, does not wait in ... ignorance, but studies.

All of this is a woman's obligation, all the more so at a time like pregnancy, when her charm is tried so much by nature.

In boys, the basic ways of relating to women develop according to their relationship with their mother. A girl develops into a mother and … wife according to the model of her mother.

Mother, be pretty, sparkling, like a clean flower, youthful, cheerful, happy … be forever a little girl and laugh! Be very strong and don't be sad, don't argue with Dad … be brave, be sunny, even if you have plenty of worries and work … even when you would like to creep into a corner and cry with tiredness or impatience. [Later, when the child is in despair, even if it doesn't think directly of the mother, the way she behaved will have an impact.]

Jana Černá describes the life of her parents together:

I think it was in 1926 that Milena met … Jaromír Krejcar, her next great love, during an excursion on the Moldau. … They agreed on everything, or at least they complemented each other.

Once they had themselves driven by taxi to Spičák [a mountain in the Bohemian Forest] without thinking of how they would pay for it.

He was born in a village, the only son of a forester … . His father died early and he remained alone with his mother … . As most men who grow up in the country and are raised by a woman, he acquired a strange, sensitive nature …

[Milena and Jaromír married with her father's approval. Jaromír applied all of his skill as an architect to creating a beautiful home for Milena. And when she became pregnant, she was completely happy for the first and last time in her life.]

She had great difficulties … [but] she was looking forward to the child. She stopped working for *Pestrý týden*, wrote again for *Národní listy*, translated as well, and together with Jaromír tried to interest people in cultivated living quarters.

In spring Milena decided to go skiing in the mountains, in spite of her pregnancy. It was … one of those heroic gestures that she herself claimed in her writing were without value … . [When she broke a leg and had to stay in the hospital for several months, until the birth,] there was fear for her as well as for the baby. During the whole thirty-two hours of labor, Milena kept her fingers crossed that it be a boy … .

Her father offered to take care of his granddaughter if anything happened, but … Milena refused … saying that … rather than entrust her to him, she would drown her child … like a puppy. …

Her right knee was stiff. For … four months the doctors tried to bend it; it hurt terribly and the only thing that helped was morphine,

Špičák, where Milena went skiing (etching from earlier period)

from which she did not free herself until she was thirty-eight … .
Milena switched from *Národní listy* to *Lidové Noviny*.

In this letter to Vondráčková, of 1928 or 1929, Milena is in great pain and unsure of her own worth:

I am always lying down, my leg always hurts, progress is at a snail's pace, and all my patience comes from vials of morphine. I feel somewhere at the bottom of something I cannot ever quite see. I don't know what the world looks like from a vertical position. Unhappy is not the right word; I feel I am destroyed. I would be immensely happy if I at least had your courage.

I admire you the most of all the people in the world, Sláva, and I look at you almost with religious envy. I love you as I loved Brunner, and I am better and braver when I think of you two. But you no longer like me … and I am always terribly sorry when you talk to me as to a small child … . You don't say anything about yourself, and you remain more of a stranger to me than to others, and, after all, despite everything I am perhaps worth more than they. I love you.—Milena.

Jana Černá continues:

Her drug addiction affected her relationship with Jaromír, which had already suffered ... during her illness. The habit was too strong to be liquidated by mere will.

In the course of a single year the beautiful, vital woman became a sick ruin, the happy marriage turned into the neurotic relationship of two people whose conflicts overstepped all bounds and bordered on madness.

Her convalescence was slow, and she still had pains ... . When she wrote an article about drug addiction, the readers in the countryside rebelled and Milena had to leave *Lidové noviny*.

When Jaromír completed the house on Francouzská Street, they moved to the highest floor ... Around the whole apartment was a terrace, and above it ... a flat roof ... . The rooms were large, and there were windows across one whole wall.

Milena wrote for the magazine *Žijeme* [We Live] ... . For a long time, she was editor-in-chief, but ... was eventually declared too left and too radical ... . I had my sandbox on the flat roof ... and my shower and my nanny, but that did not keep Milena from working for the [Communist] party. ...

... the relationship between Milena and Jaromír was no longer tenable ... . And so one day Father left for the Soviet Union, and a short time later we left Francouzská Street.

They were divorced long distance, and the three of us, Milena, Evžen Klinger, and I, moved to a new apartment. It was ... a room and a kitchen in Vinohrady.

Milena threw herself into work for the party as enthusiastically as into everything else. She worked for *Tvorba* [Creation], and was an editor of *Svet práce* [The World of Labor], and worked to the point of exhaustion ... . Several times Evžen [a Trotskyite] had to hide, and often comrades who worked illegally slept at our apartment ... .

[Although at first she spoke loudly about her reservations,] what followed was a short but intensive period of absolute faith [in Communism]. Milena ... had no doubts about being on the only right road ... .

Later she was accused of all kinds of deviations, mainly Trotzkyism, which in the

Milena with her daughter, Jana.

party dictionary meant something like eternal damnation ... . Milena was definitely not a person for whom any authority was final ... .

[Her departure from Svět práce also had to do with Jaromír's return from the Soviet Union] ... . What he told us sounded incredible then ... He reported that people were being arrested without anyone knowing why, and ... about the nonsensical cult of Stalin ... .

When the editor of *Svět práce*] asked her to leave ... Klinger ... Milena had had enough. She slapped his face and banged the door ... .

She was fond of Evžen—he was her kind of a person ... . She always fought for ... her right to decide ... for herself. ...

[So] Milena was without a job ... . She translated from Hungarian with Evžen, and her father, who did not want to see her, sent her a check for a few crowns every week ... . We often did not have money for electricity and sat by candlelight. But poverty with Milena was not poverty. She put candles into bottles [and we were in good spirits].

Milena's addiction to morphine cost money, too ... . Without ... morphine Milena changed psychologically ... and physically. Suddenly one could see her exhaustion, and she looked years older.

To improve her financial situation, she worked for a year as editor of the architects' journal *Stavitel* [The Architect], and wrote for the women's section of *České slovo* [The Czech Word]. At that time, Milena's income was minimal, and she often sent Jana to borrow money from friends, sometimes even from Ernst Polak. That graying, friendly man somehow didn't seem like Milena's legendary husband ... .

From Germany more and more refugees came with bare hands, tired eyes, and an incurable fear. Private ... problems paled against this background ... .

But when a regular income began flowing from Milena's work with *Přítomnost*,[33] things at home became much easier. Evžen also wrote for [that journal] *Přítomnost* ... . This cooperation was as strong ... as their love relationship. In him Milena found for the first time ... an equal partner ... .She never freed herself of her uncomfortable feelings about her lameness. The immobile knee ... damaged her whole outlook. Besides, the ... leg often hurt ... . The weight which she could not lose since my birth bothered her greatly ... and the fact that Evžen was ... younger than she also played a role ... .

Ever since I remember, she had two dresses, one for home and one for the street ... . The street dress was navy blue ... . In the street she usually wore a coat with deep pockets, into which she would put both hands as deeply as possible; [she went about] bareheaded [or] sometimes with a beret [which she often used to emphasize her gestures].

She cared very much about the environment in which she lived ... and went back to her old habit of stealing flowers in public places. One night a watchman caught us in Lobkowitz Square as we were cutting roses and already had a nice bouquet. Milena succeeded in convincing him that we were trimming the bushes of excess blossoms ... that weakened them. It was a pretty good rhetorical achievement ... . Finally the poor fellow thanked us and assured us that there were few such [concerned] people ... . Milena knew how to deal with people. She could talk to anybody, with villagers, with the unemployed who lived in caves, with intellectuals, with refugees ... and with the wives of her former partners ... with anybody except stupid people ... . The only person with whom she wanted to communicate and couldn't was her father.

Her work with *Přítomnost* was happy from the beginning ... . For the first time, a mature Milena did serious journalistic work unaffected by a prior viewpoint or party limitations. She established connections with new people, translated Willi Schlamm's[34] articles ... and wrote about everything that seemed urgent to her ... .

She and editor-in-chief Ferdinand Peroutka, one of our best journalists, worked well together ... . He sometimes used to say that she was so smart that surely no one else could live under the same roof with her ... .

When Jaromír ... was taken to the hospital with a heart attack, Milena of course had his charmingly decorative wife [Riva] ... whom Jaromír had brought from the Soviet Union, on her neck ... . Milena, part of whose fate was ... the burden of all the wives of her former husbands, invited her to stay with us ...

Milena realized that the turmoil ... a few kilometers from home [i.e. in Germany] was too horrible to allow any hope that it could be stopped. Assuming that she would need all her strength ... she decided to free herself of morphine once and for all ... . So ... Evžen took her to Bohnice sanitarium ... . She decided on a quick ... cure, which ... is only for people with strong nerves.

I visited her several times ... . Milena could hardly walk, her hands trembled, and her face looked worn beyond recognition. With a hoarse voice she told me [disconnectedly] that she was locked in a cage with demented women who soiled themselves, threw excrement at each other, screamed day and night ... . She returned from Bohnice worn out and thin, but the desire for morphine was gone. ...

On the 15 March 1939, when Hitler occupied Czechoslovakia, Milena burned everything which might somehow incriminate her or her friends ... . Everyone's home smelled of burned paper.

That day Professor Jesenský called. He and Milena had not been seeing each other, but he had been reading her articles … . They both knew that Evžen would have to leave the country. When Honza visited her grandfather, he handed her a little package and some foreign currency, so that Evžen would have something to start with when he went abroad.

When Milena opened the package … she cried like a baby. Apart from some dental gold, it contained the gold watch which had been given to him when he received his doctorate.

[Evžen left with the help of Milena's friend] Joachim von Zedwitz, an anarchist German count with a doctorate … after being reassured that Milena and Honza would follow him soon. Blond and blue-eyed … [Joachim] could drive people who needed to leave the country illegally.

Sometimes people on the run spent the night at Milena's apartment, and she and Jochi argued with them when they did not want to leave without their possessions.

She postponed her departure week after week, and soon began [to write for and distribute] the illegal publication *V boj* [Into Battle] … .

Early in June, 1939, Evžen Klinger wrote from England:[35]

She has almost become a symbol of resistance. The Germans know it. Two weeks ago a whole editorial about her propaganda activities appeared in *Der neue Tag* [The New Day]. When the rest is found out, Milena is irretrievably lost.

Jana Černá continues:

Things were also uncertain with *Přítomnost*. At first the censor didn't know local conditions sufficiently, and let some problematic articles pass, but later it seemed that the journal would have to cease publication.

Milena … did not want to leave [the country]. What her father had tried in vain to accomplish, the German occupants accomplished: Milena's patriotic feelings were awakened.

Lots of new people came to their apartment. Lumír Čivrny, who gave me private lessons and collaborated with Milena in her illegal activity … was one of the people of whom she was really fond in those last desperate days in Prague.

[During that summer of 1939, Milena and Honza spent some weeks at Medlov, a recreational area where many artists, journalists, etc. went.]

Milena's mood kept alternating … . She bristled with humor … sometimes she was profound, sometimes crazily happy, then again very sad. She went swimming in the pond at night … .

When war broke out, they returned to Prague. … That evening, she said:

So this is the end of peace for good. There won't ever be another hour of it. …

Přítomnost had ceased publication … and slowly there were reports about new arrests. [Milena was busy negotiating with bureaucrats for people who needed various kinds of documents. Among the friends they saw frequently at that time were the Mayers, a couple that took an interest in Honza.]

Milena … was extremely tired, fell into depressions, couldn't sleep … and kept switching stations on her radio … .

On Saturday, the 11th of November, as usual, Honza was sent to pick up the copies of the illegal paper. Although a strange voice answered when Milena phoned to announce Honza's arrival, she did not really worry. Honza was brought back to Milena's apartment by the Gestapo, which searched the apartment.

They told me that they would keep Milena for two weeks … and left with her … . She still managed to tell me that I should go to the Mayers' and stay until she returned … .

They took Milena to the Petchek Palace[36] for questioning, then to Pankrác prison, [and later] to court in Dresden … . Months passed—and Milena's health deteriorated. In addition to rheumatism and a serious paradentosis, she had an extremely painful infectious rash … .

Milena … defended herself … was cleared for lack of proof … and returned to Prague … . The Commissioner [in Prague], however, decided that it was not so much a question of what she had done but of what she might do, and decided to send her to Ravensbrück concentration camp … .

I saw her for the last time … before her departure for Ravensbrück … . I was there with grandfather, and when she finally came … I did not recognize her … . She was thin, with her hair down to her shoulders, with protruding cheekbones … . I only recognized her by her lame leg … .

I told her … how we sabotaged the instruction of German in school … . I thought she would be immensely pleased, but Milena only smiled and told me that I was a stupid little donkey, that German is one of the most beautiful languages, and that it cannot help who speaks it … .

Milena never wanted me … to kiss the hands of old ladies … . But when I sat next to her … and held her … hand with the swollen joints … I kissed the back of her hand. She looked at me askance … then … terribly lovingly, and two big tears rolled down her face.

I never saw her again.

Petchek Palace, Gestapo Headquarters in Prague

Petchek Palace, room where prisoners were detained for questioning by the Gestapo

Milena's articles in Přítomnost show her at the height of her maturity and jour-
nalistic skill. We have to content ourselves with a few selections. Here she reacts
to the Anschluss of Austria:[37]

In four years Europe has changed, and become full of Negroes.[38]
Negroes, as is known, are not allowed to touch a white woman. ...

Some time ago, the whole world was moved by understandable pity for three Negroes from Scottsborough, who were condemned to death on the false testimony of a white prostitute. ... In Vienna there are now a good half million Negroes. For the time being, nobody has hurt them much. They were "only" forbidden to work ... their property was confiscated, and they were given to understand that they should leave—unnecessarily, because they would leave if they could.

There are reports of emmigrants who go from border to border and are accepted nowhere ... Hundreds of heart-rending fates, thousands of painful farewells, suicides and wrongs ... among us.

What will England do ... France?

But mainly we have to know what we ourselves will do ... in our private sphere, the radius of which is three and a half streets, and a two-room apartment with a kitchen ... .

As a result of her travels in the Sudeten area, Milena became aware of the problems which sometimes led to Germans joining the Henlein party:[39]

I talked with a railroad man who speaks Czech very well ... . He is a German social democrat ... and has a Czech wife and two children who go to Czech school and do not speak German. He has been employed with the Czech state railroad for a full ten years ... and makes 450 Kč a month. They live with his German parents and does not pay rent ... . Two of his brothers work in Germany, two in Warnsdorf [in the Sudeten area].[40] All four have apartments of their own and help support their parents ... . Only he ... has to accept help from them. In the family of course he is ridiculed: Look at what the Czechs give you ... . He can get notice at any time and has no security. "I applied for a watchman's cottage ... . Honestly, if they turn me down, I'll join the Henlein[41] party."

With this description of the generosity of Czechs in Prague toward German anti-Nazi refugees from the Sudetenland, Milena clearly hopes to provide a model to follow:[42]

A field kitchen, lots of children who don't understand anything ... the sadness of people who have left home[43] ... their own bed, kitchen stove ... pots, and that little bit of security ... . Over there ... people lived in a kind of symbolic trench ... waiting in suspense ... with bare hands, suspecting that the enemy doesn't have bare hands.

Now the first refugees[44] are here ... many more than two thousand ... . It is good to know that the German democratic leaders all stayed in their places ... . Sometimes the Henlein people had been shooting straight into their windows ... . I saw a baby carriage with a wheel shot off ... [and] a woman who was going to have a baby in a few days. I saw lots of beautiful blond German children, women who came without underwear, some barefoot ... .

It is terrible, but ... Prague prepared a surprise for them ... . They came frightened, hungry ... . And today? It's been a long time since they ate so well and so much. Some go back for food two or three times and get it with a smile. Cream of wheat for babies, milk for children.

It was very, very nice, [children say in German] ... . I cried ... says a little girl. And why ... ? The people are so good, she sobs ... .

In front of the barracks in Nové Vysočany ... I push myself through a line of people from the places where only poor people live—they come with their arms full of gifts: a loaf of bread, a can of milk, toys, a feather bed, clothes, flowers ... a lamp. A working woman brings a pink knitted child's coat ... . They want to note down her name. "Why should you?" she protests ... and shyly ... goes away with that beautiful shyness of the poor who would like to give much ... . A ... fat, friendly woman brought a big wreath of sausages ... and distributed them to the children ... . They say that she comes every day ... . The Prague people come in large numbers, each bringing something ... . Some people phoned the director [of a factory] and asked for inexpensive children's clothing ... . And he gave two hundred pieces for free, and a doll for each child.

A while later freight trains came with [food]. Owners of big hotels daily supply milk for the children, the owner of a dairy offers cream and cheese ... . A doctor examines and treats the refugees ... .The people of Prague would gladly take the German children to their homes if it were necessary ... .

"We were told that the Czechs would spit at us ... but they welcomed us as friends ... . We won't forget it! We were afraid of you ... . " There is something very beautiful in the world ... the solidarity of people with people. ...

It is another surprise for the world that many thousands of Germans are fleeing here ... and it is clearer than the sun that ... not all Germans are alike!

In this article, Milena expressed the bitterness all of us felt about the Munich dictate: [45]

Let us look at what is going on without trembling, without wavering, and without tears. For life did not stop, and history did not end on the thirtieth of September. The world will go on for the time being, perhaps in peace, as long as there are enough mouthfuls.[46] Many will realize how bitter it is to be a mouthful. One day, however, this eternal peace, signed at ... the green table, will become shaky. And let us work earnestly, so that in the future the fates of people can no longer be decided on or over their heads.

Here Milena, whose own country was sacrificed, pleads for the German and Austrian refugees:[47]

In these pages I have pleaded for the safety of the Sudeten democrats ... as long as the Czechoslovak state was able to give it to them ... . From the Sudeten areas, occupied by the German army, the democratic Germans are coming. I am not going to dwell on what they ... experienced in their homes and what awaits them if they have to return. Many of them were dragged into the Third Reich ... . Those who ran away earlier are here without ... food, without money, without work and without prospects of work ... . In all of Prague there is hardly a house without several refugees ... . In the last five years we have seen ... how Germans live who escaped from German national solidarity ... . If there were a war, we would probably have several hundred thousand dead today. Instead, we have several hundred thousand fallen—and these fallen live. A living person wants food ... . And we, in whose front lines of peace these people fell, probably cannot give it to them permanently. In the horrors of war there is ... something like a weak glimmer of justice ... we would have fallen wherever a bullet [from our own enemies] hit us. In the horrors of peace, however, there is a ... cruel ... injustice: all who were for us fell.

Well, we didn't make this peace. It was forced on us ... . In the papers, we read about the great appreciation toward Czechoslovakia for its sacrifice to world peace. Wrong. We didn't sacrifice, that is done voluntarily ... . We were sacrificed, and we have here several hundred thousand living casualties, along with several thousand German and Austrian refugees, whom we granted the right to asylum. The responsibility for them lies with the French and English governments who wanted this peace ... . From disappointment it is a small step to the desire for revenge ... . It has always ... been taken where it was possible, it is an act of the weak against the weaker. [If that happens,] our people will receive a deep moral wound from which it will be hard to recover ... .

There are collections taken up in France and England for the democratic German refugees. Two million [crowns] have already arrived in Prague. Perhaps we should say thank you. I am sorry, but I can't ... We were silent when they took billions from us, our mountains, forests, mines, railroads, the work of twenty years ... . We feel the lack of a plan of the great Western powers which would save

the people whom they have made it impossible for us to feed permanently ... . It is a question of where to move people who stand
between the ... concentration camps of the Third Reich ... and
unemployment in an impoverished country ... . How can we be a
transit station when the borders of all countries are ... closed off, and
they only let in a few dozen people after receiving infinite capital
guarantees ... ? A fraction [of the losses France and probably England
would have suffered if there had been a war] would be enough to
guarantee [to hundreds of thousands of people] a new existence. I
think that this would be the least responsibility [to take on in
exchange for] the peace which was so cheap for you.

*When discussing the unemployed refugees, Milena is more concerned about the
humiliation of men than the problems of women:*[48]

During the Depression, wives in thousands of families went to
work—to clean, do laundry, wash windows—and the husband at
home swept ... took care of the children, and cooked dinner. You
won't find a man in the world who would consider that natural ... .
Every man considers taking the main part of the family income from
... his wife and pushing the baby carriage demeaning ... . According
to the order of the world, the household belongs to the wife and
work to the husband ... . This is so deeply engraved into men's consciousness that a man with a wooden spoon feels the bitter ridicu-
lousness of his situation, and having filled his stomach by means of
money earned by a woman bows ... his head, feeling the scorn
poured onto him by the whole world. Women often marry so that
they can work at home while the husband earns the money ... .

*Milena comments on the death of Karel Čapek a short time after the occupa-
tion of the Sudeten area:*[49]

Karel Čapek was never entirely healthy. Sick people live differently
and fear serious illness differently than healthy people. They see the
strangest beauty where other people only see something ordinary.
When fate strikes ... they crawl into loneliness, so as not to incon-
venience anybody ... . Therefore Karel Čapek only lay down when
he was already dying. I don't know if he believed in God. But he
was a religious man with a very carefully and subtly worked out philosophy of moral values, with a firm world order in his heart and in
his thinking. Like a flood, the year 1938 carried away boulders
which seemed so firm before. One blow followed another. The loss
of French friendship, of the faith in the Marseillaise, in the authors
of democratic freedom, the loss of the mountains and borders; the
crippled nation, the anxious powerlessness of the poet, and the house

crashing down … on the edge of the abyss, and the new language of the Czechs, slandering their own heritage. Too much devastation … for the poet who loved an orderly garden, blooming flowers, a hospitable house and ordinary life. He was too modest and shy to die of a broken heart. He died of pneumonia.

This is how Milena experienced the occupation of Czechoslovakia:[50]

When on Tuesday at four in the morning the phone rang, when friends called, when the Czech radio began broadcasting, the city under our window looked as it did any other night. Gradually, lights were turned on—first the neighbors', gradually in the whole street … .

As always during important events, the Czechs behaved excellently. We are grateful to Czech radio for the objectivity with which it reported every five minutes: The German army is advancing to Prague from the borders. Be calm. Go to work, send your children to school.

At seven-thirty the … children started out for school, as always. The workers and officials started for work, as always. Only [the manner of] people was different. They stood silently. I have never heard so many people be silent. In the streets there weren't any crowds … . At eight-thirty the army of the German Reich came to Národní Street. People walked on the sidewalks, as always … . The German inhabitants of Prague welcomed the soldiers.

The [Germans] also behaved decently. It is strange how things change when a body of people breaks up into individuals … . In Wenceslas Square a Czech girl met a group of German soldiers—and because it was the second day and our nerves were a little tired, she had tears in her eyes. A German soldier, a simple, ordinary little soldier, stepped up to her and said: "We can't help it." He had a German face, a German uniform, but otherwise he was no different than a Czech private. And in this terribly ordinary sentence is the key to everything. In a streetcar something else happened: a Czech youth talked big about what we'd do now and whom we'd beat up and how we'd show the world. He also had a swastika on his lapel. A German officer got up and addressed the boy in Czech: "Are you a Czech?" And the officer ripped the swastika from [the boy's] coat and said very emphatically: "Then you don't have the right to wear this."

You know, I felt like saying to the officer, "Thank you, Sir."

In this recollection from her childhood, Milena expresses her opposition to violence, her belief in self-discipline, and again her bitterness about Munich:[51]

When I was a very little girl—it was in the musty old time of Austrian-Czech tension … a time which contained the roots of many unfortunate later events … I lived at the corner of the Street 28 October and Příkopy Street, and Wenceslas Square lay before our windows. It was all actually a small provincial town with a … clean town square … . The tension could be seen in various ways, but on Sunday morning it had the character of demonstrations. On the right side of Příkopy the Germans students walked with colorful caps, on the left the Czechs in civilian clothes. Here and there it culminated in a tangle, which I didn't really understand. But then the Sunday came which I won't forget as long as I live … . From the Powder Tower the Austrian students marched in the middle of the street with their colorful caps. Suddenly a crowd of Czechs came from Wenceslas Square—and they also … walked in the middle of the street … silently. My mother held me by the hand, at the window, a little more strongly than was necessary. In the first row of those Czech people walked my father; mother was as white as a sheet, and evidently not pleased. And then things happened quickly; a group of policemen came running and stopped between the two factions. But [both] kept walking … until the Czechs arrived at the cordon of policemen and were asked to stop … . I don't remember what happened. There were loud noises, the silent crowd of Czechs changed into a screaming one, and Příkopy was suddenly empty. Only one person stopped before the guns—my father … calmly, with his arms down at his sides. Something terribly strange lay

Wenceslas Square

next to him—I don't know if you have ever seen what a person looks like who has been shot and collapses. He doesn't look human, but like a discarded rag. My father stood there for perhaps a minute. Then he bent down and began to bandage that human ruin … . Mother's eyes were half shut, and two big tears ran down her cheeks. I remember that she took me in her arms … .

Later, several times when I saw a crowd of Czech workers shot at by Czech police, when I read about Slovaks wounded by Czech police … I realized how rare it is: to be able to stand firm.

Then I saw something very similar under very different circumstances in the theater during the war. At that time we Czechs did not think of independence … . They were playing Tyl's *Fidlovačka*[52] … and in it was "Where Is My Home?"[53] You know, [it was] no … anthem … at that time, it was simply a Czech song. And … a man in front of me stood up quietly … to honor the … song. After a while another stood up … and then we all stood. We sang … the song several times … fervently, as a prayer. [It] was not against somebody, but for something, not for anybody's destruction, but for our survival. It was not a fighting song, but a song of our home, this land without a dramatic landscape, a land of hills … fields … birches, willows and spreading linden trees, fragrant among fields and quiet brooks. The land where we are at home … . I knew then that … to stand is dignified, honorable … .

We are not able and we never were able to stand up against anybody. We see clearly that it would be no use. We also cannot trust anybody anywhere in the world: when we did, in our youthful inexperience, we saw how little it took for great states—which today talk bitterly about the "wrong done to small states"—to break their word given to a small state.

Reading an article such as this, readers must have wondered how long the journal could continue to be published:[54]

I am not speaking of our losses or about our changed relationship with Germany. I am speaking about the blows which the Czech nation received and which are so painful that they can undermine its confidence in itself so destructively that it ceases to be interested in its own affairs. …

We were betrayed. The treaty in which we believed was discarded. It is natural that the nation asks itself: What are we, if we can be treated this way without punishment or echo? We are not even worth an apology to them. It is necessary to repeat … to our people: You live in a country full of enchantment, you belong to a splendid people. We prepared for battle, all of us, but the weapons were taken away from us and we were told to "go home quietly" ... . That march with guns and the return without them perhaps hurt the self-confidence of the people even more than the previous betrayal.

> *Milena suspected that country people doing traditional work can survive better than city people who have been torn from their roots. She spoke to a farmer in the country:*

So what are you doing here? I ask. Well, I have planted my potatoes, and I finished sowing the rye. In the orchard I guess I'll cut down two apple trees and plant young ones. My old woman already has young ducklings, go and see them, they are like dandelions. I'll cut that lilac bush, so that the garden looks nice this year.[55]

And, I ask, how do you get along with the Germans?

Oh well, they go along and I do my work ... .

And you aren't afraid of anything?

What should I be afraid of?

You who left the cottages of your great-grandfathers to get an education and find yourselves at an unfortunate level of development: civilization has not yet developed a hard and proud tradition in you. Go and see how to live, learn how to think, and how the nation preserves itself calmly and serenely.

> *Milena sometimes talked about leaving, but probably never seriously wanted to:*[56]

We are a nation and we have to remain one. Everyone who leaves carries away a clod of soil with him, and a piece of the roots. As long as we stay together, strength will grow out of our number ... . The spaces between us must necessarily be filled according to physical laws. There is no vacuum ... . Therefore stay ... and don't leave.

> *Jana Černá writes that when Milena arrived at the concentration camp, all the Czech women, including the communists, had received her well, until Grete Buber-Neumann arrived. She and her husband had fled Nazi Germany and sought refuge in Moscow but her husband had been executed by Stalin. When the Soviet Union signed the non-aggression pact with Nazi Germany, it had handed all surviving German Communists over to the Gestapo, including Grete.*

Milena was of course interested in [Grete's] fate. When the Czech Communists ... heard her speak about Soviet concentration camps, [and] Grete ... proclaimed, among other things ... that Ravenbrück was a resort compared to Stalin's prisons, they withdrew from her. ...

Milena and Grete became friends ... . [What she heard from Grete strengthened] her conviction that moving from fascist to Stalinist control was like going from the frying pan into the fire ... .

The reactions of the Communist prisoners are described by her friend in a letter to me: They pulled away the pots of marmalade and the bread ... . However, they did not quite succeed in isolating Milena completely ... . There were a few women ... who continued to do for her everything humanly possible.

I know that ... Milena, before her departure a convinced atheist ... in her loneliness called upon God. ...

The state of her health deteriorated, and finally she came down with a kidney inflammation. One of her kidneys was removed, but she trusted her doctor, was treated well, and received several blood transfusions; however, the other kidney was also affected, and she died on May 17 ... .

Her father could have come to take her remains to Prague, but he was in no state to travel.

Milena had written 26 September 1938 in Přítomnost:

The Communist Party left the people an unfortunate inheritance, twisted by propaganda: blind confidence in the Soviet Union ... . For some strata of the working people, the Soviet Union has become a legend, similar to the legend of Blaník.[57] If the Soviet union could and wanted to stand up in the world as the fatherland of all working people, it certainly had enough opportunity before 30 September. If it had wanted to go into a world war alone at the side of Czechoslovakia, it would have found a mouth through which to proclaim [that intention]. Nothing indicates that it considered anything but its own interests ... .

Czechoslovak worker ... ! Stop believing. No savior will come. There are no Blaniks.

Each of the following quotations helps us to round out our composite picture of Milena:

Nina Jirsíková (1910–1978), formerly a dancer and choreographer in the Liberated Theater, describes in a memoir written in 1973 the impression Milena made on her at Ravensbrück:[58]

LangenMüller

One of the best known books about Milena by her friend Grete

1942: So she walked toward me, with the sun at her back, her fine curly hair, already more gray than golden, around her head like a halo, like the delicate fluff of a dandelion. There was something fragile that radiated from her, from her glance. Her figure was rather bony and tall. She always walked erect, even later, when she pulled her stiff leg behind her. Her head had fine, noble features, with sensitive nostrils, and her eyes were particularly striking. A strong personality radiated from her, from her glance, her gestures, her diction. One felt that her strong spirit did not want to endure subjection, and that it commanded her body, which at that time was already strongly marked by illness. She seemed especially strong in an environment where there were so many people broken in body and spirit ... . Milena Jesenská loved art. We talked about art, artists, plays and books ... .

Her spontaneity carried us away, so that we could forget about our situation ... . Milena was ... able to support others spiritually ... . From what she told me, I knew that in the past she had not been strong enough to deny herself life's pleasures. She talked quite a bit about herself and Kafka ... but it was her husband Krejcar whom she still loved and hated.

Jaroslav Dresler summed up at the end of his book:[59]

Milena's greatness was neither in her "holiness" nor in her being a textbook example of an anti-Nazi fighter, but in her ability to raise herself from the dust and dirt of life to a sacrifice beyond the personal; in her ability to get over the somersaults and escapades of her journey. She came out of the cesspools and sewers of life clean and unblemished in Kafka's sense. Her nobility lies in what she finally made of herself.

Many people felt Milena's impact in a way similar to that of Eduard Goldstücker, the literary historian, expressed some important observations very concisely:[60]

Besides being a great bliss, Milena was too great a psychic burden for Kafka. In love, she was extremely self-sacrificing, but also considerably possessive ... . She was .. so active that in the passive Kafka she intensified the ... ever-present feeling of anxiety, especially in the area of sex. It was this anxiety that made their love fail ... . She was one of the handful of people who understood that by entering Bohemia, Hitler opened the door for the other dictator who was to come after him.

Many people felt Mile5na"s impact very much as Willy Haas:[61]

According to legend, ancient Bohemia was a matriarchy. One could well believe that if one knew Milena ... . In my whole life I only met one person who was born to live dangerously ... Milena. The order of the world was not for her ... . She broke it every day, every minute. She took what was due to her, even if the bourgeois called it theft ... and she gave with both hands. Nothing was impossible for her: whomever she loved, over whomever she held her protective hand could keep on marching ... . She would have been capable of murder for friendship's sake ... . I was never her lover—it would have been horrible to be married to a ... hurricane— ... [but] I was always ecstatic when I saw her.

NOTES

1. See General Introduction for a note on this nationalistic sport association.
2. These letters are in the National Literary Archives, Strahov.
3. i.e. *Thus Spake Zarathustra* by Friedrich Nietzsche
4. A novelist who was considered very emancipated.
5. 1867–1937, the foremost Czech literary critic of his time.
6. Josef Čapek (1887–1945), a painter and writer; Karel Čapek (1890–1938), a famous playwright and novelist.
7. The meeting place of the Prague German circle of writers.
8. Now Národní Street.
9. A member of the Prague German circle of writers.
10. *Prager Mittag*, 18 July 1933.
11. Munich, 1960
12. Jana Černá, *Deset adres Mileny Jesenské* [Ten addresses of Milena Jesenská], (Prague, 1959).
13. 1890–1945, a member of the Prague German circle of writers.
14. A German writer.
15. *Tribuna*, "Život ve Vídni" [Life in Vienna] 11 March 1920.
16. *Tribuna*, "Případ Jiříka Kaisera" [The Case of Georg Kaiser] 9 March 1921.
17. *Tribuna*, "Vulgární literatura" [Vulgar Literature] 4 March 1922.
18. *Národní listy*, 2 February 1923.
19. *Národní listy*, "Od člověka k člověku" (From Man to Man), January 12, 1924.
20. Czech national literary Archives, Strahov
21. Same source.
22. *Und was für ein Leben!* [And What a Life!], (Hamburg, 1979), p. 53–55.
23. Translated by Milena.
24. The Czech national colors.
25. Milena's circle of women writers.
26. Franz Kafka, *Dopisy Milené* [Letters to Milena], edited and introduced by František Kautman, (Prague, 1968).
27. *Pestrý týden*.
28. Prague, 1925.
29. With this borrowed money she went to Italy, to the sea. In Vondráčková's words: "No, debts never bothered her ... ."
30. Cesta k jednoduchosti [The Road to Simplicity], (Prague, 1926) p. 16.
31. Ibid., p. 37.

32. *Člověk dělá šaty* [Man makes clothes], Prague, 1927.
33. A very prestigious liberal weekly.
34. A refugee from Austria who became one of Milena's best friends.
35. In an article by Ulrich Weinzierl, *Frankfurter Allgemeine Zeitung*, "Wahrscheinlich bin ich traurig heute" [Today I am probably sad], 7 October 1980. The title is a quotation from one of Milena's letters.
36. Gestapo headquarters.
37. *Přítomnost*, "Soudce Lynch v Evropě" ("Judge Lynch in Europe"), 30 March 1938.
38. Milena is trying to point out that the discrimination against the Jews resembles the mistreatment of Negroes in the Southern United States.
39. "V pohraničí: Kolik bodů pro nás" [In the Border Area: How Many Points for Us?], *Přítomnost*, 7 September 1938.
40. In this article, which was written before the culmination of the Sudeten crisis, Milena concentrates on the problems of unemployment in the Sudeten German area, which, being industrialized, was hit harder by the Depression than the rest of the country. As often, she tells of a concrete experience and puts herself into the shoes of another person.
41. The leader of the pro-Nazi party in Czechoslovakia.
42. *Přítomnost*, "Pověz mi, kam utíkáš—povím ti, kdo jsi" [Tell me where you are running, and I'll tell you who you are], 21 September 1938.
43. i.e., in the Sudeten area.
44. Czechs, Jews and Germans from the Sudeten area.
45. *Přítomnost*, "Měsíc září" [The Month of September], 5 October 1938. This article is a factual, day-by-day account of the events of September, including the Munich agreement.
46. Figurative: countries sacrificed to satisfy Hitler.
47. *Přítomnost*, "Nad naše síly" [Beyond Our Strength], 12 October 1938.
48. "Nezaměstnanost za prahem domácnosti" [Unemployment Beyond the Doorstep of the Household], *Přítomnost*, 2 November 1938.
49. *Přítomnost*, "Poslední dny Karla Čapka" [The Last Days of Karel Čapek], April 1, 1939.
50. *Přítomnost*, "Praha, ráno 15. brezna 1939" [Prague, The Morning of 15 March 1939], 22 March 1939.
51. *Přítomnost*, "O umění zůstat stát" [On the Art of Standing Still], 5 April 1939.
52. See Introduction.
53. The Czech national anthem, originally an aria in that opera.
54. *Přítomnost*, "Co Čech očekává od Čecha" [What One Czech Expects from Another], 3 April 1939.
55. This is an example of "staying put" that she advocates, in this case in preference to leaving the country.
56. *Přítomnost*, "Hledat štěstí jinde" [To look for happiness elsewhere], p. 228, 1939.
57. The mountain from which, according to legend, knights will come to help the Czech people in times of stress.
58. In an unpublished manuscript by Jirsíková.
59. In Milena Jesenská: *Cesta k jednoduchosti* published by Jaroslav Dresler as "Kafkova, Milena", Eggenfelden, l982, pp.123 f.
60. Dresler, ibid, p. 124.
61. *Die Literarische Welt: Erinnerungen* [The World of Literature: Reminiscences], (Munich, 1960), pp. 38f.

Chapter 10

MILADA HORÁKOVÁ

(1901–1950)

If the Western media had a more plausible scale of values, Milada Horáková's name would be well known, rather than virtually unknown in the West. She was one of the most important activists in the Czech women's movement in the nineteen thirties. Jailed by the Nazis during most of the Second World War, she barely escaped execution, was probably the most prominent woman activist after the war, was again jailed and this time executed by the Communists in 1950, despite many telegrams of protest by world leaders.

All reports about her which I have been able to find portray her as a totally admirable person: highly intelligent, principled, conscientious. Except for her letter to her mother-in-law, here reproduced, there are no documents testifying to any inner conflicts on her part. The conflicts in her life, as I see them, were between Milada who was right, and two Unrechtsstaaten which were wrong.

Of the two trials, the one by the Communists is the more shocking: The enemy was not only the Stalinist government of her own country, but also well known intellectuals who expressed themselves against her as well as hundreds, perhaps thousands of workers who, aroused by propaganda, asked for her death.

Horáková's writings and speeches stand out as especially professional, objective and polished. At the same time she was deeply religious, much more so than any of the other women in this volume.

As the documents concerning her, including her answers in court, would fill volumes—her trial in 1950 was the largest show trial in Eastern Europe—this chapter will necessarily differ from the others. There are no memoirs or diaries from which one can compose a portrait of Milada Horáková. Therefore this chapter consists of my condensation of Zora Dvořáková's account followed by some of the letters by Horáková written days or hours before she was executed.

Milada Králová, born December 25. 1901, lived in the Prague section of Vinohrady. The large King George Square, where the … family lived, offered the curious child a colorful palette of interesting things … . Prague was growing and was being modernized … . Her father, Čeněk Král, considered himself a businessman, although technically he was not one. He worked for many years as a director of the pencil factory in České Budějovice … . This Czech concern had a difficult time competing with the well known German owned Koh-i-Noor factory.

As an enthusiastic patriot, he was intent on Czechs prevailing in comparison with Germans. That was why he [always] emphasized perfection and solidity … As the family never moved to Budějovice, the mother stayed alone with the three children during the week. This perhaps also helped Milada to act independently, and taught her from childhood on to help solve everyday problems … .If her father was rational, agile and definite, her mother was feminine, emotional and gentle … . She succeeded in creating a home which was remembered as loving and secure … .

Already as a child, Milada was aware of everything that concerned her father … she knew that he participated in every [presumably political, left of center] important demonstration. … As a strong personality, he dominated in the family and Milada, who increasingly agreed with his attitudes, was the closest to him among the children. He sympathized the most with Masaryk's Realistic Party, which in 1906 became the Czech Progressive Party … . Thus from childhood on, Milada sympathized with Masaryk's teachings … . Much later she realized that her father had the same kind of a beard and that his appearance was similar to Masaryk's.

During vacations the Králs used to go to [Mrs. Král's] native area near Kutná Hora … .The spirit of the ancient town with its Renaissance houses, Italian courtyard and St. Barbara's cathedral taught young Milada to take in the beauty of forms and to long to know the Czech past. However, her favorite holiday spot was her paternal grandfather's flour mill in Hodkov … on the Sázava river, a rural idyll where man, nature and an age-old order seemed to be in harmony … . But there also newspapers and books were read, and there were frequent political discussions … .

Although four years younger than her sister and six years older than her brother, she not only became their leader, but early was an authority among her classmates and friends. Bright, impressionable and with a strong sense of purpose, she studied languages and took piano lessons [in addition to her studies in school.]

However, tragedy struck the family. First Milada's sixteen-year-old sister became ill, and a few days later her six-year old brother. It was septic scarlet fever, complicated with encephalitis. Medical neglect seems to have played an important role, and the two children died in quick succession. Milada was deeply affected by what happened. She came to understand that life can be different from what she had experienced up to that point, and she learned pity for suffering.

When the First World War broke out, Milada was a student at the gymnasium. She became an enthusiastic debater in discussions among students about what was to happen after the war … .

When Milada's sister Věra was born, she took on much of the care for her … . As the war continued, the inhabitants of Prague lacked food and fuel. The mood was tense, from abroad came reports about Masaryk's struggle, about the creation of Czech legions in Russia; a number of the foremost political figures were arrested.

On the first of May there was an unauthorized procession in Prague, during which Milada threw a rose to the soldiers. This was considered a provocation, and Milada was expelled from the gymnasium and had to transfer to [a different one]. At the time of her graduation the Czechoslovak Republic had been founded, with T.G. Masaryk as president. The Králs welcomed independent Czechoslovakia with great enthusiasm.

Milada wanted to study medicine, but her father, prejudiced against the medical profession after the death of his two children, persuaded her that she could also help the suffering if she studied law. She finally agreed, and hoped to devote herself to social work. Therefore she also joined the Red Cross where she became acquainted with its chairperson, Dr. Alice Masaryk, the president's daughter.

In addition to law, she studied T.G. Masaryk's work systematically. In contrast to many of her contemporaries, she wanted to know his teachings thoroughly. She also studied Plato and other philosophers who had a decisive influence on him.

In those years the Králs used to spend the summer holidays in Zruč on the Sázava river, and it was then her uncle, a priest, who made a great impression on her. While she read much, she also bicycled and spent time chatting with her mother and playing with her little sister … .

With her pleasant appearance, Milada radiated a natural harmony. Of medium height, she had light brown hair, and dark blue eyes.

While a student, she became acquainted with Bohuslav Horák; he was an agricultural engineer and later completed his Ph.D. Her father agreed that they would marry after the completion of her studies. About that time she came down with scarlet fever, complicated with diphtheria; her life was hanging on a thread, and it looked as if the earlier tragedy were to be repeated. However, Milada recovered and received her doctorate in 1926.

Before Milada and Bohuslav could marry, a basic problem had to be solved. The Horáks, a deeply religious family for generations, were Protestants, and it was unthinkable that Milada would not become part of their religious community. They lived in Eastern Bohemia, where

Milada Horáková

Bohuslav's father was principal of a school. They were serious, respected people, with perhaps somewhat of a tendency to intolerance. Father Horák and his brother, a publisher, were active as lay leaders in the Protestant church. Before the couple became engaged, Bohuslav's father came to Prague and asked Milada's parents to have their daughter join his church. They deliberated for a long time, until Mrs. Král suggested that the whole family become Protestants.

The mood which prevailed in Czechoslovakia in the first half of the twenties also played a role. There was the "Away from Rome" movement, which already existed before the war, the newly founded Czechoslovak Church and the Czechoslovak Evangelical Church.

Čeněk Král agreed with his wife's suggestion, and the family became members of the Czechoslovak Evangelical Church. Milada took that step very seriously; she did not speak much about God, but she thought much about these questions ... . The wedding took place early in 1927, and Milada found herself a position with the Prague municipality. She worked in the department of social welfare under Dr. Petr Zenkl, [later the Lord Mayor of Prague], at first with foundations, then in child care. Her activities involved public housing, unemployment and in connection with that, work camps.

She devoted much time to the women's movement in the Women's National Council, solving questions connected with equal rights for women. In connection with that activity she began to go abroad, mainly to Paris, but also to England and Scotland, Sweden and Switzerland. In addition, she traveled privately to Yugoslavia, Italy and the French Riviera.

Early in her career she accompanied the Lord Mayor of Prague, Dr. Karel Baxa, to a conference in The Hague. Milada was active in the Association of Women Lawyers and collaborated on a book on women lawyers in the university and in private practice.

Among the colorful array of persons who entered Milada's life in those years, Senator Františka F. Plamínková, the chairperson of the

Women's Council, had the greatest influence on her. Plamínková was a strong personality, whose authority in Czecholovak public life was tremendous. The Women's Council became part of its international equivalent, with Plamínková as its second vice-chairperson, and a Czechoslovak delegate to the League of Nations. For Milada she was a source of new insights and a bridge to the rest of the world. Later they became close friends; Plamínková treated her as an equal partner ... .

In 1929 she joined the National Socialist Party [1] ... .

Milada wanted full equality, but also a fully satisfying family life for women ... . They should be able to seek employment on the basis of their own decision, not to help their husbands support the family. Their education should not only be directed toward professional achievement, but also toward the education of their own children. If a woman wanted to devote herself totally to her role as a mother, she was to be provided with legal and social security ... .

Bohuslav Horák had full understanding for Milada's aspirations and voluntarily stepped into the background, to allow Milada freedom for her activities ... . They had a housekeeper, so that after the birth of their daughter Jana in 1933 Milada had time to care for her and still in no way had to limit her work ... .

This was the time when Milada met president T.G. Masaryk at the invitation of his daughter Alice ... . During the discussion which took up all evening, he was interested in the Women's National Council, in the lives of Czechoslovak women and ... of young people generally ... . As a farewell gift he gave her a bunch of blooming azaleas, which in her excitement she left lying on the table ... . She considered that evening one of the most important of her life.

... The Horáks learned about Masaryk's death while vacationing in the Bohemian Forest. They immediately left for Prague and in the night stood in the endless line of people who wanted to pay him their last respects. Milada promised herself at that time to remain faithful to Masaryk's legacy.

Since December, 1935, Dr. Edvard Beneš, Masaryk's closest co-worker, was president. The Czechoslovak Republic, which during the whole time of its existence had to contend with Communist attacks and the expanding Henlein party, underwent serious trials in the second half of the thirties.

With increasing unease Milada Horáková followed Hitler's ... aggressive policies. She expected that his territorial demands against Austria and Czechoslovakia would meet with emphatic resistance from Great Britain and France ... .

The Munich agreement, which buried the Czechoslovak Republic, was a great shock for Milada. With bitterness she followed the establishment of the independent Slovak State and the German occupation of the Czech lands. When Bohuslav, who had been in the army during the mobilization, returned home, Milada was busy with the care of refugees from the Sudeten area.

Already in March of 1939, a resistance movement formed in Bohemia. There was the Political Center, which was organized immediately after Beneš's emigration. Then there was the Petitional Committee called "We shall remain Faithful," linked to the manifesto for the defense of the republic of 1938, which became an illegal network with many branches. The officers of the Czechoslovak army formed a resistance organization called "Defense of the Nation." Early in 1940 these three organizations joined to form the "Central Leadership of Domestic Resistance."

On September 1, 1939, the Nazis arrested hostages whom they selected among the leading representatives of Czech cultural and public life, among them Senator Plamínková.

On October 28th,[2] Milada watched mass demonstrations to which the Germans reacted with mass repression. They closed the Czech universities, executed nine student leaders and sent 1200 students to concentration camps. The Czechs now saw their only salvation in war.

Milada Horáková, now secretary of the Women's National Council, tried to create branches in the countryside which were to provide help with supplies. But they also were to help with the transmission of news, the finding of hiding places, housing, illegal border crossings and the illegal transmission of printed matter.

More members of the Political Center were arrested. The Petitional Committee continued with its activities and concerned itself with working out a program for the future free Czechoslovak Republic, while Bohuslav helped with its agricultural part. The Center had around forty members, most of whom did not survive the war. Milada found housing for people who had to go into hiding, and gathered information for an illegal news service. But she stayed away from bravado and unnecessary risks. Meetings took place in various places in Prague and also at the Horáks'.

On August 2, while they were on holiday, the Gestapo arrested them. Bohuslav was taken to Pardubice, Milada with little Jana to the Petschek Palace.[3] From there Jana was sent to the senior Horáks'. It took quite long before the Gestapo succeeded in discovering Milada's connection with the Petitional Council. She had to undergo hard questioning and merciless torture during which she simulated faints and seizures. The investigating commissar stuck needles into her hands to see if she was actually unconscious. She had so much self-control that she did not even react to severe pain. Sometimes at night they locked her into a special small cell similar to a chimney. The fetters cut into her flesh and deepened open wounds, but the Gestapo found out nothing from her. She claimed some of the deeds of others for herself to avert suspicion from those who were still free … .

After Heydrich's assassination, when the cruelty of the Gestapo became bestial, Milada was transferred to the "small fortress" in Terezín. There she saw her husband, and also her friend Plamínková, who was executed a short time later.

Milada lived in Terezín for almost two years. Because of a rumor that she was President Beneš's secretary, she was treated especially cruelly. For several weeks they locked her in a dark cell, then number 8, where Gavrilo Princip, the Serbian revolutionary died, who had assassinated Crown Prince Franz Ferdinand.

After the war, Milada said that during this period in her life she came to know God, and that He accepted her.

[When the Germans became convinced that she had not been] Beneš's secretary, her lot improved somewhat. She was put in charge of the quarters for the sick; in that work, her experiences with the Red Cross came her in good stead. Now she could move around in the camp somewhat more freely. Among the prisoners she found several who helped her establish contacts between prisoners and their families.

The "small fortress" in Terezín, where Milada was held prisoner for almost two years.

For that she was punished by being sent to the bunker of the Small Fortress, where people were beaten to death ... .

In October of 1944, after spending some weeks in a prison in Leipzig, where she worked in an underground munitions factory, she had to go to court in Dresden where her husband was sent at the same time. She had a small gift for him—bread she had saved in prison. During the trial she defended herself in German. The death penalty was recommended for her, but was commuted to eight years in prison ... . Milada then was shipped to the women's prison in Aichach near Munich, where she was liberated by the American army.

Having made her way to Prague on May 16, she joined the social workers at the railroad station who were taking care of former political prisoners as they were arriving. Two weeks later Bohuslav also returned, and they found themselves a new home. Family members used to hear her say: "I received the gift of life, it is not mine. I am ready to sacrifice it."

Now she considered it necessary to work politically. She understood that a strong defense against ideologies eager to establish absolute power was essential, that only a political pluralism can guarantee the freedom of the totality, of minorities and of individuals. She resumed her work in the National Socialist party, which continued in the tradition of Masaryk and Beneš.

The Horáková's house in Zapora 3, Smíchov, Prague

The Czech nation had welcomed enthusiastically the Soviet army as their liberator from the Nazi occupation ... . But the behavior of the Czechoslovak Communists from Moscow showed what they actually wanted to take over power. The National Socialist party, headed by its prewar chairperson, Fráňa Zeminová, was represented by politicians who had been in exile with President Beneš [in London.]

Milada Horáková again devoted her time to the women's movement now as chairperson of the Council of Czechoslovak Women. She also was one of the vice-chairpersons of the association of freed political prisoners. Another sphere of her activity was parliament where she sided with the female officials of several banks who lost their lifetime positions when they married and demanded that women working in the household be treated the same as other workers. Besides, she defended the rights of political prisoners.

In March of 1946 she caused an uproar among the Communist members of parliament by her defense of Dr. Feierabend who had been minister of agriculture until 1938. Milada realized that the attacks against him were part of their strategy to win the rural vote ... .

She spoke at many public gatherings organized by the National Socialist Party, and praised Beneš's negotiation of an alliance with the Soviet Union without disturbing the friendship with the West as a statesmanlike act. But the tension continued to grow, and clashes multiplied.

In the election campaign Milada Horáková ... made a number of speeches as a candidate for the district of České Budějovice ... .

In the elections, over 40% voted for the Communists who considered the 16% Social Democrats as more or less their votes. With almost 24% of the vote, the National Socialists were the second strongest party; Milada was elected on the first ballot. The democratic politicians realized that the struggle for the democratic character of the Czechoslovak Republic was beginning.

Milada was given an additional responsibility when she was put in charge of the government youth department. But her main concern was the preservation of continuity with the First Republic ... . When she visited the Soviet Union in the fall of 1947, her impressions were negative, particularly with regard to the situation of women ... . She realized that her stay was manipulated. He prewar doubts were confirmed, and she became convinced that Communist rule in Czechoslovakia would be a catastrophe. However, as a result of the elections. President Beneš [had to appoint] a new government with the Communist, Klement Gottwald, as its head.

The Soviet Union showed maximum concern for the fate of postwar Czechoslovakia. Stalin promised to equip the Czechoslovak army on the basis of credit. An important formerly German factory was given to Czechoslovakia, and air and rail connections were planned between the Soviet Union and Czechoslovakia. The time of the "indestructible" friendship with the Soviet Union began ... . Wanting to collectivize farming, the Communist party ignored parliamentary procedure to accomplish its goals.

The whole year 1947 was characterized by the increasing political crisis, and the foreign press published articles about the possibility of a violent change of the regime. In the summer months of 1947 there was an important clash about the question if the Marshall Plan which would provide economic aid from the United States would be accepted. For Czechoslovakia it was the last chance to escape the Soviet sphere of interest, but it was forced to reject the plan and to sign the long-term Czechoslovak-Soviet trade agreement in December, 1947. ..

Early in 1948 the National Socialist Party proposed early elections, assuming that the excellent results for the Communists would not be repeated. However, the Communist leadership realized this and opposed the elections.

When on February 20 the ministers who were members of the National Socialist People's Party and of the Democratic Party resigned, they assumed that the Social Democrats and the ministers without affiliation would follow suit. However, the Social Democrats remained, and so did Ludvík Svoboda and Jan Masaryk. While President Beneš refused to accept the resignations, Gottwald wanted them accepted; clearly he was going to replace those ministers who resigned with his own people.

Milada Horáková never had any illusions about the Communists, and always opposed their activities in every way possible. Knowing about her influence in the women's movement, [they] tried to gain her for their purposes. Some of her colleagues from the university and from the Council of Czechoslovak Women who had become sympathetic to the Communists also tried to pressure her to change her position ... .

When she visited Jan Masaryk in the Černín Palace, the conversation with him gave her an oppressive feeling. He seemed to deliberate before every word he spoke as if he were being watched. She asked him in vain what he meant when he said "I shall do." He seemed no longer the vital man bristling with wit that she had known.

About that time she met President Beneš several times. Shortly before the coup d'état of February he reassured her that if worst came to worst he could use the army. She made an appointment to see him a short time after Gottwald had declared publicly that the resignations had been accepted by the President. Beneš was resting in another room exhausted, and the doctor had ordered that he must not be disturbed.

The Council of Czechoslovak Women declined to yield to pressure to join the (Communist) Central Action Committee. However, the next day Milada no longer was admitted into the room of the Council, and her correspondence was confiscated. The Communist-controlled press announced that Milada Horáková had been stripped of all her public functions. In fear even organizations of which she had never been a member renounced her, as did for example the association of social workers. However, there were also many people who were not intimidated by Communist propaganda.

People of course wondered what took place in the negotiations between the Communists and Beneš, and if the signatures under the resignation of the ministers were genuine. Milada Horáková had strong doubts on that score, and also about the [alleged] suicide of Jan Masaryk who was found dead on March 10th … . Milada resigned from her senatorial post. Her closest contacts were with Hubert Ripka and Petr Zenkl[4] whom she did not hesitate to visit although they were watched by the police. Zenkl offered her the opportunity to leave the country with him, but she decided to stay as long as possible, seeing her main task in resistance within Czechoslovakia. Another reason why she did not want to leave was her close relationship to her father and the rest of her family. Her experiences with Nazi totalitarianism had taught her how to act under Communism … .At any rate, the opponents of the regime considered the results of the Communist coup as temporary.

Milada was forbidden to enter the Central Social Office where she had spent so many years. She was unemployed, but her husband still worked at the Ministry of Information, although under constant surveillance. Eventually Milada found a position in the Department of Education.

The Sokol congress which turned out to be a powerful anti-Communist demonstration improved the general mood for a short time. At the end of August, Milada went to visit President Beneš, who already was very sick; it seems that she was able to speak to him briefly.

Many acquaintances passed through the Horáks' apartment, and Milada, who was an expert in collecting information … succeeded in sending it abroad. So National Socialists, members of the People's Party and Social Democrats continued to meet at their house, but contrary to Communist claims, she did not have a leading position among them.

Using expressions such as "subversion," "espionage" and "high treason," Communist propaganda spread false rumors about arms and ammunition depots, which were to be used to murder Communists. At the meetings of the opposition which took place in various locations, there were discussions about what was to be done as well as about the increasing tension between the Western powers and the Soviet Union which could result in a new military conflict. As both last wars brought about radical changes in the world, major changes were again expected if there were another war ... .

The direction of Milada's thoughts can best be seen in a letter she sent to Petr Zenkl through illegal channels in June of 1949. She wrote that the National Socialist group was trying to maintain the continuity of the last democratically elected organs and to establish cooperation with members of the People's Party and the Social Democrats. She also mentioned approvingly "the socialist institutions which work and constitute real social progress." In conclusion she remarked: "It is sometimes very hard to live here. My husband has been out of work for a while, but I am still holding on. I think I still have a job to do here. Pray for me, so that I may know in time[when to leave]. "

Early in September Milada went to a meeting in the parsonage in Vinoře. At that time the participants were already watched by the secret police. We do not know what happened that afternoon, but when Milada Horáková returned home very excited, her husband proposed that the three of them leave immediately. However, she calmed down and they stayed.

The morning of the 27th of September the Horáks went into town together; Milada went to her office, Bohuslav returned home. He was sitting on the terrace ... when ... he saw two policemen in rain coats standing at the garden gate and ringing the bell. While they waited for additional policemen, they ordered Jana, the housekeeper and Bohuslav Horák to stay in separate rooms. Bohuslav used their temporary inattention to escape through the garden. Not realizing that Milada was arrested in her office that afternoon, he wanted to warn her not to return home. [After spending some time in hiding, Bohuslav was able to cross the border to West Germany on December l.

Since the summer of 1948 the jails were being filled with non-Communists. People who had not known each other previously were declared members of subversive groups and accused of sabotage, espionage and high treason.

Milada was taken to Ruzyně prison and police investigator Václav Pešek was put in charge of her case. He boasted that he could get any confession he wanted out of the accused. At first it seemed that the arrest of Milada and people around her would be treated as many comparable cases. There had, to be sure, already been several executions, but that was not expected in the case of Milada Horáková's group. What could they be accused of? That they met, debated about the contemporary situation, thought about solutions, and corresponded with colleagues abroad. Milada evidently guessed that her punishment would be several years of prison and forced labor.

In October of 1949 two Soviet advisors, Lichatchov and Makarov, came to Prague, who as specialists in the preparation of such major trials were supposed to provide instruction to the Czechoslovak police. Stalin wanted a major trial … . Although there was no proof, Horáková's group was labeled as a "terrorist center." When it was impossible to get the necessary admissions from the accused, Karel Šváb [a member of the security commission of the Central Committee of the Communist Party of Czechoslovakia who was executed as a member of the Slánský group two years later] beat one of the accused, Tomy Kleinerová, in the face until it bled, and screamed at her that the sentences had already been decided on, regardless whether she admitted anything or not … . For whole days the investigators rehearsed questions and answers with the accused. After every deviation from the prescribed scenario there followed further torture.

The Soviet advisers instructed the police in … what was actually horrible, absurd theater, in which all played the roles they had practiced … . To the people who knew each other, others were added who up to that point had nothing in common. So a large monster trial was created, designated as the "trial with the leadership of the terrorist conspiracy Horáková and co." … It was followed by over thirty trials which were to prove that a large network had been involved. From November 7 and 8 alone the police entered the apartments of three hundred eighty National Socialist functionaries and arrested them … .

The accused were manipulated in such a way that in the end they usually answered as the prepared scenario required. This was after they had been tortured for weeks by beatings, lack of sleep and by not being allowed to sit down in the cell.

After considering other possible candidates, the Communist government decided on Horáková as the leader of the conspiracy.

The 31 of May was the first day of the trial. [The courtroom was decorated with swastika flags, guns etc.] There were thirteen accused who had [allegedly] prepared terrorist acts and coups according to instructions of politicians in exile, and together with espionage centers in America, England, France and Yugoslavia … . Family members were not allowed in the court room, but the audience consisted of selected collectives from factories and other concerns … .

Several of the accused, and especially Milada Horáková, deviated from the prepared scenario several times. Perhaps her ability to do so stemmed in part from her experiences in Nazi jails, but she mainly had great inner strength and deep religious faith. She did not defend herself, but tried to take responsibility for the actions of others on herself.

After the third day there was a new factor: an artificially created mass hysteria was very much in evidence. In the court room there appeared baskets of almost 6300 resolutions demanding … that the heads of the leaders of the terrorist group should fall. … . As the radio spoke of the accused as of the worst criminals, they wondered which of them would escape the death penalty … .

The following text will convey some idea of the language used in court and in the media:

Karel Beran: *Před soudem lidu* (Before the People's Court), Praha, 1950, pp. 5ff.:

The trial of Dr. Milada Horáková and her twelve companions in the state court in Prague, May 31–June 8, 1950.

… Here, facing the working people, on the bench of the accused are those who followed the shameful road of the bourgeoisie, of the criminals who joined against the people of this republic in order to thrust a dagger in their back. The traitors of the republic sit here fully unmasked.

The trial of the enemies of the people took place in front of the working people of the whole republic. They were representatives of

Milada Horáková in court

the class which lost its battles on the open stage, and now it no longer returns as a political force, but as a political underworld which is preparing a new Munich and a war against its own people.

This trial however is not only ending as the unmasking of those obscure figures, but also of the gentlemen whom February blew to the West.

This trial reveals Messers Zenkl and Ripka, Hais and Majer and all the rest … as professional agents of the American, English or French imperialists, as agents [selling] the main, now American, goods, war.

After the war, the Western imperialists tried to penetrate into the Czechoslovak Republic over the bridge which was built for them by Messers Zenkl, Šrámek, Lettrich and their companions.

Then in February '48 this bridge collapsed. Messers Zenkl, Ripka and Lettrich ran away from under it and pulled Monsignor Šrámek and Hála out of the toilet of the Žatec airport, prepared to fly away on a French plane.

After February the rats crawled into their holes, and as a number of trials showed, they continued in the underground dancing according to the American whistle.

But the objective situation is not favorable to the gauleiters and little Hitlers. Our camp, the world camp of peace, democracy and socialism, lead by the powerful Soviet Union, grows and becomes more powerful every day. We are fighting, and we are fighting for peace. We are building socialism. The accused wanted to stand in the way of this building. They are preparing war. They long for … closed factories, for Zenkl's beggars, [Zenkl was mayor of Prague before the war], for … pacts with the bourgeoisie, for the occupants … .

We advise the traitors at home and abroad: keep your hands off the republic … I call on the working people to be ever watchful. May they learn from this case … to recognize the enemy, those … who prepare the new war, the servants of the aggressors. The people of our republic are not only building paradise on earth; they also will defend this paradise against the forces of the old, mean world which is condemned to destruction.

The death penalty was pronounced over Jan Buchal, Dr. Oldřich Pecl, Záviš Kalandra, and Dr. Milada Horáková. All appealed, only in Horáková's case her father and her daughter signed the appeal instead; it was in vain. Gottwald confirmed the sentences without hesitation; only in Milada's case he hesitated, because world public opinion appealed to save her life … . Among those who tried to help were Einstein, Russell, Churchill, [and Eleanor Roosevelt], but Gottwald signed the verdict on June 24 … .

ANOTHER CURTAIN 'SPY' TRIAL ENDS

DEATH SENTENCE
ON WOMAN ex-M.P.

Milada in the dock at the Prague trial.

Milada had three more days to live. She was reconciled with her fate. In her last hours she wrote letters in which she thanked for the good that had been done to her. She wrote with a firm hand, and without corrections. According to Milada's desire, she could meet with her sister and brother-in-law, and with her daughter Jana the evening before her last in a boiler room of Pankrác prison. She told them that ... she thought that she had acted right. It was only then that the members of her family could indicate to her that her husband was alive and had escaped into exile. She wanted to kiss Jana farewell, but the policeman [prevented it]. Milada ended the meeting herself. She was especially strengthened by the knowledge that her life was to be replaced by the life of the child which her sister was to have, asked them not to mourn her and said that she would not have been able to stand a long restriction of her freedom again.

It was at 4.30 in the morning on June 27, 1950, that in the inner courtyard of the prison hospital in Pankrác there appeared, next to the wall where two gallows stood, a small group of people in dark clothes; Milada's turn was the last, it seems in order to make her punishment more severe.

When she stepped on the scaffolding, her clear voice was heard: "I am falling, falling. I lost this battle, I am falling honorably, I love this land, I love this people, work for its prosperity! I am departing without hatred for you, I wish you ..." The thread of her life was cut at 5 o'clock and 35 minutes.

In the three days before she was executed, Milada wrote farewell letters to her closest relatives and to some friends. We are reproducing those which seem to contribute the most to her characterization. The first is directed to her mother-in-law, and may serve as a corrective for the reader who feels that Milada is presented too much as a paragon of perfection.

My dear Mother Horáková,
I kiss your hands—Mother of seven sorrows. I am sure you don't know how often I thought about you, how often I stood in front of you, asking your forgiveness, for I know that I am guilty of many wrongs toward you. You are a model of sacrifice and patience, with a

heart overflowing with goodness. What all came over you, and how little did the sun of happiness shine in your life! You, the embodiment of service, of service to others, in your modesty did not even notice that you were only giving, that you were giving your self along with all that care. You never asked what the others were bringing you. You were a private [i.e. soldier] of love, who only fought for the happiness of others and was not even awarded a medal for bravery. And it was and is so necessary in your life, so that you could again stand on your feet and fight for a better life, not for yourself, but for others.

This is the second time that in my heart I am asking your forgiveness. The first time it was in the fortress casemates of Terezín, almost on the threshold of certain destruction, that I realized that I did not know how to love you enough. And it was not for reasons stemming from you—I was spiritually so poor that I could not perceive that special tone of the keyboard of your character. And yet one could hear it so well. I had my ears closed by pride, jealousy and selfishness. You, dear mother, gave me from the small bundle of your personal happiness the most valuable gem, your only son Bohuslav. And you wanted nothing in return, only a little personal recognition and my permission for you to enjoy and adorn yourself with that gem. And in my young, self-assured pride, in my thoughtless competition of young, easily victorious womanhood, I was so selfish that I did not even want to let you have that little joy which you wanted for yourself. I began to compete where there was no reason to compete, for you did not want to deprive me of Bohuslav's love. And so, during all the twenty-three years of my life with Bohuslav, I somehow remained distant from you, maminko. It is a great shame, and I am telling myself this for the second time, that it took such a great trial from God for that realization, and it was not only a loss for you, it was for me also. Your dear son also suffered because of our distant relationship, for he loved both of us fervently, although each of us differently. His beautiful heart was so rich in goodness and love that I really should have been glad for you to have all he wanted to give you. And just at the time before my arrest, when Father Horák died, I was jealous and unkind to you. I thereby hurt you and Bohuslav. It was very wrong, and I am very much ashamed of myself. I was so proud and naively selfish. I felt uncomfortable because when Father Horák was dying, the two of you stayed alone with your sorrow, you did not ask me to be with you. And why should you have called me? Should I not have asked you to let me be with you? Should I not have been with you as a matter of course, just as Bohuslav always was with me when I went through difficult times … without being asked? Maminko, this is my great pain with regard to you and Bohuslav, and

I have to confess it to you today, when there must not be any falseness in my attitude. I know that I don't even have to ask you for forgiveness; your kind soul already has forgiven me …

In my mind I also have been talking to Father Horák. I was glad that his death came when he was happy and comfortable, while you again carry a cross to Golgotha. I asked him also to forgive me in his eternal abode, and I recognized that his criticisms of me were partly justified. It is true that he often wronged and hurt me, but it seems that he felt that I have certain traits of character which will cost his son much pain and sorrow … And I reacted to his correct instinct with proud and self-assured rejection, and I became obstinate when he was guilty of a wrong toward me. I needed even more humility, and therefore this test had to come. But it is tragic that you and Bohuslav again have to suffer for my correct comprehension of things. But I know that you can get up again after falling under the weight of the cross. I know that you will be victorious over your Golgotha, for you have the most powerful faith and shield. Maminko, I have it too. Therefore you perhaps more than anybody else will believe, if I say in the words of the psalm: And though I walk in the valley of the shadow of death, I shall fear no evil, for Thou art with me. You have no idea how pleased I was when my legal representative informed me that the pastor of the Protestant Congregation expressed his willingness to accompany me and to strengthen me spiritually in the hours which are awaiting me. The authorities will be asked for their permission, but even if they should not give it, the very fact that he wanted to do so strengthens and comforts me; please give him my deep thanks. I know that you are praying for me and that you prayed especially today. Continue to pray, my prayers are with you. I asked to be at least given the Králická Bible[5] and I was promised it. Of course, I don't know if they have anything like that here. Maminko, in your sorrow in which we both are alone, all of our, my, jealousies have vanished. I think I know how hard it is for you, and because you know what my and Bohuslav's love was like, you know that today my heart suffers no less than yours. And yet we have not lost him. Whether he is alive anywhere, or perhaps dead, in his heart he has not stopped loving both of us, each in a different way—and I am really not jealous any more that he loves both of us.

I have one request: spend a lot of time with Janinka. You know how much she loves you, and perhaps you will find your son in her. Help Věra [Milada's sister] to lead Jana with your knowledge of his character, for you know how similar father and daughter are—Jana and Bohuslav. Maminko, I kiss your hands. 'til we meet again. M.

To her daughter, she writes as the mother of a teenager who is concerned about her education, her health, her friends and even such mundane things as the propriety of her appearance.

My only little girl Jana,

God blessed my life as a woman with you. As your father wrote in the poem from a German prison, God gave you to us because he loved us. Apart from your father's magic, amazing love you were the greatest gift I received from fate. However, Providence planned my life in such a way that I could not give you nearly all that my mind and my heart had prepared for you. The reason was not that I loved you little; I love you just as purely and fervently as other mothers love their children. But I understood that my task here in the world was to do you good ... by seeing to it that life becomes better, and that all children can live well. And therefore ... we often had to be apart for a long time. It is now already for the second time that Fate has torn us apart. Don't be frightened and sad because I am not coming back any more. Learn, my child, to look at life early as a serious matter. Life is hard, it does not pamper anybody, and for every time it strokes you it gives you ten blows. Become accustomed to that soon, but don't let it defeat you. Decide to fight. Have courage and clear goals—and you will win over life. Much is still unclear to your young mind, and I don't have time left to explain to you things you would still like to ask me. One day, when you grow up, you will wonder and wonder, why your mother who loved you and whose greatest gift you were, managed her life so strangely. Perhaps then you will find the right solution to this problem, perhaps a better one than I could give you today myself. Of course, you will only be able to solve it correctly and truthfully by knowing very, very much. Not only from books, but from people; learn from everybody, no matter how unimportant! Go through the world with open eyes, and listen not only to your own pains and interests, but also to the pains, interests and longings of others. Don't ever think of anything as none of your business. No, everything must interest you, and you should reflect about everything, compare, compose individual phenomena. Man doesn't live in the world alone; in that there is great happiness, but also a tremendous responsibility. That obligation is first of all in not being and not acting exclusive, but rather merging with the needs and the goals of others. This does not mean to be lost in [the multitude, but it is] to know that I am part of all, and to bring one's best into that community. If you do that, you will succeed in contributing to the common goals of human society. Be more aware of one principle than I have been: approach everything in life constructively—beware of unnecessary negation—I am not saying all negation, because I believe that one should resist evil. But in order to be a truly positive person in all circumstances, one has to learn how to distinguish real gold from tinsel. It is hard, because tinsel sometimes glitters so dazzlingly. I confess, my child, that often in my life I was dazzled by glitter. And sometimes it even shone so falsely, that one dropped pure gold from one's hand and reached for, or ran after, false gold. You know that to organize one's scale of values well means to know not only oneself well, to be firm in the analysis of one's character, but mainly to know the others, to know as much of the world as possible, its past, present, and future development. Well, in short, to know, to understand. Not to close one's ears before anything and for no reason—not even to shut out the thoughts and opinions of anybody who stepped on my toes, or even wounded me deeply. Examine, think, criticize, yes, mainly criticize yourself, don't be ashamed to admit a truth you have come to realize, even if you proclaimed the opposite a little while ago; don't become obstinate about your opinions, but when you come to consider something right, then be so definite that you can fight and die for it. As Wolker[6] said, death is not bad. Just avoid gradual dying which is what happens when one suddenly finds oneself apart from the real life of the others. You have to put down your roots where fate determined for you to live. You have to find your own way. Look for it independently, don't let anything turn you away from it, not even the memory of your mother and father. If you really love them, you won't hurt them by seeing them critically—just don't go on a road which is wrong, dishonest and does not harmonize with life. I have changed my mind many times, rearranged many values, but what was left as an essential value, without which I cannot imagine my life, is the freedom of my conscience. I would like you, my little girl, to think about whether I was right.

Another value is work. I don't know which to assign the first place and which the second ... . Learn to love work! Any work, but one you have to know really and thoroughly. Then don't be afraid of anything, and things will turn out well for you.

And don't forget about love in your life. I am not only thinking of the red blossom which one day will bloom in your heart, and you, if fate favors you, will find a similar one in the heart of another person ... with whose road yours will merge. I am thinking of love without which one cannot live happily. And don't ever crumble love—learn to give it whole and really. And learn to love precisely those who encourage love so little—then you won't usually make a mistake. My little girl Jana, when you will be choosing for whom your maiden heart shall burn and to whom to really give yourself, remember your father.

I don't know if you will meet with such luck as I, I don't know if you will meet such a beautiful human being, but choose your ideal close to him. Perhaps you, my little one, have already begun to understand, and now perhaps you understand to the point of pain what we have lost in him. What I find hardest to bear is that I am also guilty of that loss.

Be conscious of the great love and sacrifice Pepík and Věruška[7] are bringing you. You not only have to be grateful to them ... you must help them build your common happiness positively, constructively. Always want to give them more for the good they do for you. Then perhaps you will be able to come to terms with their gentle goodness.

I heard from my legal representative that you are doing well in school, and that you want to continue ... I was very pleased. But even if you would one day have to leave school and to work for your liveli-hood, don't stop learning and studying. If you really want to, you will reach your goal. I would have liked for you to become a medical doc-tor—you remember that we talked about it. Of course you will decide yourself and circumstances will, too. But if you stand one day in the tra-ditional alma mater and carry home from graduation not only your doc-tor's diploma, but also the real ability to bring people relief as a doctor—then, my little girl ... your mother will be immensely pleased ... .But your mother would only be ... truly happy, no matter where you stand, whether at the operating table, at the ... lathe, at your child's cradle or at the work table in your household, if you will do your work skillfully, honestly, happily and with your whole being. Then you will be successful in it. Don't be demanding in life, but have high goals. They are not exclusive of each other, for what I call demanding are those selfish notions and needs. Restrict them yourself. Realize that in view of the disaster and sorrow which happened to you, Věra, Pepíček, grandmother and grandfather ... and many others will try to give you what they have and what they cannot afford. You should not only not ask them for it, but learn to be modest. If you become used to it, you will not be unhappy because of material things you don't have. You don't know how free one feels if one trains oneself in modesty ... how he/she gets a head start over against the feeble and by how much one is safer and stronger. I really tried this out on myself. And, if you can thus double your strength, you can set yourself courageous, high goals ... .Read much, and study languages. You will thereby broaden your life and multiply its content. There was a time in my life when I read vora-ciously, and then again times when work did not permit me to take a single book in my hand, apart from professional literature. That was a shame. Here in recent months I have been reading a lot, even books which probably would not interest me outside, but it is a big and important task to read everything valuable, or at least much that is. I shall write down for you at the end of this letter what I have read in recent months. I am sure you will think of me when you will be reading it.

And now also something for your body. I am glad that you are engaged in sports. Just do it systematically. I think that there should be rhythmic exercises, and if you have time, also some good, systematic gymnastics. And those quarter hours every morning! Believe me finally that it would save you a lot of annoyance about unfavorable proportions of your waist, if you could really do it. It is also good for the training of your will and perseverance. Also take care of your complexion regularly—I do not mean makeup, God forbid, but healthy daily care. And love your neck and feet as you do your face and lips. A brush has to be your good friend, every day, and not only for your hands and feet; use it on every little bit of your skin. Salicyl alcohol and Fennydin, that is enough for beauty, and then air and sun. But about that you will find better advisors than I am.

Your photograph showed me your new hairdo; it looks good, but isn't it a shame [to hide] your nice forehead? And that lady in the ball gown! Really, you looked lovely, but your mother's eye noticed one fault, which may be due to the way you were placed on the photograph—wasn't the neck opening a little deep for your sixteen years? I am sorry I did not see the photo of your new winter coat. Did you use the muff from your aunt as a fur collar? Don't primp, but whenever possible, dress carefully and neatly. And don't wear shoes until they are run down at the heel! Are you wearing innersoles? And how is your thyroid gland? These questions don't, of course, require an answer, they are only meant as your mother's reminders.

In Leipzig in prison I read a book—the letters of Maria Theresa [The Austrian Empress] to her daughter Marie Antoinette. I was very much impressed with how this ruler showed herself to be practical and feminine in her advice to her daughter. It was a German original, and I don't remember the name of the author. If you ever see that book, remember that I made up my mind at that time that I would also write you such letters about my experiences and advice. Unfortunately I did not get beyond good intentions.

Janinko, please take good care of Grandfather Král and Grandmother Horáková. Their old hearts now need the most consolation. Visit them often and let them tell you about your father's and mother's youth, so that you can preserve it in your mind for your children. In that way an individual becomes immortal, and we shall continue in you and in the others of your blood.

And one more thing—music. I believe that you will show your gratitude to Grandfather Horák for the piano which he gave you by practicing honestly, and that you will succeed in what Pepík wants so much, in accompanying him when he plays the violin or the viola. Please, do him that favor. I know that it would mean a lot to him, and it would be beautiful. And when you can play well together, play me the aria from *Martha* :[8] "My rose, you bloom alone there on the hillside," and then: "Sleep my little prince" by Mozart, and then your father's [favorite] largo: " Under your window" by Chopin. You will play it for me, won't you? I shall always be listening to you.

Just one more thing: Choose your friends carefully. Among other things one is also very much determined by the people with whom one associates. Therefore choose very carefully. Be careful in everything and listen to the opinions of others about your girlfriends without being told. I shall never forget your charming letter (today I can tell you) which you once in the evening pinned to my pillow, to apologize when I caught you for the first time at the gate in the company of a girl and a boy. You explained to me at that time why it is necessary to have a gang. Have your gang, little girl, but of good and clean young people. And compete with each other in everything good. Only please don't confuse young people's springtime infatuation with real love. Do you understand me? If you don't, aunt Věra will help you explain what I meant. And so, my only young daughter, little girl Jana, new life, my hope, my future forgiveness, live! Grasp life with both hands! Until my last breath I shall pray for your happiness, my dear child!

I kiss your hair, eyes and mouth, I stroke you and hold you in my arms (I really held you so little.) I shall always be with you. I am concluding by copying from memory the poem which your father composed for you in jail in 1940 ...

> *The poem expresses the exuberance Bohuslav felt at the birth of his daughter. It is followed by the list of books Milada read in jail, which contains Czech and foreign belletristic works as well as political ones by J. V. Stalin and by Klement Gottwald.*
>
> *Milada's letter to her husband must have been the hardest to write. In it she looks back on a beautiful life together and only mentions one thing that, despite the brevity of her remark, I believe really disturbed her: the fact that he left without taking Jana with him.*
>
> *It begins with the quotation of a verse Bohuslav wrote to Milada, saying that with graying temples they are hurrying along on the same road, on the way from their mother's arms to God's embrace.*

Milada Horáková from a commemorative postage stamp

On Monday, the 26.6. 1950, at 13 o'clock.

My dearest husband,

Until the 27th of September of last year, all of the almost 26 years that we loved each other this verse of your poem counted for us. Then things changed so suddenly and tragically. I am writing to you as I am to all the others and I don't even know if you are alive, and if it is even possible for you to read these words. That is the greatest pain of my heart, that … I don't have any news about you, not even sad ones, and perhaps only a few hours of my life remain. It is the first time in the long years of our life together that I face the test which fate assigned to me without you. I am so alone, and I do not understand anything about this tragedy. Perhaps it will become clear to me when our souls meet again. I only know and feel one thing: that with your great love it is not possible that you left me. But however that may be, my dear, I want to tell you: I already wrote you one letter on the threshold between life and death—in 1944 after the verdict of the *Volksgericht* in Dresden. I am happy that I do not have to revoke any of it, not a word. On the contrary, the happiness of our great, enchanted love has become more solid when we met again after our return from jail … You were the greatest love of my life—through you I have encountered so many heights of human feeling, crystalline like a jewel, that this unusual, uncommon earthly love between two people could not end in an ordinary way. You know it, I don't need to tell you about it. Do you remember that quiet evening last August, on a Saturday, when the two of us sat together in the kitchen, when the rain was murmuring in the leaves of the trees in the garden of our apartment? We were drinking tea, I was talking to you and you were listening? … I was confessing something to you from my heart. It seems that I, such a tough person, started to cry. You were silent, you kissed me and only looked at me. I told you that I know that I often sin against the goodness of your heart, I told you what you have meant to me, I asked you to forgive me if I neglected you because of my other interests. I spoke to you about strength, and about my genuine love for you. Was the discussion of that night which ended with you putting me gently on the bed, was that discussion perhaps a fateful anticipation of this letter which will never reach you? It seems to me that that is so. And therefore, even if you should not read these lines, I am certain that you know what I want to say to you. You know: I was your lover more than your wife, for a wife I lacked the necessary feeling for the exclusiveness of her tasks. I had my wings spread, and you did not keep me from flying even at the expense of your personal happiness. I had in you a perfect husband and pal who never indiscreetly pushed his way into the depth of my soul. You were so self-controlled in everything, you always stood above situations when the two of us were concerned. You are the only person in the world of whom I could believe that he understands me. I would like to be convinced that I can count on you to understand me even today. But I do not understand one thing: Why did you leave our child? In my question there is no reproach, my dear, it is only astonishment about something incomprehensible. I am all yours, as you know me, I remained faithful to our love, to you and to myself. If I leave before you do, it is only to wait for you patiently. Our love will even overcome the physical change, and it is a consolation to me that I shall always be able to be close to you spiritually. When the last hour comes, I won't be without you, you will stand next to me in the words of your poems which I shall be saying to myself … [There follows a long poem which is a confession of love to her. She ends her letter to him:] I kiss you, my husband, I press your hands, pal. If you are alive, I wish you a long and happy life. Solve your life's problems so as to be able to live fully … Your M.

At 2.30 in the morning of June 27, 1950, the day Milada was executed, she wrote once more to all her loved ones, ending with the words:

... and you my wandering, dear, only, beautiful husband! I feel that you are standing before me. Now we hold hands once more, firmly. The birds are waking up, it is becoming light. I go with my head held high. One also has to know how to lose. That is no disgrace. An enemy also does not lose honor if he is truthful and honorable. One falls in battle; what is life other than struggle? Be well. I am yours, only yours, Milada.

In all her letters, Milada said almost nothing about her activities prior to her trial, about the trial itself or about her impending death. Thus one can believe that she was resigned to her fate which she saw as God's will when she wrote to her family only hours before she died:

Don't feel sorry for me! I lived a beautiful life. I accept my punishment with resignation and submit to it humbly. My conscience is clear and I hope and believe and pray that I shall also pass the test of the highest court, of God.

NOTES

1.   A liberal democratic party which had nothing in common with the German National Socialists.
2.   The Czechoslovak national holiday
3.   The notorious Gestapo headquarters in Prague.
4.   Members of the Czechoslovak government in exile.
5.   The famous early translation into Czech.
6.   Jiří Wolker, a poet and idol of young people in the thirties.
7.   Her brother-in-law and sister.
8.   An opera by Friedrich Freiherr von Flotow.

Chapter 11

RUTH KLINGER

(1906–1989)

S*ome of my women I was bound to find, some I really found by accident. Ruth Klinger is one of the latter. My late friend Leo Brod told me about her and her autobiography years ago, when I was looking for material for my book about the Bohemian and Moravian Jews. The book did not appear in the German equivalent of* Books in Print—*I didn't know that it was self-published—and so I gave up the search. I did find it in the library of Leo Brod's son Peter who makes it one of his life's jobs to bring together literature and people, especially if they have some connection with Bohemia.*

There are many factors which make Ruth Klinger's autobiography remarkable: It provides much detailed information and deals with a Prague milieu which was a few subtle shades different from the Jewish ones which are generally known. Her parents, from a petit-bourgeois milieu with recent rural roots and not much education, raised their children in the very early twentieth century in the quarters of a former post office. They divided it into a tiny apartment without a bath—the toilet was across the yard—and a dry goods store-cum underwear production where both parents worked. There was never any talk of their daughters finishing the gymnasium, let alone going to university.

Ruth had a very difficult life which was programmed to some extent in her childhood: what was worse than the embarrassing family quarters was her father's repeatedly and angrily expressed conviction that she—in her childhood she was called Trudl—was stupid, that she had no common sense. She always feared her father, and was anxious to prove his opinion about her wrong, even as an adult when he often was her humane savior in distress.

Unquestionably the most traumatic event of her early years was the violent anti-Semitic attack of the mob in 1919 against her parents and their shop, after which her mother came down with a severe illness from which she died the following year.

It was unusual in those circles that Trudl-Ruth's father seems to have had no objections to her becoming an actress—perhaps he had so many worries that he could not concentrate on his middle daughter who seemed a hopeless case anyway.

Ruth's early photographs show her as an exotic, dark-haired, dark-skinned beauty with large eyes, more like a Yemenite than a girl from a Prague Jewish family. It seems that from childhood on, she had to be on her guard against men on the make. In her middle teens, she became a member of the Zionist youth organization Blue-White, but it seems that, except much later and under very different circumstances, she never had any romantic involvements with anybody from her own circles.

There is a pattern to her—quite a few—relationships with men: she generally describes the man, and the circumstances of their first meeting, and then informs the reader about the love affair. What is missing is the link dealing with her feelings about the man. She always told about how she felt later, when it was already plausible that she wanted the relationship to end.

Her first lover, the Germanic-looking Hans Balder, was a mystic, a neurotic and a gambler to boot who committed suicide when she left him. Next was Maxim Sakaschansky, the touchingly loving and yet violent Yiddish-speaking Russian Jew, twice married to her and twice divorced, the father of her retarded child that died early. She was a successful actress in Prague and in Berlin. How high would she have risen on the legitimate stage if she had not followed Maxim to Yiddish cabarets? In any case, that career was cut short by the Nazi seizure of power. Ruth and Maxim emigrated to Palestine where life—until after the Second World War—was an endless chain of economic and professional difficulties and frustrations. If the men in her life in Europe were about twice her age, now they were often much younger. She describes some of them as poetic or musical geniuses, but they were failures, bad neurotics, one a (bi-sexual) thief, one again a compulsive gambler. To two of them she was in times of dire poverty—as she admits in not so many words—a paid mistress.

Things looked up for her when she was able to move to Arnold Zweig's house as an unpaid secretary, and also struck up a friendship with Max Brod. Nevertheless, it does not seem surprising that at that point she accepted her sister's offer to come and live with her and her family in Prague; what seems less plausible is that she looks back on Palestine as the homeland she missed very much, and felt a total stranger in Prague.

By this time, she looks on her photograph like a very competent, middle-aged woman. In Prague there seem to have been no more romantic involvements, and despite friendships such as one with Egon Erwin Kisch, she was desperately lonely. However, she was again successful in a career. Having done well in a kind of work which was totally new to her, as a correspondent for a Tel Aviv newspaper in Prague, she was appointed executive secretary of the Israeli Embassy when the state of Israel was established.

Now we encounter a much more mature, competent Ruth who incidentally provides us with the most astutely written account of the Slánský affair and of the accompanying wave of official anti-Semitism in Czechoslovakia among the many I have read,[1] and her flight back home as she calls it, to Israel, in 1953.

Beyond that we know from friends, a relative of Ruth's and newspaper notices that she later went to work in the Israeli Embassy in Berne, married a pianist by the name of Fred Oehlgiesser and was divorced from him. In the 1970s she retired for two years to Montagnola in order to work on her memoirs, using her huge collections of clippings and notes as aids to her memory. Ruth Klinger remained a committed Zionist, but spent her last years in an old age home in Zurich, painting and giving recitals.

Unlike most of the autobiographical material I have worked with, Ruth Klinger's memoir did not lend itself to shortening so as to be left with a coherent whole. It has therefore been necessary to intersperse passages from it with many summaries and explanations. In her autobiography Zeugin einer Zeit *(Witness to an Age), Ruth writes:*

If I asked myself today, at the age of sixty-eight, if I would like to live through my childhood once more, my answer would be an unambiguous no. To suffer again so much injustice, to be defenselessly at the mercy of my surroundings?

A short time before the First World War, when Trudl Klinger was seven years old, her father rented the rooms vacated by the post-office on Jungmann Square, to remodel them for the business as well as for housing for his family. One Sunday morning, he went to the new place, several houses from their old apartment, and told Trudl that a Mr. Studnička would come and ask about him. She was to take the man to her father, but when the visitor came, he talked her out of going with him. The outcome of the episode was that her father beat her mercilessly.

Unable to say a word, I suffered the blows. Father's anger kept increasing and he kept hitting me until I lost consciousness and lay motionless on the floor. That sobered my furious father up. He carried me to the bed, fetched water ... washed my face and after a while brought me chocolate ... .

Well, this Mr. Studnička was supposed to introduce himself to father as a new employee, but had changed his mind and did not go to see him. I don't know where Mama and Fanny [Ruth's elder sister] were ... the incident was never again discussed between father and me. But: Since that day, I am paralyzed as soon as a quick explanation is expected of me. I couldn't defend myself in the decisive moment ... There always is a fearful expression on my face ... which inevitably arouses the impression that I am guilty ... Father did something to me which can never be remedied.

I was often wronged and unable to defend myself. For father, there was no doubt that I ... was mentally retarded. He hoped to be able to accomplish something with his cane.

"Leave her alone, she is only skin and bones ... " Mama used to try to mediate. Papa rolled his eyes angrily, reached for the cane and laid me over his knee ... .

One evening during supper, I pointed at the beer glass and said: "Look, if it weren't yellow, one could think that it was soda water. The bubbles rise up in the same way." That was too much for father. "A child that talks so stupidly shouldn't sit next to me. Trudl talks nothing but nonsense. Go to the kitchen ... It was terrible, terrible. And nobody ... had come to my defense. How horrible was the world where I had to live!

Mama also didn't know what she did to me with remarks like: "No grass grows for seven years wherever Trudl steps" ... Life consisted only of punishments. Did my parents have any idea what a fertile soil was being prepared for a lifelong vulnerability? (How I suffer from it to this very day!)

The "temporary" housing which was set up for the family between the store and the workshop was the family home for twenty years. The living room was, at the same time, the children's room and the dining room. Besides, there was the parents' bedroom and the kitchen which also contained the maid's bed and possessions. There was a toilet across the yard and no bathroom.

We went to the ... German grade school for five years, and then to the [non-academic] secondary school. We spoke Czech in the street, in the store and of course, with the maid. For a time, we had a Czech governess.

It was like that in many Jewish families in Prague. They were culturally German, but loved also the folksy cordiality of the Czech language. Trudl also tells of various negative experiences, such as difficulties at school as a left-handed child, and of an older man who tried to misuse her sexually.

The following text is quoted by Ruth Klinger from Selbstwehr, Independent Jewish Weekly, *Prague, May 23, 1919:*

In view of the tendentious, inflammatory and false reports of the majority of the Czech press, we give here an absolutely reliable account of the sad events which deeply shook all Jews and all who have humane feelings.

The pretext: already on Friday ... a Mrs. Chmelař drew to herself attention near the Klingers' store in the Prague suburb of Karolinental by making wild threats against the Jews. Passersby gathered around her and soon she spoke before a considerable circle of listeners, whom she incited to violence against the Jews.

On Saturday, the game began again. That day a larger group gathered, which soon displayed a threatening attitude against the Klingers' store. The proprietor went outside, called Mrs. Chmelař aside and asked her not to make her speech just in front of his store, since it could have evil consequences. He had hardly addressed her, when she attacked him wildly: "So, it is you who reported Czech women and got them to jail."

Mr. Klinger immediately returned to his store and went with his wife into the apartment located behind it. It is a matter of course for every Jew to close his store in such a situation. The multitude besieged the house and tried to enter ... the apartment. The people fanatisized each other by anti-Semitic inflammatory talk. The most unbelievable claim was sufficient to set the lowest instincts of the masses in motion, especially since the store contained ready-made clothes, i.e. "plunderable" goods.

Police did come, but they were threatened and pushed aside by the hundreds of people. In this critical situation, when the crowd was about to enter the apartment, Mr. Klinger left the house. He had hardly shown himself in the street, when the howling mob broke through the police chain and attacked the fleeing defenseless man, threw him down, and, when he stood up, mercilessly attacked him again. The police brought him to safety to the commissariat with difficulty.

Meanwhile the multitude, which had grown to thousands, continued to besiege the house and called furiously for Mrs. Klinger. Calls were heard that all Jews should be killed and thrown in the Moldau. The police lost control of the mob. They sent a messenger to the commissariat, asking Mr. Klinger to advise his wife in writing likewise to leave the house and also to go to the commissariat—that otherwise they could not vouch for her safety. They promised Mr. Klinger protection if he obeyed. What could he do but write the note? …

Mrs. Klinger was then taken to the street, protected by the police, but the mob was stronger. Despite the strong contingent which took refuge in a house after only twenty steps, they continued inciting to more rioting. Although the iron door was locked, it was broken open with bars. Mrs. Klinger, who sought protection in the apartment of an acquaintance, was dragged down the steps by her hair, again struck in her eye and mistreated. So it continued all the way to the police commissariat where she finally found peace from her bestial pursuers. The Jewish National Council contacted the police authorities several times during that day and was heard sympathetically and its president provided medical help. What he saw was pitiful. Two unhappy people who by the outbreaks of hate against them lasting from 9 am to 6 pm had totally lost their composure, disfigured by swellings and tears, bled from open wounds … And all this for no reason! For this should above all be made clear: Mr. and Mrs. Klinger have never insulted the Czech people or undertaken anything against the Czechs! Quiet, modest business people, they worked their way up to a moderate prosperity from small beginnings, through disciplined work, in more than fifteen years …

[… Ruth Klinger resumed:] I have saved this document of May 23, 1919 for 56 years, the only black-and-white proof of [those] events. Without [it], one could say that my memory probably exaggerated considerably.

The trust in Czechoslovak justice proved to be justified. In the court procedures which soon followed, my parents' total innocence was proven and the instigator, Mrs. Chmelař, was sentenced to several months in jail. Furthermore, these events which were extremely embarrassing for the newly-founded state, lead to a "list of Jewish candidates" and soon afterwards to the official recognition of the "Party of the Jewish National Minority" which received two seats in Parliament. The Klingers had paid a high price for this well-functioning representation of Jewish interests.

We children only experienced it in small part. On our way home, Fanny and I were struck by the strange behavior of the passersby. They pointed at us and whispered to each other: "Those are the Klingers' children." We reached Jungmann Square; there was an immense chorus of hellish noises that filled the air. They besieged the store and tried to open the roller blinds. Then, fortunately, our maid spotted us, took us by the arms and pushed us into the streetcar. She already had taken little Hedl [the youngest sister] to stay with friends; Fanny and I were taken to our grandparents. There we stood silently at the window and looked down in the quiet street. Here and there we heard some shreds of conversation … They thought that they had to spare us, they whispered … Did we understand what went on? Neither on that day nor later.

When we returned home … the world had changed. Our carefree childhood was over. An invisible power had struck a cruel blow. And there had been no indication before, the lightening came from a clear sky. Mother declared to father decisively that she would never again

Jungmann Square where Klinger lived as a child

enter the store, never again wait on customers and not shake hands with anyone who might have been part of the mad crowd. She would not leave the apartment, see nobody, speak to nobody. Neighbors came to express their sympathy, stressed that they had no idea, that they had nothing to do with it. Mother did not believe them a word. For weeks, the store remained closed.

In school, our presence created an uncomfortable situation about which one preferred not to speak. What would there have been to say? I remember exactly, what went through my head: Did Mrs. Chmelař think up her accusations, or was there any truth to them? But then she would have said so in court and would have brought proof. Then she would not have been sentenced to several months in jail ... She had unleashed the anger of the masses, which resulted in immense consequences, and the world did not come to an end. Wrong seems to be mightier than right, ... God knows what all is totally different than we assume ... the masses ... inspired in me fear mixed with disgust, it is still the same when I see them in the streets. I could never join a demonstration.

Well, life had to go on. Father had the glass panes of the showcases frosted, so that one could not ... look in the store from the street. The retail business was eliminated and only the production of ladies' lingerie continued. And then ... mother became very sick. After an operation she lay at home. When she began slowly to recover, there were complications ... she was operated again. This time she made no more effort to stay alive and only moaned ... . When father tried to pull mother out of her twilight state: "Regi, you have three young daughters, they need their mother!" She smiled faintly ... "They will manage by themselves ... ."

On 13 February 1920, I went to the clinic ... . Mother's room was filled with a strange sour smell. She herself had changed. Her face was waxen, her eyes deep in their sockets, her nose pointed, her breathing was heavy ... As if to hold on to her, father spoke to her lovingly: "Regi, Trudl is here, do you see her? Don't you want to bless her?" With a final effort, she raised her hands a little, I bowed my head ... close to her, she moved her lips, then her hands fell back ... Father gave me a sign to leave the room. That was the farewell; a little later, mother was dead. Father now spoke to us like to adults, between him and us children there was a good, trusting relationship.

... I want to tell more about father, mainly about the great importance which he had for me. I wonder if he may have known that my heart always pounded in his presence ... that I always wanted to show myself to him from my best side, but then ... perhaps just for that rea-

son—I always only spoke nonsense in his presence. His unjust punishments probably made me afraid of him, but I would have done anything to gain his good will ... Father ... remained ... the great
authority in my life ... And many of his principles had a decisive
influence on my development, I can still hear them ... : "One should
learn to do without things, one should ... not be greedy."

... later in life ... I was able to "do without," ... and when I had
to suffer deprivations, I did not suffer as many others did. Father did
not like us to stand in the kitchen ... to cook and clean ... I never
learned the art of cooking ... or cake baking.

In 1922–3, during the inflation in Germany ... father did not allow
us to use the opportunity for cheap summer vacations in Germany ...
"One does not benefit from the misfortune of others." Or our musical education: Although father played no instrument, he had a pronounced feeling for valuable music, and passed it on to us children.

Our knowledge of Judaism was not good, but this was the same
with almost all Prague Jews. They were very different from the Eastern Jews, for whom a feeling of closeness to the Jewish people and its
history was a matter of course. Today I know that this is something
one has to feel in one's blood, that one cannot learn from books.
During the war, when a Jewish refugee girl from Galicia sometimes
took care of us, she was horrified about our ignorance of everything
concerning Jewishness. She spoke Yiddish with us, from her I heard
for the first time—as she said proudly, "the language of the Jewish
people." I told her that it was simply faulty German full of throaty
chs, whereupon she called me "stupid." We did keep the Jewish holidays, fasted on the Day of Atonement, always sat with Mama in the
gallery of the synagogue, but were not very much concerned about
resting on Sabbath and did not eat kosher. Still, we Klingers were
proud to be Jews.

At that time we joined the Zionist youth movement "Blue-
White." Among boys and girls of my age, I felt very much at home,
all were treated alike, reference to the differences between the sexes
were avoided ... On Sunday hikes we sang folk songs. We learned
Hebrew but never got beyond a superficial knowledge. What I
liked most were the weekly ... evenings with readings from the
books of important writers. Later, we read plays with divided roles;
... by then it was already understood that "that little one" was right
for the theater.

*At the age of 17, she was hired as an actress at the New German Theater.
Hans Demetz[2] commented that "she is a terrific talent." There, Trudl met the
39-year old, German-looking Hans Balder who played "nature boy" roles. He*

was very much in love with her, and while she was not in love with him, she appreciated his interest in her and also in the mystical aspects of Judaism.

For the sake of their future together as actors, he suggested that they move to Berlin.

The idea of getting away from Prague, which had always depressed me, was … very appealing. Of course, Prague was a large city and not … narrow-minded, on the contrary … just because such high standards were applied, there were constantly guest performances of great artists from Vienna, Berlin, and Dresden. People bought tickets to Karl Kraus evenings weeks in advance, read all good books as soon as

they appeared, and the *Prager Tagblatt* had high standards. In my opinion, most Praguers were snobs, who always immediately applied their biting criticism. … When it was a question of somebody from their own circles, they had particularly high expectations.

In Berlin, Ruth and Balder performed in cabarets. When they went on tour to Spaa in Belgium, Hans totally succumbed to his gambling passion and lost all of their money. She was disillusioned about him and his selfish jealousy which was greater than his interest in her person or her career. Ruth went back to Prague, worked there as a secretary until she was called back to

Ruth Klinger at the age of 21 in Dymow's "Frühlingswahn", Berlin 1927

Berlin by a telegram, telling her of Balder's suicide. After an unsuccessful suicide attempt, Ruth returned to her secretarial position in Prague. However, by then it was 1929, and the theater in Klosterstrasse in Berlin offered her the role of Jettchen Gebert in the dramatization of Georg Hermann's famous novel. Ruth accepted the position. She felt that during the performances she became a real actress, and received rave reviews. Other successes followed, but as is inevitable for actresses, also times of insecurity.

In the Kü-Ka, an artists' cabaret, she met the man who was to give her life a new direction.

The cabaret was a cozy restaurant for Bohemians, with a podium and a piano. The m.c. announced: "Maxim Sakaschansky will now sing a few Yiddish folk songs." An about forty-year-old man of medium height with black hair and horn-rimmed glasses appeared on stage … I understood practically nothing, Yiddish was a foreign language to me

... at the entrance, new arrivals crowded together, unable to find seats. Breathless silence, then loud, unending applause ...

I looked at the people around me. This was not the usual Kü-Ka audience. There sat ... elegant ladies with glittering diamond earrings, in their costly fur coats, next to them white-haired gentlemen and listened intently, as at a ... religious séance ... They had only come because of this number.

... how visibly moved they were! Who was this man ... I approached [him], said a few ... appreciative words ... . Sakaschansky nodded, looked me in the eyes, mumbled ... "a Jewish neschomele" [soul, then]: "Miss, are you alone?" then he suggested that we meet the next morning ...

I did not feel like going to the appointment. Well, I had agreed to come ... but I would not stay long. Then I sat across from this Mr. Sakaschansky who spoke broken German and we discussed things about which ... I knew practically nothing ... I had heard this musical mixture of languages in my childhood from Galician refugees in Prague, but for me it was only hard-to-understand gibberish. Now, however, I heard about the flower of Yiddish literature and ... theater in Russia, Poland, and New York ... which compared favorably with good European literature ...

Then, Sakaschansky told me about his impoverished home town of Orsha, a Jewish shtetl in Bielorussia where he had only gone to the yeshiva until his 18th year, and how he ... after the pogroms of Kishinew ... he ... had to flee ...

From then on, we saw each other more often.

After Sakaschansky saw her on the stage, he tried to convince her to become a Jewish actress "Believe me," he said, "It won't be long and the Germans will throw out all Jewish actors." "You aren't serious? Do you really believe that?" "It doesn't take much to see that." It was October 1929.

Meanwhile, sensational reports appeared in the press about Sakaschansky's performances. Once, while walking with him in the park, she learned to sing with him their first duet: Joshke goes away.

The Kü-Ka did well. One evening ... Sakaschansky pulled me onto the stage ... and we sang our Joshke duet which earned much applause.

But ... not all Berlin Jews approved: Mr. Kurt Robitschek, the director of another cabaret, did not think he could have Sakaschansky sing in Yiddish "because he had too much of a Jewish audience."

When Ruth and Maxim rented two adjoining, elegantly furnished rooms, a new chapter in her life began. With several other people, they founded the Jewish cabaret "Kaftan." Sakaschansky played the main role in the enterprise, Ruth acted and handled the box office. The first performance was sold out, the reviews were extremely positive. The audience consisted of three parts: East European petit bourgeois, established Jewish Berliners and Zionists. But there were many Berlin Jews who felt uncomfortable in the face of so much emphasis on Jewishness.

And how did I do privately at that time? I slowly began to become accustomed to my partner's wildly theatrical scenes of jealousy—which frightened and deeply hurt me at first, for I gave him no reason ... Sakaschansky was not an average person, not to be measured by the usual standards. He was ... a burning torch on stage, in love and in anger. When after his uncontrolled scenes he apologized to me with heartrending words: "I am a Russian bear who strikes with his paws when he is aroused, but Ruthele, in my heart you lie on a wide chaise lounge."—" all was well again ... He was strange yet familiar ... since ancient times.

Unemployed demonstrated in the streets ... but we did well ... we were without competition ... there were plenty of Jews and there always would be.

On April 30, 1931, we were married in a civil ceremony . . I was sorry ... I lost my Czechoslovak citizenship ... Status: stateless.

There were guest performances—over fifty in as many cities in summer of 1931 alone—gradually she was able to perform as an equal partner of Sakaschansky's.

As clouds gathered on the horizon for Jewish Germany, the Sakaschansky-Klinger team moved their performances to other European capitals. But Ruth became pregnant, and Maxim had to perform alone. When money became very tight, she went to Prague to deliver the baby there.

From the beginning something was wrong with the child, a little boy. He turned blue, made no effort to drink and increasingly suffered from seizures. Ruth had to go on tour and continue performing—no matter how badly under the circumstances. Although two kind-hearted, simple women did their best to take care of Danielke in her father's house, his condition continued to deteriorate.

All my hopes had proven treacherous ... Now I had to free my parents' house [her father had remarried] from this burden as quickly as possible. My dear father ... what went on in your heart? "This Trudl. Could one not see it already when she was a child? There is something wrong with her mentally. She always goes by her feelings and not by her reason. Where was her little bit of common sense, when she tied herself to this man, what did she like so much about him? That he was 20 years older than she? That all he knows is to act and sing in Yiddish? ... He doesn't even know one language properly ... and besides, he is stateless ... and now you have a child without thinking about the responsibility ... you with your training as a German actress ... You don't have the healthy instinct for a suitable partner for life which every girl has. You proved that already with your first choice, with Hans Balder ... Now your father who himself is plagued by financial worries has to make up for your lack of common sense. Does one have a right to roll one's burdens onto somebody else?"

Yes, father, you are right, of course. I did everything wrong. It isn't love that ties me to this man ... his heartrending tenderness wraps me like cotton. I am his one and all ... is that worth nothing?

When Ruth and Maxim, after performances which took them all the way to Subcarpathian Ruthenia, returned via Prague to Berlin, Hitler had just become chancellor of Germany. They were refused admission to their apartment by the Nazi custodian who beat Maxim mercilessly and tore his clothes. Finally they found refuge in a Jewish pension.

Five weeks later, she received the news that Danielke had died.

... We belonged to Erez Israel, the dream of all Zionists with whom we had worked closely in recent years. They advised us to get ourselves tourist visas, in the hope that we would get the residence permits later ...

They found out that their passports had to be valid for at least a year, yet Nansen passports for stateless persons were not being renewed. ... Most of their possessions were still in the apartment with the Nazi custodian.

When on April 1, the day of the boycott, the police inquired about them by telephone, they took the earliest possible train to Prague.

It is April 2. At the British consulate, I said what the English authorities had assured us that as soon as the visa permit arrived, it would be sent on to the British authorities in Prague ... the official telephoned us that our ship ... would leave on the 12th of April from Trieste; we already had our tickets. I went to the police president and submitted an urgent application for two Czech interim passports, explaining ... the urgency of the matter. Then I went to father's apartment; he was ... in the country. His wife ... showed me the paid bills for Danielke's funeral ... At that time I was unable to part with any of the meager remnant in my wallet.

They had a farewell-performance in Mährisch-Ostrau, where finally they received a call that their visas had arrived. Back in Prague, at the police station, she was told that no interim-passports could be given to stateless persons. She requested an audience with the police president who finally agreed that she should come at 11 a.m. the next day. Then on to the British, Austrian, Italian and Yugoslav consulates. At the English consulate she was told that the Czechoslovak passports were only valid for exit from Czechoslovakia.

Back at the police president's office, after an emotional plea, she was issued two new passports and had them stamped at the other consulates. At her father's house, she found out that he would not be back in time. She was at least 400 crowns short of what they would need to get to the boat ... .

Finally, with money given her by Rabbi Arie, she and Maxim boarded the train for Trieste.

In Palestine, they were glad not to be "emigrants" but among their own, and touched by instances of kindness to them. Ruth eagerly learned Hebrew, while Maxim had difficulties—as a proud speaker of Yiddish, he sometimes met with hostility. She began to consider leaving him if he continued to be so stubborn.

Life was difficult for them and they went on a tour of kibbutzim to perform. In a kibbutz where several of her old "Blue-White" friends from Prague lived, she told Maxim that she would stay there—he could do likewise, or go back to Tel Aviv.

Then something terrible happened. Sakaschansky began to roar like a madman. He made sounds like an animal. Then he took a few heavy stones—and threw them at me. A hail of heavy stones hit me, I fell to the ground and called for help. The hail of stones did not stop. I thought my end was near. ... In a nearby vineyard, a chaver[3] noticed what was happening. He came running and with a few slaps brought the raging man to his senses, then he carried me ... to his wooden hut. There I lay on his bunk with my torn dress; blood flowed from several wounds. They took Maxim to the guest room and left him alone, but instead of calming down, he ... opened our suitcases and tore all of my clothes.

The chaver ordered a taxi ... and put him in it with the warning not to ever show up there again . ...

... I was ashamed of Maxim and of my own failure ... Why had I not had the patience to wait for a suitable moment ? ... When I had ... more or less recovered, I ... asked for work. Very well, I was told, you go to the back house tomorrow morning where the orange crates are received ...

But the work in the kibbutz was too hard for her and the members decided that she was not right for it.

Back in Tel Aviv, Maxim tearfully asked her forgiveness, but she had lost all feeling for him. After receiving a letter of rejection from the Habima,[4] she took on a job with an educated handicapped lady.

Although only 27 years old, I felt how slowly but surely I was going downhill. After all I had lived through, I felt ... worn out, my nerve was gone.

... I was about to become what I least wanted to be—a pitiful, helpless case ... I had rented a small room ... across from the maternity clinic ... Through the open window the whole neighborhood heard ... the crying of the newborn ... day and night. I saw little Danielke before me, my sick son, who was buried nine months ago ... there was no one with whom I could have a heart to heart talk ...

Without ... Maxim, who as a Russian Jew was here among his own kind, I felt totally lost.

When Maxim wrote her a desperate, loving letter, she took him back.

Deep down I breathed a sigh of relief. Let people talk all they want ... What was I to do with my longed-for freedom? ... I warmed myself in Maxim's moving, familiar devotion ...

The room ... which was small for one person, now became our home ... a narrow shelf with a curtain contained all we owned, clothing ... shoes—and on the upper shelf there were musical notes, our repertory and Hebrew language notes. On the wall there was a wire case for food. Maxim now was prepared ... to take the first job he could find. Daily, he lugged a heavy gramophone with an even heavier box of records from settlement to settlement, knocked on all doors and tried to sell record players ... .

> *This job soon ended, as did others for both of them. Ruth, along with other German speakers, felt discriminated against despite her efforts to learn Hebrew. Sometimes they presented "underground" programs, Maxim in Yiddish, she in German. They continued to live from hand to mouth. After a while, she taught Hebrew and eventually acted in the Hebrew Theater. ...*
>
> *Ruth tells about experiences in various theaters and on improvised stages in various places in Palestine. As performers, they were particularly in danger of deportation, but finally—in 1937—their stay was legalized.*

Whatever we tried, we did not get out of our financial stress. Maxim sat every morning and afternoon in the café "Ginah" ... which is where people came if they wanted to hire him as an entertainer for a wedding, barmitzvah or another joyful family occasion, but how much did that amount to?

... I had something valuable: time. I gradually borrowed from the city library all literary and philosophical standard works ... I concentrated on the wisdom of Aristotle, Plato, Spinoza, Nietzsche, Schopenhauer, and began writing in a notebook "What I have to ... remember. ..." At that time, I discovered for myself the high value of the intellectual world in which one could recover from the annoyances of everyday life, lack of money and one's own feelings of inadequacy. When I found that Plato confirmed that ideas which had often gone through my head are right, and that I only lacked the ability to formulate them clearly, this gave me a satisfaction which compensated me for much.

At that time, I began writing my own diary, ... I wrote poems, I mourned something I never had: youth.

> *It was some time in 1938 that she had met Dr. E. a former Berlin lawyer; he invited her to a gourmet meal in a hotel room.*

My initial scruples melted like snow in the sun. What then followed, was something totally unexpected. ... That evening changed me, indeed ... that evening I entered a new stage of my existence. Dr. E. introduced me to the joys of lust, of a lust of which up to that point I had no idea. I never would have dared to even dream of such sophisticated love-play. A few weeks before, I thought that my life was worth nothing. Now, I saw how much it was worth ...

Further meetings followed ... then E rented me a furnished room. There we met twice a week. At home, I said that I was teaching Hebrew ... Every time he invented new nuances, he spoiled me in a way I cannot describe. It continued ... for almost a year. I lived according to the motto: Give yourselves to nature before it takes you (... . Hölderlin) ... Of course, the motto also had an unpleasant side to it: lying. ... But, [she told herself], things are similar in many houses.

... When I began to write my memoirs, I intended, through unsparing honesty, to bring something like order into my past ... Now that I have reached the intermezzo Karli, I am besieged by very uncomfortable considerations ... must I place myself in a shamefully unfavorable light through the truthful account of my weak-willed character?

... I am ashamed to the bottom of my soul of what happened in the second half of 1940 ... But why do I seek understanding? It is more important to reach clarity about how it could happen that at that time, I let myself be turned like a rag in the wind.

> *Karli, an old friend from "Blue-White" came from Prague, and Ruth soon was involved in an affair with him. When Maxim became jealous, Ruth left him again after a knock-down, drag out fight and moved in with Karli.*
>
> *Although a pediatrician, he suggested that they peddle a cologne he thought he could produce cheaply. Karli's physical advances were also problematic. He was inhibited, confused, weak, without the least knowledge of refined sensual pleasure and tortured himself and her because of his ... inadequacies.*

During the proceedings of Ruths divorce from Maxim on the 8. of October, 1940 Maxim] repeated in Hebrew: "you are now free ... fair game" ... and I felt ... deeply humiliated ... . We sat down in a garden restaurant for the farewell meal. ... Tears fell on Sakaschansky's plate. He said (in his mixture of German and Yiddish) "I fulfilled your request because I want you to be happy, but ... I am and I remain your husband until your death."

> *She saw increasingly, what a burden she had taken on herself by moving in with Karli who soon suggested that she go back to E. She did, but E. proved to be a gambler in financial difficulties. Once again, she had acute feelings of anxiety.*

What can I do with the freedom for which I fought? It makes me afraid, that is all … . Are other women so much braver than I? Aren't they perhaps afraid to make their way through life by themselves, and therefore prefer to put up with a bad marriage? This is then called fidelity … One can't rely on anything, because I see how little I can rely on myself.

She compared the two times she left Maxim.

Always when I rattled the bars of the cage, I put myself in a pitiful situation. Father was right … I am mentally inferior … I cannot build my future on E., he is no more than a delicate enjoyment … I cannot rely on anything because I see how little one can rely on me. .. .

When she refused to give in to E. who did not want her to appear on the same program with Maxim, he had a nervous breakdown.

I felt very awkward about his nervous breakdown and was glad when he finally left.

She realized what all tied her to the ever loving Maxim

… he remained the genuine Eastern Jewish original, sure of who he was, from the small shtetl, to whom "his Ruthele" meant everything. How unshakably he believed in his God who was well disposed toward him, spoke to his guardian angel as to a … good friend!

They remarried, and although her feelings and opinions about Maxim changed frequently, she knew that nobody else gave her the same feeling of worth.

They still lived in one shabby, furnished room. Their "living" had ups and downs; for a while she played the piano in a bar for British officers, then she availed herself of an opportunity to take English lessons which lasted for several years.

Especially during the war years, Ruths account of her private life is interwoven with comments about the war, British Palestine policy and accounts about the fate of relatives. In 1941, she still had no money at all with which to help a newly arrived relative.

In 1941 she became quite successful with recitals of German literature, often with the support of Max Brod and Arnold Zweig. At that time, she also became acquainted with a musician 10 years younger than herself who made a deep impression on her. Kurt, as she called him, constantly amazed her.

There was hardly a topic about which he was not exactly informed and about which he did not express a definite view. I had made a valuable friend: intelligence coupled with youthful charm and sensuous attraction.

Kurt worked on a novel and on a play for which Ruth gave him help and encouragement. When Kurt proposed a future together, she consented, after Max Brod told her of his positive impression of Kurt. Maxim magnanimously agreed to a separation. As she wrote in a letter to Max Brod:

"I am extremely happy. It turned out that the things of which I was most afraid are absolutely delightful, daily life is all pleasure ... . Sakaschansky said as we parted " ... you will come back to me. I'll wait until you are sober again ... . This time I am not going to get a divorce." When I thought of him, I felt a stab in my heart. I felt guilty ... .

Toward the end of January 1945 ... it was he who came to ask me for a divorce, he wanted to remarry.

Soon there were problems with Kurt's literary work; she was critical of his writing, many chapters were rewritten. It all looked like patchwork. When they became critical of each other, Ruth began to work as the unpaid secretary of Arnold Zweig who urgently needed help because of his bad eyesight.

... In 1944, the newspapers first brought vague hints about gas chambers in Poland. Was something so horrible possible? ... ... just that year . . remained in my memory as the time of a never repeated artistic upswing.

She presented literary readings with texts by Arnold Zweig and others. The audiences were German speaking intellectuals in the major cities in Palestine.
 In fall of 1944, when she was 38, she met a 21-year-old struggling poet, a homosexual whom she called Wolfgang. Soon he visited her daily. Ruth fed him and clothed him; Kurt did not find him nearly so interesting as she did, but tolerated him.

The fascination of failed existences which have nothing, are nothing and yet talk big, constantly float between heaven and earth and don't know how close they are to the abyss was not new to me ... . I knew the story of the mouse and the bacon in the trap ... there was the accidental touching of hands while lighting cigarettes, an embarrassed glance ... a long silence ... lips coming closer ... a short squeeze of the hands ... and the relationship of the "motherly friend" was gone.

And then: my first visit with him, in the evening in his attic on the Carmel. The excitement on the way there. My perceptions in the small, dark room ... The dreamy mood. The blissful shudder of the boy's body during the first slight touch ... The feeling of ... eternity ... childlike, unspoiled blissful youth ... His confession: "Ruth, you are my first intimate experience with a woman." Such delight, chaste and pure ... this miracle ... then ... painfully tearing myself away ... keeping the secret which was breaking my heart to myself, pretending to be asleep in order ... not to have to talk to Kurt.

Then one day Wolfgang came, told Kurt about the affair and asked Ruth to choose. She realized that Wolfgang was a nobody, reckless and vain and asked him to leave and never to come back.

> *Kurt behaved excellently. Her explanation how this could happen: it is lit-tle more than the flirt turned into a little infidelity—well, thousands of partners in marriage do it, and it does no harm.*
>
> *She considered the affair ended, but upon Kurt's suggestion, she went on a 4-day trip with Wolfgang. Kurt was convinced that that would cure her of her infatuation with Wolfgang.*
>
> *The opposite happened. She wrote about four nights which were "filled with an indescribable sweetness." When she returned to Kurt, her relationship with him was destroyed, but it did not end until after she again deceived him with Wolfgang. This coincided with her second divorce from Maxim and with her last public appearance as an actress in Palestine.*

Wasn't the important thing that I lacked the ability to think intelli-gently about my own work? I saw my future at that time as no more than an accumulation of opaque shreds of fog ... My shaky situation was the consequence of my own recklessness and of my lack of com-mon sense ... [She wondered if she compulsively destroyed relation-ships in order not to have her partners end them? In retrospect, Ruth was convinced that she would not have had to leave Kurt.]

What would have seemed ... ridiculous a few weeks earlier hap-pened ... . Wolfgang moved into the room next door in the pension, and we shared our everyday existence.

For that which Kurt called "unsolved" about him, I found lots of excuses.

> *She realized that Wolfgang was a show-off ... that he talked sarcastically about others and took advantage of his hard-working mother. Ruth saw herself and Wolfgang like two shipwrecked people holding on to each other. They lived from hand to mouth and she worried.*
>
> *One day Maxim came, loving as ever, with an idea that was to help her out of her financial misery. Together with him and with Wolfgang, she was to com-pile a directory of all artists in Palestine; her job would mainly be collecting vital data and money from all those willing to participate. This offered her a glimmer of hope, and so she and Wolfgang went to work.*
>
> *Gradually, however, Ruth had the feeling that Wolfgang was again meet-ing his old homosexual friends. One day a ten-pound bill was missing from her purse; it was clear that Wolfgang had taken it. While looking for her money, she glanced at her little pocket mirror:*

I saw the face of an ugly woman, with yellowish wrinkled skin, her eyes wide open with fear. What had become of me, the attractive Ruth Klinger?

> *She left with her belongings and with the help of a Prague acquaintance found a place to stay—a cot in a dirty, smelly old-age home. In response to her call for help, Maxim again came to her rescue, and she continued her work on the directory. She went through a deep emotional crisis, a time of despair, at the end*

of which she decided to stand on her own feet, to avoid ever again giving a man power over herself, to surround herself with an armor of hardness, to complain to no one. At that time, she lost her fear of being alone.

She received fervent love letters from Wolfgang, again was not sure if he had stolen the money, but decided to stay alone. Finally, the job was completed and the book was received very positively.

So I finally made it on my own strength. Perhaps a higher authority, fate, had ... tried me ... to free me once and for all of my fear of the struggle for existence and also of my paralyzing fear of being alone.

She did not move back to Kurt, despite innumerable letters assuring her of his friendship and love through the years.

When she learned, after the war, that most of her family had been extermi-nated along with millions of others, she felt that ... there was only one thing which was working for: the founding of a Jewish state.

When her income from the book decreased, she became housekeeper in a boarding school, which turned out to be very humane. While she was in that fairly pleasant position, Ruth met another old acquaintance from Berlin, Otto S., a very well-to-do, orthodox, distinguished elderly gentleman. He began vis-iting her with flowers and candies.

When he took me in his arms, I had the long-missed feeling of being sheltered. His careful, somewhat soporific eroticism, his pious way of proceeding in the love-act, the long silences afterwards, all that felt good at the time. I wrote in my diary ... take me in your circle, let me, the lost sheep, take part in your peace. Will you include me in your prayers?

When S. invited her to live with him in his new home in Herzliya, Ruth accepted. But it turned out that she had to work very hard—for very little money—for S. and his son's family.

Why was I so tired? he asked. I am not only dead tired, I am ... furi-ous. Why does this man, whom I worshipped, ... pretend to be so stu-pid? Not only my love, my respect was also gone. Instead of true piety, I ... saw ... shrewdness.

... On Friday afternoons, in addition to the festive dinners, I also had to cook all the meals for the next day ... And what did grandpa Otto do? ... He busily tore toilet paper from the roll ... for the Sabbath.

Well, let us be fair ... even before I had entered the house, I had cleared the area around the entrance and thereby created my status from the first day on. This seems to be my unchangeable character—otherwise it would not have happened to me so often ... I (also) always point out what I cannot do, and belittle what I can do.

She went to visit Arnold Zweig and his wife and agreed to move in with them as their "house daughter." For some time, she was given room and board in return for secretarial work and a little household help.

In early 1947, Ruth was invited to move to Prague to live with her sister, Hedl, her English husband and their child. She was 40 years old, had no income at the Zweigs', and felt that nobody would miss her. Having found herself a job as correspondent for the Tel Aviv German-language daily, she boarded the plane to Prague.

For ... this chapter, I have voluminous aids to my memory ... How I again felt the oppressive atmosphere which Prague always had for me ... how long—familiar and yet ... impersonal the dirty-gray façades of houses, churches, baroque palaces, and monuments made me feel ... .

[It was cold and almost impossible to heat apartments, food was rationed and there were severe shortages.] There were at that time approximately 8,000 Jews living in Prague, 70% of them from Slovakia, 10% re-immigrants, 8% returned from Theresienstadt, very few were native Jews who had returned from the death camps in the East or had been spared deportation because they lived in mixed marriages.

In Prague, she was aware of anti-Semitism, but also noted a very philosemitic speech by the rector of the university, and was even more enthusiastic about one by Jan Masaryk whom she met. Egon Erwin Kisch became a good friend.

It wasn't easy to shed one's old skin and slip into a new one ... My so-called return home was difficult. Much that I took for granted turned out to be erroneous. In contrast to my sister Hedl ... who feels at home here as a Czech, I am a stranger to Czech culture, although I still speak the language quite well. I have been away too long ... I was culturally German, and what has happened in my life since then has no connection with Prague. The typical atmosphere of Prague, which I remember, the intellectual stratum of Jews and Germans doesn't exist any more.

... Each of us three sisters had a different development. Fanny is an American, I am a Palestinian and Hedl is Czech. And–she is an ... active Communist comrade.

When I left ... Palestine, I asked myself: who will miss me here ...? The question should have been: whom will I miss? Oh, I missed them all. Maxim wrote me: "Am I going to see you again in my life, Ruthele, my dearest in the world?" ... I was lonesome for Palestine ... the greater part of me remained there. ... I thought in German ... Except at E. E. Kisch's, a discussion in German was out of the question!

... She felt a gulf between those who were persecuted in Prague during the war years and people like herself who were thought of as having lead a carefree existence abroad.

The story of her father's rug throws a revealing light on the situation she encountered. From the Jewish community newspaper, she found out that the heirs entitled to a rug registered in her stepmother's name could claim it from the authorities. If her father had declared himself a German in 1930, he would have "contributed to the Germanization of the Czech fatherland," and the property would have been considered "confiscated enemy property," but it turned out that he had declared himself a "Jewish national." Ruth was asked innumerable questions about her activities during the war and had to take innumerable steps continuing for three years. However, she considered these annoyances minor; what occupied her attention, were the events in the Middle East.

As is well known, the Arab world rejected the proposal of the UN to partition Palestine. If they had agreed to it, there would not have been four bloody wars, with ten-thousand human sacrifices, there would not have been a Palestine tragedy, not thirty years of terror … .

As a newspaper reporter, Ruth had a good meeting with Jan Masaryk, whom she revered.

In November of 1947, she began to perform on a Jewish stage in a restaurant, and then went on tour with the group. At that time, interest in Jewish performances was much greater than before the war.

However, her many activities resulted in conflicts with her sister and brother-in-law who expected much more help in the household than she could give. Ruth experienced a feeling of déjà vu as she thought of earlier situations in her life.

After the coup of February 1948, her observations about which include comments on not generally known attitudes of observers including Egon Erwin and Gisella Kisch, Ruth's conflicts with her sister, a fanatical Communist, became unbearable.

I, a have-not, surely had no reason to wear mourning for the dying prosperous bourgeoisie, [but] … oh, why didn't I stay with Zweig in Haifa! I was so well off! There I gave up interesting work and left him in the lurch.

She moved to a rented room and became Hebrew secretary to the World Organization of the Palestinian Workers' Party.

As the Iron Curtain lowered, she learned to write between the lines.

As for the attitudes of the Jews: they could now be divided into two parts: those who felt like sheep without a master were … extremely vulnerable and tried to bear their Jewishness with dignity, and … those who joined the Communist Party, convinced of having thereby solved the Jewish problem for themselves for good, and of having eliminated their Jewish past. (So the party statutes promised.)

They Czechicized their names … Mr Vondrácek (formerly Kohn) lectured to me enthusiastically: anti-Semitism now belongs to the past for good. Can we not be proud of the large number of Jews in leading positions?

Ruth commented on Kisch's death: he was celebrated by the Communists as one of their own, and although he had just been elected honorary president of the Jewish Community, his wish to be buried in the Jewish cemetery was ignored.

When she recalled that Kisch had proudly introduced her as his good friend and as Arnold Zweig's secretary, she was an equal in the circle of those present ... and forgot how alone she basically was ... .

Soon after the founding of the State of Israel, Ruth was appointed secretary of the Israeli ambassador. Although she now for the first time in her life had some power along with glory, not all went smoothly. When she for example succeeded in getting an Israeli visa for a girl who had lost both legs, she made an enemy of the First Ambassador.

I became accustomed to being alone and unloved, which used to seem unbearable to me. The ridge between my eyebrows became deeper, my features harder. Common sense and responsibility marked my

Charles Bridge, LESSER SIDE

behavior in the new metamorphosis. I had come to distrust every compliment ... . My Sunday afternoons were as sad as ever. I mostly walked alone through the narrow streets of the "Lesser Side." There was hardly a building which would not be worth ... describing. If [Alexander von] Humboldt counted Prague among the five most beautiful cities of the world, he knew why. As children, we did not appreciate it ... . My days were filled with work—but at night, I often embraced the pillows and sometimes sobbed ... .

> *The atmosphere became increasingly oppressive; it was apparently a top secret letter which Ruth typed for the Israeli labor union leader Mordechai Oren suggesting restitution to the Jews by the GDR that led to Oren's disappearance.*

After the Israeli embassy was closed, in February 1953, I boarded a plane to Israel. It was a night flight, and high up in the clouds, I experienced a sunrise for the first time in my life. I could not believe that it was no dream, that after five years' absence, I returned home, that there, in the foreign ministry, a job waited for me, that I was about to begin a new metamorphosis.

NOTES

1. Reprinted in the American edition of my book, *The Jews in Bohemia and Moravia,* Detroit 1993, pp 385–390.
2. The dramaturgist at the German Theater
3. 'pal', 'comrade'
4. The best theater in Palestine

Chapter 12

JIŘINA ŠIKLOVÁ

(BORN 1935)

---

*T*here are many sides to Jiřina, and I think the reader needs to be aware of all of them.

I first heard of her almost a quarter of a century ago when she was a young instructor of sociology at Charles University in Prague. I had been providing a student in Prague with books from America, and he told me about his teacher, Jiřina, who had first acquainted him with these American works. Although he urged me to look her up, I was hesitant about imposing myself on this younger woman and did not do so. However, when a close collaborator of Jiřina's suggested around 1987 that I use her as one of the subjects of my book, I decided to visit her. At that time she was quite active in shipping samizdat[1] books from Czechoslovakia to the West and smuggling Western, mostly Czech exile literature into Czechoslovakia. I went to Jiřina's apartment close to the center of Prague. A slender, dark-haired woman with sparkling dark eyes greeted me like an old friend, fed me a meal, and welcomed me to stay with her, at that time a courageous offer to make to a "Westerner." We had hardly begun to speak when a friend came. He first told Jiřina that the police had turned his apartment upside down that very morning in a house search but then related the details of a problem immediately confronting him. I soon found myself directly involved in its solution. Jiřina's friend had just received money through illegal channels that was earmarked for a trip to Yugoslavia where he was to meet Djilas, Tito's well-known opponent, and he needed someone to go to the bank with him and testify with appropriate fictitious details that this was money they had brought with them. I was glad to help.

Jiřina was one of the very active Czech dissidents, and knew most of the others well. She was generous with her time, and although much of it was taken up with her job as a cleaning lady, caring for her senile mother and her children, and—last but not least—dealing with police harassment, she introduced me to some of her "underground" colleagues and would have done more if my time had not been limited.

A central event in Jiřina's life was the very painful break-up of her marriage which ended in divorce January 1981, after almost twenty-five years. She documented this stage of her life in the many letters she wrote at that time, some of which she sent, others not, but all of which she believes she had to write in order to get back on her feet. For lack of space mainly, I will only include her statement in divorce court and some isolated fragments of these letters to represent this time in her life. Unlike many men, who keep their interpersonal relationships and emotional life private, Jiřina is willing to explore and share her private emotional life.

Among Jiřina's remarkable qualities, her resilience matches her courage. Note that she wrote the advice column I include a month after her divorce, that she immediately continued her illegal activities as a dissident and was jailed in March that same year. In prison she wrote her essay on techniques for survival during imprisonment. Emphasizing what could or should be done, she left behind the question of personal survival and moved on to sociological observations and, while still imprisoned, reminded her friends outside to observe and celebrate the one hundredth birthday of their famous countryman, Franz Kafka, who was then tabu in Czechoslovakia.

After prison, Jiřina, with no access to international sociological literature, wrote empirical studies based in part on her work as a cleaning woman in a geriatric institution; works under various pseudonyms and also in samizdat editions. I especially like her little book, Deník staré paní (An Old Woman's Diary and Dávno, dávno již tomu (It was Long, Long Ago) in which she puts herself in Božena Němcová's place.

The Velvet Revolution in Czechoslovakia found her surrounded by a growing number of grandchildren and looking back on eight years of a relationship with a man with whom she can feel secure. She returned to Charles University and—despite financial difficulties and skeptical attitudes in her country—founded a program of Gender Studies, using help organized abroad. She has been asked to accept a political post which she refused and is flooded with invitations to serve on international boards and to lecture in many countries in the West.

As a sociologist, Jiřina of course synthesizes and theorizes, but she is primarily concerned with the application of theory to social work and beyond that is personally involved with many individual human beings and needs.

In her brief autobiography, written in the mid-eighties, Jiřina follows the requirements of the Communist regime for persons seeking employment, i.e. personal, subjective aspects of her life are largely omitted:

I was born in the family of a doctor on June 17, 1935 in Prague and ... graduated from gymnasium in ... 1953 ... I studied history and philosophy at Charles University, and graduated in 1958 with distinction ... At the university I met a large number of interesting personalities among the professors and students. Indirectly I am still in contact with some of them; they are today in various positions on both sides of the barricades.

At the university I was, among other things, interested in the Czech-Jewish movement. I studied ... Hebrew and wanted to write my thesis about [the Czech-Jewish movement] . Finally however my professors dissuaded me, saying that the purpose of a thesis is to complete one's studies and to graduate and not to ruin one's career. So I chose "The Prague Stock Exchange and its Fall in 1873"—something neutral that could pass without political complications … I am still sorry that I never returned to my favorite subject … I only follow what others write about it. By way of compensation I try to take care of a few people who returned from concentration camp, I wrote up their reminiscences of Terezín and try to help edit and translate the texts of others.

I accepted a position as a professional assistant for the *Historický časopis* (Historical Journal) of the Czechoslovak Academy of Sciences,

Hradčany from Charles Bridge

in the Historical Institute on Hradčany. My pay was small, but as compensation I had a beautiful view of Hradčany and the whole city ... I was quite bored in that venerable institution ... and shocked the other employees when I gave notice and went to teach at the former French gymnasium, where I taught ... geography, ... civics and mainly mechanical engineering, of which I had no idea. I took a course ... and received a certificate as a low-level locksmith. In the course of my life I acquired quite a number of such skills for which I never had any use later. Because this teaching ... did not satisfy me, I tried to get back to the university ... I received offers from two faculties and chose [the faculty of] philosophy, where I began working in fall of 1960 as an assistant, with a pay of 1074 kč monthly. Now, a year before retirement, I have almost the same [pay], but as a cleaning lady.

In addition to a seminar on the history of philosophy and on philosophy within the framework of Marxism-Leninism I taught seminars on oriental studies, art history, Czech, Russian studies, but also law ... I consider this period the best of my working career. At the same time I worked on my dissertation; completing it was essential for receiving a permanent position at the university ... I chose the topic "The academic YMCA, a contribution to the development of philosophic thinking during the First Republic ..." I don't know the exact title of this study, all copies were confiscated during house searches. I really liked this work, and in its course came in contact with many very

interesting people ... such as [Christian] ministers, people from the resistance [against the Nazis] ... I could pass some of the information on to my children who joined a semi-legal scouting organization in the seventies. I received the title candidate of science and a better paid position as an assistant.

Jiřina Šiklová

... At that time I lectured on the history of philosophy for non-majors ... and participated in the so-called dialogical seminar, which then, in the sixties, was conducted by Professor Milan Machovec, and where ... people from various church denominations could really freely introduce their ideas to others. That first dialog between Marxists and believers lasted almost ten years, and I was a participant, usually a passive one. Christians and pronounced atheists met there ... and later also people from abroad lectured. That seminar was the first break-through into the citadel of Marxism; there I actually learned to carry on a dialog, to understand the adherents of different views , to defend positions ... . Together with later seminars of Professor Patočka, it was as important for me as the earlier studies at the university.

Via the problems of the academic I came to the general problems of the student movement and to the sociology of youth, so that, when sociology was renewed here, I was asked if I would like to become a member of the newly founded department of sociology. Sociology had been abolished as a field after 1948, being condemned as a "pseudo-science," as a servant of Western agencies, etc. ... . It was not even advisable to use the word too much. In the first half of the sixties, when the regime became somewhat less restrictive, many realized that this attitude was outdated, and sociology was reinstituted ... Because I was abroad relatively often ... I helped to organize that department at ... Charles University, and became a member of the department ... I taught ... the methodology of research ... and in part also the history of Czech sociology ...

As at that time much was spoken in the world about the sociology of youth, and as we did not even have a basic textbook on that subject, I wrote [one] together with Dr. Eliška Freiová about youth, students, ideology and the New Left. I associated a lot with students as an observer and participant in their movement which played an important role in 1968 and 1969. During that time I became acquainted not only with the problems of the student movement in the West—about which I wrote a book which was scheduled to appear ... but didn't— but also with many spokesmen of the student movement including Rudi Dutschke, Cohn-Bendit etc. These contacts were one of the reasons for my being dismissed from the university. I was among the first group to leave the philosophic faculty ... among other things because of "informal authority among the students," which they even wrote into my evaluation. Karel Kosík, Václav Černý, Jan Patočka and Milan Machovec[2] ... were also in the group.

I began working as a cleaning lady in the State Library Klementinum. I cleaned there in the morning, and in the afternoon I sat in the professors' reading room, for which I still had a special permit, and studied and wrote. The work was good, about 2–3 hours daily, officially 8 hours, for 890 kč. a month. The core of party members at the faculty who had gotten into power did not like it, because the students made fun of it and I did also. They told me that I could look for another position. It was the time of the witch hunts in the early seventies. In April of 1971 I began working in the gerontological department of Dr. Trojan, in Thomayer hospital, in a temporary job, which was extended every three months. This was important for me, because temporary workers did not have to be approved by the district committee of the Communist Party ... I did gerontological research for the director, wrote statistical reports for the hospital, surveys etc. Dr. Trojan was an old gentleman, chairman of the Czechoslovak gerontological society, who always at the end of a five-year plan had to give reports to the Ministry of Health about what was written in Czechoslovakia about old people. I did that also. My tasks for instance were: gerontological counseling ... research on the aged in the city, psychological tests for aged patients, work opportunities for the aged, attitudes toward aged workers in a certain concern. I knew how to do different things than the doctors, and they were nice to me. It was a pleasant atmosphere ... lots of people could come and visit me in the hospital ... inconspicuously. It was also possible to have people admitted there who would have had difficulty being hospitalized elsewhere. Almost all dissidents, such as Jiří Hochman, Jiří Ruml and Karel Kyncl were among them.

I was arrested for the first time in January 1972, because of a group which published the earliest samizdat literature, because I had people around me from the Protestant Church "The New Orientation," and because my patients were visited by other dissidents. I was kept for

Jiřina Šiklová with Wolfgang Scheuer

only about 24 hours. At that time I was already working with Palach Press [in London] which at that time was still predominantly in the hands of Petr Pithart and Jiří Müller at our end … After they arrested Müller and Hýbl in December of 1971, the connection passed among others into my and Pithart's hands. [Here the interesting names mentioned are Ruda Slánský, the son of the Slánský who was executed after the show trials in the early fifties, and Jiří Dienstbier.]

In the eighties, Wolfgang Scheuer and his wife Brigitte were not only members of the diplomatic corps of the Federal German Republic in Czechoslovakia, but also our voluntary and self-sacrificing chargés d'affaires and mediators between the dissidents and our people in exile.

I used to go and see them in their apartment … at least 2–3 times monthly; each time I had letters and messages in secret pockets, manuscripts of articles and sometimes even of books in shopping bags. I used to go home from visits with them with even fuller pockets and bags …

My present man … Dr. Jiří Veselý, M.D., Dr. Sc., born 1923, … is a typical scientist, exact, very well read; he studied in Prague and Geneva … I have been living with him since spring, 1981, but we each have our own apartment. There are no tensions in our relationship.

I was jailed on May 8th, 1981 and let out on March 22, 1982. I was again in jail in October, 1988—only for sixteen days. Then they threw me out of Thomayer Hospital. Since January of 1990 I worked again as a cleaning lady in the Water Works, and since April 1990 again at the Philosophic faculty of Charles University.

During the period covered by this factually written account, Jiřina was divorced in January of 1981 at the request of her husband Zdeněk, a historian with whom she had two children. We have Jiřina's letters to Zdeněk from the period of the break-up:

December 14, 1980

Dear Zdeňku, this time I perhaps can really write you without emotions. Until yesterday I hoped that you would come back … Yesterday you told me … that you cannot and do not want to live with me, that you have rented an apartment … and that you consider it best to get a divorce. What can I do but accept it? I only ask you to apply for the divorce as soon as possible … . It will be best for you to do it … we can each pay half … . but we can do it nicely, without disgusting scenes and arguments … [then] it will be easier for us to communicate. I am going to have the feeling that things are definite and I won't think that I'll get you back if I am nice to you, I won't be hurt by your behavior. After divorce people don't bring each other flowers, and nobody expects it ... . There are lots of divorced people ... Considering that the process [divorce] was only stopped back then, they will divorce us immediately ...

In court during the divorce proceedings, Jiřina summed up her thoughts about her marriage and her divorce:

January 30, 1981 ...
I could imagine many tragedies in my life, many losses. I could imagine that there could be a war, that one would lose one's possessions ... I could not imagine getting a divorce—my parents had not prepared me for that. And because I grew up in a harmonious family, I wanted my children to have a similar home, and therefore I made the mistake of being silent and of tolerating many things in my husband, Zdeněk Šikl, which ... I should not have forgiven him ... I thought that it was all part of his personality, that a marriage is the union of two persons who are fond of each other but remain themselves, who walk hand in hand ... [and] complement and enrich each other, but don't swallow each other and limit each other's growth ... and envy each other's contentment. Besides faults, my husband had many positive qualities ... I realize that there are many things that bother him about me ... . Although we were not married in church and I am not a believer, I took the marital promise including living through good and bad with each other seriously ... . I believed that we could live together in peace and contentment even in old age. I realize that I am not going to spend thirty years of my life with anybody else, I won't have children with anybody else, and ... that the partner whom we shall perhaps find will have other faults. I did not want a divorce.

It happened because my husband in recent years began to blame me for his joylessness, for forgiving him, for wanting to control him and to play the role of his mother, etc. ... It hurt me the most that he began to torture me psychologically by pointing out repeatedly that he was trying to decide if he can live with me ... He asked for 4 months in which to decide and moved away, then he asked to extend that period by one to two years ... That was really unbearable. It is better to amputate a leg than to cultivate a gangrene. Besides, I am 45, I won't get any younger and for my old age I am going to need somebody who will be a real moral support for me ... I could not stand his continuous accusations that because of me he does not feel well in his male role. Therefore I now agree to the divorce and I want it. Apart from that, ... my husband was always an excellent father, and I experienced many nice things with him ... except for the last few years.

Even in recent years … there were times which I'll want to remember. After all, if he died I would also have to adjust.

I would rather not think about what was ugly, and here in the courtroom I sincerely thank him for what was good.

Almost immediately after the divorce, Jiřina began to "pick up the pieces:" On February 4, 1981 she wrote to friends:

… I hope you can stand one more outpouring about me. After that, I hope, it won't be necessary any more to annoy anybody … . [After a description of the divorce proceedings:] All were quite clearly on my side which was not surprising; of those six people four were women and at least three were academics … . When I said that I would not have asked for the divorce because I think that at our age it is hard to become accustomed to anybody else, the judge and her assistant said: "What would you do with him, he was shaking and all nervous, don't be crazy … ." They … actually also told me to get the divorce. Even the man present said that I should not even consider taking him back … .

… Zdeněk took me to the subway, we kissed, he bought me three carnations and we parted. It was a nice day, the sun shone, and I reminisced about everything without great emotions or pains … . I think as time goes on he is going to be quite a good friend. That same evening I went to the theater with the [Ivan] Klímas[3] … .

The following days I worked hard reading a manuscript … .

So you see, for the time being I am tolerably well, and I only take half a sleeping pill … . With all that mourning I lost a lot of time, so that now I write like crazy, by the end of March I have to complete 80 pages for a volume … . Today I bought myself material for an evening dress which I'll sew myself for the Thomayer hospital ball. Then I bought myself a typewriter … .

To another friend she wrote on the same day:

… Zdeněk said that I was too little dependent on him, too much oriented toward my work. After that they [the officials in court] asked how the children were reacting, if Zdeněk has read anything about emancipation, and in conclusion they asked him if he was not asking too much of a woman, expecting her to work, care for the household, the children, shop and be dependent on him besides … He asked if he could sometimes come home to visit. I agreed, but did not expect him to come already on Tuesday … I was surprised how little it hurt me … I don't doubt that I'll still have stupid … moods and feelings of loneliness, but I am sure that things will get better. To amuse myself, I replied to a [marriage] ad which I saw in the evening the day of the divorce …

And in a letter to Milan Šimečka, a fellow dissident: ... March 29, 1981

... people think of me as of a woman of the world standing above things, and actually I am more the type like Karolina Světlá.[4] The people who are closest to me ... would never understand that I sit here and cry into the keys of the typewriter ... so that my fingers slip ... I only know that I am dumb, ... inadequate, old fashioned ... and at the same time I tell myself thank God, despite my advanced age I am capable of experiencing things. Perhaps spring plays a role in this, the disturbance in the homeostasis of sex, although in this area we never had any conflicts to the last day that he was at home ... I can adapt very well ... Z. hates me because I always stand up again—like those children's toys that have lead in the bottom.

From Jiřina's advice column for a women's magazine of February, 1981:

If you read the letters by men or women, you get the impression that their lives were only suffering, that their former partner was "the devil in the flesh" ... . Did these people really hate each other so much [during their marriage]? ... In that case I really don't understand why they had children together ... How could they go on vacations ... together ... save up for a car together? ... they probably don't tell the whole truth ...

If your former partner had only faults ... then having been with him so long would also be proof of a shortcoming on your part ... Each of us is ... responsible for the kind of partner she/he chooses. Nobody sold us into marriage ... If your partner really had no positive characteristics, then you should be happy that it ended ... . Or are you a masochist who gets satisfaction from her sufferings? Then again you should be satisfied ... you don't want nice memories to complicate your present ... if you are convinced that your life was pure horror, you mainly hurt yourself, because you will never have another life ... . A healed scar also used to be a decoration of soldiers, past pains ... also make us wiser ... and more interesting ... . Only boredom ... is a time when we did not really live ... In the theater we sometimes see comedies and sometimes tragedies; it is important that it be a play of good quality, well acted.

Jiřina's statement in court after she was discovered transmitting books illegally is a plea for the preservation of the books:

July, 1980:

1. I would like to ask those present not to permit the destruction of the books which were confiscated in the garage in Stará Boleslav. They contain not only the creative work of the writers of part of this

nation, but also much human labor which should be appreciated. Please deposit them in a safe ... perhaps in the National Literary Archives ... and future literary historians will be looking for these "books–non-books." They will appreciate the foresight of the judge who sees to it that they are preserved. In any case, all books of that kind cannot be destroyed, the most productive "hole of memory," to use George Orwell's expression, will not extinguish them.

2. I would like to thank the Frenchman Thonon and the Frenchwoman Anis for their ... help; they sat in Ruzyně jail because of us ...

3. ... I saw nothing so terrible and harmful to socialism in acquiring books from unofficial editions and helping to transport them abroad. I only wanted to preserve the literary production of those people who are not allowed to publish here for the future.

All of my education gave me arguments for doing what I did ... According to our history books, people who were persecuted in their time were considered right later ... . It cannot hurt socialism if a few hundred people become acquainted with a different socialist view ...

As a sociologist I know that ... if this is not so, either the system is deformed, or the statistics are wrong or somebody is interested in misrepresenting reality ... I actually contributed to the good reputation of the Czechoslovak state, for I proved indirectly that ... the Czech nation consists of normal people whose opinions differ ...

While in jail, Jiřina thought about what ought to be done publicly rather than about her own situation, On January 8, 1981 she wrote a letter to friends:

Dear friends, don't be angry that, while I am wasting time in jail, I am ... telling you what to do ... I remembered that in a year, in March of 1983, will be the hundredth anniversary of Franz Kafka's birth. At the same time will be the twentieth anniversary of the first Kafka conference in Liblice, which initiated the renewal ... Did you think of that?

The present regime and the ... organization of writers will not remember this anniversary, and if, then certainly differently than we. In the world[5] ... dozens of serious books will be published, and there will be many conferences in which of course none of us will participate. And yet we should contribute ... we should publish, or rather copy on the typewriter the contributions of those ... who have something to say about contemporary culture ... Again the young generation here ... has no possibility to know him. And this although the Prague of the eighties is the city of Franz Kafka perhaps even more than before. He is extremely timely for us, and his work is not "exclusive" reading for intellectuals ... .

Here follows a long passage pointing out the parallel between her situation and those described by Kafka. This volume should be ready, so that something from it could be sent to a conference or included in volumes ... in the world ... .

Some of Jiřina's letters give a vivid impression of her life in prison. Here is one written in September, 1981:

When on May 7, 1981 they told me during a house search that I was being arrested and that we were going to Ruzyně, I took along a book of stories by Leonid Andrejev: *Satan's Diary.*

I have always wanted to be useful, "productive," I needed to work to pay for the fact that I am predominantly well off ... and even today I cannot change my way of life.

If the judge would know the prisoners at least as well as does the investigator or the guard ... he could not hand down a verdict. He would often be in the role of God in Čapek's stories ... who understands and forgives everything ... . After having come to know the environment and the prisoners, I would never want to be a psychological or psychiatric expert for the court ... I would also not want to be an educator of these people. It is a humane activity, but it is little effective. It mostly satisfies the one who does it ... who then can see himself as good ... The chance of influencing these people ... is minimal. It is much more demanding to contribute to the further development of gifted, good people, but probably better ... than to waste energy on this pathological population ... Here, I am ashamed to say, I am becoming an elitist ...

I am perhaps the only one here who [previously] had an orderly family ... . I sometimes cannot see anything positive in these people ... . But surely there is gold in them also.

... October, 1981. To save his life, Josephus Flavius greeted the Emperor Vespasianus as the Messiah. They did not crucify him ... humiliated and broken he was much more useful to the Romans ... Josephus survived the uprising ... but all his life he reproached himself for his [cowardly behavior] and tried to justify himself by claiming that he had another mission ... He never again felt well either among the Romans to whom he extended his hand or among the Jews whom he betrayed ... In reality he most betrayed himself ... This ... is actually a life sentence on oneself ... Such a situation would be unbearable to me, I would have the feeling that I gave up not only myself ... but that I am torn out of the people to whom I belong by culture and language ... Then I could do disgusting things for the rest of my life and it would make no difference ... Perhaps what I am writing will help one of my friends to avoid something irrevocable ... that would defile him ... I think that in this generation in Czechoslovakia jail is something for which one should be conditioned ... everybody should answer for himself the question: "What can I stand?"

... This place is most depressing by its ugliness, dirt and sounds. The bed linen is, to be sure, relatively clean ... about the blankets you can believe that at one time they were disinfected, and that lice and flees don't like cotton. But the straw tick does not permit this illusion ... . It is covered with grease spots, blood, sperm ... food, anything people in this kind of a situation need to wipe, including vomit ... The possibility of touching the straw tick bothered me more than steps in the hall, light ... the screaming of people newly dragged in from the street ... or the whining of the crazy gypsy woman from another cell, the stench of the toilet or the footsteps of the rats ... the dirt and grease of the food bowls ... Day can be distinguished from night only by the intensity of the light bulb behind bars in the ceiling, and from the window one can only see the dirty hall, rather a canal with pipes, and above them sometimes the ankles of the guards ... .

I was not taken to my regular cell until the eighth day. ... Perhaps they kept me here longer to soften me up ... then they put me under the shower and put in my hand two pair of stretched underpants, one terrible bra, a man's smelly shirt with the inscription Ruzyně Prison #1, brown shapeless running pants and a pair of brown socks. I wear that to this day ... The guard watched me dress ... so carefully, that she noticed that I am wearing a tampon for menstruation, which I had the foresight to bring from home. It was also checked out. Good thing that I don't have hemorrhoids ...

... A day is infinitely long here and at first you are not hungry enough to eat the food. On the 9th day of May they gave us a breaded chop ... something we won't see again until the next anniversary of "liberation." I did not eat it, it seemed to me like a hard, cold shoe sole which smelled of stale oil, and it bothered me that the "mukl"[6] handed it to me with his hand. Today I would enjoy eating it and would regret that the Red Army did not free us twice a week.

They even let me keep scissors overnight once in a while. They probably don't expect me to commit suicide. And they are right. Even here I have enough work, even here I am sometimes contented ...

... The hatred of the young fellows for the guards is frightening ... Mr. Bilák[7] should be afraid of them, not of us who were disarmed ahead of time by our education and the humanism with which we identify ... .

The past is the only thing you have left here. It is a shield, a weapon, but for some certainly also an instrument of torture. Sartre was right in his play "The Prisoners of Altona", hell is in us, and the past can be terrible … If your personal past bothers you, you will suffer much here by those unsolved, untold … problems … . This self-torture, brought about by the impossibility of occupying one's brain was described wonderfully by Stefan Zweig in his *Chess Novella* … . Its hero, an Austrian, after the Anschluss is questioned … in a hotel. He tries to get his mind off the interrogations, constantly carries on discussions with himself … tries to figure out the psychology of the interrogator … anticipates his own answers and their reactions to them … until he comes close to insanity. It seems like a game of chess, where we try to think of our opponent's future moves … .

… Another question comes up … To what am I going to return? Am I going to be able "afterwards" to be enthusiastic about anything, to love a man, to feel like starting again? Am I not going to be in people's way, will I not be too skeptical? Am I still going to understand what is going on around me? …

… We know from Mr. Hegel that everything sensible is real and everything real is sensible … .

… In normal life I can take and leave alcohol. Here I really miss it. I miss the experience of wine in a cut glass with the light shining through it on a white table cloth … I long for a nice china cup, like the one in which the Pitharts served me tea, for its fragrance, for the little spoon with which one can stir instead of using the handle of a tooth brush …

I just finished the book by the Slovenian Smiljan Rozman: *Bombs Above The City* … about people who lost everything. Only then we became conscious of ourselves … . I also sometimes feel rich here, I have more time for myself than I ever had before … .

… The consciousness that so many friends survived this gives me strength. If they, then I also … Being questioned, the escape from the cell for a few hours … was something to which I literally looked forward … .

A person from the lower strata is in the penitentiary among his own people … . An educated person as a rule loses much more …

In my previous life I looked forward to every day and often voluntarily shortened my sleep, only to live longer … .

If I had been in an accident and had my legs in a cast, perhaps I would also be excluded from life for a year … but I would know that I was healing. What is healing now? … Perhaps with our activity … we have activated [the regime's] capacity for self healing. Perhaps!

… Suffering one experiences life more intensively than when one is satisfied … I am not the type to become a sceptic … .

... Konrad Lorenz ... mentions that rats which have been confined to a small area for a long time bite each other's ears off, and the males become infertile. I don't want to bite anybody's ears off, and I unfortunately cannot determine right now if I am fertile, but I would like to hit that nightmarish Márka who constantly screams ... and digs in my grease with her fingers ... . Mr. Lorenz would be pleased with me ... the varnish of civilization is already peeling off me ... .

Dostoevski in his *Notes*[8] ... writes that nobody can live ... without some striving. If he loses ... hope, he changes ... into a monster ... .I worry about what I shall pursue later. How will I give meaning ... to the time I am spending here?

... The guards show that they have power, the prisoners with the stubbornness of children in the stage of negativism provoke them ... . Is it an international phenomenon that prisoners do not expect justice, or is it an attitude typical of Czechoslovakia and similar totalitarian regimes? I do not hope to learn the answer empirically. I would not like to become acquainted with foreign jails. I am not that curious ... .

But don't imagine that it is here like in a Nazi concentration camp or like in a prison described by Solzenycin. It is far from that. For that we are too Czech ... .

In prison, Jiřina wrote about her experiences and insights there in order to help others if they found themselves in a similar situation. She called her essay: "Defense Mechanisms, or How to Survive Imprisonment."

July 20, 1981

I miss here most of all a meaningful activity, something that would fill this estranged time ... I have begun to note down what helped me get over the earliest period. Here ... one certainly does not develop any new traits of character, at most people correct and rearrange what is in them.

All I write is of course highly subjective, but perhaps it will help Honza [her son] when he is in the army, or other friends who will go to jail ... I would like to give instructions on how to get along with people on a few square meters, and to write about positive things one can experience here. What I write should be edited ... but I am short of clean paper.

1. It is important to realize that this is an exceptional situation, and ... to change for a time ... one's hierarchy of values, to be clear on what is most important right now, and on the limits within which one can manoeuver. To realize what will happen if I say a certain thing, whether it will pay for me to go home sooner, or create problems for my conscience. One should be sure of the limits beyond which ... one will not

go even during the worst questioning. At the foundation of this is one's own moral code, the consciousness of one's responsibility toward others, not only toward oneself. None of us is his/her own God.

2. To realize ... that if I don't manage physically, I won't manage psychologically and emotionally, and after a few days I'll be saying exactly what they want. It means to eat everything, not to be repelled by the dirt or by the ugliness of the food, by the surroundings and one's own clothes and to learn to sleep and to eliminate under any conditions. To tell oneself: I am not here of my own free will, I am not responsible, I have been "thrown" into this situation ... It helps very much to realize that all the physical misery (light at night, lack of privacy, humiliation) is designed to make me nervous and to destroy me.

3. [To survive means] to subordinate almost everything to the task of managing in this new situation, and not to be excessively burdened by such questions as what will happen afterwards, how I am going to live, what I am losing ... I must find contentment in the present. After all, that is what every primitive person or animal does when threatened ... Now it is a question of survival ... It helps me, for instance, to recall how many nice things I have experienced in the past, how and when I was happy compared to incurably ill people ... Would I really want to trade this momentary reality of Ruzyně for a domesticated existence? ... How wonderful many would find it ... to simply be without pain! So why should I feel sorry for myself ... only because I have to sit in this place ... ?

4. I am helped by reflections by Søren Kierkegaard and by J.P. Sartre, that man is created, marked by "discontinuous moments" which he remembers and which provide a profile ... Without these turns and decisions life would be a mere flowing. We know from Aristotle ... that even a painful experience is more than a non-experience. And I have experiences. Many.

5. In such a situation one must not treat oneself to the luxury of self pity ... When one feels emotionally weak, and that will happen, one must overcome it by ... some activity, e.g. exercise ... washing the toilet, the floor, or by doing something for the next person. Dependence on drugs is bad in civilian life, and in jail it is literally tragic ... drugs just help those others to control us ... .

6. It is absolutely necessary to forbid oneself reflections about what would be if I had not made a certain mistake ... How many people experience misfortunes which have no meaning for anybody! What is positive in our case is that here not only coincidence played a role, but a conscious activity, that we were not only objects, but active subjects. It would be terrible to be here innocently, for nothing ...

Aldous Huxley writes in *Point Counterpoint* that things and events which change our lives substantially are never matters of chance, and that everything that happens to one is similar to the person to whom it happens … For me … it is extremely important to know that I am not a victim … .

Then … the reality which I am experiencing loses part of its absurdity for me … .

7. A great help, but a somewhat dangerous one, is creating oneself another focus … observing oneself … being curious how one is going to manage … It is a certain kind of escape, but in this situation one has the right to use certain tricks … . At home for instance I have the results of a number of tests which my colleagues made with me, when neither they nor I suspected that I would ever get into such an experimental situation … . When I return home, I'll be curious if they are valid … The knowledge that I cannot look at my watch and say "now we'll have a coffee break" is … depressing, but it also gives the matter a certain seriousness … . Otherwise one would only be like an intellectual "on brigade"[9] in a factory … Thus this is not a total waste of time … It reminds me a little of pregnancy; then I also "did something" without having to exert myself … . It is always possible to give meaning to the absurd.

8. Hegel's statement about the relationship of the master and the servant … is also helpful. When the servant realizes that … the master is dependent on him, he is freer than the master … . Sometimes I feel freer here than in civilian life.

9. It is also a good idea to … imagine the worst possible scenario, and to come to terms with it. Then anything that comes is better …

10. Another form of self-help is to imagine the motivation for the behavior of others … If I imagine what bad feelings the guard is working off, his attack does not concern me so directly.

11. All who are here with me are badly off. If I help one of them a little, it is not only an act of altruism, but also enrichment for me … And besides, I realize that I am, in these prison pants and next to this miserable toilet, still a human being … a good one … After all, I am not just a box tree that can be trimmed … A person who wanted to subject herself totally … did not have to get here in the first place. It would have been enough to shut up … and "not to get involved in anything." As a nation we have a rich tradition of that … I also need a certain amount of daily privacy … to note down a few thoughts …

12. It strengthens one immensely to give oneself a certain small … task and really to do it … It can be exercise, studying vocabulary, yoga … to fill life in one's own way, not to be guided only by commands …

13. Another joy and source of strength is … writing letters to one's family, to receive a message from friends, … to communicate illegally with other prisoners … to have one's own way …

"What Is Nice Here" *is another essay she wrote in prison:*[10]

August 11, 1981

… I am lonesome, really starved for something … a little bit nice. Here one has to manage too much by oneself. It is … loneliness in the midst of a forced collective … in which one is never alone for a second … . Adaptation is a sign of somatic and psychological health … A lot can be done with will power … . As a sociologist I should know something about the life of people in this country, [but] … until now I had no idea about this category of people … It is like in Kafka's *Trial*, only here people don't ask, they only wait … And like in Kafka's *Castle*, here the accused meet only the lowest level of officials who don't have any authority … . It would be a waste for me not to use this … opportunity to understand … .

Now I would like to write about … what is nice here … Right in the "preliminary cell" … in the cellar I heard through two cells … "Dad, do you miss Mom?" And what followed was a confession of love from son to father and from father to son, and of both for the mother and the wife, which I shall not forget …

Another nice thing here is the high degree of cohesion of the prisoners … Jirka from third floor painted a "portrait of my daughter" whom he has never seen for my birthday, and the girls from my cell painted me a dedication for it, buttered my bread with real butter … decorated my slippers with a ribbon, and knitted me a bracelet … I think this is enough for my 46th birthday … .

A friend, Helena Trojanová, wrote about Jiřina on September 19, 1981:

… She grew up … in the period and in the atmosphere which led her to the Communist Party of Czechoslovakia when she was 18. As many progressive intellectuals and students she believed that socialism would prevail … as a truly just, free and humane society … . In 1968 she took part in the large student strike. She published her works about youth and the student movement, also abroad, and lectured about these subjects in West Germany, Switzerland, Holland and England. She actively participated in the efforts to reform the Communist party and Czechoslovak society in the second half of the sixties and helped to prepare such materials for the university organization of the party, while taking an active part in important meetings and conferences … . In this work she identified with the progressive wing of the party …

and helped shape the views of the students. She did not stop her political activities even after the 21. of August, 1968, although she had several opportunities to work abroad. After the fall of Dubček she left the
Communist Party, whereupon she was dismissed from her position as
an assistant in the philosophic faculty … . The articles and larger works
which she published in the following years, mostly under her maiden
name Jiřina Heroldová, received much attention. Besides, she was co-
author of several radio and TV programs … . Dr. Jiřina Šiklová was
one of the few authors who broke through the embargo against publication and other professional work, which was the fate of so many
writers and professionals … . As a highly creative, cultured person
with strong humanitarian ideals, she tried to help those who lost their
positions in 1968 in various ways including the publication … of their
works. As a friend of hers wrote: "Sharp, educated, energetic, sensitive
and extremely self-sacrificing. And at the same time an excellent
mother of two nice children … This pure human being … sits behind
lock and key … The mediator of free cultures and information."

After leaving prison, Jiřina continued to harass the regime, and it continued to
harass her. She wrote to the Procurator on November 29, 1988:

… On October 27 at 5 in the morning a blond man with blue eyes
came into my apartment … along with other persons … to do a house
search … Upon their request I handed over to them things which had
nothing to do with the activity for which I was allegedly investigated
… . Two of the men who referred to themselves as Milan and Jirka
devoted their intensive attention to me until the November 13 … .
During that time I was in Ruzyně twice for 48 hours and two whole
days in the army barracks … all in all it was 7 days of questioning … .

Those two men threatened me with a jail sentence … although no
charges had been brought against me. They said that they wanted to
know about my contacts abroad, and if I refused, they would destroy me
professionally and hurt my children; that I would lose my job and get no
other, that they would ruin my reputation among my friends from
Charter 77, so that everybody who met me would spit out in front of
me, that somebody would attack me in the street and beat me … .

I refused to cooperate with the counter-espionage (for which they
claimed to be working) and to … sign anything. The two men repeatedly followed me on my way to and from work … took me to questioning without the preliminaries required by law … entered my
apartment and again threatened me … . The purpose of their visit was
to find out who visits me or intends to visit … . On November 13 they
again entered my apartment despite my protest. I announced to them

that if they continued to threaten me, I would report it to my friends ... abroad ... . From that day on I was no longer visibly followed ... . But on the next days they began to make good their threats ... On 15th ... I was asked by my superior not to work there any longer, because the repeated visits of the police were disturbing the peace ... As of January 21 I am without a job ... . On November 14 or 15 they came to Mrs. Anna Marvanová's apartment and played a tape, allegedly with [my] testimony against her ... . As a former worker for Czechoslovak radio she told them that it is easy to falsify such a tape ... . I have reason to believe that the aforementioned Milan and Jirka are making good their threats, and am afraid for my safety and even my life.

One of these men took DM30 from my wallet without giving me a receipt ... . Milan looked through my purse, took a letter ... and 2000kč. At the same time he asked me where I have the money with which I "finance such people" ... . He took my bank book in the amount of 12.600 kč ... . These men control my mail daily, open and read it ... They took from me the key to my apartment, and I suspect that they have duplicates ... . I ask you for protection and for a reply ... .

This letter to a friend, of April 6, 1989 shows that Jiřina still kept her sense of humor:

I again started working ... as a cleaning lady. It is a nice place to work, in Celetná Street, in a baroque building in which the Institute for Theater is located. I was inconspicuous there like a little mouse ... humble, honest and industrious ... . They did not give me a permanent job, because ... the police came and told them that it would not be appropriate for me to work there ... . So I ... began working in a similar job where there are no intellectuals who are scared shitless, but the real working class ... . I have now been cleaning an entrance hall for two months ... I can go there afternoons, which suits me because I have my 88-year-old very senile mother at home, and it is a lot of work to get her started in the morning. Then I write, do errands, and take care of my grandchild ... It turned out to be a good thing that they threw me out. In the end everything turns in my favor ... sometimes I took the little boy along to clean ... so that I looked like an over-aged single mother.

A letter to friends of October 3, 1989 tells of her life and frame of mind after the revolution:

... Recently I went on an excursion with the staff of my previous work place—it was a brigade of socialist work ... . We go by bus, drink along the way, dance etc. ... . This time we were at Mácha's Lake, the weather was beautiful, we even swam naked at night and danced on the beach ... .

I am satisfied in my new work place ... I work with my hands and feet, and actually only have time to rest when I aerobically fly through the place and perfectly clean the rooms assigned to me ... . All are enthusiastic, they never had it so nice and tidy. I clean about 16 offices, a hallway and some steps. There is linoleum everywhere, it goes quickly, the cleaning products are of good quality, and my productivity has increased since I was given large black gloves which do not adhere like condoms ...

Perhaps I have written to you about my law suit against *Rudé Právo*[11] ... Since they did not beat me up right away, I think that they won't do it. Now I am going to persecute those spies. If they do anything more against me or my children, my friends will have the task— if I cannot do it myself—of telling what all they did wrong. I am not vindictive, if they are decent and ... if RP apologizes with at least one sentence, I'll be silent. The trial was interesting, in the hall there were two colonels from the state police, lots of little spies, perhaps all of Marie Boudová's editorial office.[The woman who had made untrue statements about Jiřina in Rudé Právo.]

An undated letter to a friend, written about the same time, tells about Jiřina since the Revolution:

... If I return to the university at all, then only if they let me do a project not in the department of sociology among the original establishment rehabilitated and newly clean, but one where the young, the old, foreigners and people from other faculties can teach.

... Last Wednesday I got a telephone after 14 years. I had threatened with a newspaper article ... The next day the Water Works informed me that they have to report me to the Criminal Police, because I no longer work for them and still have their stamp in my i.d. Then a man came to the door who asked me to become a member of the Federal National Assembly. I hardly got rid of him when another came who asked me at least to become a delegate for the Czech National Council, and finally somebody came from Sokol in Budějovice, asking me to represent the Sokols. All that time my 88-year-old mother kept asking which day of the month it was, when the children were coming home from school ... and when we are going to Prague ... she thinks that we are at the cottage. On Friday I am going to Scheinfeld to make an anthology in the archives in the Schwarzenberg castle where for the last 17 years I sent all the literature ... .

In a letter to a friend of January 15, 1991, Jiřina tells how she spent part of one day:

Yesterday I moderated a discussion about the war in Kuwait; Palestinians and Iraquis were arguing ... I took care of the suggestion for an honorary doctorate for Václav [Havel] ... . Things are moving at the university, I am catching up a lot on my studies and am involved in politics whether I like it or not. I make speeches, go to the country for the Civic Forum, to the Protestant Choir ... People want an "ideal leadership" to solve everything ... . If I had been born five years earlier, perhaps they would now read my name loudly among those who committed crimes. Do I have the right to scorn others because at the time of the first Communist putsch I was more interested in pornographic pictures than in what Gottwald[12] said in Old Town Square?

... Proclaiming collective guilt is an injustice with which we must not be involved. We already made this mistake once: right after the war, in 1945, with the expulsion of the autochthonous German population from the border areas ... .

The following excerpts from letters to friends show further changes in Jiřina's life:

May 15, 1991,

... . I actually was in America and it was very interesting, but I would not want to live there. But I appreciate their courage, going across the ocean in little boats and then settling down in the mud somewhere around New York. Those great social differences there would bother me ... I was at a dinner for $2500—I did not pay for it—and in a tavern for homosexuals and lesbians, and in a shelter for the homeless. The Americans are actually to be pitied; everybody tries to get money out of them and at the same time talks badly about them because they are rich ... Having left our ... little country, I realize that there is a lot of truth in the Jewish saying [in a travel office]: Don't you have another globe? ... Meanwhile I have another grandson, so that we now have two girls and two boys ... . In general I am satisfied with my personal life apart from the total picture, but I would need four lives all at once, somehow I am always short of time ... .

On July 22, 1991, she again writes about her partner:

... My Jirka—I have been living with him for ten years. We feel well about each other ... I don't think that it is necessary to get married. He is a medical doctor and used to specialize in leukemia in children, but since there were no medicines for that ... he switched to research in the Academy of Sciences and even invented a new medicine ... . He is a bit of a "dog's snout," a rather reserved person, but nice, a sceptic, does not care about politics or any ideology including religion. He is definitely his own man in any situation. As anybody else, he has a lot of negative qualities, and he does not bother to ... smile at anybody if he does not feel like it.

More than 10 years after her divorce Jiřina writes about her former husband:

We meet occasionally, and formally send wishes for birthdays and Christmas ... Now that the possibility to write, publish and travel in the world opened up for me again, it would be very difficult to live with him. Back then he was jealous of my "successes." Could you imagine how he would carry on now? It is a good thing that he got the divorce from me.

To Editor Hirschlová of the magazine Květy:

February 6, 1991

I am sending you the article which I wrote for the French *l'Alternative* ... . I said something similar on TV on Sunday, in Radio Free Europe ... On Sunday I am going to Würzburg to train workers from the US who will be working in Eastern Europe, about what life was like here, then I'll be at a conference of sociologists in Vienna and on Wednesday I'll be at home again ... .

I am tired, nervous, ripe for the scrap heap. The only thing I enjoy, apart from my grandchildren, are the students who are studying fantastically and with a great deal of interest and come to ask for more literature ... Perhaps a better generation will grow up after all ... .

March 11, 1991 ... I am disgusted with developments and shall be glad when none of my friends will be in (political) functions any more, and only real politicians will be in politics, i.e. people equipped for it by their character ... I am glad that I refused to have anything to do with it, i.e. to have a function, but actually I am involved in politics daily ... .

I am trying to organize a chair of social work and applied sociology, which would train social workers at the university level, professionals who could really help people, organize institutions, professionally help the churches, the communities, to concentrate on urban problems. I got scholarships from all over the world, I saw teachers of this field in Holland ... and I am satisfied with that ... .

March 19, 1991 in ... a letter to a friend who is annoyed at her [own] mother:

We all have lots of faults, I for instance put my nose in things that are none of my businesses. As my mother used to say, I am the stirrer in every pile of shit ... You know, I also used to be annoyed at her and today I blame myself for not having let her feed the pigeons, and for not having given her a kiss more often ... .

From an undated letter to friends:

... I would so much like to have a little bit of quiet, not to see people, not to read the papers, only to concentrate on writing, to ... gain a philosophic perspective on what is happening, and not only to be a performing motor of daily events. Perhaps such a time will also come.

After the Revolution, Jiřina has been concerned about some of the most salient problems of our time. The lecture: "Nationalism in Eastern and Central Europe" was delivered in Franconia at a conference of Opus Dei on December 8, 1990:

Nationalism in Eastern and Central Europe is a substitute for people's lost secondary social status. We all are looking for an explanation for the sudden outbreak of nationalistic problems ... which is spreading like an epidemic in all of these devastated countries.

... Through the breaking of borders and the fall of the Communist systems not only outward barriers were broken, but also the continuity of lives, including the stereotypes of the lives of all of us who were in the opposition were disturbed. The people from the "gray zone," i.e. those who quietly and passively collaborated with the Communists and preferred not to be involved, are now looking for their ... identity ... . They will no longer be able to blame their lack of success on the gang of Communists in power ... . For years the citizens of these countries called for freedom, and now they see that for the most part they don't even have a world view or a political opinion ... .

The fall of Socialism ... is also the fall of ordinary people who lived in this system. ... Everybody who lived here also gained ... his secondary or acquired social status here, such as education, property, social position ... . He had to go along with the system in some ways —with the exception of those who were murdered and an entirely negligible number of dissidents, hardly a thousandth of the population. [The majority] is threatened by their not entirely clear conscience. Therefore they need to find a culprit ... but where can they find him in countries where actually all participated in the preservation of a nonsensical regime?

At the same time the value of the heroism of those who actively worked for the fall of the political regime is decreased, for we realize that its alleged strength was actually ridiculous ... .

When people introduce themselves, they usually mention what they became through their own efforts, their profession and education ... and realize that ... their secondary social status is connected with the ... now fallen regime ... . And so people can only claim without shame their primary social status, such as race and nationality ... It links one with those who had the same fate ... and also excuses one, for the rest of the Czechs and Slovaks ... also participated in preserving the existence of the Communist regime which failed ... .

The nationalism which is now found so frequently in Eastern and Central Europe is an expression of a total vacuum of values ... . Freedom was won, but there is nothing with which to fill it … when these poor people will have a chance to acquire a social status by their own efforts, and not by collaboration with the regime, their self-confidence will rise, they will be differentiated according to their merits and qualities, and their nationalism will fade … . But now people need a culprit, and that, of course, has to be the other … If he has a different skin color or speaks a different language, he is all the more suitable … .   Germany can be an example … . After the Peace of Versailles, the poverty of Germany changed into nationalism and fascism. After the Second World War, on the other hand, the Germans were among the first to become Europeans … . Let us hope that now also the West European states will find enough generosity, foresight and financial means for the Eastern part of their continent to weaken the nationalistic wave!

Let us also not forget that people in the post-Communist regimes grew up in the ideology of the class struggle, which was reduced to a permanent search for the enemy.

I am afraid that the biblical story about the journey from Egypt will be repeated in Europe … . The … generations living in Eastern and Central Europe will be wandering around in the desert for at least 40 years … we all will reminisce how in Egyptian slavery we were eating pots of meat … .

In 1990 Jiřina published the article "The Gray Zone And The Future Of Dissent In Czechoslovakia" in Social Research:

Jiřina Šiklová in 1994

... Specialists, journalists, artists, writers and people interested in politics differ in Czechoslovakia, not so much by what they know or by how they evaluate facts as by moral stance and courage ... whether and when they express their views. This matters much more than whether they are members of the party. Are these people progressives or reactionaries? On the left or on the right? ... my visitor asks, and I despair ... . I try to convince my visitor from the West, that the terminology taken from the meeting of the French Convention or from Cromwell's parliament, or from the Czarist Duma cannot be used now in Eastern Europe without further comments and explanations ... . These terms have been emptied ... here by repeated revolutions, overthrows, reactions, renewals ... I explain that I know many members of the Communist Party, but I personally don't know a convinced communist, that most people are not in the party out of conviction, ... but because it is to their advantage, or at least because of their conformist character, because they want to be left alone and don't have a clear opinion; they stayed in the party or were afraid to refuse when they were asked to join. It is really hard to be a member of the Communist Party after it has been reevaluated repeatedly ...

In our country only two groups are clearly definable: Those who held power and the dissidents ... . The former were so "compromised" by the contemporary political system that they cannot change their position ... and neither can the dissidents. Between them is, as in every state, the "silent majority," oriented for the most part toward consumption, people of the "gray zone" about whom I want to write ... . We mean by that a broad spectrum of people who will have an immense influence on the expected changes in this society. They could be the people who will take over its leadership. People in the gray zone are for the most part highly trained, erudite, good workers ... They soon saw the faults of the socialist system and did not have to buttress their careers by party membership ... they were minimally engaged politically and could devote themselves to furthering their education ... .

These people will never have quite clean hands, totally clear moral credit. Hesitantly and reluctantly they collaborated with the regime ... Although they agree with the dissidents, they are afraid that somebody may criticize them for having collaborated ... . They cheer Charter 77 ... but they don't play themselves ... .

The dissidents, sometimes too much in love with their own courage, do not sufficiently appreciate those who cheer ... . Most of the population ... fulfill the requirements imposed ... by the regime, but their political sympathies are with the opposition.

Class criteria are ... also blurred ... . Among today's workers you find university teachers, former politicians and journalists and vice versa ... The standard of living of the members of the gray zone is "the good middle" ... . They and their children usually swim through various loyalty checks without difficulty, get an adequate education, achieve adequate ... success ... . If they wanted to have a steep career, they would have to work clearly and emphatically for the regime ... .

The establishment was always afraid of the enlargement of the gray zone and therefore from time to time it organized purges, checks, controls etc. ... The establishment makes each of these people a fellow culprit ... and thereby regenerates its power.

We should not pass judgment on them ... each of us has his own personal limits of bravery. It is our task to win over the people from the gray zone, and not to drive them away by moralizing ... and digging in their past.

If the dissidents don't want to remain an exclusive minority, they will have to ... ask these people ... to take on leading positions. It is not right to remind them of their petty collaboration or of one's own merits ... of having suffered for years in prison ...

The people from the gray zone ... for a long time had better opportunities than the dissidents for personal growth, education ... while the dissidents lost ... the continuity with ... their original professions ... . I consider it appropriate to make it possible for near-collaborators to join the gray zone belatedly ... rather than to increase our mutual recriminations.

In an interview of about the same time, Jiřina looked back on her years as a dissident:

People of my generation for the most part chose their own fate. Each of us had the choice either to emigrate, to conform or not to agree and to be thrown out. That is what happened to me and was part of my choice. A person usually lives according to his or her intellectual capabilities and character ... . Therefore I do not consider myself a victim of circumstances.

In comparison with other dismissed colleagues I certainly was better off. It was warm in the hospital, they did my laundry, the collective of doctors treated me well ... to this day I feel well among them.

In addition to taking care of my children I was engaged in dissident activity and in my own writing. I wrote some things for a living or for pleasure, under various pseudonyms for foreign, "anti-state" journals such as *Svědectví* [13], *Listy* [14], etc. Regularly, for almost ten years, I wrote for the [women's] magazine *Vlasta* ... . There I reacted to letters by readers ... gave pseudo-learned analyses and good advice. Those letters were good sociological material ... I was paid 338 kč. for an article twice a month which was good money for me ... . Besides, I wrote a number of popular scientific books, published in *Mona*, where my friend, the editor Eva Králová made it possible to earn a living not only for me, but for many poets and writers.

I especially liked my work with patients. I did psychotherapy with the incurably ill and with the dying, and devised my own method in the area of thanatology.

I do not know if it was just luck, but I never really hit bottom. I never was really desperate. And ... I would not like to trade with my former classmates and colleagues who taught at the university these last twenty years. Bowing before power would have been worse, at least for me ... .

NOTES

1. Books published illegally in the Communist-dominated countries, usually typed and copied.
2. All internationally known scholars.
3. Klíma is one of the most esteemed Czech writers writing today.
4. A nineteenth-century novelist known for her strict morals.
5. During the Communist regime, Czechs often used the expression "in the world," as if they themselves were outside of it.
6. A person totally destroyed by imprisonment.
7. One of the most Stalinist members of the government.
8. *Notes from the Underground* .
9. "On brigade" meant doing an allegedly voluntary job apart from one's regular work or studies.
10. In the Czechoslovak Documentation Center in Scheinfeld, Germany.
11. The official Communist newspaper.
12. The first Communist president of Czechoslovakia.
13. Published in Paris.
14. Published in Rome.

POSTSCRIPT

*I*n the course of the years during which I worked on this project, I discovered many women whose activities, views and life situations aroused my curiosity, but there are only few about whom there are sufficient records for a clear picture of them. If I want to share some of my findings about those others with the reader, it is in order to convey somewhat of an idea of the variety of female experience which will never be part of recorded history.

My plan for this book underwent some changes. Some years ago, at the suggestion of the Czech poet Jan Vladislav in Paris, I wanted to assemble about ten women, born about twenty years apart, whose memoirs or letters would inform the reader about the socio-cultural history of their time. A text by the Czech writer Eliška Krásnohorská, for example, seemed promising: there she as an infant described her immediate environment: her family, her father's shop, but also the political events around 1848. It did not matter that baby Eliška was not a credible witness; the problem was rather that I did not find adequate texts about those approximate periods, written from the points of view of women. Besides, the different segments would have represented four different ethnic worlds.

Auguste Hauschner, the one Jewish woman from Prague who has somewhat of a reputation as a writer could not be included because I could not do justice to her within the confines of this book. The best of her novels, *Die Familie Lowositz,* is the clearest portrait we have of Prague Jewish society about 1870. However, the young women who appear in it clearly do not bear the author's own traits. We learn most about her from her correspondence with Gustav Landauer and Fritz Mauthner, but it can also only be fully understood in conjunction with her large and varied belletristic oeuvre.

If Hauschner was modest about her accomplishments, Hedda Sauer, whom I am mentioning in the chapter about her relative Ossip

Schubin, was even more so. Although she was well thought of as a prose writer and especially as a poet, she dealt in her memoirs much more with famous men she had known such as Rainer Maria Rilke and Gerhard Hauptmann and her husband, Professor August Sauer, than with herself.

I thought seriously about Sidonie Nádherný von Borutín, because in her the characteristics of the—mostly upper class—German gentile women as I sketched them in the introduction were the most pronounced. Despite being culturally German she imagined herself a Czech; yet unlike the Czech women I "found", she was passive, retiring and derived what fame she achieved from the men she knew. Her lonely existence in her castle and park of Janowitz near Prague was only enlivened by travels and visitors, the most important of whom were to her Karl Kraus and Rainer Maria Rilke. There is no way one can paint a lively portrait in vivid colors based on the diaries and letters of a pale, sad figure who merges into the landscape.

A portrait of Erna Haberzettl looked like a promising possibility. Born in 1901, in my then almost entirely German speaking home town of Bischofteinitz/Horšovský Týn, she was exactly twenty years older than her sister Ilse who has been my friend—with an interruption of fifty years—since grade school.

Erna was the third child of her teen age mother and a forester. The family moved a great deal, in Bohemia, Austria and in Germany. When the daughters were in their teens, they were sent away from home to take care of children in well to-do households. Erna took a two year course in nursing and then worked as a nanny in Hungary where she wrote reports about the life of a servant there. She also contributed frequently to Social Democratic papers in Hungary and in Bohemia, and it seems that under pseudonyms also to the *Arbeiterzeitung* in Vienna. Much of her verse is sensitive lyric poetry, although a small part of it is too close to political propaganda. Erna worked as a nurse, as a labor organizer and as the director of a laborers' recreation hotel in Karlsbad. Her friend Marie Günzl remembers a walk they took through the woods near Karlsbad, during which they met President Masaryk riding on a horse; she particularly remembers the reverence with which Erna spoke about him. We have another glimpse of Erna from a Social Democratic official who came to see her in Karlsbad to discuss strategy in those difficult times—it was 1938—, and found her sitting the bathroom floor of the workers' rest home she managed, trying to feed a motherless doe from a bottle.

Erna spent a large part of the war years in Prague, taking care of wounded airmen. Being in constant contact with fellow opponents of the regime, she in 1944 sought out the greater anonymity of Vienna, where she hid in her room a Social Democrat who had parachuted from England to Bohemia. She was arrested by the Gestapo and committed suicide with the cyanide capsule she had prepared for such an eventuality.

The diary which Erna kept has been lost, and only some personal letters by political co-workers, saved, it seems, haphazardly, remain along with fond testimonials in the Friedrich Ebert Archives. There are vague hints about a youthful romance in Bischofteinitz, and about a love affair with the journalist Heinrich Kalmár in Pressburg-Bratislava. Her photographs show her as an attractive, even chic young woman with a warm, open face, very unlike the heroines on postage stamps from socialist countries.

There are vast amounts of material about Božena Rotterová, a Czech, whose economic background was similar to Erna's. She was born the daughter of an unsuccessful barber in Zbraslav, a working class suburb of Prague, in 1921. In poor health from childhood on and treated badly by her mother, she could not attend a gymnasium and became a seamstress. After the Nazi occupation in 1939, she joined an underground organization of young people. It seems that her activities were betrayed to the Gestapo by her boyfriend; this breach of faith troubled Božena more than the four years in Ravensbrück concentration camp which followed.

I first learned of Božena, who was called Bibi in the camp from Sigrid Jacobeit, an East German ethnologist who wrote a monograph about that camp. Sigrid suggested that I interview Dr. Rita Sprengel in Dresden, which I did in 1987. Dr Sprengel was at that time in her eighties, a convinced communist who saw having converted Božena to her political views as the crowning achievement of her life. Through her I was able to contact Božena's second husband, the psychologist, now professor, Jan Čáp in Prague who very generously supplied me with information and photographs. From him I learned about Božena's studies and teaching career in pedagogy and educational philosophy at the university after the war as well as about her marriage to the scientist Robert Rotter.

As a woman from a poor background and a resistance fighter, Božena could have been the ideal heroine for the Communist regime. However, in subtle ways she was too much of an individualist for that role; especially from the Soviet occupation on it was clear that Bozena was, to use Jiřina Šiklová's expression, in the "gray zone". Her belletristic work reflects her increasing pessimism about the political situation. She concentrated on work with students and enjoyed spending

time at her cottage, in nature. Her letters to Rita, her friend from concentration camp, contain her reactions to èvents in her life, such as the
death of her first husband, but do not show her increasing disillusionment with Communism. Her health continued to deteriorate and she
died in 1980, just weeks after her marriage to Čáp.

Why is Božena not a suitable subject for my book, although I also
had her published books and her second husband's extensive narrative
about her at my disposal? It is because I still know too little about her
thoughts and feelings. In her autobiographical fiction, the persons
speak about, and deal with, persons and things, not about themselves.

I also considered devoting a chapter to Charlotte Garrigue Masaryk,
the American wife of the first president of Czechoslovakia. Having read
all I could find about any of the Masaryks as well as Charlotte's own
writings, her articles about Smetana and the letters she wrote during
World War I to her daughter Alice in prison. I spoke to Masarykolo-
gists in America and in Prague. She was a feminist, an active Social
Democrat, and a publishing musicologist. During the First Republic,
apart from vague praise, nothing was written about her, and since then,
of course, the name Masaryk was tabu. Since the Revolution of 1989,
previously unknown material is probably accessible, and it is to be
hoped that Masaryk scholarship will give a worthier place to the
woman who was married to Thomas Garrigue Masaryk than I could
have given her within the framework of this book.

BIBLIOGRAPHY

INTRODUCTION

Books:

Brod, Max: *Jüdinnen* Leipzig, 1915.

Jungk, Peter Stephan: *Franz Werfel A Life in Prague, Vienna, and Hollywood* , New York, 1990

Krásnohorská, Eliška: *Co přinesla léta* , pt.2, vol.2, Prague, 1928, pp.174–183.

Máchal, Jan: *O českém románu novodobém* , Prague, 1902.

Mühlberger, Josef: *Geschichte der deutschen Literatur in Böhmen* , Munich, 1981

Palacký, František: *Geschichte von Böhmen* , 5 vols., Prague, 1836–1867.

Světlá, Karolina: *Z literárního soukromí* , Prague, 1880.

Vávra, Vincenc: *O účasti žen v českém probuzení* , Brno, 1895.

Volet-Jeanneret, Helena: ' *La Femme bourgeoise á Prague: 1860–1895: de la philanthropie a l'émancipation* ', Geneva, 1988. Dissertation, University of Lausanne.

Wiechowski, Wilhelmine: *Zur Erziehung* , Prague, 1891.

____*Frau und Kind* , Prague, 1924.

____*Frauenleben und Bildung in Prag im 19. Jahrhundert* , Leipzig, 1903.

Articles:

Horská, Pavla: "K ekonomické aktivitě žen na přelomu 19. a 20. století" in *Československý časopis historický* 31:4 (1983), pp.223–7, 711–43.

Krásnohorská, Eliška: "Hlas pedagoga o ženské otázce" in *Ženské listy* , Oct 1, 1874.

Kučerová, Vlasta: "K historii ženského hnutí" in *Ženská revue* 1914, p.1 ff.

Popper, Moritz:'*Bahn frei! Ein Wort für unsere Frauen* ' Prague, 1895. Published as a pamphlet.

MAGDALENA DOBROMILA RETTIGOVÁ

Main Sources:

Rettigová, Magdalena Dobromila: *Domácí kuchařka: spolu s ukázkami z beletristického díla M.D. Rettigové a ctením o její osobnosti* ed. by Felicitas Wünschová (together with samples from the belletristic work of Rettigová and readings about her personality ...) Prague, 1986.

Rettigová's Estate in the National Literary Archives in Strahov.

Works by Rettigová:

Rettigová, Magdalena Dobromila: *Arnošt a Bělinka*, Prague, 1850.

____*Chudobičky* , Prague, 1929.

____*Domácí kuchařka aneb pojednání o masitých pokrmech pro dcerky české a moravské* Hradec Králové, 1826.

____*Kafíčko, a vše, co je sladké* Hradec Králové, 1843.

____*Křestánka vzývající Boha* n.p., n.d.

____*Koš* A Farce for Lent in two Acts, Hradec Králové, 1846.

____*Mladá hospodyňka, jak sobě počínati má, aby své i manzelovy spokojenosti došla* Hradec Králové, 1840.

____*Pojednání o telecím mase* Hradec Králové, 1843.

____*Věneček pro dcerky vlastenecké* Hradec Králové, 1875.

Secondary Literature

Nejedlý, Zdeněk: *O literatuře* Prague, 1953.

Novák, Arne: *Literatura česká 19. století* Prague, 1905.

Pospíšil, J. *Z dob vlasteneckých* Prague, 1885.

Fiction: Jirásek, Alois: *M.D. Rettigová* (a play)

BOŽENA NĚMCOVÁ

Main Sources

Němcová, Božena *Listy* vols I–IV in *Knihovna klasiků* Prague, 1951.

____*Korespondence* Prague, 1930.

Němcová, Božena: *Karla: Obrázek z okolí domažlického* Prague, 1940.

____*Pohorská vesnice* Prague, 1856.

____*Obrázky z cest v Uhrách Sebrané spisy* Prague, 1897.

____*Pověsti a povídky slovenské* Prague, 1857, 1858.

Záhoř, Zdeněk: *Vyběr z korespondence Boženy Němcové* Prague, 1917.

Secondary works:

Černý, Václav: *Knížka o babičce* Prague, 1963.

Frič, Josef Václav: *Paměti* Prague, n.d.

Roth, Susanna: "*Babička* im Urteil tschechischer Gegenwartsautoren" in Guski, Andreas: *Zur Poetik und Rezeption von Božena Němcovás Babicka* Berlin, 1991 p.260 ff.

Havel, Rudolf, ed.: *Božena Němcová ve vzpomínkách* , Prague, 1961.

Kubka, František and Novotný, Miloslav: *Božena Němcová* , Prague, 1941.

Lelek, Josef: *K románu Boženy Němcové* , Prague,1921.

Novotný, Miloslav: *Prízpěvky k životopisu Boženy Němcové* , Prague, 1951.

Otruba, Mojmír: *Božena Němcová* Prague , 1964.

Podlipská, Žofie: *Životopis Boženy Němcové* Prague, 1891.

Pospísil, J. *Z dob vlasteneckých* Prague, 1885.

Sobková, Helena: *Nové úvahy o narození a původu Boženy Němcové Marginálie Sborník k osmdesátému výročí spolku českých bibliofilů*, Prague, 1988.

Světlá, Karolina: *Z literárního soukromí* , Prague, 1880.

Tille, Václav; *Božena Němcová* , Prague, 1911.
Vávra, Vincenc: *Korespondence a zápisky Boženy Němcové* , Prague, 1913.
Záhoř, Zdeněk: *Božena Němcová: Hlasy o osobnosti a o díle* , Prague, 1927.

Secondary Literature:
Article
Neruda, Jan: "Feuilleton" in *Národní listy* January, 1887, pp. 87ff.

Fiction
Jeřábek, Čestmír: *Život a sen* , Brno, 1974.

JOSEFA NÁPRSTKOVÁ

Main Source:
Josefa Náprstková's unpublished diary, 1890–1894, in the Náprstek Museum in Prague.

Secondary Literature
Kodym, Stanislav: *Dům u Halánků* Prague, 1955.
Novotný, Miloslav: "Katinka Naprsquaw, komunistka a rebelantka", in *Lidové noviny*, 31.5. 1936.

OSSIP SCHUBIN

Main Sources:
Ossip Schubin: "Erinnerungen einer siebzigjährigen Frau" in *Westermanns Monatshefte*, vol. 68, July–August, 1924, pp. 485–545.
Franzos, Karl Emil, ed: Die Geschichte des Erstlingswerks Leipzig, 1906, pp. 259–267.
Sauer, Hedwig: Unpublished memoirs in the estate of August Sauer in the archives of Charles University in Prague.

Books by Ossip Schubin
Schubin, Ossip: *Asbein. Aus dem Leben eines Virtuosen* Braunschweig, 1990.
_____*Bludička Erzählung aus dem slavischen Volksleben* Braunschweig, 1990.
_____*Boris Lensky* Berlin, 1889.
_____*Bravo rechts. Eine lustige Sommergeschichte* . Jena, 1884.
_____*Der arme Nicki Die Geschichte eines aus der Reihe Gefallenen, Berlin,* 1906.
_____*Die Flucht nach Amerika Berlin,* 1914.
_____*Die Geschichte eines Genies* (The Story of a Genius) Berlin, 1890.
_____*Ehre* Dresden 1883.
_____*Erinnerungen eines alten Oesterreichers* Jena, 1886
_____*Es fiel ein Reif in der Frühlingsnacht* Berlin, 1892.
_____*Finis Poloniae* Dresden, 1892.
_____*Gräfin Erikas Lehr-und Wanderjahre* Braunschweig, 1891.
_____*Heil Dir in Siegerkranz!* Braunschweig, 1891.
_____*Thorschlusspanik* Dresden , 1892.

BERTA FANTA

Main Sources:

Bergmann, Else: 'Familiengeschichte' Manuscript, n.d. in archives of the Leo Baeck Institute in New York.

Fanta, Bertha: Unpublished diary, 1900–1911, in the possession of her grandson Dr. Martin Bergmann, New York

Assorted papers in the Hugo Bergmann archives in Jerusalem.

Fanta, Otto: "Die Handschrift" in *Dichter, Denker, Helfer. Max Brod zum 50. Geburtstag* Mährisch Ostrau, 1934.

Secondary Literature:

Kowalewski, Gerhard: *Bestand und Wandel Meine Lebenserinnerungen* Munich, 1950.

HERMINE HANEL

Main Source

Hanel, Hermine: *Die Geschichte meiner Jugend* Leipzig, 1930.

Letters from her children Lilli and Georg Deiglmayr.

GISA PICKOVÁ-SAUDKOVÁ

Main Source:

Picková-Saudková: 'Deník židovské dívky', unpublished, in the Town Archives of Kolín, Czech Republic

Book:

Picková-Saudková, Gisa: *Hovory s Otakarem Březinou* Prague, 1929.

Secondary Literature:

Rabbi Richard Feder: *Židovská tragedie* Kolín, 1947. In it eulogies by Dr. Erwin Winternitz (p.145) and by Rabbi Feder, p.156.

GRETE FISCHER

Main Source:

Fischer, Grete: *Dienstboten, Brecht und andere Zeitgenossen in Prag, Berlin, London* Freiburg, 1966.

Other Books by Grete Fischer:

Amiel, Joseph: (Pseudonym of Grete Fischer) *Palästina, das erlaubte Land* Paris, 1934.

Fischer, Grete: *Die Schuld der Gerechten* Darmstadt, 1974.

____*Vermächtnisse* Darlington, n.d.

Articles in *Berliner Börsenkurier* , especially 1930–33.

Milena Jesenská

Main Sources:

Vondráčková, Jaroslava: *Kolem Mileny Jesenské* edited by Dr. Marie Jirásková. Prague, 1991.

Černá, Jana: *Deset adres Mileny Jesenské* Prague, 1959.

Milena Jesenská's articles in *Tribuna, Národní listy* and *Přítomnost*

Jesenská, Milena: Unpublished letters to dr. Albína Honzáková in the National Literary Archives in Strahov.

Books by Milena Jesenská:

_____*Cesta k jednoduchosti* first published Prague, 1926, edition of Eggenfelden, 1982 contains essay by Jaroslav Dresler: "Kafkova Milena".

_____*Clověk dělá saty* Prague, 1927.

_____*Mileniny recepty* Prague, 1925

The most important journals and newspapers in which Milena Jesenská published other than those listed as main sources:

Pestrý týden 1926–27
Svět práce 1933–34
Kmen 1920–21
Rozpravy Aventina 1926–
Lidové noviny 1929–1930
Tvorba 1930–33
Žijeme 1932–33
Světozor 1928–29

Secondary literature:

Buber-Neumann, Margarete: *Milena, Kafkas Freundin* Munich, 1977.
Jirsíková, Nina: untitled unpublished manuscript, Prague, 1973.
Kafka, Franz: *Dopisy Mileně* Introduction by František Kautman. Prague, 1968.
Kaus, Gina: *Und was für ein Leben!* Hamburg, 1979.
Binder, Hartmut: "Ernst Polak. Literat ohne Werk" in *Jahrbuch der deutschen Schiller-Gesellschaft* 23. Year, Stuttgart, 1979, pp. 366-415.

Milada Horáková

Primary literature:

Horáková, Milada. *Dopisy Milady Horákové 24.-27.6.1950* Praha, 1990.

Secondary literature:

Dvořáková, Zora. *Milada Horáková.* Praha, 1991.
Beran, Karel. *Před soudem lidu.* Praha, 1950.
Rada, Svobodného Československa. *Milada Horáková: k desátému výročí její propravy.* Washington, 1960.

Ruth Klinger

Main Source

Klinger, Ruth: *Zeugin einer Zeit* Zurich, 1977.

An abbreviated edition of this book appeared under the title *Die Frau im Kaftan* edited by Ludger Heid, Gerlingen, 1992.

Jiřina Šiklová:

Main Sources

Letters by Jiřina Šiklová to various addressees including the author, a brief autobiography, an advice column and other unpublished writings.

_____*Akademická YMCA v Československu* doctoral dissertation, unpublished, 1961.

Articles

_____"Universitní profesor dr. Emanuel Rádl" Acta universitatis Carolinae-Historia universitatis Carolinae Pragensis, 1968, vol. IX, fac. 1, pp. 79–94.

Šiklová, Jiřina: "Adaptace na smrt partnera ve stáří" in Zdravotnická pracovnice, Oct. 1979, p. 10.

_____"Sociology of youth in Czechoslovakia" in Zeitschrift für Soziologie , yr. II, Heft 2, April 1982.

_____"Save these Books" in Index on Censorship, vol. 12, no 2, April 1983.

_____"Mládež v ČSSR a náboženství" in Svědectví, yr. XX, number 79, 1986, p. 513ff.

_____"Nationalism in Eastern and Central Europe" lecture delivered at conference of Opus Dei in Franconia 8.12. 1990

_____"'The Gray Zone and the Future of Dissent in Czechoslovakia" in Social Research no 2, vol. 57 1990, Summer, 347–363.

_____"Verteidigungsmechanismen oder wie man die Haft überlebt" in Antworten zum hundertsten Jahrestag der Geburt Franz Kafkas am 3. Juli, 1883 collected by Hermann v. Bothmer, Hanover, 1983.

Books under pseudonyms:

Heroldová, Ph.Dr. Jiřina: *Co všechno snese žena* Prague, 1978.

Matulová, Nina: *Deník staré paní* Prague, 1988.

Pavlíček, František: *Dávno, dávno již tomu* , Praha, 1979.

Secondary Literature:

Trojanová, Helena: "Kdo je Jiřina Šiklová?" unpublished manuscript, in Czechoslovak Documentation Center, Scheinfeld, Germany.

Sources of Illustrations

♣

From the Department of Prints and Photographs, Library of Congress, Washington, D.C. : pp. 1, 3, 5, 41, 47, 72, 147, 268, 347, 348.

From A.D. Šubert and F.A. Borovský: *Čechy* 1, part a, Praha, 1993, pp. 6, 52, 97, 280.

Čechy III, pt. 2, Praha, 1994, pp. 25, 206, 226.

Čechy IV, Praha, 1934, p. 10, Polabí, Praha 1894, p. 104.

Čechy X, 1896. p. 182.

From Zdeněk Wirth: *Praha v obrazech peti století,* Praha, 1934, p. 10

Stará Praha, Praha, 1940, pp. 117, 138, 139, 146.

Ratibořice, Praha, 1967, p. 68.

From Pavel Scheufler: *Fotografiké album Čech,* 1848-1914, Praha, 1989: pp. 16, 19, 110.

From my collection: pp. 19, 53, 57, 65, 66, 74, 85, 128, 138, 154, 172, 186, 252, 268, 302.

From M.D. Rettigová: *Domácí kuchařka,* Praha, 1985.

From Rudolf Skopec: *Dějiny fotografie od nejstarších dob k dnešku,* Praha, 1963, p. 49.

From J.V. Frič: *Paměti,* p. 51.

From Miloslav Novotný: *Život Boženy Němcové,* Praha, 1959, p. 82.

Printed with permission from Náprstek Museum, Prague, pp. 91, 102, 107.

From the book *Hrady a zámky,* p. 116.

From the Czech National Literary Archive, Strahov, p. 142.

From the photographer Jiří Ployhar: p. 147, 150, 199, 200, 250, 274, 293, 294, 318.

From Hermine Hanel: *Meine Jugendjahre,* Leipzig, 1930L 177, 191.

From Lilli Deiglmayr, Wiesbaden, Germany: p. 196.

From a painting in Kolín town museum: p. 198.

From Elisabeth Wolf, Darlington, England: pp. 226, 246.

From a Unicef postcard, p. 229.

Printed with permission from Eric Mossel: *Een litrerair gids van Praag*, Schoten, Hadewijch, 1988, pp. 236, 252.

From Marta Marková-Kotyková: *Mýtus Milena*, Primus, Praha, 1993, p. 249, 253, 256, 269.

From Margarete Buber-Neumann: *Milena, Kafkas Freundin*, p. 289

From Miroslav Ivanov: *Justiční vražda aneb smrt Milady Horákové* Nakladatelství Betty, Praha, 1991, 290, 300.

From a Czechoslovak postage stamp: p. 310.

From Ruth Klinger: *Zeugin einer Zeit*, Zurich, 1979, p. 321.

From Jiřina Šiklová, pp. 339, 341, 260.

INDEX

WOMEN, FAMILY AND SOCIETY IN MEDIEVAL EUROPE
Historical Essays, 1978–1991

David Herlihy

Edited and with an Introduction by Anthony Molho

Until his untimely death in February 1991, David Herlihy, Professor of History at Brown University, was one of the most prolific and best-known American historians of the European Middle Ages. Author of books on the history of thirteenth- and fourteenth-century Italy, Herlihy published, in 1978, his best-known work in collaboration with Christiane Klapisch-Zuber, *Les Toscans et leurs familles* (translated into English in 1985, and Italian in 1988). For the last dozen or so years of his life, Herlihy launched a series of ambitious projects, on the history of women and the family, and on the collective behavior of social groups in medieval Europe. While he completed two important books – on the family (1985) and on women's work (1991) – he did not find the time to bring these other major projects to a conclusion.

This volume contains essays he wrote after 1978. They convey a sense of the enormous intellectual energy and great erudition which characterized David Herlihy's scholarly career. They also chart a remarkable historian's intellectual trajectory, as he searched for new and better ways of asking a set of simple and basic questions about the history of the family, the institution within which the vast majority of Europeans spent so much of their lives. Because of his qualities as a scholar and a teacher, during his relatively brief career Herlihy was honored with the presidencies of the four major scholarly associations with which he was affiliated: the Catholic Historical Association, the Medieval Academy of America, the Renaissance Society of America, and the American Historical Association.

Anthony Molho is Munro Goodwin Wilkinson Professor of European History at Brown University, and has written several works on the social, political, and economic history of late medieval and early modern Italy.

430 Pages, ISBN 1-57181-023-4 hb, ca. **$59.95/£46.00**
ISBN 1-57181-024-2 pb, ca. **$17.95/£12.95**

165 Taber Ave., Providence, RI 02906 • Tel: 401-861-9330 • Fax: 401-521-0046
E-Mail: BerghahnBk@aol.com *or* BerghahnUS@aol.com

Bush House, Merewood Ave., Sandhills, Oxford OX3 8EF • Tel: (01865) 742 224 • Fax: (01865) 744 978
E-Mail: BerghahnUK@cityscape.co.uk

Sexual Subordination and State Intervention
Comparing Sweden and the United States

R. Amy Elman

One would expect a welfare state such as Sweden to compare favorably with the United States regarding the implementation of public policies and programs. Surprisingly, the author comes to quite different conclusions: in studying the treatment of battered, raped and sexually-harassed women in the two countries, she has found that, contrary to conventional expectation, the ability of the decentralized American state to innovate effectively has been consistently underestimated, whereas Sweden's ability to do the same has often been exaggerated. One explanation seems to be that the very structure of Sweden's centralized, corporatist state does not permit women to make claims on it that do not directly relate to work-force participation. By contrast, the American state is more permeable to the interests of women (as women) in instances where those interests are not economically determined.

By focusing on issues specific to women, this study transcends the emphasis on class which is the traditional basis for social reforms and discussions of the state. Thus, it establishes a more comprehensive comparative political perspective than those presently offered by political analysts concerned with public policy and state structure.

Contents: The Analytic Context: Gender Specification & State Structures – The Comparative Context: States, Structures & Movements – The States & Woman Battering – The States & Rape – The States & Sexual Harassment – Conclusion.

R. Amy Elman is Assistant Professor of Political Science at Kalamazoo College, Michigan, where she also serves as the Director of the Women's Studies Program and as Associate Co-Director of the Center for European Studies.

September, 1995 • ca. 128 pages, bibliography, index
ISBN 1-57181-071-4 hb, ca **$35.00/£25.00** ISBN 1-57181-072-2 pb ca. **$14.50/£10.50**

165 Taber Ave., Providence, RI 02906 • Tel: 401-861-9330 • Fax: 401-521-0046
E-Mail: BerghahnBk@aol.com *or* BerghahnUS@aol.com

Bush House, Merewood Ave., Sandhills, Oxford OX3 8EF • Tel: (01865) 742 224 • Fax: (01865) 744 978
E-Mail: BerghahnUK@cityscape.co.uk

Women in Contemporary Russia

Edited by **Vitalina Koval**

The position of women in Russia has always been difficult. In spite of the Revolution in 1917, the legal, economic, social and political inequalities between men and women have remained severe. For more than seventy years the official propaganda of the Soviet system deliberately concealed form the public, in the West as well as in the East, the actual position of women, presenting it in rose-colored hues and proclaiming that, under socialism, the issue of the position of women in society had been resolved once and for all. However, the opposite was true: women increasingly suffered from overt and covert discrimination. In fact, the discrepancy between the official and actual position of working women became so acute that it led to serious social problems. The democratic reforms of the mid-1980s brought some positive changes at last; for the first time, the "women's issue" was recognized as an urgent socio-political problem requiring serious investigation and practical measures.

The authors of this collection of original essays, most of whom are social scientists at the Moscow Academy of Science, examine those aspects of the life of women in Russia today which are most pressing, not least those arising from the multi-ethnic composition of the Russian Federation that comprises more than one hundred different nationalities and in which women constitute fifty-three percent of the population.

Contents: Introduction – L.M. Drobizheva / L.V. Ostapenko, The Women of Russia: Some Demographic and Ethno-Cultural Characteristics – V.V. Koval, Women and Work in Russia – L. Rzhanitsyna, Women's Attitudes to the New Economic Reforms and the Market Economy – Y.B. Klinova, Women and Legal Rights in Russia – Y. Azarova, Social Security for Women and Children in Russia: The Situation and the Problems – V. Perevedentsev, Women, the Family and Reproduction of the Population in Russia – T.Y. Zabelina, Young Women of Russia: Studies, Work, and Family – M.G. Kotovskaya, Women and Religious Consciousness in Russia – O. Kuchkina, Women in the Arts.

Vitalina V. Koval is Senior Fellow in Politics and the Labor Movement of the Russian Academy of Science.

July, 1995 • 144 pages
ISBN 1-57181-885-5 hb, ca **$35.00/£25.00**

165 Taber Ave., Providence, RI 02906 • Tel: 401-861-9330 • Fax: 401-521-0046
E-Mail: BerghahnBk@aol.com *or* BerghahnUS@aol.com

Bush House, Merewood Ave., Sandhills, Oxford OX3 8EF • Tel: (01865) 742 224 • Fax: (01865) 744 978
E-Mail: BerghahnUK@cityscape.co.uk